Canada: The State of the Federation 2008

Open Federalism and the Spending Power

Edited by
John R. Allan
Thomas J. Courchene
Marc-Antoine Adam
Hoi Kong

Institute of Intergovernmental Relations
School of Policy Studies, Queen's University
McGill-Queen's University Press
Montreal & Kingston • London • Ithaca

The Institute of Intergovernmental Relations

The Institute is the only academic organization in Canada whose mandate is solely to promote research and communication on the challenges facing the federal system.

Current research interests include fiscal federalism, health policy, the reform of federal political institutions and the machinery of federal-provincial relations, Canadian federalism and the global economy, and comparative federalism.

The Institute pursues these objectives through research conducted by its own staff and other scholars, through its publication program, and through seminars and conferences.

The Institute links academics and practitioners of federalism in federal and provincial governments and the private sector.

The Institute of Intergovernmental Relations receives ongoing financial support from the J.A. Corry Memorial Endowment Fund, the Royal Bank of Canada Endowment Fund, and the governments of Manitoba and Ontario. We are grateful for this support, which enables the Institute to sustain its extensive program of research, publication, and related activities.

L'Institut des relations intergouvernementales

L'Institut est le seul organisme universitaire canadien à se consacrer exclusivement à la recherche et aux échanges sur les questions du fédéralisme.

Les priorités de recherche de l'Institut portent présentement sur le fédéralisme fiscal, la santé, la modification éventuelle des institutions politiques fédérales, les mécanismes de relations fédérales-provinciales, le fédéralisme canadien au regard de l'économie mondiale et le fédéralisme comparatif.

L'Institut réalise ses objectifs par le biais de recherches effectuées par son personnel et par des chercheurs de l'Université Queen's et d'ailleurs, de même que par des congrès et des colloques.

L'Institut sert comme lien entre les universitaires, les fonctionnaires fédéraux et provinciaux et le secteur privé.

L'Institut des relations intergouvernementales reçoit l'appui financier du J.A. Corry Memorial Endowment Fund, de la Fondation de la Banque Royale du Canada, et des gouvernements du Manitoba et de l'Ontario. Nous les remercions de cet appui qui permet à l'Institut de poursuivre son vaste programme de recherche et de publication ainsi que ses activités connexes.

ISSN 0827-0708
ISBN 978-1-55339-197-5 (bound)
ISBN 978-1-55339-196-8 (pbk.)

To the Memory of

Tom Kent

Outstanding Public Servant and Public Intellectual

CONTENTS

PREFACE

This 2008 edition of *Canada: The State of the Federation* examines "open federalism" and the federal spending power, topics that were given increased prominence, if any were necessary, by the commitment by the Conservative Party in its 2005–06 campaign and subsequently, to the pursuit of "open federalism" and "strict constructionism", i.e., to a strict adherence to the division of powers set forth in the Constitution. The organizers of the conference perceived that the Harper government's first years in office presented an opportunity to examine afresh the controversy over the spending power, to enquire whether it was in fact being used differently by the new government, and to consider other, potentially less controversial ways, of sustaining the federal role in the Canadian welfare state. Accordingly, Dr. Thomas J. Courchene and Dr. John R. Allan, then respectively the Director and Associate Director of the Queen's Institute of Intergovernmental Relations, Marc-Antoine Adam, a Director in the Secrétariat aux affaires intergouvernementales canadiennes, Québec, and then a Visiting Fellow at the Institute, and Hoi Kong of the Faculty of Law, Queen's University, undertook to organize the conference and seek presenters for the selected topics. In addition to the Institute, the conference was cosponsored by the Faculty of Law of Queen's University. I would like to say how very much we appreciate their efforts.

The conference itself was held at Queen's University on January 25–26, 2008, in Kingston. General financial assistance for the conference was provided by the Province of Ontario and by the Forum of Federations, while funding in support of the publication of the proceedings was provided by the Department of Justice, Canada. We very much appreciate the support of all three sponsors and are pleased to acknowledge our indebtedness to them. We would also like to thank our presenters: Marc-Antoine Adam, Marc Chevrier, Sujit Choudhry, Thomas J. Courchene, Tom Kent, Hoi Kong, Andrée Lajoie, Harvey Lazar, Roderick A. Macdonald, Errol P. Mendes, Alain Noël, Andrew Petter, and John D. Whyte. Not only have they contributed excellent papers, they also participated actively in the discussion prompted by their papers, thereby adding greatly to the value and stimulus of the conference.

Four years have passed since the conference was held. The gap between the conference and the publication is largely explained by the uncertainties resulting from the transition from one Institute director to another. Nevertheless, the editors and I are confident that the debate over the use of the federal spending power is still alive and that this publication remains timely. It should also be pointed out that a version of the conference papers was published in 2008 by the *Queen's Law Journal*.

In addition to the presenters, the success of the conference also owed much to the staff of the Institute, who were responsible for all conference arrangements. In particular, I should like to thank Patti Candido, then the Administrative Assistant to the Director, and Mary Kennedy, the voice and face of the Institute to all conference participants. Under their skilful management, conference arrangements were faultlessly executed. They were most ably assisted by Dr. Nadia Verrelli and by Ryan Zade, then our post-doctoral fellow and research assistant respectively.

Preparation of the text for publication was expertly undertaken by Sharon Sullivan, of the John Deutsch Institute at Queen's, and we are grateful to the JDI for making Sharon available. Ellie Barton was our most thorough copy editor. Once again our cover design was undertaken by Mark Howes, and we are most appreciative of his efforts and patience, and for the assistance of his colleagues at McGill-Queen's University Press.

It is with sadness that we note the November 15, 2011 death of one of our presenters, Tom Kent, an extraordinary public servant, one of the principal intellectual architects of the Canadian welfare state, and Fellow of the School of Public Policy at Queen's University. It is an honour to dedicate this book to his memory.

André Juneau
Director

I

Introduction

1

Introduction[1]

John R. Allan and Thomas J. Courchene

Ronald Watts has defined the federal spending power as "the power of Parliament to make payments to people, institutions or provincial governments for purposes on which Parliament does not necessarily have the power to legislate, for example, in areas of exclusive provincial jurisdiction" (Watts 1999, 1). The combination of no clear constitutional authorization but widespread, at times coercive, use of the federal spending power in building and sustaining the Canadian welfare state, has been a potent source of controversy both in intergovernmental relations and in academic consideration of Canadian federalism. Indeed, its capacity to generate divergent views was clearly evident at the 2008 conference on "Open Federalism and the Spending Power" held at Queen's University, and co-sponsored by the Queen's University Institute of Intergovernmental Relations and the Queen's Faculty of Law. The conference brought together a distinguished group of political scientists, constitutional lawyers and economists many of whom have been actively involved in the intergovernmental controversies involving the spending power, and virtually all of whom have contributed to the voluminous literature dealing with this most disputed concept.

The rationale for the 2008 conference was found in the commitment by the Conservative party in its 2005-06 campaign and subsequently to the pursuit of "open federalism" and to "strict constructionism" – i.e., to respecting the division of powers laid out in the *Constitution Act* and to restraint in the use of the spending power (Young 2006, 8). The conference presented an opportunity to revisit the controversy over the spending power, to assess whether it was in fact being used differently by the new government, and to consider alternative ways of sustaining the federal role in social Canada. More specifically, the conference reviewed the variety of ways the federal government and the provinces share roles and responsibilities in the day-to-day operation of the Canadian federation, and then compared these practices with the institutional framework provided by the constitution. Finally, and in the light of the practices of "open federalism", it examined the potential for providing more principled approaches to power sharing.

The papers generated by the conference are organized in four sections. Those in the first section place the spending power in context, both historically

[1]Parenthetical Arabic numerals unaccompanied by text refer to the pages in this volume.

and in terms of practice and principle, with the final paper in the section focusing on the perception and use of the spending power by the Harper government. The papers in the second section are devoted primarily to legal considerations, with particular emphasis on the constitutional considerations usually cited by those opposed to the use of the spending power. This is followed by another preponderantly legal group of papers, this time with the focus on positive law. The final section contains two papers that emphasize the changing political and economic environments in which the spending power must operate. We note that the first of these is by the late Tom Kent, to the memory of whom this book is dedicated.

The conference papers are discussed in somewhat greater detail in the balance of this introduction.

THE SPENDING POWER: CONTEXT

The conference key-note address was delivered by **John Whyte**, and the paper from which it was derived is presented in Chapter 2. The premise underlying this chapter is that "a nation's constitutional character is more a function of ethical vision, or even aesthetic rendering, than it is a product of statecraft design" (19). Moreover, he notes that what Canada truly is, as a political community, is historical and contingent, and best perceived through our historical narrative. Caution is necessary, however, in discerning the tropes – most particularly irony – by means of which the narrative is constructed. Using the narrative of the Treaty 8 negotiations between the aboriginal peoples and the newly formed nation of Canada as an overarching trope, Whyte goes on to relate narratives of four critical episodes of constitutional change or elucidation: first, the contrast of Macdonald's view of a strong national government with Cartier's emphasis on minority nationality and provincial independence; second, the evolution following the Second World War of our constitutionalism in the expression of a national welfare state; and third, Prime Minister Trudeau's failed attempts to further centralize power at the federal level. His fourth narrative concerns the Harper government's turn to "pure federalism" – "the idea that each level of government should stick to its constitutional mandate" (35).

Whyte categorizes Harper's federalism as resting on two related policies: first, a plan to move away from shared-cost programs and conditional grants (the principal instruments by which the federal government has imposed its ideas of an appropriate national social role on provinces); and second, the embrace of asymmetry under which different provinces enjoy different treatment on a number of matters. He observes that this raises a number of fundamental questions. For example, are we better off as a nation if the challenges of the current age are seen as impinging on the entire nation, putting everyone at risk, or should the challenges be viewed from a regional or provincial perspective, one that demands differing federal-provincial responses to maximize regional advantage? And does seeking to meet the needs of regions and communities jeopardize the inclination and ability to protect the vital interests of all citizens?

Indeed, does the very idea of national well-being, like that of nation-building, belong to a simpler and more cohesive age?

While he concedes that a move to a federalism based on a diminished national responsibility and more accommodation of asymmetry may appear to be a purer federalism, Whyte concludes it is not necessarily so: federalism is not purer simply because the nation is more fractured. Rather, what is necessary are principles of co-ordination that allow established political communities and multiple political identities to work together to create a cohesive nation. He concludes on an unambiguous note:

> We scorn the constitutional idea of watertight compartments not just because they so soon grow dated or because they under-represent our experience (although they may do both), but because constitutions were never designed to keep our interests apart. Rather, we make constitutions to describe how we will work together to keep a nation – to build a better nation. (38)

In the second paper in this section, **Roderick A. Macdonald** notes that capturing the essence of the spending power requires analysis that "goes to the links between the theoretical foundations of liberal-democratic states and to the instrumentalities by which governance agendas are pursued in such states". In tracing these links, he notes that a constitution comprises both an explicit text and an unwritten set of implicit understandings. The latter, in turn, comprise our constitutional inheritance and our political practices and constitutional conventions. Understanding the spending power requires siting it in this broader, more comprehensive constitutional context, and not being fixated on the explicit constitution.

As did Whyte, Macdonald notes the contingent nature of our constitutional situation: the roles of the different branches and orders of government are constantly shifting, as are the normative and financial tools by means of which government agendas are pursued. With respect to the spending power, he observes that direct spending by the federal government in areas of provincial jurisdiction (a practice he describes as "the bane of federal constitutionalism") to compel or induce provinces to adopt those welfare programs or program features that the federal government is prepared to finance, is being made obsolete by changes in what citizens expect of government. In consequence, he notes that, in the opinion of many commentators, the welfare-state politics of the type that have given rise to conflict over the spending power may have just about run their course.

Among the factors that Macdonald believes are contributing to less acrimony regarding the spending power are globalization and the emergence of identity politics in which personal assertion focused on language, culture, religion and ethnicity dominates conceptions of multi-cultural citizenship. He foresees an end to large-scale redistributive programs mediated by substantial bureaucratic structures, and, in their place, increasing use of targeted programs focused on individuals. Such changes, he observes, invite scholars to consider what conceptions of citizenship will drive governance in the future. The emerging governance challenges, he believes, will result in increased focus on the problem of marginalized populations and inequality of life chances. Citing

Courchene (this volume), he observes that the issues confronting governance simply do not map easily onto discrete subject-matter constitutional jurisdiction: issues of national significance fall into areas of provincial responsibility. The outcome is likely to be a transformed spending power, one that empowers citizens to realize their increasingly diverse identities and aspirations. Macdonald believes that a constitutional foundation for this is to be found in Section 36 of *The Constitution Act, 1982*.

In his paper, presented in Chapter 4, **Thomas J. Courchene** provides a comprehensive review of the parallel evolutions of the practices and principles relating to the federal spending power and its use in the Canadian constitutional context. He follows this with an assessment of alternative perspectives for addressing the spending power in a broader context, one that recognizes the evolving nature of decision-making in an increasingly integrated national and global situation. Throughout, his approach is primarily a public-policy one, rather than one focused on constitutional law. In passing, he notes that the spending-power issue is, in large measure, one of fiscal imbalance: absent superior revenue access, the federal incentive to spend in areas of provincial jurisdiction would be much attenuated. He also observes, in common with Macdonald and Kent, that the spending power is increasingly directed to individuals and institutions rather than transferred to or through the provinces, a change that is surely conducive to improved accountability.

Section 94 of the *Constitution Act, 1867*, which Courchene suggests might better be titled "Transferring Constitutional Authority", receives attention in his paper as providing a possible constitutional underpinning for the exercise of the spending power. Since transferring some aspects of property-and-civil-rights powers to the federal government pursuant to this provision requires the concurrence of the participating provinces, and is not subject to a Quebec veto, a suitably modified version of the section would permit the common-law provinces to opt *into* pan-Canadian programs, while leaving Quebec to mount, with fiscal compensation, its own version of the pan-Canadian program. He notes, however, that the process would likely fail for want of federal support should some of the larger common-law provinces choose to follow the Quebec model and mount their own versions of the pan-Canadian program.

A strong case is made that the evolving context in which the federation operates presents substantial new challenges. In particular, Courchene argues that while the major problems respecting human capital, the knowledge economy and the environment may fall substantially into areas of provincial jurisdiction, they unquestionably have very significant national implications and dimensions. What is needed is a federal model that both recognizes this and is able to deal with it effectively.

Courchene concludes that despite its objections to the use of the federal spending power, "Quebec has been able to carve out for itself a remarkable degree of political and policy space, so much so that it is the envy of sub-national governments everywhere. And for the most part this has been accomplished through political rather than constitutional channels" (115).

The final chapter in this section is by **Harvey Lazar**, who focuses particularly on the policies and practices of the Harper government respecting the spending power. He provides first of all a way of thinking about the spending power, and then applies the framework developed to the record of the Harper government in the period up to the time of the conference. The framework is predicated on the idea that the spending power serves two overlapping but distinct purposes: first, it is an instrument of public policy that the federal government can use to advance particular policy objectives. Beyond that, it is also and secondly a symbol, signalling the kind of federation that the federal government wants for Canada. In both capacities, however, it is contested, and there are competing views on whether, to what extent, and in what ways Ottawa should use the spending power to construct and maintain the federation. He notes, in particular, the constraints imposed by the fact that Quebec authorities see the spending power as unconstitutional or at least politically illegitimate. They therefore tend to argue that, if the other provinces and territories hold a different view, the appropriate remedies are asymmetrical arrangements in which Quebec can opt out with fiscal compensation. Above all, there is a need for flexibility and recognition that, in some circumstances, the exercise of the spending power may require more of an opt-in than an opt-out approach.

Lazar notes that while the Harper government has embraced "open federalism" and spoken of placing formal limits on the use of the spending power for new shared-cost programs in areas of exclusive provincial jurisdiction, its track record in office belies the fear that it would create a firewall between federal and provincial governments and abandon, at least to some degree, those aspects of federal social policy that depend on the spending power. Indeed, as he notes, the Harper government's 2006, 2007 and 2008 budgets showed considerable continuity with the policies of previous governments. In particular, with respect to the direct spending power – i.e., making payments directly to individuals and institutions, rather than relying on transfers to provincial governments – he concludes that the Harper government has made no significant departures from the approach to the direct spending power taken by previous governments. Indeed, this is largely true with respect also to the indirect spending power, leading to the conclusion that the fears of the firewall scenario are, at best, overstated. He also notes, however, that the government's cuts to the Goods and Services Tax curtailed substantially the fiscal capacity to introduce new programs through the spending power. Freedom of action has also been constrained by the government's recognition of the legitimacy of the diverse opinions concerning the spending power: he observes that a federal government that privileges one position too strongly relative to competing views is unlikely to remain in office very long.

THE SPENDING POWER: LEGAL CONSIDERATIONS

The chapters in this section are devoted primarily to legal considerations, with particular emphasis on the constitutional considerations usually cited by those opposed to the use of the spending power. The first chapter is by **Marc Chevrier**, who examines the origins of federalism from both historical and political perspectives. This analysis leads him to suggest that, taking as it does the form of an asymmetrical pact between an imperial power and a smaller nation with limited autonomy, the use of the spending power is at odds with the spirit of federalism. In the case of Canada, Chevrier states that understanding the constitutional regime founded in 1867 requires that attention be focused on the relatively neglected political aspect of federalism, as distinct from its constitutional dimension. Canadian federalism, he notes, grew out of the evolutionary British Constitution and its tradition of accommodating historical nations. Seen in this manner, political and intellectual leaders in Lower Canada saw Confederation as an act of retrocession that was favourable to Quebec's nationalist discourse.

Regarding the use of the spending power from the 1950s onward, to build the postwar welfare state, Chevrier sees this as involving the gradual emergence of the idea that the federal government had responsibility for the well-being of Canadian citizens, a vision he believes was transformed into constitutional dogma by the constitutional reform of 1982. Based on an analysis of other countries, Chevrier concludes that Canada now has two choices that it may make: either it chooses to become an imperial federation or, alternatively, it may choose to limit the *dominium* of the federal government by adopting a constitutional amendment prohibiting or limiting the conditional use of the spending power. He concludes that it remains unclear which of these two outcomes will prevail in Canada's future federal dynamic.

In the following chapter, **Alain Noël** argues, as the title of his chapter makes clear, that the federal spending power is a power that does not exist. The omission of any reference to it in the *British North America Act*, he states, was not an oversight, but rather the result of the framers of the *Act* intending to create a multinational and not a territorial federation: federal institutions that preserved the autonomy of the constituent peoples were required if the resulting country were to be sustained. Despite this deliberate omission and, for example, the 1937 decision of the Judicial Committee of the Privy Council that federal spending legislation – in this case, that relating to unemployment insurance – remained subject to the division of powers, Ottawa has regularly invoked a federal spending power in areas of exclusive provincial jurisdiction.

Noël reviews the political developments that led to the exercise of the purported federal spending power, and considers in greater detail more recent events, in particular, the attempts to arrive at political solutions to govern its use. These attempts, he notes, were complicated by Quebec's insistence that any proposed solution avoid conferring any explicit or implied legitimacy to a federal spending power. He considers the Harper government's pronouncements on open federalism, particularly the 2007 Throne Speech proposal to formally limit the use of the federal spending power for new shared-cost programs. Since shared-costs programs were by then largely an anachronism, and since the proposal failed to address the actual and diverse manifestations of the spending power, he states that it lacked credibility as a serious solution.

Noël goes on to detail the inadequacies of the various proposed solutions to the abusive use of the spending power from the Meech Lake Accord to *A Framework to Improve the Social Union for Canadians* (the Social Union Framework Agreement, i.e., "SUFA"), concluding that they were all undesirable because, in attempting to limit the federal spending power, they implicitly recognized a power he contends did not in fact exist. The most constitutionally compliant option would be an approach that eliminated conditional federal transfers and expenditures in areas of provincial jurisdiction, while compensating provinces directly for the associated loss of revenue. He notes that, for those provinces who so wished, an element of flexibility might be provided by the use of section 94 of the *Constitution Act, 1867*. Noël acknowledges the likely negative response such a comprehensive solution is likely to receive; he concludes, therefore, that solutions to the spending power that may be adopted will be political rather than legal.

In Chapter 8, **Andrew Petter** revisits his 1989 analysis of the federal spending power, where he concluded that it was unconstitutional and could not be defended by means of contemporary political justifications (Petter 1989). In that analysis, he argued that the federal spending power could be attacked on the grounds of legal doctrine, constitutional values, and *realpolitik*. More specifically, he argued that he could see "no basis in language or in logic for suggesting that when Parliament authorizes expenditures of funds with respect to some matter it acts any less 'in relation' to that matter than when it regulates with respect to the same matter" (ibid., 456). He believes this view was supported by the decision of the Privy Council in the *Reference Re Employment and Social Insurance Act (Can.)*. Respecting constitutional values, he maintained that the spending power threatened both the federal nature and the democratic character of the Canadian state. His assessment in respect of *realpolitik* was dualistic: on the one hand, he argued that it was not necessary to counter regional disparities, compensate for provincial fiscal incapacities, or maintain progressive politics in Canada, as some defenders of the spending power claim. On the other, he argued that, after four decades of political development predicated on the use of the spending power, it was beyond the capacity of the courts to invalidate the power itself or the structures of government to which it had given rise.

Petter's prescription for these difficulties was a four-part program of constitutional reform. First, a prohibition of conditional transfers between governments, with the tax room required to fund the transfers being given to the government with legislative jurisdiction. Second, end the use of other conditional grants, loans and tax expenditures by the federal and provincial governments where these are used to promote policies falling outside their respective legislative jurisdictions. Third, a constitutional formula to ensure current levels of equalization, including that embedded in existing conditional-grant programs. His final prescription was for the adoption of a formal procedure to make the process of constitutional amendment more flexible.

Revisiting his earlier analyses and prescriptions, Petter finds his earlier concern about the dangers posed by the spending power to federal and democratic values undiminished. His views on legal doctrine, however, have been changed by recent case authority; he now feels that there can be no doubt that the spending power has been authorized by the courts. Moreover, even if the courts were so disposed, it would be even more difficult for them to now invalidate some sixty years of political development. He continues to believe that, given a sufficiently robust system of unconditional, regional equalization payments, the spending power is not required to address regional disparities, compensate for provincial fiscal incapacities, or advance progressive politics in Canada. He is more convinced than ever that we need a Constitution that is easier to amend as social and political needs require. In this context, he notes that the extensive use of the federal spending power over the last sixty years is clear evidence of the inability of the Constitution to adapt to circumstances. Indeed, he now feels that the problem of constitutional inflexibility has been compounded over the intervening years, and now constitutes a deficiency that he believes "surpasses those of the spending power" (176).

Petter is not optimistic regarding the prospects for constitutional reform. As noted above, he does not regard simple judicial invalidation as being either likely or feasible. Reliance on section 94, as elaborated by Mark-Antoine Adam in Chapter 11, he also finds lacking, and no more likely to find judicial favour than simple invalidation. Its use would require asking the courts to ignore their jurisprudence of the last twenty years, bring into play a previously unused provision of the Constitution, and transform it in three significant ways. He characterizes acting in this manner as "more an act of political invention than constitutional interpretation" (177). Moreover, he believes a revitalized section 94, with full rights of compensation for non-participating provinces in federal legislative schemes, could lead to "a dangerous and destabilizing degree of asymmetry in federal arrangements, with Parliament exercising varying degrees of authority over social policy in different provinces" (177). While in the abstract he still finds his own proposals for constitutional reform appealing, he concedes that the extent of our current constitutional rigidity is such as to make them increasingly unattainable.

Petter concludes by noting that, given current conditions, the Constitution is likely to remain in a state of stasis and the exercise of the spending power will expand and contract over time in response to political exigencies. Resort to the federal spending power he considers a poor alternative to constitutional flexibility, but, absent the latter, he has difficulty seeing how Canada could function without a federal spending power. While this may compromise the constitution, he notes that the only thing worse than a constitution that can be compromised is one that cannot be changed.

The final chapter of Section II is contributed by **Hoi Kong**, who relates the federal spending power to section 36(1) of the *Constitution Act, 1982* and considers it in the light of New Governance Theory. In so doing, he addresses two long-standing issues in constitutional theory: legal indeterminacy (reflected in reasonable disagreement about what the law requires) and limited institutional competence (where cases may strain the institutional capacity of courts). These issues, he notes, are often pertinent to disputes about the constitutionality of specific government actions. In effect, authors or agencies may disagree about the constitutionality of some exercises of the federal spending power, and the complexity of fiscal federalism may pose institutional challenges for courts that would oversee the power.

Kong begins his analysis by outlining the contours of the contemporary debate over the federal spending power; he then justifies judicial oversight of the exercise of the spending power; and concludes the first section of the chapter by arguing that section 36(1) is the appropriate locus of constitutional authority for some controversial exercises of the spending power. More specifically, he argues that it provides a normative framework for particular instances of a long-standing practice and for balancing the relevant interests. Such an approach to the spending power, he reasons, is more sensitive to the range of interests at stake and, absent persuasive arguments against adopting this approach, it is superior to alternatives that would require the courts to engage in a wholesale override of the presumption of constitutionality.

In the second part his paper, Kong elaborates an interpretation of section 36(1) that draws upon the literature on judicial minimalism, while in the final section he proposes, for the implementation of his interpretation, a doctrinal rule that draws on New Governance theory. He concludes by observing that the proposals he has offered are grounded in constitutional values and in the political experience of the Canadian and other federations, and suggests that the questions he has raised are central to any adequate contemporary analysis of the spending power in Canada.

THE SPENDING POWER AND POSITIVE LAW

The three chapters in this section deal with the spending power and aspects of positive law. In the first, Andrée Lajoie argues that, under existing constitutional doctrine, all exercises of the federal spending power that intrude on provincial jurisdiction are unconstitutional. In the second chapter, Marc-Antoine Adam shares Lajoie's opinion on the unconstitutionality of the federal spending power, and seeks a remedy in section 94 of the *Constitution Act, 1867*, arguing that this would authorize a flexible relationship between federal and provincial governments, one based on consent. The final chapter in the section is by Errol Mendes, who rejects the arguments of both Lajoie and Adam for doctrinal reasons that lead him to conclude that the constitutionality of the spending power is not substantially in doubt. Moreover, he rejects the version of federalism implicit in the policies of the Harper government, preferring an alternative version of federalism and the spending power predicated on section 36(1) of the *Constitution Act, 1982.* These chapters are discussed in somewhat greater detail in what follows.

Andrée Lajoie begins her chapter by observing that "In federations, especially in former British colonies, centralization is the name of the game. ... [and] Canada is a constant winner at that game" (233). While the federal spending power is but one of an array of centralizing tools, she notes that it has become the federal government's preferred instrument of centralization. She argues, however, that neither it, nor its use as an instrument of centralization, is justified by the text of the Constitution. Rather, the current centralization of both the legislative powers and the related executive powers are the result of judicial interpretations of the division of powers and the ensuing government practices.

Lajoie believes that both the legal scholarship and jurisprudence are divided on the question of the constitutionality of the federal spending power. In particular, she notes that the question of the constitutionality of the spending power is still open for want of a binding Supreme Court decision. This has not, however, deterred the federal government from spending in areas of provincial jurisdiction, but the manner in which the federal spending power is exercised has changed. Rather than relying on conditional transfers to the provinces, the more recent tendency has been for the federal government to make direct transfers to provincial entities and individuals. All such exercises, she suggests, entail direct invasion of provincial jurisdiction, and hence are constitutionally invalid. Lajoie contends that truly unconditional grants lack favour with the federal government because it is difficult for it to derive electoral benefit from them. Targeted grants to the provinces that are tied to politically significant areas, such as health and social welfare, are more attractive and constitute a second way in which the federal government bypasses the authority of the provincial governments. She concludes by noting that however much the federal government and some provinces – but not all, and most certainly not Quebec – may wish for increased centralization, for the wish to become a reality the Constitution itself must be altered. Until that occurs, conditional federal spending in the realm of provincial jurisdiction is both unconstitutional and disruptive to the federal principle and national harmony.

The second chapter in this section is by **Mark-Antoine Adam**, who was a Visiting Fellow at the Institute of Intergovernmental Relations when the chapter was written. His concern is that the unlimited-spending-power thesis has long been used to justify federal spending in areas of provincial jurisdiction. This thesis, which is predicated on a distinction between spending and regulating, requires that it is only the latter that is subject to the division of powers. Adam contends that the unlimited-spending-power thesis has little foundation both in the Canadian Constitution and jurisprudence. Nor does it accord well, he argues, with the principles underlying Canadian constitutional interpretation. Finally, he notes that it is difficult to reconcile with the realities of Canadian intergovernmental relations where federal spending in areas of provincial jurisdiction typically involve discussion and negotiation, rather than federal unilateralism. Adam argues that it is public support for federally funded programs that has caused these difficulties to be largely overlooked, although not by many of the provinces, most particularly Quebec, which have resisted federal encroachments on their jurisdiction.

As an alternative to the present, questionable use of the federal spending power, Adam proposes an approach that would rest on provincial consent, one the provinces could either opt into or, alternatively, reject but with fiscal compensation. With respect to the latter, it would appear that there would be no requirement for provinces that do not opt-in to offer a program similar to that received by those that do; the result might therefore be a considerable increase in the asymmetry of the federation, depending on the number of provinces that chose not to opt in.

After a review of several co-operative mechanisms, Adam settles on section 94 of the *Constitution Act, 1867*, as the most promising constitutional foundation for a federal spending power predicated on consent. Although previously unused, he believes that what this section provides is essentially a legislative inter-delegation mechanism, one that could be read expansively enough to include all the common-law provinces, a wide range of subject areas, and an authorization for the payment of compensation to provinces that chose not to opt in. Once having opted in, he believes there would be nothing to prevent a province from subsequently withdrawing, thereby causing the relevant federal legislation to be no longer operative within that province. He concludes by noting that, by respecting the division of powers, a federal spending power based on section 94 would respect the autonomy and diversity of the provinces, and so promote intergovernmental co-operation.

The chapter by **Errol P. Mendes** concludes the section of papers dealing with the federal spending power in relation to positive law. The title of the chapter – "Building Firewalls and Deconstructing Canada by Hobbling the Federal Spending Power: The Rise of the Harper Doctrine" – highlights the primary concern of the author, namely, that the rhetoric of the Prime Minister suggests a desire and intent to build "firewalls" between the responsibilities of the federal and provincial governments, thereby "hobbling" the federal spending power and the role it has played in minimizing inequality across Canada. Mendes labels this unlegislated policy "the Harper Doctrine". In pursuing this doctrine, the author suggests that the Prime Minister is promoting the kind of federal policy that Quebec political leaders have traditionally demanded, that is, the severe restriction or elimination of the federal government's ability to spend in areas of provincial jurisdiction. Such a policy, he suggests, would be inimical to the role that the federal government and Parliament must play in protecting the quality of life and social opportunities of Canadians wherever they may reside in Canada.

Mendes briefly reviews the role of the federal government in the development and expansion of the Canadian welfare state in the post-World-War II period, noting that the favoured mechanism in realizing this nation-building was federal fiscal transfers in the form of equalization, direct grants or through the use of the federal spending power. This, of course, generated tensions between the federal government and the provinces, most particularly Quebec. Several attempts were made to resolve these tensions, most particularly with the Meech Lake and Charlottetown Accords. He suggests, however, that the desire to reconcile the federal interest in promoting national standards of social development with respect for provincial-spending priorities reached a zenith in 1997-98, in the discussions leading to the signing of the Social Union Framework Agreement ("SUFA") in 1999. He notes that while this agreement represented a non-constitutional, non-legislated consensus between the federal government and the provinces (other than Quebec, which refused to sign), such federal-provincial agreements are a fundamental part of Canadian constitutionalism and the rule of law. He therefore dismisses the charge that the strictures against the use of the spending power are not part of an entrenched constitutional framework and hence violate constitutionalism and the rule of law.

The possibility of providing a clear constitutional foundation for the spending power by means an expanded reach of section 94 of the *Constitution Act, 1867* is also dismissed. Rather than relying on a "tortured interpretation" of section 94 combined with a "kind of penumbra entitlement to compensation based on section 36(1)", he suggests it would be much better to rely on the ordinary meaning of section 36 to give constitutional support to a federal spending power "that is exercised responsibly in the interests of a common Canadian citizenship, while SUFA works with section 36 to avoid as much as possible the undermining of provincial autonomy and spending priorities" (298).

He concludes with the warning that Harper's legacy may be a severe curtailment and political sterilization of the ability of future governments to exercise the federal spending power in the interests of strengthening the social fabric of the country.

THE SPENDING POWER IN FUTURE PERSPECTIVE

The final two chapters, by Tom Kent and Sujit Choudhry, are forward looking in their consideration of the federal spending power. Believing the use of the spending power in shared-cost programs to have been irreparably broken by the failure of past federal governments to uphold the contracts implied by their entry into shared-cost initiatives, Kent sees the future exercise of the federal spending power increasingly tied to direct transfers to individuals and organizations. For his part, Choudhry sees future debates about the use of the federal spending power being driven by the demographic shifts that will characterize the 21st century. These final two chapters are now discussed in more detail.

In the chapter "The Federal Spending Power Is Now Chiefly for People, Not Provinces", **Tom Kent**, who was present at the conception of some of the most innovative uses of the federal spending power in building the post-World War II Canadian welfare state, provides an insider's account of these developments. Resort to the spending power was necessary, he suggests, because "strict equalization" was both beyond the fiscal capacity of the federal government and the tolerance of the so-called "have provinces". There was thus need for other federal-provincial collaboration that required the use of the federal spending power. In the late 1950s, for example, Kent suggests that Canadians were both ready and eager for the welfare state, but that the fiscal capacities of the provinces were too disparate to permit advance at comparable rates. A Canada-wide welfare state could thus be achieved only with federal cost-sharing by means of the spending power. This required federal legislation stating only broad principles, and not the prescribing of provincial programs. Despite some inevitable grumbling – Kent notes, for example, that the Social Credit government of Alberta disliked Medicare in principle – Canada's social programs were "created by federal and provincial governments in a consensus driven by democratic will", and with "no word of objection to the spending power as such" (309).

This intergovernmental harmony over the use of the federal spending power was not to last, and, as he has noted elsewhere (Kent 2008, 14), the fault lay with the federal government. Kent attributes a growing disenchantment with shared-cost programs and the federal spending power to a new generation of federal politicians, one that took the welfare state for granted and did not perceive sufficient political credit to compensate for raising federal taxes to be spent by provincial politicians. As he observes, "the political foundations of cost-sharing had cracked" (309) and the damage has been enduring. The Social Union Framework Agreement, requiring as it does nothing more demanding than "agreed Canada-wide objectives" and providing easy opt-out with fiscal compensation, also contributed to the demise of prospects for continuing transfers for new social programs. Block-funding initiatives he considers to be equally doomed. The obituary, however, was for transfers to the provinces, but not the federal spending power. On the contrary, Kent sees both an opportunity and a need for new uses of the federal spending power in making transfers directly to individuals and organizations. Such direct transfers, he observes, are unfettered constitutionally and by SUFA; rather, their use is limited only "by considerations of practicality and sustainability, by finance and by the collaborative spirit within federalism" (311). The chapter concludes with a comprehensive program for the use of such direct transfers that, if implemented, would "promote equality of opportunity, mobility, and other Canada-wide objectives" (ibid.).

The concluding chapter both of the section and of the book is by **Sujit Choudhry**, who looks forward to probable constitutional change in the 21st century and the ways in which the debate over the federal spending power is likely to evolve. Choudhry begins his analysis by exploring the original purposes of our 19th century Constitution and its evolution in the 20th century. This evolution was triggered by Canada's changed place in the world, and by a changed perspective on what a modern state should be, and the functions it should perform. Saddled with a Constitution providing in sections 91 and 92 lists of "exclusive" areas of jurisdiction predicated on a 19th-century conception of what the state does, ways had to be found to adapt the Constitution to the demands of the regulatory and redistributive state. He notes that this adaptation seldom involved explicit constitutional amendment, and this never on a comprehensive, large scale. Rather, adaptation was achieved by ad hoc constitutional interpretation in the litigation process, and by executive and legislative action, these being driven by the gap between the 19th century text and the state functions required in a modern, independent Canada.

The gulf between text and reality forced governments into a complex mix of competition and collaboration, court battles and policy co-ordination, executive federalism and inter-governmental agreements. The result has been to layer, on top of the 19th century *political* Constitution, a 20th century *fiscal* Constitution "consisting of constitutional doctrine, intergovernmental agreements, and federal statutes creating shared-cost programs and equalization" (321). The latter constitution, he states, clearly divorces the federal government's regulatory jurisdiction from its fiscal jurisdiction, and it is this that has permitted the conditional exercise of the federal spending power.

Viewed historically, Choudhry concludes that the constitutional politics of the spending power are the product of a larger process of constitutional adaptation. This prompts the question of how the constitutional politics of the spending power are likely to change in response to the emerging pressures of the 21st century. Change will come, he suggests, because our Constitution is increasingly "out of sync" with key demographic developments, namely, disproportionate population concentration in certain provinces; the increasing urbanization of population; and the aging of our population. He concludes by observing that debates over the conditions attached to the exercise of the federal spending power are debates of the 20th century. "We are now in a new century, and new issues are already upon us. How we talk about the spending power will necessarily change as part of a larger reconfiguration of political and economic power" (326).

REFERENCES

Kent, T. 2008. "The Harper Peril for Canadian Federalism", *Policy Options* 29(2): 12-17.

Petter, A. 1989. "Federalism and the Myth of the Federal Spending Power", *Canadian Bar Review* 448.

Watts, R.L. 1999. *The Spending Power in Federal Systems: A Comparative Study*. Kingston: The Institute of Intergovernmental Relations, Queen's University.

Young, R. 2006. "Open Federalism and Canadian Municipalities", in K. Banting, R. Gibbins, P.M. Leslie, A. Noël, R. Simeon, and R. Young (eds.), *Open Federalism: Interpretations, Significance.* Kingston: The Institute of Intergovernmental Relations, Queen's University.

II

The Spending Power: Context

2

Federalism Dreams

John D. Whyte

Le fédéralisme est envisagé dans ce chapitre en tant que récit socio-historique. Faisant des négociations du Traité 8 entre les peuples autochtones et la nation nouvellement constituée du Canada un tropisme déterminant du dynamisme constitutionnel, l'auteur retrace quatre temps forts d'une évolution épique de la Constitution. Il oppose tout d'abord la vision de Macdonald d'un gouvernement national fort à celle de Cartier, qui privilégiait la nationalité des minorités et l'autonomie provinciale. Il décrit ensuite l'incidence de la Seconde Guerre mondiale sur l'engagement du gouvernement fédéral en faveur des programmes sociaux. Il revient en troisième lieu sur les tentatives ratées de centralisation politique de Pierre Elliott Trudeau. Il examine enfin le retour au « fédéralisme pur » opéré par Stephen Harper. Ce qui l'amène à conclure que la seule fragmentation n'engendre pas nécessairement une forme épurée de fédéralisme. Car ce ne sont pas les règles de répartition de l'autorité qui sont au cœur de l'État fédéral, mais les principes de coordination qui incitent les diverses communautés du pays à renforcer de concert la cohésion d'une nation performante.

INTRODUCTION

A nation's constitutional character is more a function of ethical vision, or even aesthetic rendering, than it is a product of statecraft design. Often, federalism scholars seek to describe a nation's constitutional core by placing its structures within the taxonomies and models of federal theory.[1] Of course, what we truly are as a political community is historical and contingent, best grasped through understanding our national narrative. Creating a narrative is an exercise that proceeds through tropes, those literary devices that select and highlight the purposes behind the language of description. Chief among the tropes is irony – the common process of presenting life's messy and diffuse events as revealing deep purposes and reflecting established themes, while expressing all the while a

[1]Undoubtedly, there is great value in the exercise of describing and organizing various federalism mechanisms. For an excellent recent work describing federalism's varieties, see Anderson (2008).

deep skepticism about the inevitability (or naturalness) of such claims of order.[2] It is this recognition that our ordering is flawed or fallible, and this skepticism over the continuing validity of our sense of purpose, that drive the urge to reconstruct, revise, and reconstitutionalize. Hence, it is through an ironic view of our national traditions that we find our licence to be self-determining. Humankind never stops emulating the gods, and in the realm of statecraft this godliness means we tend to ground the search for political order in the virtues and principles that have become our established faith.[3] But, also following the gods, it means never suspending our critical recognition that the forms and structures we use have already begun to fail – that they no longer capture our hopes or meet our changing needs.

In the narrative of our constitutional experience, in the solid metaphors of state and constitution, we hide our uncertainty about what parts of our history matter, and our uncertain grasp of what the choices we make will mean for the nation. These metaphors represent our striving for stability; they represent the normative anchor that we hope will bind us to the common purpose of sustaining a political community. While this national narrative may seem to result from a god-like freedom to select which past endeavours we choose to honour and which commitments we want to carry into the future, we must also remember that it is a narrative and represents a limit on what we next prescribe. We are not entirely free to take leave of the accumulated weight of our lived experience or to devise whole new structures of political relationships. The very discursiveness by which we create narrative, and gain meaning and purpose from it, depends on established structures – the regimes of both openness and constraint that we dare not subject to revolutionary destruction (unless, of course, we have decided to give up on the political community and there is no further need to seek history's meaning). Notwithstanding the weight of our past, our common history must be, ultimately, that this nation is a self-determining community capable of adapting to a changing world, and that we are capable always of reforming our constitutional order. It is the constitution's fate to reflect that which we have already chosen, but also to mediate the struggle that arises from the paradox of fidelity through dynamism.[4]

In the tensions between fate and purpose, between event and meaning, between past choices and current context, between the weight of commitments and self-determination, it is wise to be modest in shaping our constitutional purposes. This is not just because we have inherited so much from others and invent only in small measure, but rather because we understand so poorly the effect of today's choices in tomorrow's context. Wise counsel suggests modest

---

[2]For an examination of the role of irony in human understanding and development, see Rorty (1989). Rorty, however, doubts that irony – so personal and so based on specific experience – is well suited to public philosophy and public purposes (ibid., 73-95).

[3]For a strong version of the place of established virtues (or moral claims) in the public order, see Nussbaum (2007, 4).

[4]This theme is ubiquitous in the academic literature on constitutional theory. See, e.g., Khan (1992).

constitutionalism, and that is best practised through the adoption of simple political goals. The most basic of political goals, at least for the liberal democratic state, is to enable all to flourish.[5] Realizing this simple political ambition depends on two further conditions: fairness (or justice for all) and stability. These conditions are related. Many political communities (perhaps, at some point, all political communities) restrict entitlement to full membership, allowing the flourishing of only a few by giving special privileges to some and exploiting others. Not only are the states for which this has become the constituted purpose oppressive and damaging to their members, but they are bound to be short-lived. The inherent instability of tyranny gives rise to a second order of tyranny: that of radical dislocation, in which one's plans, commitments, and achievements are nullified and supplanted by revolution's inevitable arbitrariness.[6] Canada is not such a country. It is not designed to favour only a few, empower only some, and privilege a limited class. The making of Canada may have been strategic, but it was not opportunistic. Canada was meant, first and foremost, to become a stable nation, and its stability and peaceableness were to be grounded on justice and expressed through constitutionalism.

CONSTITUTIONALISM IN CONTEXT

Canada's plan for justice was not proclaimed in the abstract but was based on the idea of just relations between existing peoples and their political communities. The constitutional design made no dominant claim to be uniting Canadians around a single national loyalty but only to be uniting an array of communities, whose members would become Canadians who might possibly become a single united people under a national government.[7] Cultural and

---

[5]This is not simply an arbitrary moral principle or a bit of wisdom imparted through divine revelation, but a reflection of the rational calculation that it is logically consistent to treat others with consideration and respect if one intends to claim that one's situation and needs ought to be treated seriously (see Pinker 2008).

[6]In the actual paper I delivered at the Open Federalism and the Spending Power conference, I referred to the then recent attempt by Fidel Castro to confirm his political legitimacy by being elected to the Cuban Congress. I argued that this underscored the waning force of Cuban totalitarianism. Specifically, I made the claim that for Cuba, tyranny will last just half a century, a time frame that does not count as genuine political stability. More boldly, I declared half a century to be the approximate (or natural) lifespan of tyrannies, a claim that is frequently enough borne out, but for which there are certainly exceptions. The implication is that if the basic state aim is to enable the flourishing of all, then tyranny is a bad choice both substantively and structurally.

[7]Of course, this version of the Canadian narrative is just that – a version – and not one that Canada's first Prime Minister, Sir John A. Macdonald, would have accepted. Macdonald preferred that Canada be a single legislative union and believed that the federalist derogations from that model would do little to impede "the almost imperial authority of the federal government to build the nation" (Vipond 1991, 4). Macdonald's version of Canadian Confederation met effective resistance from the start, thereby adding

ethnographic pluralism has been a major political project of European settlement for most of Canada's colonial history.[8] Our political *leitmotif* has been intersocietal reconciliation, more than overt conflict or the vanquishing of minority communities.[9]

Reflections on the Treaty 8 Negotiations

Here is one, perhaps unexpected, story of Canadian reconciliation.[10] In the summer of 1899, Federal Treaty Commissioners Laird, Ross, and McKenna met in what is now Alberta and northwest Saskatchewan with three First Nations tribes: the Wood Cree, the Beaver, and the Chipewyans. All sides met to enter into what became Treaty 8, an agreement designed, among other things, to acquire land for Canada on which settlement by Europeans could take place. From the beginning there were two certain outcomes of these negotiations.

First, it was implicit in the treaty process itself that there would be colonial settlement on First Nations' territory.[11] Second, when this settlement took place, Canadian criminal law was to apply to members of the First Nations. The Federal Treaty Commissioners' report stated:

> We showed them that, whether [a] treaty was made or not, they were subject to the law, bound to obey it, and liable to punishment for any infringements of it. We pointed out that the law was designed for the protection of all, and must be

---

a chapter to our national narrative that significantly altered our constitutional culture (ibid., 47-82).

[8]This history is explored in Cameron (2007, 71-94).

[9]The actual history of a nation and its narrative themes are, of course, two different *leitmotifs*. The latter one represents a choice about which version of history should be allowed to form the defining and normative story. With respect to colonialism's earliest intercultural dealings – those between European settlers and indigenous peoples – we have starkly contrasting histories to draw upon. The narrative selected and presented below is flattering to the honour of the new nation of Canada. Many would object to this choice and would argue that, without defining our nation by the stories of oppression and cultural homicide, there can be no subsequent story of repentance and reform and, hence, no serious national project of thoroughgoing decolonization. Indeed, it is hard to know which of these strategies would best lead to positive intersocietal reform. One would guess that both are needed to purge the continuing perniciousness of colonization.

[10]This story is drawn from the judgment in *Benoit v. Canada* (2003), 228 D.L.R. (4th) 1 (F.C.A.), 242 F.T.R. 159 at para. 7 [*Benoit*]. I adapt this story from an earlier essay (see Whyte 2007a, 128).

[11]In the history of Canadian prairie treaty-making, it is unlikely that governmental representatives always made it clear that the underlying and non-negotiable purpose of treaties was to have First Nations cede most of their traditional territory or that, after 1875 (under the federal *Indian Act*) nationwide state control and First Nations submission had been legislated. It appears that the Treaty Commissioners for Treaty 8 were more forthright in naming the government's essential conditions (see Miller 2004, 129-142).

> respected by all the inhabitants of the country … requiring them to live at peace with the white men who came into the country.[12]

In these negotiations, however, the First Nations were not without purpose. As the commissioners reported:

> They … asked for assistance in seasons of distress.... There was expressed at every point the fear that the making of the treaty would be followed by the curtailment of the hunting and fishing privileges, and **many were impressed with the notion that the treaty would lead to taxation** and enforced military service. They seemed desirous of securing educational advantages for their children, but stipulated that in the matter of schools there should be no interference with their religious beliefs. (ibid., emphasis in original)

These demands for the continuation of their economic and cultural practices, for exemption from the most onerous obligations of citizenship (taxation and conscription), for receipt of social benefits, and for preservation of religious and cultural integrity comprise an eminently sensible list on which to construct the intercultural accommodation between settlers and First Nations that was being sought.

The terms of Treaty 8 gave full consent to the First Nations' requests. It seems that long before there was a developed theory or template for the recognition of intra-state group rights, wise people understood that a nation and its constitution are built on actual needs and interests, formed in specific contexts, expressed through representatives, reflecting self-determination and expressed in formal agreements. The organizing ideas of a constitution are not prior to, or constitutive of, the agreements that are formed. They reflect relationships between political communities that are created through reconciliation of competing interests. Behind a constitution constructed in this way is not just the belief that existing peoples and existing communities have a moral right to endure and to sustain their cultural integrity,[13] but the idea that the recognition, accommodation, and protection of existing political communities is what best serves basic state goals of general well-being, universality of membership, and (most of all) security and stability.

Basing a claim for the presence in Canada of statecraft values of accommodation, equal justice, and stability on the story of treaty-making with

---

[12]Extracts from the Commissioners' Report are reproduced in *Benoit, supra* note 10 at para. 8.

[13]This chapter's primary concern is with political accommodation for a state's good political purposes – the main purpose being the promotion of state stability through just treatment. States will also adopt specifically moral views and will base constitutional provisions on these views. This basis of constitutional inclusion will correspond to inclusion on prudential grounds when it is wise for a nation to respect moral claims. Some might object to group-based moral rights on the ground that any authentic recognition of them presents the possibility of an entitlement to erode individual moral claims, and as a matter of coherent moral theory, moral claims belong exclusively to the realm of the individual. This view is examined and rejected in Newman (2004; 2007, 743-752).

First Nations may strike some as callous. Perhaps it should not serve as a story of actual statecraft or of a genuine constituting process because it was not principled; rather, it was conducted on the basis of calculations of power and with the intention to abridge the treaty relationship as soon as the political capacity of the state permitted. In particular, until 1982, the results of treaty-making did not enjoy the full force of constitutionalism's chief instrument of effectiveness: legalism – the application of the rule of law through a constitutionally independent judiciary.[14]

While there is much truth in this claim (and in claims based on the many other forms of violation of aboriginal rights), the underlying value of accommodation between communities has not been refuted by the aboriginal/non-aboriginal narratives that collectively comprise Canadian history. When a nation puts aside both its original promises and its concern for the well-being of one of its minority communities, it invites instability and disorder. In due course it will face a reckoning for the damage that has ensued. This reckoning is here with us now. It is being faced in many ways: in the desperate and costly grappling with crime and social dysfunction; in the bitter negotiations among governments, resource developers, and indigenous peoples with claims over traditional lands; in the protracted struggle to have land claims resolved; in the attempts through compensation and intercommunity engagement to provide a healing response to atrocious cultural degradation; and in the halting (and, perhaps, insincere) efforts to begin to realize the promise of aboriginal self-government. These challenges offer the Canadian state an opportunity to provide redress for its deviation from the constitutional understandings that it once so correctly adopted and practiced. Canada lives in a redemptive moment. It can now recall and reinstitute the original promises based on respect for, and recognition of, entitlements to cultural integrity and economic sufficiency that flowed from the indigenous presence.

It might also be claimed that, although the story of treaty-making with the Treaty 8 First Nations is illustrative of state-building, it is not truly a story of Canadian federalism. This, I think, is not correct. In the summer of 1899, representatives of the Canadian government were busy forming a political community based on a political union under which there would be a common citizenship not only with specific obligations and entitlements but also with recognition of distinct political identities, giving rise to named arrangements and protections. Federalism is the formal splitting of political identity in order to harvest political loyalty and stability most effectively from the competing ideas of political membership that each citizen carries into union – and that most citizens continue to carry indefinitely. These ideas of membership come from cultural and linguistic distinctiveness, from geography, from the history of settlement, and from already existing political structures.

But ideas of political belonging also come from dreams and hopes for a larger polity with the capacity to defend and expand a new nation, meld its parts

---

[14]This was achieved through the constitutional recognition of aboriginal treaty rights in s.35(1) of the *Constitution Act, 1982*, being Schedule B to the *Canada Act 1982* (U.K.), 1982, c.11.

into a coordinated whole, and grow to be independent. Federalism is a trick for capturing (and creating) an *animus* for a large and capable political community while not squandering or destroying the deeper and older political commitments that, if denied, will lead to resentment and political splintering. In fact, federalism is one answer to the abiding conundrum of political communities: Do we best build national political solidarity by creating a single dominant political identity, or are we wiser to build a national identity by making space for, and accepting, the legitimacy of the communities that have been brought into the nation? Federalism in this general sense is simply a mode of creating political pluralism within a master regime of political ordering, and it has no single formula. Nor, once the initial structure is created, does it have fixity. The arrangements we so carefully devise are invariably ambiguous (if not conflicted). They are expressed loosely, perhaps casually, and they are subject to ever-changing contexts and shifting ascendancies among the competing ideas of national needs and national well-being.

FOUR NARRATIVES OF CANADIAN CONSTITUTIONALISM

Canadian federalism was built on the contingencies arising from the existence of two founding settler communities, two languages, two cultures, and two legal systems. The new nation reflected these contingencies and many other unique features: a spread-out population that posed unbearable cost to one imperial power and unbearable temptation to another; the reality of several colonies marked by sectarian conflict; an erratic democratic condition; vast unrealized potential; abysmal infrastructure; and palpable forgone market efficiency. The constitutional reflection of all this was imperfect, in the way that legal texts inevitably do not fully reflect political complexity, and it was unclear, in the equally inevitable way that legal texts do reflect irresolution. Instead of settling statecraft conflict, the constitutional form produced strong competition over what would be its ascendant parts. Furthermore, many of its attempts to establish easy or unilateral solutions to conflicting senses of what the country should become proved to be inappropriate, and so became moribund.[15]

Like written constitutions the world over, Canada's faced the challenges posed by social and political dynamism. There is no element of constitutionalism so perplexing, and yet so important to the continuing political influence of both constitutional law and the rule of law, as the question of how a constitution adapts to social changes. While we have a general sense of how constitutions change, the deeper question is complex: which processes for making change are legitimate, or legal, or permanent, or consensual or even recordable? Constitutions can take on changes in various ways. One way is through formal constitutional amendment – a process which Canada, up to 1982, was reasonably adept at initiating, mainly through judicial interpretation – and which

[15]For a description of the elements of the constitution that have lost their force, as well as a general theory of informal deconstitutionalization, see Whyte (2007b).

has, without doubt, been Canada's greatest source of constitutional revision. Other changes have taken place through political adoption of new restraints on power,[16] through consistent practices of disuse,[17] through indirect restraints such as popular referenda,[18] and through structural compulsions.[19]

Notwithstanding the potential richness of this conceptual approach to constitutional change and adaptation, I would prefer to look at Canadian constitutional development by examining four significant moments of constitutional change and the roles of a handful of influential persons who shaped Canadian federalism. These instances stand as illustrations of how susceptible a constitution can be to the needs and ideas of the moment and to the predilections of a few.[20]

Macdonald and Cartier

If we start at the beginning, two protagonists sought to shape the new Canadian state – Sir John A. Macdonald and George-Étienne Cartier.[21] Under the Macdonald plan, once the new nation was unleashed, the force of the motives for its being would continue to define the nature of nationhood and shape its energies and needs. The new nation's legitimacy and the power of the narrative of its birth would sweep all before it; they would gain for Canada all the roles and all the powers of a great nation. In contrast, the Cartier plan was based on the sense that although geopolitical, economic, and historical realities made impossible the severing of the two settler communities, nationality could maintain its political integrity and cultural identity forever through a constitution that precluded its complete absorption into a political union and held at bay the

---

[16]There are many examples of this new curtailment of power, such as the establishment of legislative officers like electoral commissioners and public auditors, or restraints on executive discretion in the appointment of judges.

[17]One such power that has been consistently disused is the federal power to supervise provincial sectarian education.

[18]For example, constitutional protection for Newfoundland and Labrador's denominational schools came to an end because of a popular referendum in the province.

[19]Structural compulsions that act to restrain the constitution can be seen in the expansion of the federal conditional spending power and, more recently, in the recognition of a provincial role in international relations.

[20]Of course, one does not wish to adopt a naïve form of historicism, one in which historical actors float above, and are untouched by, systems of thought, structures of power and social values. To describe the history of Canadian federalism through vignettes of heroism can be only a limited explicatory device, but one that illustrates the theme of shifting conceptions of nationhood.

[21]Macdonald and Cartier were antagonists in that they had different preferences for a legislative union or a federation, respectively, and also in the way they envisaged the nation unfolding. Otherwise, however, they were strong political allies for nearly two decades.

annexing ambitions of a national majority.[22] These were large and competing visions. Each one reflected a noble dream: Macdonald's dream of effective nationhood and Cartier's dream of constant accommodation of a distinct minority. The Constitution incorporated two texts to match these visions. Madonald's text was filled with general powers, appointing powers, overarching authorities, supervisory roles, and declaratory mechanisms. The other text, the one that Cartier relied on to persuade the people of Quebec to join Confederation, more subtly included sectarian recognition, language recognition and, most significantly of all, jural recognition – the preservation of a legal system different from that of the rest of the nation, one which created a distinct normative sense of private relations that underscores Quebec's social uniqueness.

From the early years of Confederation, Macdonald's idea of a powerful national government seemed not to be the one that shaped constitutional life. Provincial autonomists such as Oliver Mowat and Edward Blake strongly resisted early Supreme Court decisions, which took the view that provincial governments were subordinate bodies.[23] Notwithstanding the clear preferences of the Prime Minister and the support that his views enjoyed in these decisions, federalism in the form of thoroughly divided regulatory power was not swept away by a new national consciousness. Perhaps the decision that best holds to Cartier's purer federal vision was Sir Montague Smith's 1881 decision in *Citizens Insurance v. Parsons*.[24] In this case, the Privy Council was asked to strike down a provincial law that sought to regulate the conditions under which insurance contract terms would or would not be enforced. The claim against the validity of this law advanced by the insurance company (whose exculpatory clauses failed to satisfy its requirements) was that this sort of regulation properly fell to the federal government under its jurisdiction over the regulation of trade and commerce. Sir Montague Smith saw in this claim the potential for usurpation by Parliament of the authority to write and rewrite the rules of contract. This could have given Parliament the capacity to amend significant elements of civil law – the very capacity that Cartier and others believed had been denied to the national level of government.

Sir Montague Smith's judgment in *Citizens Insurance* seems as technical and dry as the insurance policy that had grounded the legal dispute. However, beneath the parsing of constitutional language and the painstaking application of

---

[22]The radically different ways that Macdonald and Cartier cast the essence of Confederation are described in Silver (1982, 36-38).

[23]See, e.g., *Lenoir v. Ritchie*, [1879] 3 S.C.R. 575. Of course, it was not just the Supreme Court that frustrated the provincialists. The Judicial Committee of the Privy Council, in *Russell v. The Queen* (1882), 7 A.C. 829, granted the federal order jurisdiction over temperance regulation under the highly improbable analysis that it fell within a federal residual jurisdiction. As expansionist of federal power as this might have become, the Privy Council did not, however, adopt the ideas that provincial legislatures were subordinate to Parliament and that provincial governments did not enjoy normal governmental prerogatives.

[24][1881] 7 A.C. 96 [*Citizens Insurance*].

interpretive maxims was a pragmatic view of the Confederation bargain. He stated that if the insurance company's claim of provincial incapacity to regulate insurance contracting based simply on insurance being a trade were to prevail, Parliament would be entitled to regulate most contracting, with the result that "the province of Quebec though now governed by its own civil code, founded on the French law . . . would be subject to have its law on that subject altered by the dominion legislature and brought into uniformity with the English law (ibid., 111). Ultimately, to prevent the constitutional purposes behind the provincial list of jurisdictions from being defeated, Sir Montague Smith appealed to an interpretive principle of mutual modification, under which broad descriptions of federal legislative jurisdiction are not given their widest face value but are restricted in scope.

The *Constitution Act, 1867* sets out two large, overarching federal powers: the regulation of trade and commerce, and the making of laws for the peace, order and good government of Canada in relation to matters not assigned to the provinces.[25] The "peace, order and good government" power is extensive in two ways. First, it is a trumping power that supports the idea of a national jurisdiction to meet national needs or to secure the national good. Second, it carries the implication that provincial powers are less general, that they refer to more specific regulatory projects or purely local interests,[26] leaving for the central government an unnamed and as yet unimagined and unrealized residual field of governmental action. The view expressed so forcefully in *Citizens Insurance* is that the lists of legislative powers must be read with an eye to preserving the specific idea of Confederation as a political bargain to preserve the integrity of legal systems, as well as the legislative authorities responsible for them, and that it would be fatal to the plan to preserve distinct political communities to give full scope to any of the big concepts on which broad federal jurisdiction could be grounded. A large power over market regulation and commercial activity was denied, and the federal trade power was reduced to the functions that national governments are well-suited to play, and indeed must play. First, the federal level of government should legislate to prevent provincial regulation of the movement of goods across interprovincial and international borders that would create trade advantages for the regulating province and would therefore produce market inefficiency.

Second, the federal level should act to forestall trade practices by individual enterprises that would be anticompetitive or would distort market behaviour and thereby erode the strength and vitality of the national economy.[27] As for the

---

[25](U.K.) 30 & 31 Vict., c. 3, reprinted in R.S.C. 1985, App. II No. 5.

[26]Ibid., s.92(16). This section's application to "Generally all Matters of a merely local or private Nature in the Province", while undoubtedly a general provincial power, is cast in the language of relative regulatory insignificance.

[27]Sir Montague Smith did in fact clearly identify these regulatory functions of the national level in a short paragraph that has shaped constitutional interpretation since. This paragraph contains a charming, but misleading, expression of judicial modesty: "Their Lordships abstain on the present occasion from any attempt to define the limits of authority of the dominion parliament in this direction" (*Citizens Insurance*, *supra* note 24, 113).

peace, order and good government clause, the general reasoning behind *Citizens Insurance* was carried over in subsequent Judicial Committee decisions to create a judicial bar to recognizing a sweeping national power that would destroy the provinces' jurisdiction over civil law. In *Citizens Insurance*, and the line of cases that followed it, that jurisdiction was raised from the narrow conception of the making of rules for conducting private transactions and establishing private liabilities to a general jurisdiction for managing a provincial legal system (apart from enacting crimes) and, as a consequence, for managing the economic and social fabric of the provinces. Of course, *Citizens Insurance* did not carry the entire burden of decentralizing the Canadian federation; constitutional jurisprudence over the following decades continued to ensure that the national government could not erase the Confederation promise of protecting existing political societies.

The League for Social Reconstruction

The second moment of federal reshaping came nearly two-thirds of a century later, during and after the Second World War. What emerged was an ambitious federal program of social reconstruction that tied together the development of federal social programs, Keynesian macroeconomic management, higher federal taxation levels, and the use of both direct and conditional federal grants to provinces. This alteration of the federal role was achieved through political and constitutional innovation, and in the case of unemployment insurance in 1940, through constitutional amendment.[28] But behind these bureaucratic manoeuvres lay a changed spirit of political purpose and a vastly changed idea of the role of the national government. Perhaps the source of these changes was the growth of democratic socialism, with its belief that the free market consistently fails to meet economic and social needs. In Canada, social democracy's war with capitalism was never pursued wholeheartedly or with much effect,[29] but its concern with the social welfare of all, its determination that the state intervene in job markets to protect workers, and its commitment to social welfare programs all seem to have had a transformative political effect.

The most visible early expression of democratic socialism came in the form of the League for Social Reconstruction, formed in 1932 and lasting just ten years, which sought to redefine the state's social purpose. The giants of this

---

[28]*Constitution Act, 1940*, 3-4 Geo.VI, c. 36 (U.K.), reprinted in R.S.C. 1985, App. II No. 28. This former constitutional amendment currently is reflected in s.91(2A) of the *Constitution Act, 1867*, *supra* note 25.

[29]*The Regina Manifesto (1933)* was the founding document of the Co-operative Commonwealth Federation. This document was, however, unequivocal in its declaration that capitalism should be replaced by "a planned and socialized economy in which our natural resources and principal means of production and distribution are owned, controlled and operated by the people": *The Regina Manifesto (1933)*, quoted in Zakuta (1964, 160).

movement were F.R. Scott,[30] Frank Underhill, Eugene Forsey, and Leonard Marsh. In 1943, Marsh published his *Report on Social Security in Canada* (Marsh 1943) – perhaps the most important book ever published in Canada on the welfare state – for the federal Advisory Committee on Reconstruction.[31] Soon after the League was founded, many of the same people were joined by the leaders of prairie socialism (J.S. Woodsworth and T.C. Douglas) to form a national political party called the Co-operative Commonwealth Federation. This party pursued the familiar social democratic themes, in particular the view that inevitable economic cycles of the free market visit the most extreme hardships on labourers and the poor, and that state planning and political commitment to eradicating class inequality were needed to overcome this fate. The federal political and bureaucratic actors who in due course were responsible for implementing Canada's social reconstruction through national social programs could hardly be labelled socialists. They were, however, motivated by the same sense that the state's role needed to be expanded in order to alleviate the social hardships visited on individuals by economic shifts, and the hard personal fates experienced in labour markets. This motivation may have come from something akin to the social gospel ideas of compassion and caring that motivated many Canadian social democrats, but more likely it came from a sense that the members of a national workforce and their families deserved a decent life and, perhaps more to the point, that a decent life needed to be guaranteed in order to ensure the ongoing commitment of workers to participate enthusiastically in the economy and society. The elements of a decent life for Canadians came to include allowances to support families, insurance against unemployment, decent pensions, and protection against the economic devastation of ill health.

The dramatic growth in social welfare programs in Canada in the 1940s and 1950s under federal Liberal governments provided an important element of national identity, but it also marked a significant change in Canadian federalism. In short, social reconstruction defined not only a new sense of public function, but a new sense of national responsibility. This occurred in a complex way. On the one hand, the League for Social Reconstruction, and social democrats more generally, were convinced that legislative power had to be centralized, and they launched an attack on the crippling effect on Canadian well-being of the long line of Privy Council decisions. This campaign was bolstered by three decisions in the 1930s striking down federal initiatives on the ground that they violated provincial jurisdiction over contracting, even though the regulatory schemes were cast as general national programs designed to produce labour and goods, market stability, and (in the case of two of the schemes) greater protection for workers in a harsh labour market environment.[32]

---

[30]For an examination of Frank Scott's contribution to the work of the League for Social Reconstruction and to Canadian socialism, see Horn (1983, 71).

[31]"Marsh believed that governments should be responsible for constructing a postwar social order in which the responsibility of physical security would give way to an essential role in the provision of social security" (Maioni 2004, 21).

[32]*Canada (A.G.) v. Ontario (A.G.)*, [1937] A.C. 355 (P.C.) [*The Employment and Insurance Act*]; *Reference Re Natural Products Marketing Act*, [1936] S.C.R. 398, (*sub.*

On the other hand, Canada's great public policy response to the Depression, the *Rowell-Sirois Report* (Canada 1940), made it clear that the provinces were responsible for meeting the new social needs that had arisen. While the *Report* offered a strong defence of provincial rights, it also recognized that provinces were fiscally incapable of meeting the social demands created by the Depression. It therefore recommended the transfer of all direct taxation to the federal level and the institution of a system of federally funded adjustment grants to provinces to allow them to pay for social programs. From the standpoint of federalism, the significance of this recommendation lies in its wholesale endorsement of a federal spending power to support new social programs. It is interesting, however, that the *Rowell-Sirois Report* did not recommend conditional grants. On the contrary, it defended the provinces' autonomy in deciding whether to institute or fund programs. It placed the hope for provincial social intervention on political values rather than federal jurisdiction. The report noted that "no provincial government will be free from the pressures of the opinion of its own people" (ibid., Book 2, 84).

Between the centralizing arguments of the social democrats and the purer federalism policies of the *Rowell-Sirois Report*, the Mackenzie King government opted for a stronger national role, using the newly vitalized spending power to initiate family allowances and extend old age pensions.[33] Later, as the idea of social welfare programs was extended to education, welfare, and health care, the federal government accepted the place of provincial programs but with the policy hammer of federal conditional grants.

Perhaps the most significant aspect of social reconstruction was its striking redefinition of the Canadian state and Canadian federalism. The reconstruction

---

nom. British Columbia (A.G.) v. Canada (A.G.)) [1937] A.C. 377, 389 (P.C.) [*The Natural Products Marketing Act*]; *Reference Re Weekly Rest in Industrial Undertakings Act, Minimum Wages Act and Limitation of Hours of Work Act*, [1937] 1 D.L.R. 673 (P.C.), (*sub nom. Canada (A.G.) v. Ontario (A.G.)*), [1937] A.C. 326 [*Labour Conventions*]. The social welfare reform centralizers were particularly discouraged by Lord Atkins's observation that "while the ship of state now sails on larger ventures ... she still retains the watertight compartments which are essential to her original structure" (*Labour Conventions*, ibid., 354).

[33]The federal spending power rests on the assumption that governments enjoy both the jurisdiction and entitlement to act based on their corporate personhood. That is, a government's ability to act as purchaser, entrepreneur, employer, and owner is derived from this personhood. These bases for governmental action find expression in the spending provisions of the *Constitution Act, 1867, supra* note 25, and in particular in s.91(1A). These governmental actions can, and do, intrude on provincial jurisdictions, and the spending power is used to induce (or compel) specific features in provincial regulation and funding. There does not seem to be a clear constitutional restraint on the federal spending action even when it influences the exercise of provincial jurisdictions. The tolerability of this jurisdiction-altering capacity rests on the idea that national governments can pursue national aims through the soft mechanism of spending national wealth. Parliament's money can promote Canadian objectives even when direct regulatory power cannot be used with respect to many purely political objectives. Federal spending, therefore, has become a device to attenuate the limitations of jurisdiction-based federalism.

that was put in place amounted to nothing less than the creation of a modern activist state – a state that is not content to be a victim of fate but seeks actively to shape its economic and social destiny through the clever use of fiscal policy, taxation, insurance, spending, and social programs. At least for a time the ideas (and dreams) of reconstruction became Canada's Constitution – and they may still be in the minds of many Canadians. Social welfare programs became the way we understood how the basic state aims of well-being, equality, and stability could be pursued. These instruments were, by and large, the result of federal policies, or provincial policies that became adopted as federal programs. What was being reconstructed in this period was not so much our social and economic condition as our political identity. Following a period of social vulnerability, Canada created a richer social citizenship, and sustaining that citizenship became a national imperative.

Trudeau's Dream of Nationalism

In this narrative of federalism's development, we come next to Pierre Elliott Trudeau. Of the heroes of this story, it is he who most wears the mantle of failed heroism. He was driven by a single political ambition for the Canadian state, and he pursued that vision to lengths that, if not tragic, were at least costly. He saw Canada as a strong nation comprised of citizens with a strong national identity, presided over by a strong central government. He believed that it was primarily the national capacity that would allow Canada to have stability and would ensure the well-being of all.[34] The national markers of true national sovereignty that he pursued were constitutional patriation, national bilingualism (not language-defined regionalism), cultural pluralism as a form of interculturalism (and not as a channel to legal and political pluralism), and entrenched human rights that would both form a common political condition for all Canadians and stand as a source of pride throughout Canada.[35]

There was one further instrumental aspect to Trudeau's search for strengthened national capacity and this was to bring about an expansion of federal jurisdiction. He attempted this in two ways. First, he sought to have the Supreme Court of Canada revise the country's federalism jurisprudence. Perhaps this goal was evident in the federal government's intervention in *Canadian*

---

[34]This, however, does not capture the subtlety of Trudeau's idea of federalism. He was not a promoter of a Canadian unitary state, and he expressed frustration with the social democrats' seeming indifference to the value – indeed, the necessity – of federalism for the Canadian state (see Trudeau 1968, 124).

[35]At the November 1981 First Ministers' Conference, at which the plan for constitutional patriation was agreed to by ten of these ministers, participants reported that Prime Minister Trudeau was adamant in his refusal to accept a provision that would allow Parliament and legislatures to block the application of the Charter to specific legislation. He conceded to the inclusion of this clause (the "notwithstanding" clause) only when he realized that without it he risked losing all provincial support. For a general description of the events leading to patriation, see Romanow, Whyte, and Leeson (2007).

Industrial Gas and Oil Ltd. v. Saskatchewan[36] and its decision to become a party in *Central Canada Potash Co. Ltd. v. Saskatchewan*.[37] In these cases, the federal government was determined to prevent any recognition of provincial resource-management jurisdiction that would result in diminished federal power over taxation or diminished federal authority over international trade. The ambition to expand federal jurisdiction was certainly evident in the federal defence of its mid-1970s wage and price legislation in the *Anti-Inflation* case.[38] The piece of legislation at issue in that case[39] had been enacted due to the dire circumstance of a very high national inflation index. A federal legislative response could easily have been constitutionally justified as emergency legislation if Parliament had clearly cast the legislation in this way; clear parliamentary declarations of emergency are lightly scrutinized by the Supreme Court. Instead, the federal government characterized the *Anti-Inflation Act* as a response to a national concern, and expressed its purpose in these terms in the *Act*'s preamble. Furthermore, when the validity of the *Act* came before the Supreme Court, the government chose to defend it primarily on the basis that inflation was a national concern and this gave rise to an inherent federal power to regulate market prices and wages in order to bring it under control. Had this argument prevailed, the federal peace, order and good government clause – the textual home of federal power to take on the regulation of matters that had national dimensions – would have been released from ninety years of narrow construction and could have become a licence for the national government to assume jurisdiction over matters traditionally within provincial power, merely through claiming overwhelming national interest. Notwithstanding the stout attempt by Trudeau's great judicial ally, Chief Justice Bora Laskin,[40] a majority of the Supreme Court would not go along with such dramatic revision of the traditional interpretation of the peace, order and good government clause. The federal government's claim of constitutional validity prevailed, but only on the non-jurisdiction reforming basis that the wage and price legislation was just an instance of emergency legislation and was valid for only so long as the country suffered under an inflation emergency.

The same centralizing pair – Trudeau and Laskin – were similarly confounded by a majority of the Supreme Court in the *Patriation Reference*.[41] Although that case presented no obvious opportunity for durable constitutional

---

[36][1978] 2 S.C.R. 545.

[37][1979] 1 S.C.R. 42.

[38]*Reference Re Anti-Inflation Act*, [1976] 2 S.C.R. 373 [*Anti-Inflation*].

[39]*Anti-Inflation Act,* R.S.C. 1974-75-76, c.75 [*Anti-Inflation Act*].

[40]I make no suggestion of political collusion. As Trudeau himself acknowledged: "I never talked politics with Bora Laskin, and I have no idea how he voted before he was on the bench, nor how he might have voted had he not become a judge" (Trudeau 1991, 295).

[41]*Reference Re Resolution to amend the Constitution*, [1981] 1 S.C.R. 753 [*Patriation Reference*].

revision of federal powers, it did engage the general Trudeau claim that the courts must recognize the national government's capacity to act in situations of clear national interest. In Trudeau's mind, the Supreme Court, through a perverse cobbling together of ambiguous historic incidents and vague federal declarations of self-restraint, had fashioned a constitutional norm that threatened Canada in its direst hour and allowed provincial frustration of a clear national will to establish national independence. Chief Justice Laskin and two other justices accepted this essential, salvific role of the national government, but the rest of the Court did not. Trudeau's frustration with what he saw as the Court majority's weak grasp of vital national purpose as the basis of federal constitutional authority was evident a decade later when he spoke of the decision in the *Patriation Reference* at the opening of the Bora Laskin Law Library at the University of Toronto. The majority, he said frequently "chose to turn a deaf ear and a blind eye to the legal arguments which might have led them in another direction" (Trudeau 1991, 299). Laskin's view, he claimed, "was not only the better law, but the better common sense, and consequently it was also wiser politically" (ibid., 295). Getting right to the heart of his view of constitutional interpretive purpose, he asserted that if Laskin's view had prevailed, "Canada's future would have been more assured" (ibid.). As much as Trudeau hoped for a judicial turning away from the long tradition of reading federal powers narrowly, the Supreme Court had resisted the call to invigorate the power of the national government.[42]

Trudeau made one other attempt to create new federal powers. In the summer of 1980, after four years of constitutional negotiations in which the provinces sought an array of expanded (or at least clearer) powers, Trudeau presented a proposal for a new federal jurisdiction, and the proposal was not trivial. He suggested that Parliament be granted a jurisdiction that he labelled "powers over the economy".[43] It had many elements, such as economic stabilization, economic development, and income distribution, but its heart was federal regulation of the Canadian economic union. In response, some provinces

---

[42]Some might argue that the post-Trudeau era Supreme Court engaged in judicial expansion of federal jurisdiction that the Laskin Court did not. See, e.g., Leclair (2003, 411). In n. 21 of his article, Leclair lists eight other articles that have pursued the same theme. In spite of all these academic authorities, I remain skeptical of the argument they espouse. Certainly, the decisions in *R. v. Crown Zellerbach Canada Ltd.*, [1988] 1 S.C.R. 401 and *General Motors of Canada v. City National Leasing*, [1989] 1 S.C.R. 641 both upheld, respectively, the federal peace, order and good government jurisdiction as well as the federal regulation of trade and commerce jurisdiction. They did so in contexts and through legal reasoning that suggested there was new scope for federal legislation under these powers. However, I argue that in each case the base for federal power was so narrowly and carefully delineated, and the national interest that supported the decisions was so scrupulously described, that they hardly represent a radical new jurisprudence of Canadian federalism. Nor have these decisions led to further significant cases that recognize expanded federal power.

[43]This phrase was the shorthand used during the constitutional negotiation to describe the federal government's introduction of a proposal to strengthen the Canadian economic union or common market (see Canada 1980; Courchene 2003, 51).

agreed to a new multigovernment trade-monitoring regime; however, Trudeau's sole interest was in federal authority to prohibit all laws that directly or indirectly impeded open trade. This would have overwhelmed provincial jurisdiction over local commerce and internal trade and all forms of provincial regulation that could have an impact on markets.[44] The scale of constitutional disruption in this reform initiative, its lateness in the negotiation process, and Trudeau's disinterest in revised versions of his proposal with attenuated federal dominance all suggest that this proposal may not have been a considered attempt to secure vital new national powers. It was removed from the reform table within weeks. The proposal may have been advanced by Trudeau as a bitter reminder that the federal-provincial constitutional patriation process had become too dominated by provincial jurisdiction-seeking; for this reason, he had lost confidence in the relevance of patriation to national development.

The proposal represents the underlying theme of this narrative. Trudeau was seized by the sense that a real nation (a capable and stable nation) needs strong, effective national powers – powers that will both allow the nation to meet existential challenges and enable it in its daily pursuit of national well-being. He was right to maintain that a nation's constitution must be a dynamic instrument, able to adapt to new contexts and needs. But a constitution is also a manifestation of the people's consent. It is not the product of an unmediated ideal, no matter how grand and compelling that ideal may seem to be.

Stephen Harper's Federalism

The next stage of the constitutional narrative is now upon us. It features the displacement of judicially mediated jurisdictional conflict,[45] shifting the focus of federal-provincial political competition from disputes over regulatory authority and program priorities to disputes over money – over the adequacy, fairness, and good sense of various governments' spending and taxation policies. The debate has often been rancorous and seems mostly unaffected by principle. This is not to say, however, that Prime Minister Stephen Harper (who is indeed the last of our federalism heroes) lacks substantive ideas on Canadian federalism or on the essential purposes of the nation-state. In fact, for him, these two sets of ideas correspond. Harper seeks to resolve federal-provincial tension largely by turning to pure federalism – the idea that each level of government should stick to its clear constitutional mandate and not become engaged in political projects that, under the original constitutional arrangement, were assigned to the other

[44]The fate of this proposal in constitutional negotiations is described in Romanow, Whyte, and Leeson (2007, 68-73).

[45]Of course, judicial supervision of federal relations is hardly a thing of the past. In recent years the Supreme Court of Canada has issued two important decisions developing constitutional rules for coordinating federal and provincial regulatory initiatives. See *Rothmans, Benson & Hedges Inc. v. Saskatchewan*, [2005] 1 S.C.R. 188 (which refined the doctrine of federal paramountcy); *Canadian Western Bank v. Alberta*, [2007] 2 S.C.R. 3 (which limited the scope of interjurisdictional immunity).

level of government. This approach has been called "classical federalism",[46] but in truth it is not accurate to say that Canadian federalism is classical – that is to say that it is governed by the principle that each jurisdiction is fully accountable only for its own fields of authority, or that each level of government makes decisions independent of the other levels. This is indicated by the federal government's constitutional obligation to equalize fiscal capacity among the provinces,[47] and by the fact that already established coordinated programs, such as pensions and health care, have been continued. Nor is it accurate to describe the new federalism as "shared-cost federalism" (see Banting 2006, 79). The Harper plan is keen to diminish the role of shared-cost programs under which "the federal government decides when, what and how to support provincial programs and provincial governments decide whether to accept the money and the terms" (ibid.).

However, the idea of a purer federalism – one in which the national government declines to take on responsibility for a range of social support programs[48] – matches Harper's conception of the prime duties of the nation-state. These duties entail promoting national security (in particular, participating in the global "war on terror"); promoting public safety (through more effective criminal justice measures, assuming punitive measures are effective in reducing crime); promoting a trade-regulation environment that may, from some perspectives, be conducive to market investment and innovation; and reducing the tax burden on earners and consumers of goods. What is interesting from a federalism perspective is that while these essentially neo-liberal policies well serve the detachment of the national government from the social role of the modern activist state, they do not entail any novel conception or reformulation of federal powers. International affairs and defence are federal responsibilities, as are enacting criminal law and criminal penalties. The federal level also has full discretion over both direct and indirect taxation. It is true that an aggressive and comprehensive market policy that is designed to make Canada economically competitive in every way – reducing restraints on investing, promoting high productivity, removing trade barriers, developing human capital, and creating a stable social network – would certainly involve the federal government in many areas of provincial responsibility. In fact, however, the federal plan for economic development under the Harper government seems simply to pursue the objective of allowing the world's capital agreements to operate unencumbered by regulatory conditions. This, of course, is not constitutionally innovative. The Harper policy is to reduce restraints on investing, promote high

---

[46]This term is used and explained in Banting (2006, 79).

[47]See *Constitution Act, 1982*, *supra* note 14, s.36(2). This section states that the federal government is "committed to the principle of making equalization payments to ensure that provincial governments have sufficient revenues to provide reasonably comparable levels of public services". This is strangely attenuated language for a constitution, but the somewhat blunter s.36(1)(a) states that governments are committed to "promoting equal opportunities for the well-being of Canadians".

[48]Refusing to support an early childhood care structure is the best known instance of the Harper government's backing away from social programs.

productivity, remove trade barriers, develop human capital and create a stable social network. Therefore, the Harper plan for federalism incorporates the aims of the global market state but pursues this objective with mostly hortatory efforts at tackling the challenges of productivity, taxation, regulation, labour protection, capital investment, education, and the environment, thus avoiding federal-provincial confrontation. In fact, the complex and vital interactions between social conditions and economic competitiveness are more thoroughly explored within international organizations and agreements than through federal policies (see Robinson 2003, 228-230).

Harper's federalism rests on two related policies. The first is the announced plan to move away from shared-cost programs and conditional grants – the mechanisms by which the federal government has imposed its ideas of an appropriate national social role on provinces as the providers of social care. The second is the embrace of asymmetry under which different provinces enjoy different treatment on a number of matters, most notably with respect to participation in international affairs. Asymmetry is also evident in new descriptions of fundamental constitutional relationships and in the treatment of provinces under the equalization program. Asymmetrical relations within the federation, as opposed to maintaining formal equality among all provinces, may well be the right device to secure national stability in that it can be seen as an accommodation of political communities' differences. However, it also weakens (and perhaps makes irrelevant) the practice whereby all governments in Canada work together to coordinate responses to national needs.

This of course raises our most basic question: Are we better off as a nation to see the challenges of the current age as bearing down on all of the nation, putting all at risk, or should we see these challenges as impacting in a different way each region and province and thus requiring each substate unit to recruit its distinct federal-provincial arrangement for its own advantage? Is it the case that the more Canadian federalism seeks to meet the needs of regions and communities, the less it will be inclined, and be able, to protect the vital interests of all citizens — the interests of economic security, equitable treatment, shared well-being, and enjoyment of rights? Or does the idea of general national well-being, like the idea of nation-building, belong to a simpler and more cohesive age?

CONCLUSION

The shift from policy coordination (and hence policy competition) to federalism based on a diminished national responsibility for public goods, greater federal unilateralism, less diplomacy, and more accommodation of diversity[49] may be

[49]For a very perceptive analysis of Canada's changing federal-provincial dynamic, see Jeffrey (2006, 117). Jeffrey, however, locates the origin of the change in Canadian federalism away from national policy and toward the practice of appeasement by the Liberal governments under Prime Minister Jean Chrétien and, especially, Prime Minister Paul Martin.

said to accord with both a purer conception of federalism and the new political virtue of empowering every person and every social collectivity to shape their own identity. But in fact, it seems to accord with neither assumption. In the ways that matter to most people – caring adequately for themselves and their families, developing a valued social role, and living with a sense of a secure and stable future – Canadians are not actually shaping their own lives as much as they are bearing their own fate. Federalism is not purer just because we are a more fractured nation. At the heart of the federal state are not domains of authority but principles of coordination that allow established political communities and multiple political identities to work together to create a cohesive nation. The thrusts and initiatives of the national government do not destroy federalism: they reflect its promise of a richer citizenship. While placing at the core of the idea of Canada the focus on fiscal transfers and the simple equalization precept of equal governmental capacity might seem to represent a new respect for federal theory, it may actually manifest disrespect for the real future of Canada. This future is built on addressing the needs of children, meeting challenges of productivity and competitiveness, reforming the delivery of health services, preventing social disorder and dysfunction, and reducing environmental harms. There well may yet be reason for a national dream.

What is at the heart of constitutionalism is not division or separation, although both are essential conditions for the political mediation that sustains a nation. What a constitution most aspires to do is build the agencies and define the roles that can reflect the interests, the identities, and the virtues and gifts that must be brought into the national discourse. These must be made part of the national narrative and must be built into the great arch of national destiny. A constitution saves a nation from death by political opportunism and compels a constant mediation among a nation's players. We scorn the constitutional idea of watertight compartments not just because they so soon grow dated or because they under-represent our experience (although they may do both), but because constitutions were never designed to keep our interests apart. Rather, we make constitutions to describe how we will work together to keep a nation – to build a better nation.

REFERENCES

Anderson, G. 2008. *Federalism: An Introduction.* Don Mills: Oxford University Press.

Banting, K.G. 2006. "Open Federalism and Canada's Economic and Social Union: Back to the Future?" in S. Conway *et al.* (eds.), *Open Federalism: Interpretations, Significance.* Kingston: Institute of Intergovernmental Relations, Queen's University.

Cameron, D.R. 2007. "An Evolutionary Story", in J. Gross Stein *et al.* (eds.), *Uneasy Partners: Multiculturalism and Rights in Canada.* Waterloo: Wilfrid Laurier University Press.

Canada. 1940. *Report of the Royal Commission on Dominion-Provincial Relations*, Books 1, 2 and 3. Ottawa: King's Printer [*Rowell-Sirois Report*].

— 1980. *Securing the Economic Union in the Constitution: Discussion Paper*, by the Honourable Jean Chrétien, Minister of Supply and Service. Ottawa: Ministry of Supply and Services.

Courchene, T.J. 2003. "Analytic Perspectives on the Canadian Economic Union", in M.J. Trebilcock *et al.* (eds.), *Federalism and the Canadian Economic Union.* Toronto: Ontario Economic Council and University of Toronto Press.

Horn, M. 1983. "F.R. Scott, The Great Depression and the League for Social Reconstruction", in S. Djwa and R. St J. Macdonald (eds.), *On F.R. Scott: Essays on His Contributions to Law, Literature and Politics.* Kingston: McGill-Queen's University Press.

Jeffrey, B. 2006. "From Collaborative Federalism to the New Unilateralism", in H.J. Michelmann and C. De Clercy (eds.), *Continuity and Change in Canadian Politics: Essays in Honour of David E. Smith.* Toronto: University of Toronto Press.

Khan, P.W. 1992. *Legitimacy and History: Self-Government in American Constitutional Theory.* New Haven: Yale University Press.

Leclair, J. 2003. "The Supreme Court of Canada's Understanding of Federalism: Efficiency at the Expense of Diversity", *Queen's Law Journal* 28.

Maioni, A. 2004. "New Century, New Risks: The Marsh Report and the Post-War Welfare State in Canada", *Policy Options* 25(7).

Marsh, L. 1943. *Report on Social Security for Canada.* Ottawa: King's Printer, reprinted Toronto: University of Toronto Press, 1975.

Miller, J.R. 2004. *Lethal Legacy: Current Native Controversies in Canada.* Toronto: McClelland & Stewart.

Newman, D.G. 2004. "Collective Interests and Collective Rights", *The American Journal of Jurisprudence* 49.

— 2007. "You Still Know Nothin' 'Bout Me: Toward Cross-Cultural Theorizing of Aboriginal Rights", *McGill Law Journal* 52.

Nussbaum, M.C. 2007. "Foreword: Constitutions and Capabilities: 'Perception' Against Lofty Formalism", *Harvard Law Review* 121.

Pinker, S. 2008. "Does Science Make Belief in God Obsolete?" Online: John Templeton Foundation at www.templeton.org/belief/essays/pinker.pdf, May 29.

Robinson, I. 2003. "Neo-Liberal Trade Policy and Canadian Federalism Revisited", in F. Rocher and M. Smith (eds.), *New Trends in Canadian Federalism*, 2d ed. Peterborough: Broadview Press.

Romanow, R., J. Whyte, and H. Leeson. 2007. *Canada ... Notwithstanding: The Making of the Constitution, 1976-1982*, 25th anniversary ed. Toronto: Thomson Carswell.

Rorty, R. 1989. *Contingency, Irony, and Solidarity.* Cambridge: Cambridge University Press.

Silver, A.I. 1982. *The French-Canadian Idea of Confederation 1864–1900.* Toronto: University of Toronto Press.

Trudeau, P.E. 1968. "The Practice and Theory of Federalism", in P.E. Trudeau (ed.), *Federalism and the French Canadians.* Toronto: Macmillan.

— 1991. "Convocation Speech at the Opening of the Bora Laskin Law Library", *University of Toronto Law Journal* 41(3).

Vipond, R.C. 1991. *Liberty and Community: Canadian Federalism and the Failure of the Constitution.* Albany: State University of New York Press.

Whyte, J.D. 2007a. "Identity, Community and the Charter", *Canadian Issues/Thèmes canadiens* 8(3).

— 2007b. "Sometimes Constitutions Are Made in the Streets: The Future of the Charter's Notwithstanding Clause", *Constitutional Forum constitutionnel* 16(2).

Zakuta, L. 1964. *A Protest Movement Becalmed: A Study of Change in the CCF.* Toronto: University of Toronto Press.

3

The Political Economy of the Federal Spending Power

Roderick A. Macdonald

Toute constitution comprend à la fois un texte explicite et une série d'ententes implicites qui déterminent les modalités d'exercice du pouvoir. Les rôles de chaque branche et – dans un État fédéral – de chaque ordre de gouvernement varient constamment, tout comme les instruments qui servent aux gouvernements à réaliser leurs objectifs. Les instruments normatifs (les statuts et autres instruments réglementaires) édictent les règles tout en régissant ou en facilitant les conduites. Les instruments financiers (qui servent à produire les recettes et à les dépenser) ont aussi des effets normatifs, que ce soit en guidant directement la conduite des gens ou en influant sur le choix de leurs activités. Or l'évolution des attentes des citoyens à l'égard du gouvernement a rendu désuet ce fléau du constitutionalisme fédéral, c'est-à-dire les dépenses fédérales destinées à contraindre ou influencer les provinces et à financer les programmes de l'État-providence dans les domaines de compétence provinciale. De sorte que pour conserver sa légitimité, l'action gouvernementale doit désormais amener les citoyens à prendre conscience de la diversité grandissante de leurs identités et aspirations. Le principal défi consiste donc à créer une institution qui, à l'exemple des rapports entre les gouvernements fédéral et provinciaux, permette d'équilibrer le pouvoir de générer des recettes et de les dépenser. L'article 36 de la Loi constitutionnelle de 1982 offre à cet égard les fondements d'une argumentation normative sur les buts et instruments du pouvoir fédéral de dépenser.

INTRODUCTION

Understanding what has come to be called the "spending power problem"[1] in Canadian constitutional law is no mean trick. Despite assertions that its scope,

I should like to thank Kimberley Brooks, Fabien Gélinas, Hoi Kong, Robert Leckey, and Robert Wolfe for their helpful comments on an earlier version of this chapter.

[1]The literature on this subject is robust, and much emanates from Quebec. For a recent conspectus, see Lajoie (2006).

scale, and uses and abuses are easily identified, to capture the issue, assess its pertinence, and develop appropriate policy responses require analysis that goes both to the theoretical foundations of liberal-democratic states and to the instrumentalities by which governance agendas are pursued in such states. This chapter seeks to trace the links between these two frameworks of inquiry. Its fundamental premise is that today's preoccupation with the spending power is tributary to a constellation of myths: about the nature and purposes of constitutions; about the central features of constitutional interpretation; about the relationship between regulatory instruments and fiscal instruments; about the rationales for government action in Canada since the nineteenth century; about the policy tools that governments should now deploy; and about the policy role of the federal government in the early twenty-first century. The chapter begins by linking constitutional theory, tools of governance analysis, and the general framing of concerns with the spending power. It then shows how governing instruments are shaped by overall policy choices, how federal spending is just one locus of contestation of federal jurisdiction, and how recent changes in citizen expectations of government and in instrument-choice theory shape constitutional decision-making.

THE SITES OF GOVERNANCE

Human beings are social animals who find meaning in the relationships they build with others. Sadly, these relationships are not always bilateral or equitable, for human beings in the Western cultural tradition also appear to have an insatiable appetite to project their views about life, community, social organization, spirituality, and justice onto others. Sometimes they accomplish this through war, terror, or episodic violence; sometimes through brainwashing and other forms of psychological manipulation; sometimes through religious crusades, pogroms, and jihads; and sometimes by economic coercion wrapped up in the guise of free market exchanges. In contemporary Western societies, the primary vehicle for self-assertion and domination of the other is the political state. The state is idealized as a reflection of the will of the people to be a "nation", and this "nation" is imagined as a singular collective project to which all who inhabit a specific territory must adhere.[2]

But let us be clear. The fact that the state is idealized as a monolithic aspirational project, and that the intersubjective violence it authorizes in pursuit of this project is disciplined by institutions and procedures supposedly made legitimate by the consent of the governed, in no way diminishes either the intensity or the extent of the coercion. Whether exercised for malignant or

---

[2]There is, admittedly, an alternative vision of the political state. The state can also be theorized as providing the institutions and processes through which human beings may achieve fulfillment in pursuit of their own purposes without either subsuming themselves in the will of others or sating their appetite to dominate. Both visions are always reflected in the governance practices of liberal democracies, and the dominance of one or the other varies over time, and from state to state. For a helpful exposition of the point in the context of Canadian constitutionalism, see Abel (1976).

benign purposes, political power no less than economic and religious power tends toward authoritarian subjugation. Hence the rationales for requiring political power to be explicitly delegated to the state by the people, and for dispersing this power both functionally and by subject matter. Sharp distinctions between the authority of the legislature, the executive, and the courts are meant to provide institutional and procedural checks on each of these organic branches of government.[3] So, too, independently legitimated political units (component states of a federation, most notably, but also municipal councils and school boards) are designed to ensure the existence of discrete sources of power that also will compete for authority, and that often are able to wield effective coercion only by acting in concert – a concertation of effort that normal political processes will, it is believed, usually prevent from becoming tyrannical.[4]

The constitution is the most visible legal mechanism by which these manifold sources of violence are disciplined in liberal democracies. Not just the constitution as canonical text that may have been written at a particular moment to achieve particular congeries of purposes, but also the constitution as the implicit set of beliefs, practices, and understandings by and through which power is actually wielded. So understood, a constitution serves two complementary purposes. First, it recognizes, authorizes, and constrains those (including political majorities) who would impose their will on others. Second, in doing so, it offers a panoply of discrete institutions, processes, and instruments for translating this will, when appropriately conceived and legitimated, into action. In federal states particularly, the further assumption is made that the smaller the aggregated units, the greater the chance that national heterogeneity will be possible and that diverse subnational and communal aspirations will flourish without limiting or suppressing personal self-fulfillment.[5]

This said, a certain form of constitutional fetishism stands as a great threat to liberal democracies. Preoccupation with constitutional jurisdiction has become the opiate of both the political right (those who would disperse and constrain state power so as to prevent tyranny in the name of freedom) and the political left (those who would consolidate state power in a central government so as to build a nation). Yet the constitution being fetishized is typically only the explicit, textual constitution – those documents (and judicial decisions

[3]Of course, distinctions among these organic components of government that may be sharp in theory are in practice not so sharp – a point that jurists often have trouble understanding. See notably, Ontario, Royal Commission (1968, 15-65).

[4]See Madison (1987). The theory of dispersed, competitive institutions of governments as guarantors of civil liberties is conventionally ascribed to James Madison, as expounded in the Federalist Paper #10.

[5]The risk to federations, however, is that too great a deference to "particularisms" will lead to dissolution, while too great a deference to the liberating power of the larger unit will prevent achievement of the human potential it makes possible, as the hegemony of the central authority asserts itself. The issue is helpfully explored in May (1970).

interpreting such documents) that bear the label "constitution".[6] The implicit, non-textual constitution is relegated to the realm of (a) the historical common-law constitution; (b) non-justiciable constitutional conventions; and (c) ordinary political practices, which under the classical definition are neither law nor conventions.[7]

By formulae like "we the people", the explicit constitution of a state habitually identifies who is establishing the new political order and the justifications for doing so. It also structures the organic components of government, and typically (although not fully in Canada) it establishes the processes whereby each of these components derives its legitimacy – election, appointment, heredity, and so forth. Third, it usually elaborates constraints on legislative and executive action in the form of voting supermajorities, guaranteed constituencies, bicameral legislatures, bills of rights, and complex amendment processes. In geographically dispersed or socioculturally diverse states, the textual constitution often also allocates power as between a federal authority and the constituent substate units. Finally, given the history of democratic liberalism and responsible government, constitutions invariably elaborate how the state may raise revenue – for example, by taxation, borrowing, joint venture, and receipt of a donation or subsidy – although they invariably do not at the same time speak to the authority of the state to spend any revenue it generates.[8]

What, then, of the implicit constitution? Viewed as a matter of purpose rather than as a matter of pedigree, the unwritten constitution has two main components. The first is the constitutional inheritance. To understand constitutional documents for example in Canada – United Kingdom statutes such as the *Quebec Act* of 1774, the *Constitutional Act* of 1791, the *Act of Union* of 1841, the *British North America Act* of 1867 and the *Canada Act* of 1982 – is to recall that they each presuppose constitutional principles that pre-date them. Every written constitution, no matter how revolutionary, is tributary to the existing common-law (or unwritten) constitution of the political community to which it bears witness. To assert continuity, however, is not to assert stasis. Through its texts and their application, a living constitutional order constantly mediates the claims of history and the claims of necessity. Thus, we have the second dimension of the implicit constitution: political practices and constitutional conventions. Certain texts become obsolete – for example, in

[6]In Canada, of course, the explicit constitution comprises, at a minimum, those documents that are recited in s.52(2) of the *Constitution Act, 1982*, being Schedule B to the *Canada Act 1982* (U.K.), 1982, c. 11.

[7]The relevance of these distinctions, apparently well understood at the time of the *Reference Re Resolution to amend the Constitution,* [1981] 1 S.C.R. 753 [*Patriation Reference*], is much less clear following the *Reference Re Secession of Quebec*, [1998] 2 S.C.R. 217. See the fine discussion in Gélinas (2008).

[8]I have elaborated upon the general features of explicit constitutions in Macdonald (1996a).

Canada, the powers of reservation and disallowance, or educational appeals[9] – because other political processes and conventions have overtaken them. Meanwhile, certain governance practices develop precisely because there never were texts to address a felt need.[10] Examples of such practices are geographic representation in cabinet, limitations on Crown immunity, responsible government, cooperative federalism, the judicial appointment prerogative of the Prime Minister, and the protection of judicial remuneration.

The upshot of these observations is that one should not be transfixed by the explicit Constitution.[11] The fundamental interpretive and performative choice is not between two extremes: (a) a constitutional order that comprises only a frozen, written constitution drafted in language particular to a conjunctural event in the past, and subject to amendment only through formalized processes; or (b) mere political pragmatism unconstrained by text, history, and principle. Rather, because constitutions in their fullest sense are about the basic distributional terms under which constant and continuing negotiation of coercive authority within a state takes place, constitutional interpretation requires a rich interweaving of textual arguments – arguments grounded in the need to respond to changed circumstance, arguments about the best reading of the constitution based on normative demands, and historical arguments about the nature of a federal state.[12] Constitutions are, substantively, about competing visions of the relationship between personal fulfillment and collective endeavour; they are also about the balance to be struck between instrumental concerns (the means for facilitating human interaction) and policy concerns (the prescription of specific ends to be pursued through that interaction).[13] Procedurally, constitutions are about competition for jurisdiction, authority, and power: competition between Parliament and the executive; between Parliament and the courts; between the executive and the courts; among courts; among executive agencies; and, in federal states, between actors at both the federal and provincial levels, as well as across the various provinces.[14]

---

[9]See *Constitution Act, 1867* (U.K.), 30 & 31 Vict., c. 3, ss.56, 90, 93, reprinted in R.S.C. 1985, App. II, No. 5. Likewise, many principles of the common-law constitution – the unconstrained exercise of the royal prerogative of mercy, the non-justiciability of conventions, and the delivery of the "Speech from the Throne" in Quebec – have been overtaken by practice or convention, quite independently of explicit legislation that modifies them.

[10]The discussion of Gelinas (1997) is particularly insightful on this point.

[11]See Arthurs (2004) for an exploration of this point.

[12]The implications of this interpretive approach for understanding the federal spending power are discussed in the fourth section.

[13]It will be obvious that I am drawing heavily on the work of Lon Fuller. The best expression of his understanding of the issue may be found in Fuller (2001).

[14]In signalling these competitions between the formal institutions of a given constitutional order, one should not be unmindful of similar competitions between institutions of the state and institutions of the multiple other normative orders that seek out the loyalty and commitment of citizens. Greater attention is now being paid to non-

Recognition of the multiple, overlapping, polycentric commitments through which a political state is constituted and given institutional expression leads to a final point about constitutionalism: these distributional judgments, whether grounded in the explicit or implicit constitution, need not be driven by an identical logic. In federal states especially, there are various ways of allocating the legislative, executive, and judicial jurisdiction on the one hand, and of distributing the powers to tax, to borrow, to spend, to subsidize, to effect intergovernmental transfers, and to divide the public debt on the other hand. So, for example, there is no impediment to dividing the judicial power jurisdictionally along different fault lines than the legislative power. Nor is it necessary to frame the reserved or personal prerogative powers of the executive identically between federal and substate units.[15] The sites of governance and the boundaries between these sites are both inescapably plural and continuously shifting.

THE TOOLS OF GOVERNANCE

The competition for governance in political states today is played out not just in a variety of institutional sites; it also takes place through the deployment of a variety of modes and instruments.[16] Not all governance is direct and not all regulation is explicit – not today, not ever. "Deregulation" and "privatization" are shallow labels to capture the change in governance brought about through a re-regulation from state to citizen. This re-regulation occurs by way of the delegation of authority from politics to markets and by way of the transformation of a multifaceted, contextualized, and overt distributive justice to a unique, universalized, and covert allocation of benefit and burden through a logic of corrective justice.[17] Conversely, "governmental regulation" and "big government" are shallow labels to capture either the internormative trajectories between non-state and state legal orders or the delegation of governance from citizens to political actors rather than to family, cultural, religious or informal

---

state legal orders, whether in theories of interstate federalism as applied to aboriginal peoples (see, e.g., Otis 2006) or in theories of legal pluralism (see Macdonald 1998).

[15]In this respect Canada is typical. Under the *Constitution Act, 1867*, *supra* note 9, the executive powers of the Queen's federal and provincial representatives are not identical, as attested by, for example, the differences in the powers of reservation and disallowance (ss.56 and 90), and the constraints on the power to appoint judges (inapplicability of ss.96-100 to the provincial judiciary). The powers of the judicial branch to hear and determine cases do not follow the same logic as the distribution of legislative powers under ss.91-94A. The powers of taxation allocated to federal and provincial legislatures are not identical (ss.91(3) and 92(2)), nor are their powers to deploy the penal sanction (ss.91(27) and 92(15)).

[16]An excellent inventory of the possibilities is presented in a list of thirteen different tools in Salamon (2002a, 21).

[17]For an early study, see Macdonald (1985).

agents.[18] In other words, the very idea of constitutional government – the state – can be seen as both a site and a mode of governance. As much as diverse regulatory institutions and policies can be understood as tools of government, government can be seen as one regulatory tool among others that populations deploy to effect a governance agenda.[19]

Political theory typically does not, however, shape the details of institutional design. So, for example, in keeping with most contemporary "theories of justice" speculations, the "tools of governance" literature in public administration simply presupposes the state, rather than non-state actors, as the sole originating site of governance.[20] At the same time this "instrument choice" literature tends to be relatively agnostic about the precise political institution that actually makes use of any particular tool. The analysis is formal. Indeed, scholars observe that all the organic components of government are able to deploy most of these instruments of governance. Courts do not just decide disputes: they may make rules, they may undertake managerial functions (for example, in bankruptcy) and, increasingly in constitutional cases, they may require government expenditure.

Parliaments and legislative assemblies not only legislate: they may adjudicate disputes through bills of attainder and like strategies, and they may regulate through procurement strategies. The executive, in addition to deploying a range of managerial instruments such as orders-in-council in governmental agreements and contracts, may both legislate and adjudicate. Likewise, in a federal state, the full range of governing instruments, both direct and indirect, are assumed to be available to both federal and constituent governments, even though in some cases (notably the use of the penal power, the power to tax, the power to disburse, the power to create adjudicative institutions, and the power to appoint judges) governments may be textually constrained.[21] Even more

---

[18]See generally Eliadis *et al.* (2005) for an excellent overview of alternative frameworks for understanding these internormative trajectories.

[19]In the Canadian context, the *locus classicus* for such analysis is Confederation itself: Was Sir John A. Macdonald's first National Policy as announced in 1878 a government initiative to build the Canadian state by promoting the commercial empire of the St. Lawrence, or was the idea of a confederated Canada a governance tool of the Montreal commercial bourgeoisie? For a brief discussion, see Fowke (1988).

[20]While nothing in the classics of modern political theory requires that the analysis be limited to "justice within the state", the standard works all focus on the political state. See, e.g., Rawls (1971); Nozick (1974); Sandel (1998); Taylor (1992). A similar point may be made about "choice of governing instrument" literature. See, e.g., Trebilcock *et al.* (1982); Salamon (2002a); Eliadis *et al.* (2005).

[21]Again, the Canadian example is instructive. So, for example, s.91(27) of the *Constitution Act, 1867*, *supra* note 9, reserves the "criminal law power" to the federal Parliament; s.92(2) restricts provincial taxation power to "direct taxes"; s.96 provides that all Superior Court judges are to be appointed by the Governor-General; and s.101 provides that only the Parliament of Canada may create statutory courts vested with the authority of a superior court of record. Of course, over the years, many of these differences have been attenuated through judicial interpretation. On s.91(27), see Hogg

generally, a similarly broad array of tools are available to delegates of these governments, be they federally constituted territories, Indian bands, municipalities, school boards, armies, police forces, regulatory agencies, or public corporations.

One further feature of modern approaches to tools of governance is particularly important for understanding the spending power. Scholars recognize that these various modes of governance are fundamentally bivalent. On the one hand, the vast bulk of them have normative implications: either explicitly or implicitly, either canonically or inferentially, they are instruments aimed at "subjecting human conduct to the governance of rules".[22] On the other hand, tools of governance all have economic implications: either explicitly or implicitly, either canonically or inferentially, they are fiscal instruments that involve the getting or the giving of money.[23] Just as every tax and every subsidy is a regulatory tool implying an economic sanction or reward meant to produce normative consequences, every tool of governance that is not directly a tax or expenditure is at the same time an instrument that produces economic consequences and redistributes costs. To illustrate the idea of regulatory bivalence, one need only examine how states now deploy diverse governance tools.

Normative Tools

Historically, the most important governance tool in liberal democracies has been legislation. But legislation is a multi-purpose instrument and plays many roles. So, for example, a central premise of constitutional governance in the parliamentary tradition is that state action can be founded only on the Royal Prerogative or on a grant of authority by a legislative body. Moreover, once Parliament has occupied a particular field through statutory enactment, the Royal Prerogative in the field is to that extent suppressed.[24] Constitutional law requires that one look first to legislation as a source of regulatory authority. Yet a distinction must be drawn between the concept of legislation as a necessary constitutional foundation for executive action and as a normative phenomenon –

(2005a), c. 18; on s.92(2), see ibid., c. 31; on s.96, see ibid., c. 7.1; on s.101, see ibid., c. 7.2(b).

[22]The expression is from Fuller (1969, 106). On the taxonomy of normativity suggested in the text, see Macdonald (1986).

[23]These two dimensions of regulation have not, however, been theorized generally. Typically, the literature focuses on the "cost of regulation", rather than "cost as regulation". For a recent analysis in the traditional mode, see External Advisory Committee on Smart Regulation (2004).

[24]Particularly relevant to the present discussion is the fact that the executive (the Crown) also exercises those powers and enjoys those privileges possessed by natural persons (for example, the power to contract, to own property, and to speak) independently of a grant of authority by legislation or under the prerogative, although Parliament may constrain the exercise of these powers by legislation. See Hogg (2005a).

a regulatory tool. Insofar as the idea of legislation as an instrument of the rule of law is concerned, in Canada one must begin by attending to basic constitutional principles, and do so before turning to the division of powers in the *Constitution Act, 1867*.[25] Sections 91 to 95 allocate legislative jurisdiction by subject matter, but otherwise do not constrain how Parliament chooses to frame statutes and delegated legislation.[26]

When Parliament deploys legislation normatively, it matters little whether the legislation is directed at citizens and enforced by courts, or whether it establishes an administrative agency with the delegated authority to make rules, adjudicate claims, and inspect or license activity. In both cases, Parliament is pursuing a governance agenda. Moreover, in both cases the regulatory endeavour has significant financial consequences for citizens and for the country. For example, when the Canadian Radio-television and Telecommunications Commission regulates the activity of Bell Canada, it imposes compliance costs that are then passed on to customers. Requirements that Bell Canada provide certain services at certain rates often amount to an enforced cross-subsidy of its operations. Furthermore, statutes that create or protect a patent as a form of property provide a subsidy to patent holders and transfer costs to users. The establishment of civil causes of actions or new liability regimes, and the use of the criminal law to prohibit activity, also impose such costs. In other words, regardless of whether governance through legislation aims at command and control regulation, licensing, inspection, the creation of new torts, property rights, or crime, its deployment is not cost-free. Conversely, the elimination or abolition of forms of property, or civil causes of action arising from the private law of general application such as, for example, the elimination of tort claims relating to asbestos use, is a regulatory strategy that redistributes costs.

Governments also regulate by establishing Crown corporations. The doctrine of corporate ultra vires sits uneasily with the modern business corporation, even though there are important differences between public and private spheres, as modern Crown corporations can perform significant regulatory functions, either by analogy to business corporations or by virtue of broadly cast statutory powers. Typically these regulatory functions have significant economic consequences, either through excess pricing protected by a monopoly power or by discount pricing that provides an indirect subsidy. So, for example, when Air Canada or VIA Rail signs an agreement with an intra-provincial bus company to provide for "flow through" discount fares that enable the company to offer non-market rates, or when Canada Post Corporation offers over-the-counter services only marginally related to the post office, the regulatory effect is both normative and financial.

---

[25]*Supra* note 9. Two such principles, deriving from the notion of responsible government, are pertinent. Both the power to tax and, more generally, to collect revenue, and the power to disburse money from the Consolidated Revenue Fund must be authorized by Parliament – that is, by legislation.

[26]There has been surprisingly little normative scholarship by Canadian legal authors directed to teasing out the underlying structure of the division of powers sections of the *Constitution Act, 1867*, ibid. For one notable exception, see Abel (1969).

The use of contract as a governing instrument, a feature of Canadian public life since the era of land-grant companies, canals, and railways, is becoming increasingly visible. Today, collateral spending occurs whether the contract is with a private agency to establish a public-private partnership (PPP), with another government, with a private citizen (as, for example, a mortgage insured through the Central Mortgage and Housing Corporation), or with a non-governmental organization (NGO) such as the Red Cross. Moreover, government procurement policies, such as the federal contractors program, not only have an impact on employment policies, labour standards, unionization, minimum wages, and so on: they also involve expenditures that may exacerbate or relieve corporate expenditures. The latter is particularly true where contracts are deployed to establish exemptions from legislation regulating language of work, labour standards, environmental degradation, product safety, and so forth.

Finally, there are a range of mega-regulatory instruments. These include monetary policy, interest rate regulation, and foreign exchange controls as well as "behind the wicket" requirements such as mandatory insurance, mandatory labelling, tradable permits, and franchising. All of these instruments govern citizen behaviour, all have financial consequences for regulated parties, and all involve indirect government expenditure.

It follows that no state regulatory activity is free. Every program costs the enacting government something, if only in the form of an "opportunity cost": in this sense, all government programs are expenditure programs. Moreover, all regulation imposes costs – on the regulating government, on regulatees and their customers and suppliers, or on other governments:[27] in this sense, all regulation is a form of taxation. Since all taxation and all government expenditures are redistributive, so too all regulation is redistributive.

There is a further point. Most government programs also involve indirect subsidies, whether simply by providing an information hot-line, a brochure, a service at below cost, or by exempting particular persons or service providers from costly regulatory compliance. Frequently, however, the costs and the benefits are not indirect consequences of regulatory activity, but are the primary tools of a regulatory strategy. To these instruments – taxation and expenditure – this chapter now turns.

---

[27]Increasingly, the imposition of regulatory costs on other governments has become the subject of scrutiny. Downloading of service provisions on municipalities is just a particular example of what is known as the "unfunded mandate" problem. Consider that federal criminal or regulatory legislation within s.91 normally must be enforced by provincial police or other agencies and applied by provincial courts. Likewise, provincial legislation within s.92 (for example, labour standards and the provision of municipal services) may impose costs on federal agencies like the Employment Insurance Commission or the Canada Lands Corporation. The obverse is also true. If a mandate is fully funded (or over-funded), the impact is a federal expenditure for provincial purposes. For example, the funding of criminal legal aid at a rate in excess of what is actually spent on criminal or federal legal aid services means that provincial legal aid plans are being subsidized by the federal government.

Financial Tools

The traditional tools of governance focus on the channelling of human action and interaction through commands, rules, and the offer of services. Public purposes are achieved directly either by proscribing and regulating conduct, or by facilitating human interaction through the creation of institutions, processes, and services.[28] A regulatory purpose may also be pursued indirectly by use of financial levers: notably the power to raise revenue by means of an involuntary transfer to government (taxes, fees, licences, levies, etc.) and the power to disburse (broadly conceived as the offer of subsidy, exemption, or benefit).

As noted, the exercise of both the power to raise revenue by involuntary charges and the power to disburse require legislative authorization. In Canada, these powers are textually asymmetric, both as between taxing and spending and as between federal and provincial governments. So, for example, the *Constitution Act, 1867* grants Parliament the authority (unconstrained except by the convention that money bills must originate in the House of Commons) to raise revenue by any means of taxation (section 91(2)), or to borrow on the public credit (sections 91(3) and (4)). In contrast, it grants the provincial legislatures only the authority to impose direct taxes within the province, to borrow on the credit of the province, and to raise money by imposing licensing fees (sections 92(2), 92(3), and 92(9)). Nowhere is the federal power textually limited in purpose, while in sections 92(2) and 92(9) direct taxation and licensing fees may be imposed only to raise revenue for "provincial purposes", although provincial borrowing under section 92(3) is not so limited. Likewise, section 91 does not explicitly constrain the power of Parliament to authorize federal expenditures, although section 92 limits the authorization to disburse that may be granted to the provincial government by provincial legislatures.[29]

Consider first of all the power to raise revenue. Every decision of this character (and notably, every decision about taxation) has implications for human behaviour.[30] A decision to tax income produces different behavioural consequences from a decision to tax wealth. A decision to tax consumption produces different consequences from a decision to tax debt. A decision to tax imports through excise duties produces different consequences from payroll

---

[28]On this general point, see Fuller (1975).

[29]Since provincial taxation is limited as to purpose, presumably provincial disbursements are also limited as to purpose. As for the federal power to disburse, the rule of law requires Parliament and legislatures to authorize departmental budgets and to approve disbursements from the Consolidated Revenue Fund, but s.91 otherwise does not further constrain the purposes for which such authorization is granted. Whether these textual differences should, or according to the courts, actually do, matter to the interpretation of the federal and provincial taxation and spending powers is discussed in the last three sections of this chapter.

[30]The point is trite, but is exhaustively elaborated in Parliament (1969). The present discussion will focus on taxation, although borrowing and the sale of assets such as land, broadcast licences, and airline routes are also important facets of the power to raise revenue.

taxes. And a decision to raise revenue by imposing mandatory insurance requirements produces different consequences from a decision to raise revenue through excessive licence fees. Even where governments explicitly claim that the purpose of taxation or the imposition of a levy is merely to raise the revenue necessary to finance services and programs, the choice of taxation strategy is a regulatory decision with distributive consequences that are often direct.[31]

The regulatory policy implications of taxation and other mechanisms for raising revenue are, however, infinitely more complex than the simple decision about whether or not to tax; whether or not to impose a fee, a toll, or a levy; whether or not to borrow; and whether or not to dispose of government property. These implications also embrace decisions about the tax unit (whom to tax): a person, family units, partnerships, corporations, trusts, and so on. Within those categories, decisions will have to be made on issues such as the following: (a) the scope and definition of the tax base (What is a good or service? What is income? What is wealth? What is an import? Who is an employee?); (b) the structure of deductions, credits, and reclamations (deductions for GST paid earlier in the process of manufacture and general GST rebates, as well as income tax deductions, whether from taxable income or credits from tax payable); (c) rates of taxation – should differential tax rates be imposed for different kinds of goods, such as luxury goods, necessaries, or other consumables? Should different kinds of income (investment income, capital gains, interest income) attract different rates of taxation? Should rates of taxation be progressive depending on levels of income?; (d) when income should be taxed (When it is earned, or when it is received?); and (e) administration (Who will administer the tax system?).[32] Similar choices confront governments in adopting borrowing strategies: How high should the interest rate be set? Should the borrowing instrument be offered at a discount? Should it involve a mix of capital gain and interest?

---

[31] In tax literature the expression "redistributive" rather than "distributive" is often used. For the purposes of this chapter, however, the word "distributive" will be used in the generic sense. The distributive consequences of revenue-raising measures can be traced in two dimensions. First, people will often change their behaviour to avoid or minimize tax or other levies. For example, when faced with higher gasoline taxes, they may drive less or take public transit more frequently. Faced with differential taxes on income and capital gains, they will direct investments to low-dividend, but high-accretion investments. But taxation and levies also sometimes change basic patterns of human interaction. If income is taxed, people may engage in informal barter. If sales and services are taxed, people may exchange services. Even though the tax system may seek to impose tax on these actions, it is much harder to enforce reporting and collection. Moreover, in many cases, the reciprocity is not explicit. People may choose to live together in a commune where there is simply an informal division of labour. In other words, in this second dimension, pure revenue-raising taxation may not only create the conditions for, but also encourage the development of deeper bonds of social solidarity. See Cheal (1988); Mauss (1989).

[32] On the basic structure of taxation and the policy choices open to governments, see Hogg, Magee, and Li (2007).

What, then, of the power to disburse? Even though all regulatory actions and programs involve expenditures, some instruments of governance seek to achieve their regulatory results through direct disbursements. Like taxation, direct spending has practically an infinite array of instantiations. One may begin with an inventory of recipients of the spending. Sometimes the spending is directed to citizens, sometimes to corporations, associations, unions, charities and NGOs acting in their own names and sometimes to these entities acting as intermediaries, or to government agencies, regulatory bodies and public corporations acting in such a fashion.

The form of the spending is also various. Sometimes it is unconditional and takes the form of an *ex gratia* cash payment or a voucher. Sometimes it is conditional and is managed through a claims process. Sometimes the expenditure involves the provision of insurance, a pension, a rebate, a grant, a loan at favourable (or no) interest, or a loan guarantee. Sometimes it is a contractual commitment in the form of a favourable procurement contract. Sometimes the expenditure is unilateral. Sometimes it is meant to be a contribution-matching expenditure by the recipient. Sometimes it takes the form of a gift in kind, of equipment (a flag), or of services (translation), or of an immunity or a compromise or a write-off of an existing debt.

Often, of course, expenditure is indirect. A favourite of contemporary governments is tax expenditures: for example, through general or particularized income tax deductions and credits (including tax deductions for contributions made to political parties or registered charities), GST rebates, waiver of payroll tax contributions, subsidized licensing fees, or tax relief contracts. Other forms of indirect expenditures include regulatory relief expenditures in the form of tradable permits, exemption from requirements that would otherwise increase costs of production, and franchises and PPPs that authorize the collection and retention of a percentage of tolls.

These various types of disbursements – direct or indirect, through the tax system or otherwise – produce a normative effect in two ways. The first is by direct steering, as with most tax expenditures, conditional subsidies like child benefits, loan guaranties, and tax relief contracts. This assumes that people will act as profit maximizers and will, therefore, orient their actions to derive maximum benefit from the program in question. The second way, just as often deployed, is through abeyance, as with old age security, disability pensions, child benefits, employment, and similar insurance programs. Many of these types of disbursements do not presuppose that the human conduct lying behind the disbursement will directly change; it is hard to imagine how one could decide not to grow older, or decide to regrow a severed limb. Rather, these disbursements produce their effects by enabling eligible recipients to reorient expenditures away from an activity that they might have previously felt obliged to attend to, and toward an activity of their choosing.

All tools of governance and all governmental actions (including inaction) are complex in their structure and impact. All generate both normative and economic consequences, and can increase or decrease the cost of goods and services. Consequently, the amount of disposable income available to citizens may increase or decrease, and the allocation of personal spending may be influenced. The character of daily activity may be changed as the practices of self-reliance, barter, or gift loom larger. In other words, a theory of regulation presumes that human beings are largely rational actors who respond to incentives of various descriptions. Whether these incentives aim at liberty constraints or psychic levers, they will inevitably involve costs and lead to government expenditure.

THE SPENDING POWER IN LAW AND MYTHOLOGY

Given that every conceivable governmental operation involves economic consequences and every tool of government involves redistributive spending, the exact parameters of any government's exercise of its "spending power" as a separate regulatory instrument are hard to specify. To act is to spend. Nonetheless, when Canadian constitutional lawyers talk of the spending power, the object of their concern historically has been considerably narrower than a tools-of-government analysis would suggest. They refer to state action that involves (a) direct program spending, (b) by the federal government, (c) in areas where the legislature of a province has been given exclusive jurisdiction to enact legislation, (d) otherwise than by unconditional transfer, (e) without the express consent of the government of an affected province, and (f) where the revenue source is taxation or levies internal to Canada.[33] To reach meaningful conclusions about the constitutional dimensions of the spending power, it is necessary to elaborate upon each of these definitional constraints.[34]

Direct Program Spending

All state action in deploying a tool of government involves the direct or indirect expenditure of money and produces normative consequences, even where direct spending in pursuit of a policy is envisioned. However, only a portion of these actions involve what might be called targeted program spending. Neither indirect spending consequent upon the deployment of a non-fiscal instrument, nor direct disbursements in the form of tax expenditures, nor even spending by virtue of direct subsidies outside the income tax system, fits the classical definition of direct program spending. Direct expenditure outside the income tax

---

[33]The above criteria are derived from articles by both those who acknowledge the constitutionality of a federal spending power so conceived, and those who contest its constitutionality. See, e.g., Lajoie (1988); Tremblay (2001); Petter (1989); McCoy and Friedman (1988); Choudhry (2002); Maher (1996).

[34]The issue has become more complicated in recent years, as concern about federal spending has shifted considerably to also embrace the larger context of what has come to be called the "fiscal imbalance". A comprehensive discussion is presented in Commission on Fiscal Imbalance (2002a). To capture this additional dimension of constitutional contestation requires a brief excursion into the law and practice of "fiscal federalism" – an endeavour that will be taken up in the fourth section. See generally Lazar (2005).

system might involve, for example, subsidies to hydro corporations, the post office, municipal mass transit services or VIA rail; GST and PST rebates for low-income earners; and various forms of information on health, nutrition, recreation, housing safety standards, and so on, provided free through pamphlets and the Internet. Nonetheless, the primary focus of debate about the spending power has been on direct program spending in areas like health, welfare, pensions, infrastructure, research and post-secondary education, through shared-cost programs, conditional grants to provinces, mediated payments to institutions for redistribution to citizens, and direct grants to citizens.[35]

Federal Spending

The second limitation on the scope of the spending power that generates scholarly concern is the limit that the federal government must be the source of the money spent or the channel through which that redistributed money flows. In other words, critics are less concerned with direct program expenditures as a tool of government *per se* than with expenditure by the federal government in particular.[36] The argument is not one of political theory (that governments ought not to tax and spend), but rather one of constitutional law. The claim is that there are constitutional limits on the authority of the federal government and its agencies to engage in direct program spending. No such limits, however, attach to such spending by other governments or agencies. So, for example, any spending by a provincial government or one of its agencies (municipalities, school commissions, and regulatory commissions) is not seen to raise constitutional concerns. There may be political concerns, but if so, the remedy is political.[37] In addition, there is little concern over program spending by foreign

---

[35]In the literature on the spending power prior to the Meech Lake Accord, there was only rare discussion of disbursements in the form of tax expenditures, operating subsidies, or favourable procurement policies. For the exception that proves the rule, see Petter (1989). Discussions at that time also did not address spending by way of the direct gift of property to citizens. Examples of such gifts might include the gratuitous disposal of excess Crown assets, the allocation of shares in privatized Crown corporations, or the distribution of Crown lands.

[36]Each of the critics, *supra* note 33, and the various studies prepared for the Commission on Fiscal Imbalance (2002a), focus on spending by the federal government.

[37]For example, extra-provincial spending in the manner of the original sixth point raised (but quickly abandoned) in the run-up to the Meech Lake Accord, namely, the special role of Quebec in promoting the welfare of francophone communities outside Quebec, has not generally been seen to be constitutionally illegitimate. On this sixth point see Hogg (1988). An early example of Quebec spending to this effect can be found in *An Act to authorize school commissions to make contributions from their funds for patriotic, national or school purposes*, S.Q. 6 Geo. V (1916) c. 23, s.1, under which the Quebec legislature undertook to assist the financing of patriotic, nation, or scholarly endeavours in Quebec, or elsewhere. A recent case of extra-territorial provincial spending in which the court held the spending to be within provincial legislative competence is *Dunbar v. Saskatchewan (A.G.)* (1985), 11 D.L.R. (4th) 374 (Sask. Q.B.) [*Dunbar*]. For further

countries (for example, through cultural exchanges, scholarship programs, and financing of research consortiums, as well as through direct expenditures and gifts to their non-resident nationals). Program spending by international agencies such as the World Bank, the International Monetary Fund, or the United Nations Educational, Scientific and Cultural Organization, or even by foreign or extra-provincial charities, corporations, unions, and NGOs also escapes the censure of constitutional scholars preoccupied with the spending power.

Exclusive Provincial Legislative Jurisdiction

The key to the constitutional concern, as conventionally formulated, is that federal spending must be related to a matter over which provinces are given exclusive legislative jurisdiction. Where jurisdiction is exclusively federal under an enumerated head of power, or an explicitly shared responsibility – for example, agriculture and immigration – the constitutional concern does not arise. Of course, what constitutes a matter of exclusive provincial legislative jurisdiction can only be determined by a careful consideration of what the limits of federal power may be. The question has two dimensions. The first is to determine whether the limits on the federal power to spend are identical in scope to the limits on the power of the Parliament of Canada to enact legislation.[38] The second is to determine the limits of federal legislative jurisdiction where expenditure arises as a collateral or ancillary effect of the exercise of an enumerated federal power. Historically, the "watertight compartments" metaphor of Lord Atkin dominated the analysis of constitutional jurisdiction.[39] Today, a different metaphor of constitutional jurisdiction controls the discussion. Jurisdictional frontiers are no longer to be established by what look like *ex ante* bright-line rules, but are rather to be determined by a functional logic under which the scope of federal legislative jurisdiction is capable of

discussion of the implications of this point for the rationale and scope of limitations on the federal spending power, see the section "Federal Jurisdiction" below.

[38]It is often claimed that the speeches of Lord Watson in *Liquidators of Maritime Bank v. Receiver General of New Brunswick*, [1892] A.C. 437 (P.C.) and Lord Haldane in *Bonanza Creek Gold Mining Co. v. R.*, [1916] 1 A.C. 566 (P.C.) [*Bonanza Creek*] settled this question. While the court in *Bonanza Creek* held at 580 that "the distribution under the new grant of executive authority in substance follows the distribution under the new grant of legislative powers", this conclusion is not definitive on the extent of the power to disburse. This point will be considered in greater detail in the final section.

[39]*Reference Re Weekly Rest in Industrial Undertakings Act, Minimum Wages Act and Limitation of Hours of Work Act*, [1937] 1 D.L.R. 673 at 684 (P.C.), (*sub nom. Canada (A.G.) v. Ontario (A.G.)*), [1937] A.C. 326 [*Labour Conventions Case*]. It is important to note that the "watertight compartment" view does not demand that constitutional interpretation be grounded in an "original intent" ontology. Rather, the watertight compartment view seeks to reduce (if not eliminate) the possibility of concurrent legislative jurisdiction, and is usually accompanied by a narrow reading of the ancillary powers doctrine. For further elaboration of the point, see the section "Federal Jurisdiction" below.

significant enlargement.[40] As the Supreme Court moves to an expansive reading of the ancillary and national dimensions doctrines, the limits of jurisdiction in each order of government become much more difficult to pin down.[41] While the same type of expansive reading can be given to provincial jurisdiction, much of the constitutional concern about federal spending is now expressed not just in terms of limiting such spending to areas within federal legislative authority, but also in terms of contesting recent judicial decisions that are seen as enlarging Parliament's legislative jurisdiction.[42] In other words, if one's policy or political objective is to constrain federal regulatory action by limiting the spending power to federal heads of legislative jurisdiction, one's purposes can be defeated if courts give a continually broadening interpretation to the extent of that legislative jurisdiction.

Otherwise Than By Unconditional Transfer

In its most general form, the critique of the federal spending power is directed to all direct federal program spending in areas of provincial jurisdiction, regardless of how the spending occurs. Under one version of this critique, even if the federal government were simply to give money to a province as an unconditional transfer, this would be an unconstitutional expenditure, and its acceptance by the province would also be unconstitutional.[43] However, most critiques of the spending power imagine that what is constrained by the Constitution is not the federal spending in itself, but its conditional or directed nature. The problem arises because the offer of money, either in the context of a shared-cost program or as a conditional transfer, will impliedly drive provincial policy in an area of provincial jurisdiction.[44] Even some unconditional transfers can have important, though indirect, steering effects. If the transfer is to citizens, this may undermine provincial economic redistribution policy; for example, the

---

[40]See Leclair (2003). He argues that "bright-line" jurisdictional frontiers are necessary to prevent federal encroachment on provincial authority. For further discussion, see text at note 76, *infra*.

[41]See, for example, *General Motors of Canada Ltd. v. City National Leasing*, [1989] 1 S.C.R. 641 [*General Motors*]. Some scholars also observe that the waning of doctrines of interjurisdictional immunity such as propounded in *Bank of Montreal v. Hall*, [1990] 1 SC.R. 121 are further evidence that the Supreme Court no longer respects "bright-line" jurisdictional frontiers and is prepared to tolerate increasing encroachment on what was previously considered to be exclusive provincial or federal jurisdiction.

[42]See notably, Brouillet (2005).

[43]For an early argument to this effect, see Beetz (1965, 113). Since the enactment of s.36 of the *Constitution Act, 1982*, *supra* note 6, this argument about unconditional grants is probably no longer tenable.

[44]Other problems are that it forces provinces to commit to programs that may then be underfinanced in the future; also if the program is accepted by others, and there is no opt-out, it penalizes the recalcitrant province. See generally, Abel (1978), and especially Part IV of this unfinished work entitled "Spending: Scope of the Spending Power" at 313.

federal transfer of a substantial fixed amount in the form of a gift or interest-free loan to all taxpayers could well compromise the effectiveness of policies favouring a steeply graduated income tax. This is even truer for unconditional transfers to corporate entities such as hospitals, hospital foundations, universities, food banks, and so on. Unconditional gifts to any non-universal recipient group are redistributive, however widely the net is cast. Taken to the limit, unless a formula were found such that the amount returned to a province was identical to the amount raised within the province, the transfer of funds would have an impermissible regulatory effect. Here the policy steering arises because all transfers imply a transfer formula. Moreover, if the chosen formula involves explicit equalization of some sort, this is redistributive federal spending that has implications for provincial capacity to raise revenue and to target spending as the province sees fit. [45]

Without the Express Consent or Possibility of Fully Compensated Opt-Out of the Affected Province

One reason why critics disparage even unconditional federal spending is that it puts provinces under enormous pressure to accept the funds. Consider first conditional spending. The only way in which a province can be truly free to consent is if it will receive, through an opt-out, exactly the same amount of money from the federal treasury that it would have received had it consented to the shared-cost program or the conditional transfer. Moreover, if some provinces agree to a conditional transfer and others do not, it may be difficult to control for externalities. Imagine a direct subsidy to citizens for certain prescription drugs. Even with an opt-out, given the difficulty of enforcing interprovincial trade barriers, cheap drugs in Saskatchewan could easily be marketed in any other province, and this would have an impact on policy formation in those provinces. Where the subsidy is to a provincial health agency, this implies policy steering as long as interprovincial mobility of citizens is possible. Moreover, unless the amount of the transfer by opt-out is exactly equal to a province's pro-rated share of tax collected in the province, then even an unconditional transfer via an opt-out can mean foregone revenue for the province and a cross-subsidy to other provinces. Consequently, even with express consent or the right to an unconditional opt-out, program expenditures may be interprovincial equalization expenditures in disguise. Put slightly differently, in order for the federal spending not to have a redistributive effect, the amount of the compensated opt-out would have to be the greater of the amount the province would have

[45] This latter position must rest on a different constitutional footing than the conditional transfer critique, however, for in this case the federal expenditure in no way trenches on provincial jurisdiction or otherwise seeks to "guide" provincial policy. Rather, the argument must be to the effect that the federal government should not have the capacity to *raise* revenue beyond that required to finance strictly federal purposes. Accepting the legitimacy of this claim, however, merely displaces the issue: is economic redistribution a legitimate federal purpose? On this issue, see the discussion on s.36 of the *Constitution Act, 1982* in the final section.

received under the scheme or the province's share of the total tax bill necessary to fund the program.[46]

Revenue Source Is Tax or Levies within Canada

A further issue relating to the source of the money that sustains direct federal program spending remains. Initially those who contested the existence of a federal spending power focused on expenditures of tax and other revenues raised by the levies on Canadian taxpayers.[47] Presumably, the foundation of this narrowly cast objection was that expenditure of money raised by taxation had negative impacts on the capacity of provincial governments to fund their own programs. Today, however, because concern has shifted to the steering effect of federal expenditure, the objection embraces all federal spending regardless of the revenue source: gifts by Canadians to the federal government; transfers by foreign governments or international agencies to the federal government for redistribution; taxation of offshore taxpayers who do not reside in any particular province; spoils of war; profits of Crown corporations; and so on.[48] Consider the following example. A multimillionaire could set up a charitable foundation and distribute scholarships to post-secondary students as he or she saw fit (subject, of course, to applicable Human Rights Code restrictions); the criteria for awarding the scholarship might, conceivably, be identical to those adopted by the Social Sciences and Humanities Research Council of Canada (SSHRC). But on the broad understanding of federal spending, the multimillionaire's foundation could not give the money to a federal agency such as the SSHRC to do the spending, even if the norms adopted by the foundation were identical to those employed by the SSHRC. Nor could the federal government spend even where there was no impact on the capacity of provinces to raise revenue, because the revenue source would be a type of taxation exclusively available to the federal Parliament (for example, indirect taxation) or levies that only the federal government could impose (for example, customs duties). The root of the complaint at this point clearly has only a tenuous connection with a concern about undermining provincial public policy, or even with compromising the possibility of raising provincial revenue. Rather, it has to do with competing

---

[46]The rationale is this: *ex hypothesi* these programs are not "equalization programs" justified as falling within federal jurisdiction under s.36. Consequently, the federal government should have no authority to raise, in an opting-out province, revenue that is greater than the amount received in compensation. If it did so, it would be engaged in an unauthorized equalization program by conscripting taxpayers in a province that has opted out into financing the program in "have-not" provinces.

[47]Notwithstanding the express language of s.91(2), courts have sometimes doubted that properly collected tax revenues can be spent in any manner the federal executive might choose. See *Reference Re Employment and Social Insurance Act (Can.)*, [1937] 1 D.L.R. 684 (P.C.), (*sub nom. Canada (A.G.) v. Ontario (A.G.)*) [1937] A.C. 326 at 366 [*Unemployment Insurance Reference*].

[48]For a helpful discussion, see Lajoie (2006, 153-154).

understandings of federal citizenship, which is why this argument has particular resonance among Quebec scholars.[49]

From this discussion, it is apparent that there is a significant difference between what might constitute the federal spending power were a sophisticated "tools of governance" analysis to be adopted, and what constitutional critics of federal spending in Canada have traditionally seen as the main issues. This difference has long obscured a number of important substantive inquiries: (a) Why do governments spend? What are the justifications for government spending? (b) What is the nexus between taxation and expenditure? Is the argument really about federal spending or about federal taxation? (c) What is the impact of the changing environment of instrument choice: is federal spending really an issue for the future? These inquiries are addressed in the next sections of this chapter.[50]

POLICY CONTEXTS OF FEDERAL SPENDING

All governments spend money; all Canadian governments have done so since 1867. However, the "federal spending power" became a significant issue for most Canadian constitutional lawyers only in the period after World War II. Some believe that the first exercise of the narrowly defined federal spending power arose in relation to agricultural subsidies in 1912, and that such federal spending was pursued systematically throughout the next quarter century.[51] However, the general deployment of the power to spend in fields of provincial legislative jurisdiction dates from the beginnings of the welfare state, or from what many policy analysts have called Canada's second National Policy.[52]

---

[49]For further development of the idea that federal social spending carries deep implications for the meaning of federal citizenship see Weinstock (2005; 2006).

[50]Some scholars see the "federal spending power" problem as (a) a particularly Canadian problem that (b) is essentially a consequence of the expansion of the welfare state in the mid-twentieth century. It is neither. The problem of federal spending is present in all federations and has been evident for at least two centuries. Consider the following example. Toward the end of the American Civil War, the Confederate government found itself desperately short of soldiers. It proposed to conscript slaves into the army, offering them and their families freedom at the conclusion of the war. While critics of the plan acknowledged that the Confederate government could conscript slaves for war purposes (and even arm them), they contested whether it lay within the power of the government to "free the slaves". Slaves were property, and manumitting them would be an exercise of the spending power: it would be to give away federal property. There was no authority in the Confederate government to do so for any non-federal purpose, and the Constitution explicitly forbade the government to interfere with the "institution" of slavery – a power reserved exclusively to the several states. For a discussion of this point, see Currie (2004, 1300-1306).

[51]See Sécretariat aux affaires intergouvernamentales canadiennes (1998). See also Commission on Fiscal Imbalance (2002b).

[52]For a brief discussion, see Fowke (1988).

Two factors account for this, one of them economic and centripetal, one of them ideological and centrifugal. First, the nineteenth-century conception of the role of government, and the consequent allocation of responsibility as between provincial legislatures and the Parliament of Canada in 1867, proved ill-adjusted to the needs of twentieth-century states. Second, the post-World War I (Treaty of Versailles) conception of nationalism, and the claims of nations for political presence, sparked a general desire for self-assertion by provincial governments and especially by the government of Quebec.

Consider the economic, centripetal explanation. Canadian constitutional lawyers typically tell one of two stories of Confederation. One of these stories, dominant among francophone scholars in Quebec, suggests that the *Constitution Act, 1867* was simply a further iteration of a permanent compact between two nations.[53] The second story, dominant elsewhere, suggests that Confederation was simply a means for the Colonial Office to get rid of the burden of England's North American colonies, yet temporarily maintain their colonial status: Confederation was a step on the road from "colony to nation" (see Lower 1958; Stanley 1956; Lower 1946). There is also a third story, offered mainly by political economists and historians: Confederation was the vehicle by which the Montreal anglophone bourgeoisie were enabled to pursue policies of high tariffs, immigration to the prairies, and transportation infrastructure in furtherance of building what has come to be called "the commercial empire of the St. Lawrence".[54] On this interpretation, the primary question was how to generate the political authority necessary to build a coast-to-coast economy against the natural north-south economic flow. The Canada of the *British North America Act* – the particular configuration of political institutions and the particular allocation of legislative jurisdiction – can be seen as an instrument of economic policy, rather than economic policy being seen as an instrument deployed by the federal government in a state-building endeavour.[55]

By the mid-1930s, however, all governments of the Atlantic area were confronted with the Great Depression and the need to deploy macro-economic levers to resuscitate the economy and protect the welfare of citizens. Hence, the Rowell-Sirois Commission and its attendant second National Policy's strong federal spending on social welfare and the institutions of cultural and economic nationalism. In pursuing this twin policy of open global markets to ensure that trade was not a source of conflict and, as a concomitant local counterbalance, the creation of a robust welfare state in Canada followed a similar course to that

---

[53]I have attempted my own analysis of compact theory – one that emphasizes the difference between a compact between two peoples and a compact between the Government of Quebec and the Government of Canada – in a number of articles. See Macdonald (1991a; 1991b; 1996b); Macdonald and Szilagyi (2005).

[54]See generally Dales (1966); Norrie (1974); Smiley (1975); Eden and Appel Molot (1993); Tupper (1993); McFetridge (1993).

[55]In this light, Lesage's *Maîtres chez nous* rallying cry of 1962 was fundamentally no different from Macdonald's National Policy slogan of 1879. See Macdonald and Wolfe (2008-2009).

of other North Atlantic states.[56] But economic and political stability required more. It also called for a central bank to manage economic shocks coming from outside Canada, and for the formal instruments needed to allow resources to flow gracefully between slower-growing and faster-growing regions of the country. This federal action was not achieved easily, given the reluctance of the Privy Council to adopt an expansive reading of Parliament's jurisdiction.[57]

The economic shock of the 1930s was accompanied by the political shock of the early 1940s, in the form of World War II. The federal government found itself politically unable to raise the revenue needed to finance the war in the absence of provincial cooperation. On both the spending and taxation fronts, the arrangements of 1867 appeared to be inadequate to deal with these two crises.[58] Apart from occasional constitutional amendments,[59] the preferred vehicles of the second National Policy became tax rental agreements; direct federal spending through subsidies to citizens, groups, and corporations; multiple shared-cost programs; interprovincial equalization transfers; and, increasingly, complex tax expenditures.[60]

From the federal response to these crises, and particularly from the refusal of the federal government to desist from such policy initiatives once the economic and political crises were met, came the second explanation of concern about federal spending – the ideological and centrifugal explanation. The components of the first National Policy were national in the sense that they applied to the whole country. Any action not required for building a transcontinental state and economy was left to the provinces. The story of the second National Policy, however, is one of continual conflict between orders of government. The 1867 arrangement did not imagine that the state, whether provincial or federal, would enter the social terrain occupied by religious and charitable institutions and by rural and neighbourhood collective-assistance organizations. Nor were the Fathers of Confederation prescient as to the policy instruments and jurisdictional allocations necessary to manage a national economy in the mid-twentieth century. When Canadians and their governments felt the need to create the institutions and programs of what became the welfare state, few provinces had the tax base, the population, and the governance

---

[56]This idea is based on the "double movement" elaborated in Polanyi (1967). See also Ruggie (1982).

[57]See *Labour Conventions Case*, *supra* note 39; *Unemployment Insurance Reference*, *supra* note 47.

[58]Abel (1978), especially Part III entitled "Taxation" at 293 and Part IV entitled "Spending: Scope of the Spending Power" at 313.

[59]See *Constitution Act, 1867*, *supra* note 9, ss.91(2A) (added in 1940), 94A (as originally enacted in 1951). These amendments related to unemployment insurance and old age pensions, respectively.

[60]For a good review of these initiatives, see Courchene (1997).

capacity to manage them. As a result, with the concurrence of most provinces, Ottawa took the initiative in developing social welfare policy initiatives.[61]

Many Quebec scholars see all these instruments of the second National Policy, and not just the spending power as understood in the classical sense, as an unwarranted and unjustifiable trespass upon provincial jurisdiction.[62] The principal normative argument, most often implicit, is that of appropriate governing structures for diverse and dispersed political communities. Scholars who argue that social spending programs that directly emanate from, or are seen to originate with, the federal government should be curtailed often make the argument primarily because they cannot conceive of Canada as their nation – only as their state.[63] The basic premise is that the initial allocation of social policy to the provinces should be maintained even when Canadian state-building calls forth a more thickly conceived conception of federal citizenship.[64] Nowhere has this understanding of federal-provincial relationships been better explored than in the *Tremblay Commission Report* of the 1950s.[65] While the policy goals of the first National Policy benefited Quebec, neither the goals nor the instruments encroached on provincial legislative powers. They did not, moreover, challenge the ability of Quebec City to hold itself out as the political centre for francophone identity. The tools and objectives of the second National Policy, by contrast, brought to light differing conceptions of the role of the state, initially, and differing conceptions of the locus of responsibility for nation-building, subsequently. Until the 1950s, Quebec resistance to federal action was grounded in ideological conflict between a small-government regime in Quebec and a welfare-state regime in Ottawa about the respective roles of the state and the institutions of civil society. After 1960, the conflict was about which government should take responsibility for providing the policies and programs of the welfare state that were definitive of a nation.[66]

---

[61]For a perspective on the creation of many of these initiatives by an insider at the time, see Kent (2008).

[62]To my knowledge, the only non-Quebec scholars who take an uncompromising position against the "unlimited" federal spending power are Abel (1978) and Petter (1989). Most acknowledge both the existence of and the necessity for federal spending that goes beyond the jurisdictional constraints of federal legislative authority, even though some also attempt to find normative justifications for constraining its exercise. On the latter point, see particularly Hoi Kong, this volume.

[63]This is a recurring theme in much scholarship emanating from Quebec. For an insightful reflection from a jurist see Woehrling (1988). For an equally insightful reflection from a political scientist, see Dufour (1989).

[64]The point is nicely explored in Taylor (1993a, 1993b).

[65]See Quebec (1956). The Report is often seen as an intention to justify the establishment of a provincial income tax to generate revenues to compensate universities for the government's refusal to permit them to receive federal money directly. Nonetheless, the overall thrust of the Report aims at justifying the role of the provinces as the centre of gravity for social citizenship.

[66]This latter conception of the role of the state is true as much for Liberal Party premiers Lesage, Bourassa, (Daniel) Johnson, and Charest as for Parti Québécois

This discussion of ideological conflict around federal spending raises more fundamental questions. One might begin by asking, "Why do states act?" It is obviously beyond the scope of this chapter to essay a theory of the state and the citizen, but insight into the character of the issue can be gained by thinking about spending as a question of instrument choice. Here there are two broad explanations. One is the public choice explanation: governments in liberal democratic states imagine and pursue policies to get elected. When financial resources are thin, governments tend to spend *law*, enacting statutes that ostensibly solve a problem by externalizing and redistributing the costs of dealing with it onto someone else. When financial resources are more plentiful, governments tend to spend *money*, establishing programs that overtly involve redistributing benefits. The other explanation is less conspiratorial: governments in liberal democratic states imagine and pursue policies that ensure a fair balance between market liberalism and social welfare. When social welfare can be assured by building externalities directly into the costs of production, governments act by way of regulation, and by according franchises and contracts. When social welfare cannot be assured in that way, governments act by means of taxation, spending, state corporations, and similar instruments. When neither of these forms of direct governance is possible, states act by way of indirect regulatory instruments (see Peters 2002, and Salamon 2002c).

The desire of the Quebec government to act as a state (implicitly denying that it is a province within a federal state) is manifest in both these strategies. The Duplessis government of the 1950s spent law to act as a state; the promotion of a socially conservative and largely Roman Catholic rural society was not an issue of expenditure as much as it was an issue of control of public morality.[67] However, the very different view of the state adopted by the Lesage government and its successors required resources and money; on this view, it was possible to assert a national project of state-building in diverse regulatory fields by spending money within the traditional jurisdictional framework of section 92, and without trespassing on federal jurisdiction. The only constraint upon state-building action in Quebec was the provincial government's capacity to raise revenue.

Expenditures, especially direct program expenditures, are a powerful policy instrument. They can be used for economic projects, whether by a province or by the federal government. They can be used for political projects, as in the

---

premiers Levesque, (Pierre-Marc) Johnson, Parizeau, Bouchard, and Landry. After 1960, any federal action that appeared to challenge the ability of the Quebec government to shape patterns of interaction or to promote Canadian citizenship necessarily ran counter to Quebec self-affirmation, whether merely nationalist or overtly sovereigntist. In this light, the fundamental problem with the patriation endeavour of 1982 was less the amending formula than the attempt to use the Canadian Charter of Rights and Freedoms as a Canadian nation-building strategy. The best contemporary analysis of this point remains Russell (1983).

[67]Many of these attempts to control public morality – notably the control of religious and political speech – were found by the Supreme Court to trench upon the exclusive jurisdiction of the Parliament of Canada in matters of criminal law and, more generally, upon certain constitutional principles relating to civil liberties. See Hogg (2005b, c. 34.1–34.4.).

competition to put either the Quebec or the Canadian flag on a cheque, in Quebec's spending in support of extra-provincial francophonie and in Ottawa's promotion of the "no" option in Quebec's referendum. They can be used to serve social projects, whether local, provincial, or pan-Canadian. Historically, neither the federal government, nor scholars favouring federal social spending, have objected to non-section 92 provincial spending.[68] But federal spending evokes a different response. Increasingly, both in Quebec and in the newly minted "have" provinces in Canada, the objection is not to the existence of federal spending but to its scope, its scale, and especially its modalities. Unilaterally imposed shared-cost programs, non-negotiated conditional transfers, and abusive exploitation of tax room ground the current concerns. But the present Canadian Constitution offers little room for normative arguments addressing these objections. Only arguments about the constitutional division of powers appear to provide a meaningful bulwark against federal fiscal and regulatory imperialism. And these prophylactic arguments have most purchase when combined with an originalist conception of federal constitutional jurisdiction as constrained within watertight compartments.[69] This chapter now turns to a brief consideration of the relationship between federal spending and federal jurisdiction.

FEDERAL JURISDICTION, FEDERAL TAXATION, AND FEDERAL SPENDING

Many of the most persistent critics of the federal spending power are also among those from Quebec who contest the very idea that Canada is, or ever was, a federation.[70] For these critics, there is irrefutable evidence that Sir John A. Macdonald's initial ambition to create a unitary state is slowly being realized – evidence that can be found in various features of the *Constitution Act, 1867*, in various practices of the federal government since then, and in various interpretive doctrines of the Supreme Court.[71] There are two key normative concerns: formally, that the original distribution of legislative powers was a binding contract between "two founding peoples"; and substantively, that the expansion of federal jurisdiction undermines the government of Quebec's pursuit of its distinctive mission as heartland and homeland of Canada's francophone population.

[68]See, e.g., Scott (1955). It is a different question whether a citizen might object to provincial expenditures for non-section 92 purposes. For one unsuccessful attempt to constrain provincial spending on this basis, see *Dunbar*, *supra* note 37.

[69]For a thoughtful and balanced review of the arguments for and against this mode of constitutional interpretation, see Leclair (2005 and 2002).

[70]This is not the occasion to explore what exactly the claim "Canada is not a federation" means in the light of federalism theory. For a recent exploration, see Gaudreault-DesBiens and Gélinas (2005, 51).

[71]For the best summary of this position see Lajoie (2006, 145-151). For a further elaboration, see Tremblay (1991).

As evidence of the "un-federal" character of the very terms of the *Constitution Act, 1867*, these critics cite, notably, these facts: (a) the Lieutenant-Governors of the provinces are vested with a power of disallowance of legislation or reservation of Royal Assent for the pleasure of the Governor-General; (b) the Parliament of Canada may declare a work or undertaking to be for the "general advantage of Canada", and therefore assume jurisdiction over it; and (c) the federal government has an unlimited power to acquire property for public purposes, and when it does so, it can largely subject such property to exclusive federal jurisdiction.

Had they wished, they might also have noted that (d) the Lieutenant-Governors are appointed by the Governor-in-Council; (e) the Governor-in-Council, and not the courts, has jurisdiction to hear appeals in education matters; (f) all superior court judges are appointed by the Governor-General; and (g) some matters central to the concept of "property and civil rights", and unconnected with the national economy – notably marriage and divorce – are vested in the federal jurisdiction.[72]

The brief goes further. Since 1867, the situation has deteriorated as a result of three interconnected sets of developments. The first set consists of unwise or inappropriate amendments to the Constitution. Among them are (h) amendments relating to unemployment insurance and pensions that transfer provincial jurisdiction to the Parliament of Canada.[73] The second set consists of amendments to the Constitution that are not only unwise but also arguably unconstitutional in the sense that they violate other, more fundamental principles of the Constitution. Among them is (i) the "unilateral" patriation of the Constitution in 1982. The third set consists of amendments that are inconsistent with the Constitution. Among these are (j) the federal government's constant encroachment on provincial jurisdiction through unilateral interventions, such as what is disparaged as the "Canadian Social Union without Quebec"; (k) Parliament's use of the spending power to encroach upon provincial jurisdiction; and (l) Parliament's abuse of its taxation power to create a fiscal imbalance that paralyzes provincial initiatives. The normative judgments reflected in this enumeration reflect the richer view of the Constitution as always, and necessarily, more than text.

Finally, critics contend that over the past half-century the Constitution has been interpreted in a manner that consistently enhances the legislative powers of Parliament at the expense of the provinces. For example, it is noted that (m) the Supreme Court now has final constitutional authority, and unlike the Privy Council its members are appointed exclusively by one of the necessary parties to

---

[72]On these seven points, see respectively the *Constitution Act, 1867*, *supra* note 9, ss.90, 92(10)(c), 91(2), 58, 93(3), 96, 91(26). While the point has not been previously raised in critical commentaries, it is also the case that the power of the Parliament of Canada to establish courts for the better administration of the laws of Canada under s.101 permits the federal government to unilaterally withdraw vast areas of jurisdiction from the competence of provincial courts established under s.92(14).

[73]See *Constitution Act, 1867*, *supra* note 9, ss.91(2A) (as added in 1940), 94A (as initially added in 1951).

division of powers litigation; (n) interpretive doctrines such as federal paramountcy, the extended residuary power, the national dimensions doctrine, and the emergency power provide cover for federal legislation that intrudes upon areas believed to have been assigned exclusively to provincial jurisdiction; and (o) the relatively recent change from an exclusive category theory of federal and provincial jurisdiction to a much looser ancillary powers doctrine opens the door to jurisdictional overlap, and because of the doctrine of federal paramountcy, it potentially subordinates provincial legislative authority to federal initiatives across almost the entire range of provincial jurisdiction.[74]

What, then, can be made of this inventory of concerns about the undermining of Canadian federalism through enlargement of federal powers? More particularly, what is the relationship of federal spending and federal taxation to this alleged expansion of federal jurisdiction?

Six observations about the character of the critique are pertinent. First, the arguments are essentially formal. Rarely are either substantive or normative questions addressed. Take the declaratory power, for example. One might ask how many of the almost five hundred exercises of that power have been beneficial to Canadians and how many have not. Or whether the existence of the declaratory power is compatible with the theory of federalism as a mode of political governance. Or whether the declaratory power is simply another way of exercising Crown ownership or operating a Crown corporation. Or one might ask whether the exercise of the power has ever prevented a provincial government from pursuing its own regulatory purposes.

Second, the arguments are, for the most part, textual and historically frozen. Only some variant of "creationism" or "original omniscience" theories of constitutionalism can justify the claim that the vision of the state adopted in 1867, and the vision of the legislative, executive, and judicial powers necessary for building that state, are unchanging and unchangeable by practice. But the frozen constitution is frozen only insofar as the frontiers of federal power are concerned. Is it consistent to claim, for example, that the power of reservation and disallowance is evidence of an imperfect federalism simply because it exists (although it is unused), and at the same time to claim that other governance actions are illegitimate because they are non-textual?[75]

Third, the arguments have little reference to the implicit constitution, and they occasionally appear to attribute an animus that does not seem to have been present at the time of action. Is it true, for example, that federal power caused

---

[74]Given the policy justification for the national dimensions (*R. v. Crown Zellerbach Canada Ltd.*, [1988] 1 S.C.R. 401), emergency power, and ancillary power (*General Motors*, *supra* note 41) doctrines, the only heads of provincial legislative competence that would probably be immune from interference by federal legislation would be those relating to the provincial constitution; direct taxation within the province; the borrowing of money on the credit of the province; the establishment, tenure, and remuneration of provincial officers; and the management and sale of provincial lands and resources (*Constitution Act, 1867*, *supra* note 9 at ss.92(1)-(5)).

[75]In other words, it is not obvious that "originalism" is coherent as an intellectual position when the type of polycentric political negotiation that led to the enactment of the *Constitution Act, 1867* is at issue.

provincial incapacity to deal with the Depression? The assumption is that explicit amendment is the only way in which the assumptions and practices of a constitution may change. Were this the case, there would be no idea of a cabinet (as opposed to a Privy Council), there would be no role for the Prime Minister in nominating judges of superior courts or Senators, and there would have been no consequence for Canadian federalism flowing from the Balfour Declaration. All constitutions are in constant evolution to meet the felt necessities of the time and changing perceptions of political authority.[76]

Fourth, the arguments presume a univocal theory of citizenship, which sees the lives of Canadians as sharply divided between orders of government. This is especially apparent where the arguments shift from a critique of shared-cost programs and conditional spending mediated through provincial governments, to a critique of direct federal expenditure on citizens. The claim is that the federal government has no authority, by way of tax expenditures, subsidies, and payments, to enhance the meaning of Canadian citizenship beyond the formal (as reflected in a passport) or the economic. This means that people can be full citizens only of provinces, and that their relationship with the federal government must be mediated exclusively through the provinces. On this view, there is no true federal citizenship, and all nation-building by the Parliament of Canada necessarily diminishes a person's "root" or "true" provincial citizenship. Even the "states-rights" reservation of the Tenth Amendment to the United States' Constitution does not rest on such a thin and intermediated view of federal citizenship.

Fifth, the arguments are vaguely conspiratorial. The assumption is that the common thread of all federal action since 1867 has had no purpose other than to diminish the power of the provinces. Every exercise of the federal spending power is meant to reduce provincial sovereignty. Admittedly, some federal spending is designed to enhance the presence of the government of Canada. Since 1995, for example, the federal government has spent massively in support of its own nation-building project. Why should it not have? Has not the Quebec government spent massively for exactly the same purposes, often seeking to mirror the institutions and trappings of a sovereign state?

Sixth, the arguments are sometimes cast in very strong terms. The language tends to be either warlike or uncompromising, with expressions like "invasion" and "complete absorption" characterizing the motives and predicted outcomes of federal action (see, e.g., Leclair 2007, 39-40). Rather than being a reasonably balanced attempt to think through the exercise of federal power over time, and to assess the benefits and detriments of the spending power as exercised to date, the arguments are invariably teleological. While framed as arguments about federalism and the proper exercise of powers by orders of government in

[76]The argument is, fundamentally, that there is no clear, unambiguous meaning that can be given to constitutional texts that advert to the power of the federal government to disburse money. As earlier sections have attempted to show, there are good textualist arguments in favour of the unlimited spending power. Those who assert that the *Constitution Act, 1867* contains a clear "bright-line" rule limiting federal spending are, in short, using what purports to be a textualist argument to shore up an unarticulated normative agenda. On this point see, e.g., Weinstock (2006).

Canada, for some scholars the arguments are really about Quebec nationalism, if not the achievement of Quebec's independence.

To summarize, the arguments involve, at once, (a) textual comparison of the *Constitution Act, 1867* to some idealized model of compact confederalism; (b) a critique of a particular theory of constitutional interpretation that has become predominant in Western democracies over the past half-century; and (c) a state-building aspiration that involves a particular unitary vision of citizenship, nation, and state action. The significance of this last point may be best appreciated by comparing the shifting ground on which arguments about federal spending have been most recently built. Until the mid-1980s, the major critique of implicit federal incursion into provincial jurisdiction was directed at the federal spending power itself.[77] Ottawa was compromising provincial autonomy by committing provincial governments to massive investments in programs that they could not thereafter control, or scale back as the need arose. Following the cutbacks of the early 1990s, the ground of complaint changed.[78] Rather than simply being an evil in and of itself, the spending power was also an evil because it produced what has come to be called a fiscal imbalance. To take a classic statement from the Séguin Commission:

> Fiscal imbalance exists when the federal government invokes a "spending power" to intervene in the provinces' fields of jurisdiction. ... [T]his power limits the decision-making and budgetary autonomy of the provinces, has a direct influence on their level of spending and is facilitated, on practical terms, by excess revenue of the central government in relation to its spending within the jurisdictions allocated to it by the Constitution. (Commission on Fiscal Imbalance 2002b, 16)

The argument is somewhat more complex than this statement suggests. To begin with, the argument is that federal spending by conditional transfers for federally designed programs undermines provincial policy-making.[79] Second, the argument is that transfers under shared-cost programs not only commit the provinces to federal policy, but also to expenditures they might otherwise not make.[80] Third, the argument is that whenever the revenue raised from general

---

[77]Occasionally, other themes not related to fiscal policy were evoked. For an illustrative example, see Lajoie (1969).

[78]Some argue that Ottawa first began to renege on its commitments in the late 1970s and that the massive readjustments of the 1990s merely exacerbated the trend. See Tom Kent, this volume.

[79]Whether this is in fact the case is an empirical question that would require asking the following: Are these programs unilaterally imposed by Ottawa? Are they so detailed in their requirements that provinces have no room to manoeuvre? Do these programs meet a need that citizens of a province actually want fulfilled? To my knowledge, none of the studies for the Séguin Commission actually sought answers to these questions.

[80]This too is an empirical question. Here the evidence of an improper federal influence is easier to marshal. Even if a shared-cost program were to pass the tests for a legitimate conditional grant program just noted, once the federal government began to

federal taxation strategies within a province is over and above the amount required for federal purposes, the province's capacity to levy taxes for its own purposes will be paralyzed. Viewed in this light, one of the fundamental problems with the federal spending power is that it can be exercised today only through the tax system, which has a significant impact on the ability of provinces to manage their own fiscal policy.[81] This observation helps to situate the normative basis for limiting federal spending and federal taxation.

Imagine the following situation. The Parliament of Canada unwinds all shared-cost programs, eliminates conditional transfers (except, for the sake of argument, unconditional equalization grants to provinces under section 36 of the *Constitution Act, 1982*),[82] and withdraws completely from direct program spending in relation to provincial jurisdiction and even in relation to federal jurisdiction grounded in the ancillary power, the residuary power, or the national dimensions doctrine. Instead, Parliament directs the federal government to maintain current levels of taxation but to double spending on the Canadian Armed Forces, upgrade Canada's rail network, airports, and harbours, and substantially increase Old Age Security payments and so on. Or imagine that Parliament directs the federal government to deploy such newly freed-up revenue to eliminating the accumulated federal debt, and thereafter to building a federal equivalent to the Alberta Heritage Fund. In these situations, on the assumption that Ottawa continues to raise revenue to the same extent as it has so far, but uses all such revenue for indisputably federal purposes, there is no exercise of the federal spending power, no attempt to direct provincial expenditures or shape legislative policy, and no indirect exercise of federal jurisdiction under expansive interpretive doctrines. Yet there is just as significant a potential (if not actual) paralysis of provincial taxation power as if Parliament had directed the federal government to embark on new shared-cost, conditional grant, or even unconditional transfer programs.

A similar conclusion could be reached in relation to tax expenditures. Presumably, the Parliament of Canada could continue to tax citizens at source (or through instalments) at a very high marginal rate, and then, at the moment of filing, return large sums to citizens as tax expenditures. The return to citizens

---

renege on its funding commitments, there would be an illegitimate downloading of expenses onto the provinces. On this point, see Kent (2008).

[81]For one of the earliest expressions of this concern, see Quebec (1956). An excellent assessment of the tax-expenditure nexus in diverse federal states is offered in Abel (1978), especially Part III entitled "Taxation" at 293 and Part IV entitled "Spending: Scope of the Spending Power" at 313.

[82]The argument to be presented is no less persuasive even if equalization payments were to be curtailed or eliminated. Indeed, it is doubtful that s.36 provides provinces with any justiciable rights to a claim in the federal treasury. Moreover, when the Government of Canada transferred tax room to the provinces in 1995, there was little provincial uptake, which suggests that the real problem of fiscal imbalance may be that provinces are reluctant to raise provincial tax rates for fear of having economic activity flee to another jurisdiction. If this is the case, then there is a strong argument to be made for having Ottawa occupy the most tax room for raising revenue, and then act as a transfer agent to the provinces.

could be in the form of basic personal deductions, targeted deductions for designated expenditures, Canada Savings Bonds, a tax-refunded guaranteed annual income, or interest-free (and ultimately forgivable) draws on a general loan fund similar to the Alberta Heritage Fund. Here again, as long as this type of tax remission were directed to all taxpayers without distinction, the federal government would be acting within its constitutional powers, even on the most restrictive of interpretations heretofore advanced. Yet, given the high rate of initial taxation required to raise the revenue and the return of revenue in the form of non-taxable benefits (gifts, loans, and guarantees), tax expenditures of this kind would have an equally significant impact on provincial revenue sources.

The above examples are, of course, implausible in today's economic and political climate. But their implausibility is for political reasons, not constitutional reasons. The current federal government seeks to reduce expenditure, not transform it. Resource-rich provinces do not want to see revenue from their resources being deployed to finance current account expenditure. Resource-poor provinces do not want to see their entire federal subsidy reduced to the intergovernmental equalization formula, but wish to maintain federal transfers to their residents through shared-cost programs. Moreover, these examples illustrate that the fundamental problem of managing the revenues and disbursements in a federal state is not simply one of federal spending per se, nor simply one of federal taxation per se. The central problem, common to both unitary and federal states, arises when the democratic impulse induces governments to disanchor any power or any regulatory instrument from its normative moorings. Within a federation, there is an additional problem. Neither an inventory of legislative powers assigned to each order of government, nor the democratic impulse itself, provides any mechanism for determining the appropriate fiscal share that each unit of government should receive.[83] How then might taxation and spending by the federal and provincial governments be brought into line? Are there normative principles and institutional forums that can serve this goal? This is the topic of the final section.[84]

---

[83]In addition, the decision about expenditure is not simply tributary to ordinary politics. Sometimes extraordinary events require a (temporary?) readjustment to accepted distributional principles: on occasion the shift may flow to the federal government (as in the case of financing a war); on occasion it may flow to the provinces (as in the case of a health pandemic). On the complexity of these federalism rules, see Simeon (1982-83).

[84]Political economists and historians have tracked various mechanisms by which issues of fiscal federalism have been managed in the past in Canada. See, e.g., Courchene, this volume; Watts (1999). To my knowledge, none have sought to explore issues of institutional design: i.e., by what instruments and through what institutional processes distributive determinations should be made. Moreover, the only example of where a constitutional lawyer has offered a proposal for achieving such a balance is Abel (1978), Part V entitled "Spending: The Canadian Equalization Fund and Council" at 338.

THE CHANGING ENVIRONMENT FOR INSTRUMENT CHOICE

Today, a number of commentators argue that welfare state politics of the type that gave rise to the conflict over the spending power have now just about run their course. Canadian perspectives on regulatory governance are moving away from the approaches characteristic of the second National Policy and toward an emerging third National Policy.[85] It was not insignificant to the framing of the *Constitution Act, 1867*, and to the conception of government it instantiated, that the first National Policy of the late nineteenth century was the project of an imperial colony seeking to locate its frontiers and to stitch together its diverse units into a single economy. Likewise, constitutional adjustments in Westminster and in Canada, as well as the social programs of the second National Policy that accompanied them, were a project of an emerging state defining itself as politically independent and sovereign while coming increasingly under the economic hegemony of the United States. The third National Policy is emerging in an era of (a) globalization – when the links between sovereignty and territory are becoming ever more problematic; and (b) identity politics – where personal assertion through language, culture, religion, and ethnicity are predominating over conceptions of multicultural citizenship.[86]

Any national policy is a story about how members of a political state (or for that matter, any political community that collectively self-identifies as a political community)[87] frame or characterize problems of governance, as much as it is about how they tackle those problems. Even though multiple political communities can coexist within the same geographic boundaries, there is often a high degree of commonality in how they imagine the aspirations and instruments of policy. So, for example, just as the policies of Mercier and Taschereau in Quebec mirrored those of Macdonald and Laurier, so too the policies of Lesage, Johnson, and Bourassa mirrored those of St. Laurent, Pearson, and Trudeau. The same observation applies to the policy pursuits of Bouchard, Landry, and Charest and to those of Chrétien, Martin, and Harper.[88]

---

[85]See, e.g., Courchene, this volume; Choudhry (2002); Kent (2007). However, the above authors do not explicitly use the notion of a third National Policy, nor do they relate their analyses to emerging trends noted in contemporary governance theory (see, e.g., Salamon 2002b, 1). For an initial attempt to do so explicitly, see Macdonald and Wolfe (2008-2009).

[86]On these complementary valences, see Ruggie (1993); and Klotz and Smith (2007).

[87]The caveat is necessary because, from a governance perspective, the state is one institutional option for political communities, and not all such communities have such institutions (whether as UN states or as substates, provinces, autonomous regions, etc.). For a legal pluralist perspective on post-national governance, see Macdonald (1998).

[88]In other words, the political stripe of a government (PQ or Liberal in Quebec; Liberal or Conservative in Ottawa) has little bearing on the construction of what is described as a National Policy and on conception of policy instruments by which that policy is pursued. Likewise, the issues are addressed in broadly similar terms whatever

To date, however, no politician, poet, or pundit has yet come up with an enduring label for this new National Policy for the twenty-first century. Still, we can detect its elements emerging in the actions of governments across the political spectrum in all parts of Canada. The end of redistributive programs based on large aggregates managed by large, mediating bureaucratic structures and an increasing use of targeted programs focused on individuals are suggested by the constraints of the Canadian Charter of Rights and Freedoms, by the Canada-US Free Trade Agreement and the North American Free Trade Agreement, by the GST, by the end of block-program funding, by the transformation of the concept of marriage, and by signals from the Supreme Court about the design of the *Canada Health Act*.[89] These developments do not necessarily mean the end of Canada as a collective project that seeks to put an east-west continental economy and the institutions of the welfare state to the service of the dreams and aspirations of every Canadian. Rather, they invite scholars to ask what conceptions of citizenship will drive governance in the future, and what principles are likely to guide instrument choice over the next few decades.[90]

Too much policy analysis is premised on economic efficiency being the litmus test of acceptability, perhaps with some subsidiary consideration of effectiveness.[91] An awareness of the importance of public administration might also lead one to consider whether a proposed action is actually manageable.[92] But the first governance question should be about the relations among citizens, and the second should be about their relations with the state. Citizens constitute the state, and they do so to serve their purposes. Some efficient policy choices demean citizens by imagining them only as individuals, while other equally efficient tools enable citizens to lead self-directed lives by enhancing their capacity to act in concert with others. Analysis of contemporary trends in policy proposals and governance instruments, whether by political parties of the left or right, suggests that there are four normative pillars of Canada's third National Policy, and that government programs will increasingly privilege those pillars: (a) self-directed citizen agency rather than status- or territory-driven

---

the province – be it Danny Williams's Newfoundland and Labrador, Dalton McGuinty's Ontario, Ed Stelmach's Alberta, or Gordon Campbell's British Columbia. On this point, see generally Macdonald and Wolfe (2008-2009).

[89]It follows that I am not convinced by the "Chicken Little"-type arguments that followed the decision in *Chaoulli v. Quebec*, [2005] 1 S.C.R. 791. See, e.g., Flood, Roach, and Sossin (2005).

[90]In this respect, I think that Choudhry (2002), asks the right questions, although I disagree with some of the answers. Similarly, Tom Kent is right to contest how the Harper government is using the issue of "federal spending" to emasculate the redistributive social-welfare role that the federal government must promote. See Kent (2008) and Weinstock (2006).

[91]This, of course, is the message of the "instrument choice" literature of the early 1980s. See Trebilcock (1982).

[92]See the essays in Eliadis *et al.* (2005).

entitlements; (b) real choice about personal identity; (c) the mediation of multiple, fluid, and overlapping commitments through the lifespan of citizens; and (d) lateral interest-based affiliations rather than totalizing institutions.[93] Consequently, the formal instruments of the third National Policy will increasingly be those of "indirect" rather than "direct" governance: programs and services managed by centralized bureaucracies (both public and private) will be unbundled; equalization of life chances will be explicitly pursued, along with the dismantling of entrenched institutions that distribute rights and entitlements differentially; and networks will be built among public, private, NGO, domestic, and international agents to accommodate a plurality of perspectives, and these networks will overtake state monopolies.[94]

Some years ago the Law Commission of Canada commissioned a series of studies on the governance challenges confronting Canadians at the outset of the twenty-first century. Five challenges, none of which is controversial today, were explicitly identified: (a) urbanization and the rise of global cities; (b) immigration and its attendant diversity of ways of being and expectations of government (new identity claims); (c) significant differentials in growth rates among provinces, and in particular the declining percentage of the population of Canada speaking French as a first language and residing in Quebec; (d) increasing citizen concern about issues relating to quality of life, health, and the environment; and (e) an aging population and issues of intergenerational equity.[95] The common thread running through these challenges is the problem of marginalized populations and inequality of life chances – whether for an urban underclass, for religious, ethnic, and racial minorities, for discrete language communities, for the youth and the elderly, or for those of lesser education and poorer health status.

What does this mean for instrument choice, and especially for the future of the federal spending power? A first point is that these issues all raise what Tom Courchene (this volume) characterizes as the "national dimension/provincial jurisdiction" dilemma: the governance challenges today simply do not map easily onto discrete subject-matter constitutional jurisdiction.[96] Moreover, many

---

[93]The argument in the text does not presume either that other aspects of earlier National Policies will disappear or that the instruments by which policy was then implemented will whither away. Economic management, transportation, and communications infrastructure, and population policy (including immigration) will remain preoccupations, and instruments like crown corporations, franchises, regulatory agencies, and aggregated spending programs will still be found. They will, however, be less important in the overall policy and instrument mix. For a longer discussion, see Macdonald and Wolfe (2008-2009).

[94]A fine study of the challenges is Kettl (2002).

[95]These five challenges were recognized by the Law Commission of Canada in a working document entitled *The Governance of Human Agency* (1999). This document appeared on the Commission's website until December 2006, when the Government of Canada terminated funding for the Commission and closed its website.

[96]Inescapably, constitutional doctrines like "national dimensions" will be increasingly significant in defining federal authority; inescapably, courts will tolerate provincial

of the identified exclusions are cumulative, but they are cumulated differently across the population.[97] Furthermore, in contrast to crises, these challenges are almost all non-episodic, and they do not lend themselves to once-off or even transitional interventions.[98] This means that the appropriate responses are likely to be highly individuated: some challenges will require the type of territorial response appropriately managed by provinces; others will call for a response more appropriate to local or municipal intervention; and yet others will require a direct response to particular citizens, whether from the federal or the provincial government.[99]

It follows that the policy rhetoric of Canada's second National Policy – national standards, monopolistic delivery systems, conditional grants – is inapt to deal with the continuing national dimension/provincial jurisdiction dilemma. In the overall framework of Canada's third National Policy, Ottawa should tax and spend only at the ends of the policy-response spectrum whenever a proposed fiscal measure cannot be justified by a direct appeal to a head of legislative power assigned to Parliament. In my view, section 36 of the *Constitution Act, 1982* now provides both the idea of, and ample justification for, so constraining federal spending: the federal role is to ensure that all provinces have sufficient resources to *be* provinces (section 36(2)), and that all citizens have sufficient resources to *be* citizens (section 36(1)). It is nothing more.[100] In other words, while the text of the Constitution does not explicitly constrain federal spending, for the reasons given in the previous section, I believe that there is both a policy argument and a moral argument for limiting federal spending along the lines suggested by section 36.

In the case of spending under section 36(2), the expenditure must be unconditional, for the end in view is equality of governance opportunity (not uniformity of outcome) and the instrument – the allocation of money – is to be used to empower provincial agency (not to impose regulatory discipline on

---

trespass on the criminal law power, will continue to expand the category of direct taxation, and will validate provincial adjudicative bodies that exercise s.96 powers.

[97]The point is hardly new and has been a commonplace in the "access to justice" literature for at least 40 years. Moreover, the implications for institutional design to facilitate access to justice have also been long recognized. For an overview of the literature, see Macdonald (2005a).

[98]On the differences between strategies for addressing these differences, see Iacobucci, Trebilcock, and Haider (2001).

[99]For my attempt to address this multiplicity of necessary responses, see Macdonald (2005b). The point is also captured in the *Framework to Improve the Social Union for Canadians: An Agreement between the Government of Canada and the Governments of the Provinces and Territories*, Canada, 4 February 1999, Part 5: "These transfers support the delivery of social programs and services by provinces and territories in order to promote equality of opportunity and mobility for all Canadians and to pursue Canada-wide objectives." Not surprisingly, this thought – spending to achieve pan-Canadian "social citizenship" – is anathema to some in Quebec. For a helpful discussion, see Tremblay (2001).

[100]As grounding for policy analysis with regard to s.36, see Kong, this volume.

provinces). The focus of equalization spending directed to provinces should be on ensuring the management of core governmental functions; there should be no conditional transfers to provinces, nor any shared-cost programs where the provinces are conscripted as disbursing agents for money collected through federal taxation.[101]

Given the policy challenges of overcoming inequality of life chances and providing support to marginalized populations, a different approach should be taken to section 36(1) equalization spending: the spending will typically be conditional, not unconditional. The focus of citizen-equalization spending should be on opportunity: early childhood and family support, young adult educational and vocational training, a negative income tax for all citizens, and a targeted focus on preventative health measures.[102] In other words, direct transfers to citizens should be conditional and should enhance the capacity of all citizens to participate equally in the life chances that define Canadian citizenship. This means, in particular, that equalization transfers to citizens should explicitly seek to occupy tax room to ensure that pan-Canadian norms are not defeated by competitive economic pressures on provinces. The problem with prohibiting this type of federal spending and permitting provinces to tax and spend with such an end in view is that it creates a fiscal race to the bottom as provinces compete to reduce provincial taxation and expenditure. Conceiving the federal government as a collection agent for provinces under a broadly conceived citizen-focused equalization scheme facilitates the provision of a minimum level of economic well-being consistent with the history, practices, and aspirations of Canada as a political community. Only where a province or territory can assert a unique interest in defining what equal citizenship might mean in a manner that cannot be accommodated by a direct federal transfer should an opt-out against tax room be permitted. Such distinctive claims are most likely to arise in Quebec and in territories like Nunavut, although the simple fact of Quebec being a "distinct society" on one dimension does not necessarily mean that it has a relevant distinctiveness for any particular federal direct expenditure program. Nor does it necessarily mean that no other province may have its own "distinctiveness" on a particular issue sufficient to sustain an opt-out. Each claim for a special autonomy interest must be addressed on its own merits, and in the light of its specific relationship to the proposed expenditure.[103]

These arguments for a renewed and refocused federal spending power deal with only half of the contemporary fiscal nexus: disbursements. The other half is

---

[101]The core governmental funding functions through s.32(2) would include the costs of running a legislature, a public service, a police force, the judiciary, key administrative agencies, retransfers to municipalities, and like institutional measures.

[102]Interestingly, others (including some of the architects of Canada's second National Policy) have reached similar conclusions. See notably the works of Kent (2007, 2006; and this volume).

[103]This second-order decision-rule to determine if direct spending under s.36(1) is legitimate coheres with Nancy Fraser's vision of resource distribution to facilitate recognition, not just egalitarian redistribution. See Fraser (1997).

taxation: how to ensure that the federal government does not then try to achieve an indirect regulatory agenda by expropriating available tax room from provinces. This is an issue that has been unsuccessfully addressed in almost every federation. It is almost impossible to resolve through detailed constitutional rules or even through a formula. Like the question of whether a particular provincial claim for a distinctive autonomy interest is sufficient to sustain an opt-out, the question of the appropriate tax room does not lend itself to constitutional adjudication.[104] Indeed, no better proposal seems today to be on offer than the imperfect idea advanced by Albert Abel to establish an "Equalization Fund and Council", which would serve as another constitutional forum like the Senate (in theory) and the Supreme Court (in practice).[105]

CONCLUSION

The fundamental premise of this chapter has been that the contemporary preoccupation with the spending power contributes to a constellation of myths: about the nature and purposes of constitutions; about the central features of constitutional interpretation; about the relationship between regulatory instruments and fiscal instruments; about the rationales for government action in Canada since the nineteenth century; about the policy tools that governments should now deploy; and about the policy role of the federal government in the early twenty-first century.

It may be that Canadians generally (perhaps even including a majority of francophone Canadians in Quebec) supported successive federal interventions by way of the "spending power". This merely attests to a failure of political wisdom and statesmanship among federal leaders. After all, history teaches that bad policies (even many egregious or genocidal policies) have attracted popular support. The rhetoric of many discussions of the spending power is also flawed. To say that Quebec is opting out of programs that Ottawa has no constitutional authority to impose by legislation is Orwellian. In reality, in tolerating these federal programs, other provinces are indirectly delegating authority upwards to Ottawa. Moreover, attempts by Ottawa to herd provinces, generally by threatening a bilateral deal with one or more provinces individually, are an abuse of the federal principle. Either the one-off deal is equity-disrupting as between the provinces – the difficulties caused by the attempt to buy Nova Scotia and New Brunswick with "revenue-replacement grants" in 1867 are an

[104]It follows that, although I agree with the normative foundations for federal spending that he asserts, I am skeptical about the approach to institutional design – referring the matter to the courts under a set of *ex ante* decision rules backed with default presumptions. See Kong, this volume.

[105]See Abel (1978), Part V entitled "Spending: The Canadian Equalization Fund and Council" at 338. The concern, of course, is to find an institutional forum to provide stability and genuine policy exchange in relation to matters now dealt with episodically through "first ministers' conferences" or federal-provincial-territorial sectoral meetings on economic issues.

object lesson – or it is jurisdictionally invasive because it coerces participation through the fear of "losing out".

In the years ahead, Canada may at last move beyond the simplistic formula by which "deux nations" as a founding myth has been corrupted into a "deux états" condominium of Quebec and the Rest of Canada (ROC). If anything, a primary consequence of coming to terms with the aspirations and instruments of a third National Policy will be the recognition that there is no ROC. There are multiple ROCs, and many of them are within Quebec. If there is merit in the analysis of the goals and instruments of Canada's third National Policy, it will apply to programs of provincial governments as much as to programs of the federal government. The policy future does not imagine a "weakened" third National Policy federal state and a "strengthened" second National Policy provincial state. It points to strengthened federal and provincial governments appropriately deploying appropriate policy instruments.

Thirty years ago, Albert Abel discerned the central features of constitutionalism in Canada (see ibid.). The underlying argument of this chapter flows from his analysis, although it deviates from his prescriptions. That argument can be summarized in the following series of propositions:

- States are the product of peoples, not the inverse. Once states are established, however, they tend to recreate peoples.
- Constitutions have both explicit and implicit elements, neither of which is fixed, and they intersect to modify each other.
- Federal constitutions are the result of particular conjunctural processes, and the distribution of powers they envision is historically contingent.
- Legislative power, judicial power, and executive power in the form of taxing and spending do not always track the same logic.
- All tools of government have both normative (directly or indirectly regulatory) and fiscal implications.
- If the sum of regulation in a state is constant, so is the sum of fiscal activity. Only the forms and justifications for political action change.
- The bane of federal constitutionalism – direct program spending by the central government in fields of primary provincial responsibility – is only a small part of the fiscal dimensions of federalism.
- Spending is a function of political bidding between levels of government, and in Canada at least, the arguments against the federal spending power today are political and moral, not constitutional.
- The key question for a federation is the relationship between sources of revenue and the policy empowerment left to provinces after federal taxation has been levied.
- Overt welfare-state program spending is a product of a particular historical moment that is rapidly passing (or has already passed).
- The changes in the world economy, in Canada's sociodemographics, and in citizens' perceptions of the goals and instruments of government are irreversible.

- Governments will increasingly undertake actions that focus on citizen empowerment, fluid identities, unbundled delivery mechanisms, and a multiplicity of policy networks.
- Section 36 of the *Constitution Act, 1982* provides a textual basis for a normative argument about the aims and instruments of federal spending.
- The central issue for the future will be how to design a federal-provincial-territorial institution to discipline the allocation of taxation and borrowing room as between the federal and provincial governments.
- Current controversies about the federal spending power in support of shared-cost programs and conditional transfers are yesterday's news, and have little bearing on the design of tools and policies necessary for the flourishing of Canada's third National Policy.

REFERENCES

Abel, A.S. 1969. "The Neglected Logic of 91 and 92", *The University of Toronto Law Journal* 19(4).

— 1976. "A Chart for a Charter", *University of New Brunswick Law Journal* 25.

— 1978. "Constitutional Charter for Canada", *The University of Toronto Law Journal* 28.

Arthurs, H. 2004. "Constitutional Courage", *McGill Law Journal* 49.

Beetz, J. 1965. "Les attitudes changeantes du Québec à l'endroit de la Constitution de 1867", in P.-A. Crépeau and C.B. Macpherson (eds.), *The Future of Canadian Federalism.* Toronto: University of Toronto Press.

Brouillet, E. 2005. *La négation de la nation: l'identité culturelle québécoise et le fédéralisme canadien.* Sillery: Septentrion.

Cheal, D. 1988. *The Gift Economy.* London: Routledge.

Choudhry, S. 2002. "Recasting Social Canada: A Reconsideration of Federal Jurisdiction over Social Policy", *The University of Toronto Law Journal* 52.

Commission on Fiscal Imbalance. 2002a. *Fiscal Imbalance in Canada: Historical Background, Report – Supporting Document 1.* Quebec: Bibliothèque Nationale du Québec.

— 2002b. *The "Federal Spending Power" Report – Supporting Document 2.* Quebec: Bibliothèque Nationale du Québec.

Courchene, T.J. 1997. "Proposals for a New National Policy", in T. Kent (ed.), *In Pursuit of the Public Good.* Montreal: McGill-Queen's University Press.

Currie, D.P. 2004. "Through the Looking-glass: The Confederate Constitution in Congress 1861–1865", *Virginia Law Review* 90(5).

Dales, J.H. 1966. *The Protective Tariff in Canada's Development.* Toronto: University of Toronto Press.

Dufour, C. 1989. *Le défi québécois.* Montreal: L'Hexagone.

Eden, L. and M. Appel Molot. 1993. "Canada's National Policies: Reflections on 125 Years", *Canadian Public Policy* 19(3).

Eliadis, P. *et al.*, eds. 2005. *Designing Government: From Instruments to Governance.* Montreal: McGill-Queen's University Press.

External Advisory Committee on Smart Regulation. 2004. Final Report. *Smart Regulation: A Regulatory Strategy for Canada.* Online: Government of Canada at www.smartregulation.gc.ca.

Flood, C.M., K. Roach, and L. Sossin, eds. 2005. *Access to Care, Access to Justice: The Legal Debate over Private Health Insurance in Canada.* Toronto: University of Toronto Press.

Fowke, V.C. 1988. "The National Policy – Old and New", in W.T. Easterbrook and M.H. Watkins (eds.), *Approaches to Canadian Economic History: A Selection of Essays.* Ottawa: Carleton University Press.

Fraser, N. 1997. "From Redistribution to Recognition? Dilemmas of Justice in a 'Postsocialist' Age", *Justice Interruptus: Critical Reflections on the "Postsocialist" Condition.* New York: Routledge.

Fuller, L.L. 1969. *The Morality of Law*, 2d ed. New Haven: Yale University Press.

— 1975. "Law as an Instrument of Social Control and Law as a Facilitation of Human Interaction", *Brigham Young University Law Review* 1975(1).

— 2001. "Means and Ends", in K.I. Winston (ed.), *The Principles of Social Order*, 2d ed. Oxford: Hart.

Gaudreault-DesBiens, J.-F. and F. Gélinas. 2005. "Opening New Perspectives on Federalism", in J.-F. Gaudreault-DesBiens and F. Gélinas (eds.), *The States and Moods of Federalism.* Montreal: Yvon Blais.

Gélinas, F. 1997. "Les conventions, le droit et la Constitution du Canada dans le renvoi sur la 'sécession' du Québec: le fantôme du rapatriement", *Revue du Barreau du Quebec* 57(2).

— 2008. "La Cour suprême du Canada et le droit politique", *Cahiers du Conseil Constitutionnel* 24.

Hogg, P.W. 1988. *Meech Lake Constitutional Accord Annotated.* Toronto: Carswell.

— 2005a. *Constitutional Law of Canada*, 5th ed., vol. 1. Toronto: Carswell.

— 2005b. *Canadian Constitutional Law*, 5th ed., vol. 2. Toronto: Thomson Carswell.

Hogg, P.W., J.E. Magee, and J. Li. 2007. *Principles of Canadian Income Tax Law*, 6th ed. Toronto: Thomson Carswell.

Iacobucci, E.M., M.J. Trebilcock, and H. Haider. 2001. *Economic Shocks: Defining a Role for Government.* Toronto: C.D. Howe Institute.

Kent, T. 2006. "Priorities for a Progressive Canada", *Policy Options* (April-May). Online: Institute for Research on Public Policy at www.irpp.org/po/archive/apr06en/kent.pdf.

— 2007. *Federalism Renewed.* Ottawa: Caledon Institute of Social Policy.

— 2008. "The Harper Peril for Canadian Federalism", *Policy Options* (February). Online: Institute for Research on Public Policy at www.irpp.org/po/archive/feb08/kent.pdf.

Kettl, D.F. 2002. "Managing Indirect Government", in L.M. Salamon (ed.), *The Tools of Government: A Guide to the New Governance.* New York: Oxford University Press.

Klotz, A. and B. Smith. 2007. "State Identity as a Variable", unpublished, presented at the American Political Science Association, August 2007, Chicago.

Lajoie, A. 1969. *Le pouvoir déclaratoire du parlement: augmentation discrétionnaire de la compétence fédérale au Canada.* Montreal: Presses de l'Université de Montréal.

— 1988. "The Federal Spending Power and the Meech Lake Accord", in K.E. Swinton and C.J. Rogerson (eds.), *Competing Constitutional Visions: The Meech Lake Accord.* Toronto: Carswell.

— 2006. "The Federal Spending Power and Fiscal Imbalance in Canada", in S. Choudhry, J.-F. Gaudreault-DesBiens, and L. Sossin (eds.), *Dilemmas of Solidarity: Rethinking Redistribution in the Canadian Federation.* Toronto: University of Toronto Press.

Lazar, H., ed. 2005. *Canadian Fiscal Arrangements: What Works, What Might Work Better.* Montreal: McGill-Queen's University Press.

Leclair, J. 2002. "The Supreme Court of Canada's Understanding of Federalism: Efficiency at the Expense of Diversity", *Queen's Law Journal* 28.

— 2003. "The Supreme Court of Canada's Understanding of Federalism: Efficiency at the Expense of Diversity", *Queen's Law Journal* 28.

— 2005. "The Elusive Quest for the Quintessential 'National Interest'", *The University of British Columbia Law Review* 38.

— 2007. "Vers une pensée politique fédérale: la répudiation du mythe de la différence québécoise 'radicale'", in A. Pratte (ed.), *Reconquérir le Canada: un nouveau projet pour la nation québécoise.* Montreal: Voix parallèles.

Lower, A.R.M. 1946. *Colony to Nation: A History of Canada.* Toronto: Longmans, Green.

— 1958. "Theories of Canadian Federalism – Yesterday and Today", in A.R.M. Lower *et al.* (eds.), *Evolving Canadian Federalism.* Durham: Duke University Press.

Macdonald, R.A. 1985. "Understanding Regulation by Regulations", in I. Bernier and A. Lajoie (eds.), *Regulations, Crown Corporations and Administrative Tribunals.* Toronto: University of Toronto Press.

— 1986. "Pour la reconnaissance d'une normativité implicite et 'inférentielle'", *Sociologie et Sociétés* 18(1).

— 1991a. "... Meech Lake to the Contrary Notwithstanding: Part I", *Osgoode Hall Law Journal* 29.

— 1991b. "... Meech Lake to the Contrary Notwithstanding: Part II", *Osgoode Hall Law Journal* 29.

— 1996a. "The Design of Constitutions to Accommodate Linguistic, Cultural and Ethnic Diversity: the Canadian Experiment", in K. Kulcsar and D. Szabo (eds.), *Dual Images: Multiculturalism on Two Sides of the Atlantic.* Budapest: Hungarian Academy of Sciences.

— 1996b. "Three Centuries of Constitution-Making in Canada: Will There Be a Fourth?" *University of British Columbia Law Review* 30(2).

— 1998. "Metaphors of Multiplicity: Civil Society, Regimes and Legal Pluralism", *Arizona Journal of International and Comparative Law* 15(1).

— 2005a. "Access to Justice in Canada Today: Scope, Scale, and Ambitions", in J. Bass *et al.* (eds.), *Access to Justice for a New Century: The Way Forward.* Toronto: Law Society of Upper Canada.

— 2005b. "Kaleidoscopic Federalism", in J.-F. Gaudreault-DesBiens and F. Gélinas (eds.), *The States and Moods of Federalism.* Montreal: Yvon Blais.

Macdonald, R.A. and S. Szilagyi. 2005. "Constitutional Hockey: *Canadiens* and *Habitants* in the *Imaginaire* of Quebec", *University of British Columbia Law Review* 38(2).

Macdonald, R.A. and R.D. Wolfe. 2008-2009. "The Real Constitutional Question: Canada's 21st Century National Policy", *Policy Options* December/January.

Madison, J., A. Hamilton, and J. Jay. 1987. *The Federalist Papers.* New York: Penguin Books).

Maher, M. 1996. "Le défi du fédéralisme fiscal dans l'exercice du pouvoir de dépenser", *Canadian Bar Review* 75.

Mauss, M. 1989. *The Gift: The Form and Reason for Exchange in Archaic Societies*, trans. by W.D. Halls. London: Routledge.

May, R.J. 1970. "Decision-Making and Stability in Political Systems", *Canadian Journal of Political Science* 3(1).

McCoy, T.R. and B. Friedman. 1988. "Conditional Spending: Federalism's Trojan Horse", *The Supreme Court Review* 1988.

McFetridge, D.G. 1993. "Rent-Seeking as Nation-Building: A Comment on 'Canada's National Policies: Reflections on 125 Years'", *Canadian Public Policy* 19(3).

Norrie, K.H. 1974. "Agricultural Implement Tariffs, the National Policy and Income Distribution in the Wheat Economy", *The Canadian Journal of Economics* 7(3).

Nozick, R. 1974. *Anarchy, State, and Utopia.* New York: Basic Books.

Ontario, Royal Commission. 1968. *Inquiry into Civil Rights*, Report Number One, vol. 1. Toronto: Queen's Printer.

Otis, G. 2006. "Territorialité, personnalité et gouvernance autochtone", *Cahiers de droit* 47(4).

Parliament. 1969. *Report of the Royal Commission on Taxation.* Ottawa: Supply and Services Canada.

Peters, B.G. 2002. "The Politics of Tool Choice", in L.M. Salamon (ed.), *The Tools of Government: A Guide to the New Governance.* New York: Oxford University Press.

Petter, A. 1989. "Federalism and the Myth of the Federal Spending Power", *Canadian Bar Review* 68.

Polanyi, K. 1967. *The Great Transformation.* Boston: Beacon Press.

Quebec. 1956. *Report of the Royal Commission of Inquiry on Constitutional Problems,* vol. 1. Quebec: Government of Quebec.

Rawls, J. 1971. *A Theory of Justice.* Cambridge: Harvard University Press.

Ruggie, J.G. 1982. "International Regimes, Transactions, and Change: Embedded Liberalism in the Postwar Economic Order", *International Organization* 36(2).

— 1993. "Territoriality and Beyond: Problematizing Modernity in International Relations", *International Organization* 47(1).

Russell, P.H. 1983. "The Political Purposes of the *Canadian Charter of Rights and Freedoms*", *Canadian Bar Review* 61.

Salamon, L.M., ed. 2002a. *The Tools of Government: A Guide to the New Governance.* New York: Oxford University Press.

— 2002b. "The New Governance and the Tools of Public Action: An Introduction", in L.M. Salamon (ed.), *The Tools of Government: A Guide to the New Governance.* New York: Oxford University Press.

— 2002c. "The Tools Approach and the New Governance: Conclusion and Implications", in L.M. Salamon (ed.), *The Tools of Government: A Guide to the New Governance.* New York: Oxford University Press.

Sandel, M. 1998. *Liberalism and Limits of Justice.* New York: Cambridge University Press.

Scott, F.R. 1955. "The Constitutional Background of Taxation Agreements", *McGill Law Journal* 2(1).

Sécretariat aux affaires intergouvernamentales canadiennes. 1998. *Québec's Historical Position on the Federal Spending Power, 1944-1998.* Quebec: Gouvernement du Québec.

Simeon, R.E. 1982-83. "Criteria for Choice in Federal Systems", *Queen's Law Journal* 8.

Smiley, D.V. 1975. "Canada and the Quest for a National Policy", *Canadian Journal of Political Science* 8(1).

Stanley, G.F.G. 1956. "Act or Pact? Another Look at Confederation", in J.S. Moir, A. Pouliot, and L. Lamontagne (eds.), *Report of the Annual Meeting Held at Montreal, June 6-8, 1956.* Ottawa: Canadian Historical Association.

Taylor, C. 1992. "The Politics of Recognition", in A. Gutman (ed.), *Multiculturalism and the 'Politics of Recognition'.* Princeton: Princeton University Press.

— 1993a. "Why Do Nations Have to Become States?" in G. Laforest (ed.), *Reconciling the Solitudes: Essays on Canadian Federalism and Nationalism.* Montreal: McGill-Queen's University Press.

— 1993b. "Alternative Futures: Legitimacy, Identity, and Alienation in Late-Twentieth-Century Canada", in G. Laforest (ed.), *Reconciling the Solitudes: Essays on Canadian Federalism and Nationalism.* Montreal: McGill-Queen's University Press.

Trebilcock, M.J. *et al.* 1982. *The Choice of Governing Instrument.* Ottawa: Minister of Supply and Services Canada.

Tremblay, A. 1991. "Judicial Interpretation and the Canadian Constitutional Reform Dilemma", *National Journal of Constitutional Law* 1.

— 2001. "Federal Spending Power", in A.-G. Gagnon and H. Segal (eds.), *The Canadian Social Union without Québec: 8 Critical Analyses.* Montreal: Institute for Research on Public Policy.

Tupper, A. 1993. "Canada's National Policies: Reflections on 125 Years – A Commentary", *Canadian Public Policy* 19(3).

Watts, R.L. 1999. *The Spending Power in Federal Systems: A Comparative Study.* Kingston: School of Policy Studies, Queen's University.

Weinstock, D.M. 2005. "The Moral Psychology of Federalism", in J.-F. Gaudreault-DesBiens and F. Gélinas (eds.), *The States and Moods of Federalism.* Montreal: Yvon Blais.

— 2006. "Liberty and Overlapping Federalism" in S. Choudhry, J.-F. Gaudreault-DesBiens, and L. Sossin (eds.), *Dilemmas of Solidarity: Rethinking Redistribution in the Canadian Federation.* Toronto: University of Toronto Press.

Woehrling, J. 1988. "La reconnaissance du Québec comme société distincte et la dualité linguistique du Canada: conséquences juridiques et constitutionnelles", *Canadian Public Policy* 14.

Reflections on the Federal Spending Power: Practices, Principles, Perspectives

Thomas J. Courchene

Le rôle et l'étendue du pouvoir fédéral de dépenser occupent une place nettement plus importante dans le programme d'élaboration des politiques du pays depuis que le gouvernement Harper s'est fait le chantre d'un « fédéralisme ouvert » et que la Chambre des communes a unanimement proclamé que « les Québécois forment une nation au sein d'un Canada uni ». Or, sans circonscrire le pouvoir fédéral de dépenser, cet engagement d'Ottawa de respecter la répartition constitutionnelle des pouvoirs au profit d'un fédéralisme ouvert échouera le test de crédibilité.

Sur la sinueuse voie des approches de rechange visant à brider ce pouvoir de dépenser, l'auteur retrace les politiques et principes qui lui ont été associés depuis la Seconde Guerre mondiale. Un vaste éventail qui va des mesures de décentralisation de l'impôt sur le revenu au renforcement du tissu social du pays en passant par le maintien et la promotion d'une union économique, sociale et fiscale, sans oublier évidemment la création d'une gouvernance harmonisée pour la fédération la plus décentralisée du monde. Dès lors, le défi du pouvoir de dépenser consiste à choisir, parmi l'ensemble riche et diversifié de nos principes et instruments, ceux qui selon les besoins permettent à la fois les accommodements et les limites.

INTRODUCTION AND OVERVIEW

The federal spending power (FSP) has returned to centre stage in public policy debates, in large part due to Stephan Harper's call for "open federalism" replete with a commitment to respect the constitutional division of powers on the one hand and to the subsequent Parliamentary proclamation that "the Québécois form a nation within a united Canada" on the other. Watts (1999, 1) defines the spending power as "the power of Parliament to make payments to people, institutions or provincial governments for purposes on which Parliament does not necessarily have the power to legislate, for example, in areas of exclusive provincial jurisdiction". However, for purposes of this paper the exercise of the federal spending power will be viewed more broadly and will encompass areas like federal regulation that can also affect the division of powers. In any event, the key issue here is that for Prime Minister Harper's commitment to respect the constitutional division of powers to be credible it follows that the exercise of the federal spending power in selected areas must somehow be circumscribed. Not surprisingly, therefore, the October 2007 Speech from the Throne contained the following undertaking with respect to the narrower conception of the spending power:

> ...guided by our federalism of openness, our Government will introduce legislation to place formal limits on the use of the federal spending power for new shared-cost programs in areas of exclusive provincial jurisdiction. This legislation will allow provinces and territories to opt out with reasonable compensation if they offer compatible programs.

While this undertaking reflects the concerns normally associated with the exercise of the federal spending power, in the ensuing analysis the spending power issue will be viewed as having two related yet distinct components. The first is the one referred to in the above quotation, namely that any legislation relating to the spending power should provide the provinces with protection against arbitrary and unwanted federal intrusion in areas of exclusive provincial jurisdiction. The second is that any reworking of the spending power principles should also be flexible enough to allow for federal-provincial co-determination or collaboration on matters in provincial jurisdiction in order to build pan-Canadian programs where desired, including the possibility of delegating provincial powers upward and perhaps even federal powers downward.

With this brief overview as context, the ensuing analysis proceeds along three avenues. The first of these (*The Spending Power and Canadian Policies and Practices*) traces the evolution of Canadian policies/practices as these relate to the interaction between the federal spending power and selected elements of provincial constitutional powers. The story begins with the Quebec's decision in 1954 to adopt its own personal income tax (PIT) and with the many spending-power ramifications that flowed from this decision. This is followed by an elaboration (in more or less chronological order) of a series of specific spending power initiatives: the shared-cost programs; UI/EI; the tax-collection agreements; the CPP/QPP; the 1995 federal budget and the CHST; the Council of the Federation and the pharmacare proposal; the 2004 First Ministers' healthcare agreement, among several others. Among other purposes, this litany will serve to highlight some of the many roles that the spending power has played in the evolution of socio-economic policy, e.g., creating national versions of provincially administered social programs; creating a decentralized yet harmonized income tax system (with important recent steps in PST/GST harmonization as well); preserving and promoting the Canadian economic union; creatively experimenting with concurrency with provincial paramountcy (henceforth CWPP) as an approach to the spending power; embracing "opting out" with compensation as an approach to "deux-nations asymmetry" and so on. To an important degree, these can be summarized by noting that Canadians and their governments have shown themselves to be masters of the art of managing a federal system in that most of the above accomplishments have been achieved without much, if any, alteration in the written constitutional word.

The second avenue (*The Spending Power and Institutional/Constitutional Principles*) presents a comparable survey of formal principles or proposals relating to the spending power – Section 94 of the Constitution; pre-Patriation spending-power proposals; the *Constitution Act, 1982* (including equalization and s.92A relating to resources); Meech; Charlottetown; the Calgary Declaration, again among several others. The message here is quite similar to that of the next section: we Canadians are a creative bunch and over the years we have found a rich and diversified set of principles by which to accommodate and/or inhibit aspects of the exercise of the federal spending power, writ large.

The final substantive section (*Perspectives and Options*) situates the preceding analysis within a broader context, one that reflects the evolving nature of our increasingly integrated societies. For example, while the "network" has emerged as the pre-eminent and pervasive organizational form in the Information Age (Castells 2004), it does not sit well within an open-federalism framework. Nor does what I shall refer to as NI/PJ, namely areas that in the new global era are in the national interest but are under provincial jurisdiction. Attention is then directed to articulating a series of options, institutional and constitutional, for limiting the exercise of the federal spending power. The chapter concludes with two observations. The first relates to Quebec. While recognizing the substantive and symbolic importance to Quebec of finding formal approaches to limiting the federal spending power, the demonstrated and quite dramatic achievements of Quebec's use of the political route in this regard suggests that the province must ensure that a legislative or constitutional approach to the FSP will not end up reducing its considerable *existing* room to manoeuvre. The second emphasizes the enduring nature of our struggle with the federal spending power: it is fast becoming centre-stage in the already politically loaded energy-environment tug-of-war between Ottawa and the provinces.

By way of a final introductory comment, while reference will be made to various constitutional provisions and even to some court cases, the analysis adopts a public policy approach to the spending power issue, not a legal or constitutional approach. Hopefully, however, it will serve to complement the more legal/constitutional perspectives, such as those referenced below – Adam (2008), Hogg (1985), Kellock and Leroy (2007), and Petter (1989).

THE SPENDING POWER AND CANADIAN POLICIES AND PRACTICES

The 1954 Quebec Personal Income Tax

Under the provisions of the 1942-47[1] *Wartime Tax Agreements* the provinces "rented" their personal income tax base to the federal government. In the post-war period Ottawa, infused with the spirit of Keynesian stabilization, desired to retain control of the overall PIT. Accordingly, at the 1945 Conference on

[1]Canada's fiscal arrangements agreements tend to be renegotiated every five years; hence the reference to 1942-47 agreements.

Reconstruction, the federal government offered various further rental options to the provinces, which eventually became the 1947-52 *Tax Rental Agreements*. While all provinces signed on to this arrangement in 1945, by 1947 Ontario and Quebec had established their own corporate income tax (CIT) systems. More problematic for Ottawa was Ontario's announcement in 1950 that it intended to introduce a 5 percent PIT. In response, the federal government "sweetened" the provincial rental options under the 1952-57 arrangements. In addition to the earlier options, Ottawa added a fourth – the yield of the personal income tax at 5 percent of the federal rates, plus the yield of 8.5 percent of corporate profits earned in the province, plus the average-per-capita revenues from succession duties, plus the existing 1948 statuary subsidies. Ontario signed on to these enriched agreements and abandoned its CIT as well as its intention to implement a PIT. Quebec refused to sign.

All of this is preamble to one of the watershed moments in Canadian fiscal and political federalism, specifically the introduction in 1954 of Quebec's PIT, with its 15 percent marginal tax rate. The triggering factor was Ottawa's decision in 1951 to exercise the federal spending power in the form of transferring monies directly to universities. Not surprisingly, Premier Duplessis viewed this as an unwarranted intrusion into an area of Quebec's exclusive jurisdiction, an intrusion made possible in large measure because of Ottawa's superior revenue access. Duplessis' approach to countering this exercise of the federal spending power (i.e., to providing a revenue source to compensate Quebec universities for the province's prohibition from accepting federal grants), was the creation in 1953 of the Royal Commission on Fiscal Relations (headed by Thomas Tremblay and, therefore, usually referred to as the Tremblay Report), a reproduction of which appears in the Carleton Library series (Kwavnick 1973). One reason for the commissioning of the Tremblay Report was to provide the rationale for the 1954 PIT. Intriguingly, the initial role of the PIT as a symbol of Quebec's fiscal autonomy had as much to do with providing a bulwark against the exercise of the federal spending power as with providing an instrument for generating revenues, *per se*.

As Chair of the Ontario Economic Council and as scribe for its 1983 position paper (*A Separate Personal Income Tax for Ontario*) I drew from an excellent study by Claude Forget (1984) to provide additional perspective on the introduction of the Quebec PIT (Ontario Economic Council 1983, 30):

> There can be little doubt that Quebec's move in 1954 to establish its own PIT was the outcome of a power struggle between Quebec and Ottawa. However, as our background research [by Claude Forget] makes clear, and as is also very evident from the report of the influential Tremblay Commission, what was at stake was not only the power to tax but also the power to spend for provincial purposes. By implementing its own autonomous PIT, Quebec was in effect challenging Ottawa's implicit claim, based on superior financial resources, that it had the right to determine areas of provincial jurisdiction where the national interest required that more monies be spent. Quebec saw the constitutional authority to levy direct taxes as the foremost symbol of fiscal autonomy at the provincial level. To be kept on a tight fiscal leash by Ottawa was, in the province's view, equivalent to subordination to the federal government across the entire fiscal front. Thus, as the Forget background study suggests, to the

> extent that a provincial PIT was a symbol, *it was initially less a symbol of fiscal autonomy in the field of taxation than a symbol of autonomy in the field of public expenditure.* (emphasis added)

The longer term implications of Quebec's PIT turned out to be both dramatic and wide-ranging. First, Quebec's PIT effectively asserted (perhaps reasserted is better since some provinces had versions of the PIT prior to World War II) the principle that under s.92(2) of the Constitution Act, 1867 a province can implement whatever PIT policies it deems appropriate with respect to tax rates, bracket structures and deductions, for example. Second, Quebec's PIT system forced radical changes in the fiscal arrangements. In 1957, the tax rental arrangements were replaced by the *Tax Sharing Arrangements* (1957-62), whereby all provinces were given the further option of levying their own taxes and receiving an abatement of federal taxes equal to 10 percent of the federal PIT, 9 percent of the federal CIT and 50 percent of succession duties, with the federal government agreeing to collect the provincial taxes free of charge. However, because these revenues were allocated to the provinces on the basis of the derivation principle (i.e., on the basis of what was actually raised in the province), they generated very different per-capita revenues across provinces. This led to one of the defining moments of Canadian fiscal federalism – the creation in 1957 of Canada's system of equalization payments. The overall result was i) that Quebec maintained its separate PIT while the remaining provinces "piggy-backed" on the federal PIT, and ii) that the equalization program became a permanent fixture in federal-provincial fiscal relations, eventually evolving to include all provincial revenues.

Two other spending-power implications of the Quebec's PIT merit highlight. The first is that the introduction of the Quebec PIT in order to have a revenue base to counter the federal spending-power initiatives emphasizes an obvious, but oft-unstated, reality, namely that the spending power issue is, in large measure, a fiscal imbalance issue. Without the existence of superior revenue access, Ottawa would have much less incentive to use its scarce resources to spend in areas of provincial jurisdiction. Along these lines, Quebec's launching of the Séguin Commission on fiscal imbalance in 2003 and the Commission's subsequent recommendation that the provinces take over the GST are also inherently about the fiscal vulnerability of the provinces to Ottawa's exercise of the spending power in the wake of the 1995 federal budget's slashing of cash transfers to the provinces.

The second was more immediate and had a more far-reaching impact on the evolution of the federal spending power, let alone the federation, as Forget (ibid., 194) noted:

> In the years before 1954, Ottawa made a long series of important decisions that brought about spending programs entirely financed, regulated, and administered by the federal government in areas of provincial jurisdiction. These programs were unemployment insurance, family allowances, and old age pensions. Two of the programs required constitutional amendments to which Quebec (in one case under Duplessis) consented. After 1954 came even more significant spending programs: hospital insurance, Medicare, and social

> assistance. *All of these later programs were to be cost-shared with the provinces, but provincially administered.* (emphasis added)

Arguably, therefore, this post-1954 shift from federally funded, regulated and administered programs to shared-cost programs under provincial design and administration is also part of the legacy of the Quebec PIT. To be sure, there is a fascinating irony here: federal shared-cost programs in this era served as a bulwark against federal *takeovers* on social programs in provincial jurisdiction, whereas in the fullness of time these shared-cost programs themselves became viewed as having the potential for trampling on areas of provincial jurisdiction.

By way of some final comments, Quebec's revealed preference for own-source taxes over federal cash transfers led the province in the 1960s to demand and receive 16.5 additional tax-points of the federal PIT instead of an equivalent amount of cash transfers.[2] The other provinces were also offered the same opportunity, but there were no takers. This would not happen today, which is no doubt why Ottawa's offer has never been put back on the table. Forget's (ibid., 208) observations are appropriate in terms of a "what-if" conclusion to this fascinating episode:

> Had the federal government continued in the early 1950s to spend only for its own purposes, the provincial PIT would probably never have seen the light of day, since it was by no means likely that the Quebec government could have obtained an offset for its [15 percent] tax from the federal government beyond the 5 percent that was already on offer [from the 1952-57 *Tax Rental Arrangements*] ... At any rate, it should be clear that the Quebec PIT was a defensive reaction to the federal [spending power] initiative and not a forerunner of some separatist drive.

Prior to focusing on the spending-power-driven shared-cost programs and the resulting development of much of the Canadian welfare state, it is worth directing attention to the two programs that were, via constitutional amendment, transferred to the federal government – UI/EI in 1940 and the contributory public pension plan in 1964.

Unemployment Insurance

In the 1937 *Unemployment Insurance Reference*, the Judicial Committee of the Privy Council ruled that unemployment insurance fell under "property and civil rights" and, therefore, outside the competency of the federal Parliament. Indeed,

---

[2]Of these 16.5 PIT tax points, 8.5 related to hospital insurance, 5 points related to the Canada Assistance Plan and the remaining three to the former Youth Allowance Program. Now that all of these programs have been superseded, these tax points remain as part of Quebec's PIT and are offset via a corresponding decrease in Ottawa's other cash transfers to the province. This is why Quebecers pay considerably less in the way of federal taxes and more in the form of provincial PIT than the residents of the other provinces. Note that a tax point is 1 percent of federal personal income taxes at the time of the tax-point transfer.

as Kellock and Leroy (2007, 15) recount, Lord Atkin concluded that even if the compulsory contributions required by UI were to be considered a valid federal tax, Parliament could not disperse those funds as it saw fit because this would afford an easy federal passage into the provincial domain. All in all, a landmark decision and a strong defence of provincial jurisdiction against the exercise of the federal spending power.

As noted by Forget above, until the advent of cost-sharing in the wake of the Quebec PIT, constitutional amendment (i.e., passing s.92 powers upward) was the only way to make Ottawa a key social-envelope player. For unemployment insurance this occurred very quickly after the Supreme Court decision: As a result of a 1940 amendment to the Constitution, unemployment insurance became a federal head of power. Therefore, Ottawa's UI/EI (i.e., UI then, but now referred to as EI) program, per se, does not constitute an exercise of the federal spending power of the sort contemplated in this paper, since UI/EI is now a federal responsibility. However, what may well still fall under the rubric of the generalized spending power is Ottawa's use of UI/EI to venture into the areas such as training, and maternal/parental leave. Spending by the federal government in these areas may well go beyond the strict definition of unemployment insurance and intrude, arguably, in areas of provincial jurisdiction. However, the 2005 Supreme Court decision supported Ottawa by ruling that maternity benefits "are consistent with the essence of the federal jurisdiction over unemployment insurance" and it went on to say the same thing about parental benefits.

Nonetheless, as DiGiacomo (2008) has noted, prior to this Court decision Ottawa entered into a deal with Quebec that devolved the maternity and parental benefits of EI to the province. This Canada/Quebec agreement decreased federal EI premiums for Quebecers by an amount essentially equivalent to what these benefits were costing Ottawa in Quebec. This deal was designed to come into force irrespective of the eventual decision of the Supreme Court. Obviously, Quebec felt that Ottawa was using the EI program to regulate/spend in areas that Quebec believed remained in the provincial jurisdiction. Presumably, other provinces can follow in Quebec's footsteps should they so wish.

By way of a final observation that runs in the opposite direction, one might note that a majority of Canadians probably are in favour of EI embodying maternal and parental leave, since these initiatives represent advances in the ambit of our welfare state and may have been unlikely to have been put in place by the provinces. This may be yet another role for the federal spending power, namely to use programs already within federal jurisdiction to initiate new social programs in areas of provincial jurisdiction. Such programs, once established, might eventually be transferred back to the provinces.

CPP/QPP

Section 94A of the Constitution (added by the *Constitution Act*, 1964) reads as follows:

> The Parliament of Canada may make laws in relation to old age pensions and supplementary benefits, including survivors' and disability benefits irrespective of age, but no law shall affect the operation of any law present or future of a provincial legislature in relation to any such matter.

In constitutional jargon, the responsibility relating to old age pensions is concurrent with provincial paramountcy (CWPP). In 1966, while all of the other provinces signed on to the newly created Canada Pension Plan, Quebec exercised its paramountcy and established its own separate QPP.

The reason why the CPP/QPP is so interesting is that CWPP represents one way of addressing concerns relating to the exercise of the federal spending power. Suppose (for illustrative purposes) that CWPP were to characterize all of the programs comprising Canada's social envelope. Ottawa would then be free to legislate with respect to these programs, but the provinces could trump this by passing their own legislation. And if the opting-out provinces received compensation, then concurrency with provincial paramountcy would be, at least in principle, one way to circumscribe the exercise of the federal spending power. Obviously, however, the federal government would be loathe to engage in this process unless it was confident that all or almost all of the provinces would remain on side.

As will also become clear, the process that led to the CPP and QPP is quite similar to the amending procedure explicit in s.94 of the Constitution which, as elaborated later, would allow the common law provinces (all except Quebec) to transfer to Ottawa areas that fall under s.92(13), i.e., "Property and Civil Rights in the Province". Although not framed in terms of s.94, this is exactly what happened with the CPP/QPP. Given this, it is certainly appropriate that the numerical section of the Constitution for the 1964 pension amendment is s.94A.

The Shared-Cost Programs (The Established Programs and Canada Assistance Plan)

While hospital insurance (introduced in 1958), post-secondary education (in 1967), and Medicare (in 1968) were all 50 percent shared-cost programs, the actual sharing differed markedly across each program. For PSE, Ottawa offered to share PSE operating expenses dollar-for-dollar with each province. However, three Atlantic provinces (all except Nova Scotia) accepted the alternative $15-per-capita option. For hospital insurance, each province received 25 percent of the per capita insurable hospital expenses in the province and 25 percent of the *Canadian average* per capita insurance expenses. And for Medicare, Ottawa calculated the total costs of the program of all provinces combined and then distributed 50 percent of these costs to the provinces on an equal per capita basis.

Because of the cost-sharing formats, the financing for these three so-called "established programs" was open ended, so that Ottawa's spending on them was essentially determined by the collective decisions made in the provincial capitals. By way of an aside, might it be said that since it was the provinces that were triggering the increases in the federal spending, it was also the provinces that were triggering increases in the exercise of the federal spending power! In any event it should come as no surprise that Ottawa took advantage of the 1997 *Fiscal Arrangements Act* to "block fund" these established programs. In other words, the overall financing for the three programs was henceforth to be evenly split between cash transfers and tax-point transfers, where a tax point is 1 percent of the relevant federal tax. The number of tax points to be transferred was determined to be 13.5 for the PIT and 1 for the CIT. Since the provinces were already in receipt of 1 CIT tax point and 4.357 PIT points, the net tax-point transfer amounted to 9.143 PIT tax points. The transfer was implemented by a reduction in the federal income tax rates and a revenue-equivalent increase in the provinces' PIT rates. By way of example, before block funding Ontario's tax rate was 30.5 percent of the federal tax rate; after block funding, it became 44.0 percent (see Courchene 1979, for details).

The Canada Assistance Plan (CAP) was established in 1966 as a 50-50 shared-cost program. While the CAP eligibility criterion is "needs", regardless of cause, provincial welfare levels differ markedly in terms of how this criterion is implemented and in levels of income support. Because one of the conditions of Ottawa's 50 percent funding share is that the provinces cannot impose residency requirements for eligibility, one result of the exercise of the federal spending power is that these independent provincial programs became linked together in a national grid – an internal social union, as it were.

Prior to turning to the further evolution of these social programs in the wake of the 1995 federal budget, some perspective on the relationship between the exercise of the federal spending power and our social envelope is appropriate. In particular, the following observations seem apt:

- The genius inherent in the exercise of the federal spending power in these areas was that it allowed the provinces to administer these programs which, with federal co-funding and CEU-related conditions, effectively became national programs.
- Over time many of the initial conditions were relaxed (e.g., the move from shared-cost to block-funded programs) so that the provinces progressively became responsible for the design as well as the delivery/administration of these programs.
- In terms of how governments reacted to these joint programs, the provinces could complain that spending 50-cent dollars on social programs, but 100-cent dollars elsewhere in their budget, tilted spending toward the social programs. For its part, Ottawa was presumably pleased with this leverage, but not too happy about the fact that most of the credit associated with these programs was showered on the provinces.
- In spite of the presence of federal funding for the social programs (whether cash or tax-point transfers), what allowed these programs to provide reasonably comparable public goods and services to all Canadians (and what allowed these programs to remain in provincial jurisdiction) was the presence of the generous equalization program. However, it is important to note that the benefits of equalization went beyond the "have-not" provinces: this is so because the decentralization of the CIT and PIT would never have progressed as far as it has without the presence of an equalization program

that allowed the poorer provinces to share in the returns from devolving taxation to the provinces.

- Finally, from a provincial vantage point and even from a states rights perspective, the exercise of the FSP might well be celebrated. This is so because, as Forget's earlier-referenced comments indicated, without the shared-cost approach these programs may have ended up in the federal domain as did family allowances and UI/EI. In contrast, the provinces are able increasingly to exercise full control over these programs.

The provincial counter-argument here would run along the lines that Ottawa was anything but a reliable partner in terms of this sharing. Specifically, once the programs became "established" (i.e., embraced by citizens) the federal government could, and did, withdraw funds unilaterally and arbitrarily. The best examples of this are the early 1990s cap on the Canada Assistance Plan and the freezes on the health and PSE transfers. The most arbitrary and punitive of all, however, were the cuts unleashed by the 1995 federal budget, to which we now turn.

The 1995 Federal Budget and the Federal "Savings Power"

While Paul Martin's historic 1995 federal budget will be remembered on the economic front as putting an end to 27 consecutive deficits and ushering in a decade of surpluses, on the social front it will be remembered as lowering the boom on the provinces. Specifically Martin rolled EPF and CAP into the newly created Canada Health and Social Transfer (CHST), which he then cut by $6 billion (from $18.3 billion in 1995-96 to $12.5 billion by 1997-98), and obviously by much more on a cumulative basis. In a paper concerned with the federal spending power, this dramatic reduction of cash transfers to the provinces is probably best viewed as an exercise of what might be termed the *federal savings power*! By way of an aside, many of the provinces, and no doubt a majority of Canadians, would very much prefer the exercise of the federal spending power to this exercise of the federal savings power.

The 1995 budget also merits the designation of a watershed in the evolution of Canadian fiscal federalism. This is so because while the deficit downloading to the provinces led, as already noted, to a remarkable turnaround in federal fiscal fortunes, on the provincial fiscal front the short-term consequence was that monies had to be transferred from here, there and everywhere in order to satisfy the health-care demands, the consequence of which was that the non-health-care areas were being fiscally starved. The end result was hardly surprising: the intergovernmental fiscal balance turned quickly and sharply in Ottawa's favour. Fiscally, therefore, Ottawa was now more than able to employ the spending power in areas of provincial jurisdiction and, for their part, the cash-strapped provinces were more than willing to accept this federal largesse. This would eventually set the stage for the rather spectacular spending power binge orchestrated by Prime Minister Paul Martin, e.g., for cities, day care, infrastructure, health, and equalization.

The Report to Premiers and the APCs

But this is getting too far ahead of the storyline. As part of the 1995 federal budget, Ottawa requested that the provinces work with the federal government in developing mutual-consent principles to underpin social Canada. The provinces responded by revitalizing the Annual Premiers' Conferences (APCs) and by commissioning the Ministerial Council on Social Policy Reform and Renewal to frame a response to Ottawa's request. The result was the impressive *A Report to Premiers* (1995). The first part of this report articulated a comprehensive set of social policy principles, many of which found their way into the 1999 Social Union Framework Agreement (SUFA). The second part was a framework and an agenda for investigating whether the provinces, acting collectively, could make progress in the direction of designing, delivering and setting standards for what might be called pan-provincial social programs. This was in response to the realization on the part of the provinces that in order to maintain their decentralized social programs they would have to move in the direction of creating an internal (i.e., pan-provincial) social union or else Canadians might ask Ottawa to do it for them.

The *Report to Premiers* also made the case for federal-provincial cooperation in launching a nationwide child-tax benefit. The result was Ottawa's introduction of the Canada Child Tax Benefit (CTTB) in the 1997 federal budget. Apart from being a welcome social policy innovation, this was also a "federalism friendly" program in that the provinces were allowed, if they wished, to reduce their spending on welfare benefits to families with children by the value of the CCTB provided that they re-directed these savings to other programs that also focused on low-income families with children. As already noted the first section of the *Report to Premiers* helped frame the principles underlying SUFA while the second section served to inform the spending powers provisions of SUFA, on which more later.

In the present context, three further observations appear warranted. The first is that while the CCTB can be viewed as a welfare program, it is delivered via the federal PIT and, therefore, falls under Ottawa's jurisdiction. Relatedly, with the CCTB and subsequent enrichments there appears to be a *de facto* re-arrangement or re-allocation of responsibilities in the social policy arena – Ottawa is now largely responsible for the children and the elderly, leaving the provinces largely responsible for working-age adults (especially since Ottawa, in the aftermath of the 1995 Quebec referendum, devolved aspects of training to the provinces). The third observation is that there appears to be a trend for Ottawa to pull back on its transfers to and/or through the provinces in favour of dealing directly with citizens, a trend continued with the Harper Conservatives (with daycare for example). Again, more on this development later.

While Quebec was not a formal participant in the APC process (it had observer status) and was not a signatory of SUFA, it was nonetheless active along roughly similar lines. Specifically, the province launched the earlier-noted *Commission on Fiscal Imbalance*, headed by Yves Séguin, which reported in 2002. The newly elected (2003) Jean Charest government, with Yves Séguin as the Minister of Finance, proposed that the Annual Premiers' Conferences be folded into a new organization, the *Council of the Federation* (COF), with membership restricted to provincial and territorial premiers. All provinces agreed, and the COF was created in December 2003, with its initial mandate directed, along lines suggested in the Séguin report, toward restoring fiscal balance in the federation.

The Council of the Federation (COF) and the 2004 Pharmacare Proposal

At the (post-federal-election) June, 2004, meeting of the COF at Niagara-on-the-Lake, the provincial and territorial premiers proposed to transfer responsibility for pharmacare upward to the federal government. Intriguing, the COF was also unanimous that the province Quebec would be opting out (with compensation) of this pharmacare plan. From the COF Press Release: "It is understood that Quebec will maintain its own program and will receive a comparable compensation for the program put in place by the federal government". This proposal corresponds closely to the wording and spirit of the s.94 amending formula which (as will be elaborated later) allows all common-law provinces to transfer aspects of "property and civil rights in the province" (which would obviously include pharmacare) upward to the federal government, while civil-law Quebec would retain its existing program. While compensation is not mentioned in s.94, this is arguably due to the reality of 1867: if updated to the present day compensation would almost surely be included (see the late spending power proposals as well as Adam [2008]). It is noteworthy that this pharmacare proposal is relevant for all three of practices, principles and prospects relating to the federal spending power.

The 2004 First Ministers' Meeting and the Health Care Agreement

At the First Ministers' Meeting in September of 2004, Prime Minister Paul Martin and the provinces signed a 10-year, $41 billion health care agreement. Apart from the importance of this deal in terms of restoring much of the provincial fiscal shortfall arising from the 1995 federal budget, the agreement is memorable in that Ottawa formally recognized Quebec's specificity. While Quebec agreed to work in collaboration with Ottawa and the provinces, Quebec's own policies would be determined "in accordance with the objectives, standards, and criteria established by the relevant Quebec authorities" (cited from *Asymmetric Federalism that Respects Quebec's Jurisdiction* [Canada 2004], a Canada-Quebec addendum to the health care agreement).

In effect, this addendum can be viewed as the federal counterpart to the provincial recognition of Quebec's distinctiveness contained in the above pharmacare proposal. However, since this addresses the reigning-in of the spending power only to the extent that the issue relates to Quebec, it is not likely to be viewed as an acceptable approach to the spending power by the other provinces. Indeed, apparently in the final countdown to the September 2004 health care deal, Ottawa verbally agreed that Alberta and British Columbia (and, by extension, one would presume all the provinces) could have the same deal as that offered to Quebec. Since the other provinces have not acted on this option, what transpired may best be described as *de jure* symmetry but *de facto* asymmetry. However, the reality that Quebec could be finessed by an asymmetric side deal served to open the way for Prime Minister Paul Martin's relentless exercise of the federal spending power during the remainder of his tenure.

Paul Martin's Fiscal Cafeteria

With the Quebec issue thus finessed, the Martin Liberals went about devoting much of their remaining time in office to a seemingly unrestrained exercise of the federal spending power in terms of one-off (time-limited) bilateral deals across a bewildering array of policy areas, a process that I have elsewhere (2006) referred to as *bilateral or contractual* federalism. As noted earlier this should not be all that surprising since, in the wake of the 1995 federal budget, Ottawa was fiscally flush and the provinces were cash-starved. *The Economist* (2005) likened this spending spree to operating a "fiscal cafeteria" for the provinces.

This interesting episode merits further attention. Were the provinces so cash-strapped that they signed any and every federal deal available, or were we witnessing rest of Canada (ROC) expressing a desire to work much more closely with Ottawa to create national programs? To the extent that the latter cannot be ruled out, this suggests that the rethinking or reworking of the federal spending power must recognize that the ability of consenting provinces to pass powers upward (e.g., pharmacare) may be as important as constraining Ottawa's power to intervene in exclusive provincial jurisdiction.

Stephen Harper's Open Federalism

While there were plenty of issues that separated the Conservatives from the Liberals in the 2006 election, the battle was ultimately decided in Quebec, where Stephen Harper's promise of "une Charte du fédéralisme d'ouverture" garnered enough seats in the context of a Liberal collapse to give the Harper Conservatives a minority government. "Open federalism", as reflected in Harper's now-famous Quebec City speech [December 19, 2005], represented much more than a swing back to the middle in that it was a sharp move in the direction of classical federalism. *Inter alia*, open federalism embraced the following: a recognition and a respect for the constitutional division of powers; a recognition that there exists a fiscal imbalance in the federation; a commitment to redress this vertical fiscal imbalance; a related commitment to rein in the federal spending power in areas of exclusive provincial jurisdiction; and, finally, a commitment to work with the Council of the Federation to improve the management and workings of the Canadian federation. And all of this was cast within the Conservatives' political rhetoric of bringing a halt to the "domineering and paternalistic federalism of the Chrétien-Martin Liberals".

Transitions: "Opting Out" vs. "Opting In"

To this point, the analysis follows Canadian practice in utilizing "opting out" to describe the situation where Quebec is taking a different approach to what are otherwise pan-Canadian policies or programs. Thus, Canadians are prone to say that Quebec has opted out of the PIT, that Quebec has opted out of the CPP, that Quebec has opted out of some cash transfers in favour of additional tax transfers, that Quebec has effectively opted out of the 2004 health care accord, and that Quebec was to be permitted to opt out of the provincially proposed pharmacare program. However, there is something fundamentally wrong with this terminology. These are all areas that fall under Quebec's constitutional jurisdiction (some exclusive, some concurrent). *It is not opting out to operate a program that is within your own constitutional competence!* The institutional and/or constitutional reality is that the rest of the provinces have *opted in* to federally-run (or jointly-run) programs. There is more than mere semantics involved here, since there is normally a negative connotation to opting out, one that portrays Quebec as forever pleading for special treatment when the opposite is closer to the truth. As the focus of the analysis shifts from practice to principle so too will the opting-in/opting-out terminology. Indeed, the focus on s.94 of the BNA Act (the quintessential opting-in provision) is an ideal launch point for the evolution of selected *principles* associated with the exercise of the federal spending power.

PRINCIPLES UNDERPINNING THE EXERCISE OF THE SPENDING POWER

With the above overview of Canadian practice with respect to the spending power as background, attention now turns to a comparable evolution of selective spending power *principles* as reflected in various federal, provincial and federal-provincial agreements and declarations. Because the line between what falls into the domain of *practices* as distinct from *principles* is in several cases a matter of judgment, readers may well have allocated the various events and agreements differently as between the practices previously discussed and the principles that follow. This also implies that some repetition is inevitable.

The Constitution Act, 1867: s.94

In terms of the "passing powers up" or "opting in" aspect of reworking the spending power, s.94 of the *Constitution Act, 1867* is an oft-overlooked provision that may have considerable potential. Entitled *Uniformity of Laws in Ontario, Nova Scotia and New Brunswick,* s.94 reads as follows:

> Notwithstanding anything in this Act, the Parliament of Canada may make Provision for the Uniformity of all or any of the Laws relative to Property and Civil Rights in Ontario, Nova Scotia, and New Brunswick, and of the

> Procedure of all or any of the Courts in those Three Provinces, and from and after the passing of any Act in that Behalf of the Parliament of Canada to make Laws in relation to any Matter comprised in any such Act shall, notwithstanding anything in this Act, be unrestricted; but any Act of the Parliament of Canada making Provision for such Uniformity shall not have effect in any Province unless and until it is adopted and enacted as Law by the Legislature thereof.

More detail on the potential role of s.94 in terms of the spending power issue appears in Adam (2008). For present purposes we note that the late Frank Scott (1977, 114) suggested that the Fathers of Confederation, unable to obtain a unitary state, included this clause so that an easy way would be available for the provinces other than Quebec to pursue a more uniform and unified future. Samuel LaSelva (1983) suggests that one reason why section 94 has received so little attention, both from the courts and from constitutional experts, has to do with its misleading label. Rather than "Uniformity of Laws ..." it should have been entitled "Transferring Constitutional Jurisdiction" to make it clear that it is in fact an amending procedure. Although s.94 mentions only three provinces, it would presumably apply to all non-Quebec provinces.[3]

Therefore, section 94 was designed to allow the common-law or non-Quebec provinces to transfer selected powers pursuant to property and civil rights to Ottawa, without requiring the consent of Quebec. In an important sense, the earlier-referenced 2004 health care deal can be viewed as a non-constitutional way to accomplish a similar goal. It allows the nine provinces to opt into a more uniform and unified approach to the Canada Health Act while at the same time allowing for asymmetric (essentially status quo) treatment for Quebec. And the pharmacare proposal is an even better example since, on the one hand, it explicitly transfers to Ottawa aspects of property and civil rights for all provinces except Quebec and, on the other, it assumes that Quebec will maintain its existing program replete with federal compensation. This reference to compensation could be viewed as "updating" s.94 to reflect the reality of the 21st century. Attention will be directed back to s.94 in the later section dealing with options for addressing the spending power.

Treaties and the Division of Powers: The 1937 Labour Conventions Case

Can the signing of international treaties serve to undermine the constitutional division of powers? Or, as University of Melbourne's Greg Craven (1993,11) put it: "Can the central [federal] government, simply through the exercise of its capacity in the field of foreign relations, significantly alter what otherwise

---

[3]Marc-Antoine Adam (2008) notes that when it seemed possible that Prince Edward Island and Newfoundland might be part of founding Confederation partners, s.94 included these two provinces in addition to the three in s.94. This seems to suggest clearly that s.94 would include all non-Quebec provinces.

would be the constitutional balance of power?" For Australia, Craven's answer is clearly yes: "the federal balance achieved by the Constitution is now at the mercy of the treaty making power of the federal executive" (1993, 22). This also appears to apply to other federations, such as the Swiss and the American, where the federal governments have relatively free reign to manoeuvre and in the process to force the compliance of sub-national governments. Any counter to this tends to be political, not constitutional.

However, Canada is a clear exception, since prevailing constitutional precedent points in the other direction. Specifically, in the *Labour Conventions* case (1937.A.C. 326 (P.C.)), the Judicial Committee of the Privy Council decided that Canada's status as a signatory to the International Labour Organization Convention did not confer on Parliament the power to implement those aspects of the Convention relating to matters coming under provincial constitutional responsibility. By way of an aside relevant to the overall spending power issue, it was in this case that Lord Atkin penned his famous "watertight compartments" metaphor: "while the ship of state now sails on larger ventures and into foreign waters she still retains the watertight compartments which are an essential part of her original structure".

Kellock and Leroy (2007, 17) argue that *Labour Conventions'* reasoning ought to extend to the spending power issue:

> ...governments do not spend money as an end in itself, just as governments do not implement treaties as an end itself (Petter, 1989). As Lord Atkin explained in the 1937 *Labour Conventions Case*: "there is no such thing as treaty legislation as such. The distribution [of legislative, TJC] powers is based on classes of subjects; and as a treaty deals with classes of subjects so will the legislative power of performing it be ascertained".

In contrast, Hogg (1985, 253) suggests that *Labour Conventions* "is a poorly reasoned decision", although he adds that it may not be undesirable as a matter of policy within a federation such as Canada.

My hunch is the environment is the most likely issue to trigger a challenge to *Labour Conventions*. The reality that markets are progressively global, that social-policy and labour-policy "riders" are increasingly attached to trade agreements, and that the environmental challenge knows no jurisdictional boundaries means that we are almost certain to find ourselves in a federal-provincial jurisdictional tug-of war which could easily involve revisiting *Labour Conventions*. This is not meant to downplay its importance past, present and even future, in terms of the exercise of federal policies – regulatory or spending – in areas of provincial jurisdiction. Rather, it is to note that environmental federalism may at base be viewed more as an inherently international issue than a federal-provincial issue.

Trudeau and the Spending Power

Faced with provincial concerns about the exercise of the federal spending power, initially by Quebec (following on from Jean Lesage's establishing the

QPP and receiving additional tax points in lieu of cash transfers), but gradually spreading to other provinces, Prime Minister Trudeau tabled a set of spending power principles/guidelines at the 1969 First Ministers Conference (FMC). These guidelines were (reproduced from Watts 1999, 2):

- The federal spending power should formally be entrenched in the constitution;
- Parliament should have an unrestricted power to make conditional grants to provincial governments for the purpose of supporting their programs and public services; and
- Parliament's power to initiate cost-shared programs involving conditional grants in areas of provincial jurisdiction should require both a broad national consensus ... and a per capita reimbursement of the people (not the government) of a province whose legislature decided not to participate.

This would come close to importing the Australian approach to its spending power. Specifically, s.95 of the Australian constitution states that Parliament "may grant financial assistance to any State on such terms and conditions as Parliament thinks fit". Since Quebec has never accepted the constitutionality of the federal spending power (Telford 2003, 4), there was no chance that formal recognition, let alone entrenchment, of the federal spending power would ever find acceptance.

A more acceptable approach from the Trudeau government emerged a decade later in the context of the 1978-79 constitutional discussions with the provinces. Again from Watts (1999, 2):

> ... the exercise of the federal spending power would have been made subject to a provincial consent mechanism (a majority of provinces with a majority of the population), with unconditional compensation for non-participating provinces (though there was no agreement on whether compensation was to be paid to non-participating provincial governments or directly to their residents).

While enshrining this version would also create problems for Quebec, one should note that this was part of a "best efforts draft" relating to overall constitutional change that was much more "province-friendly" than what resulted, post the 1980 Referendum, from Trudeau's promise to Quebecers of a "renewed federalism".

The Constitution Act 1982 and Equalization (s.36)

As part of the 1980-82 constitutional negotiations, the "gang of eight" (all provinces except Ontario and New Brunswick) proposed that the overall patriation package include a provision whereby a province would be able to opt out from federal programs with full compensation. Although this proposal fell by the wayside, the concept of "opting out with full compensation" would resurface on several later occasions. What did become enshrined were the s.36 equalization principles:

> Equalization and Regional Disparities
>
> 36. (1) Without altering the legislative authority of Parliament or of the provincial legislatures, or the rights of any of them with respect to the exercise of their legislative authority, Parliament and the legislatures, together with the government of Canada and the provincial governments, are committed to
>
> (a) promoting equal opportunities for the well-being of Canadians;
>
> (b) furthering economic development to reduce disparity in opportunities; and
>
> (c) providing essential public services of reasonable quality to all Canadians.
>
> (2) Parliament and the government of Canada are committed to the principle of making equalization payments to ensure that provincial governments have sufficient revenues to provide reasonably comparable levels of public services at reasonably comparable levels of taxation.

While the generally-accepted view is that s.36 is non-justiciable, it nonetheless does provide constitutional underpinning for the exercise of the spending power to achieve interprovincial fiscal equity (s.36(2)) and for the promotion of equality of opportunity and of access to public services for individual Canadians (s.36(1)). This latter is evaluated more fully in the discussion on the Social Union Framework Agreement, and in the contributions by Tom Kent (2008 and this volume).

The National Energy Program and s.92A

If Quebec felt betrayed by the 1980-82 patriation process, the same can be said with respect to Alberta and the 1980 National Energy Program (NEP). On the tax front, the following initiatives were part of the NEP: the Natural Gas and Gas Liquids Tax; the Petroleum and Gas Revenue Tax; the Petroleum Compensation Charge (on consumers); and a Canadian Ownership Charge for purposes of financing an increase in public ownership of the energy sector. Beyond these measures, depletion allowances were to be phased out and replaced by the Petroleum Incentive Program grants (PIP grants) which Canadian-owned companies operating on Canada Lands (as distinct from provincial lands) could access. Finally, but not exhaustively, the NEP included two "nationalization" provisions: the federal government reserved for itself (or a federal crown corporation) a 25 percent interest in all existing and future petroleum rights on Canada Lands (i.e., the controversial "back-in provision"), and the federal government's intention to purchase several large foreign-owned oil and gas firms.

Not surprisingly, the reaction from the energy patch, and particularly from Alberta, ranged from negative to outright hostile. The NEP was viewed as a frontal attack on the energy sector and an exercise of the federal regulatory power, as it were, in areas that the provinces viewed as their exclusive jurisdiction. The constitutional patriation process offered the energy provinces an opportunity to push for a confirmation of provincial powers over resources in return for their support of the overall constitution package. As a result, the *Constitution Act. 1982* added s.92A to the *Constitution Act, 1867*. Beyond granting (or in some areas probably re-affirming) the provinces exclusive legislative authority over the development, conservation and management of natural resources, s.92A also includes the provision that the provinces can make laws in relation to the raising of money by any mode of taxation in respect of natural resources and electricity generation.

Overall, therefore, the NEP was a policy with ramifications that transcended the energy patch and the western provinces to profoundly influence Canada's political, constitutional and federal evolution as well as to play a catalytic role in the introduction of the Canada-US Free Trade Agreement. The relationship between the NEP and the FTA arose because Alberta became a strong supporter of the FTA in part because the energy pricing provisions of the FTA would make it very difficult for Canada to ever unload another NEP-type program on the energy patch. Nonetheless, given the economic and financial stakes associated with the energy-environment nexus in the context of global climate change, a further Ottawa-Alberta confrontation over the exercise of the federal spending power or the federal regulatory power may be difficult to avoid (Courchene and Allan 2010).

The Meech Lake Accord (1987-90)

At the 1986 Mont Gabriel conference "Rebuilding the Relationship: Quebec and its Confederation Partners" (co-sponsored by *Le Devoir* and by Queen's Institute of Intergovernmental Relations and its then Director, Peter Leslie), Quebec's Minister for Canadian Intergovernmental Affairs, Gil Rémillard, advanced five conditions that needed to be met before the province would sign on to the 1982 constitutional amendments. Included among these five points was the "limitation of the federal spending power". Rémillard's conference presentation became the catalyst for federal-provincial agreement in the *1987 Meech Lake Accord*. This *Accord*, requiring unanimous ratification by Ottawa and the provinces within three years, was intended to be enshrined in a *Constitution Act, 1987*. As Telford (2003, 38) notes, this represented the first attempt to limit the federal spending power constitutionally. Section 106A was to read as follows:

> 106A. (1) The Government of Canada shall provide reasonable compensation to the government of a province that chooses not to participate in a national shared-cost program that is established by the Government of Canada after the coming into force of this section in an area of exclusive provincial jurisdiction, if the province carries on a program or initiative that is compatible with the national objectives.

Telford (2003, 37-38) also points out that Premier Robert Bourassa was comfortable with this wording because (quoting Bourassa) "the new section 106A is drafted so that it speaks solely of the right to opt out, without either recognition or defining the federal spending power ... so Quebec keeps the right to contest before the courts any unconstitutional use of the spending power". I will revisit this way of finessing the spending power later in the paper. For the record, the *Meech Lake Accord* failed when Manitoba and Newfoundland withheld their legislative support, thereby allowing the three-year ratification period to expire without achieving unanimous provincial ratification.

The Charlottetown Agreement

The failure of Meech triggered yet another round of constitutional activity. The resulting federal constitutional proposals, in *Shaping Canada's Future Together* (Canada 1991), included spending power provisions which, after negotiations with the provinces, were then included in the 1992 *Charlottetown Agreement*:

> A provision should be added to the Constitution stipulating that the Government of Canada must provide reasonable compensation to the government of a province that chooses not to participate in a new Canada-wide shared-cost program that is established by the federal government in an area of exclusive provincial jurisdiction, if that province carries on a program or initiative that is compatible with the national objectives.
>
> A framework should be developed to guide the use of the federal spending power in all areas of exclusive provincial jurisdiction. Once developed, the framework could become a multilateral agreement that would receive constitutional protection. The framework should ensure that when the federal spending power is used in areas of exclusive provincial jurisdiction, it should:
> (a) contribute to the pursuit of national objectives;
> (b) reduce overlap and duplication;
> (c) not distort and should respect provincial priorities; and
> (d) ensure equality of treatment of the provinces, while recognizing their different needs and circumstances.

The *Charlottetown Agreement* went down to defeat in a national referendum by a 54.3 percent to 46.7 percent margin overall, and with 6 of the provinces also rejecting the *Agreement* (the four westernmost provinces plus Quebec and Nova Scotia).

From the 1995 Quebec Referendum to the Calgary Declaration

On October 30, 1995 the federalist forces won a razor-thin (50.58 percent vs. 49.42 percent) victory in the Quebec independence referendum. This led to olive-branch initiatives on the part of both Ottawa and the provinces. At the federal level, the Jean Chrétien Liberals, obviously reeling from the referendum near-miss, included a reference to the spending power in the 1996 *Speech From the Throne*. Specifically, the government declared that it would only create new shared-cost programs once it obtains an agreement from a majority of the provinces. In addition, it promised to allow provinces to opt out of such programs with compensation if they set up an equivalent program.

The provinces' approach to reaching out to Quebec after the 1995 Referendum took the form of the under-appreciated *Calgary Declaration* (1997). This *Declaration* was orchestrated by Premier Ralph Klein in his role as the chair of the Annual Premiers' Conference and was signed by all provinces except Quebec (in large measure because this was to be a response on the part of the other provinces to Quebec's concern over its role in the federation). The *Calgary Declaration* was then taken back to each of the nine provinces for further consultation and discussion and was eventually (1998) given assent in all nine provincial legislatures, in several cases with considerable fanfare. Of the 7 articles of the *Declaration*, three are of importance for present purposes:

> 5. In Canada's federal system, where respect for diversity and equality underlies unity, the unique character of Quebec society, including its French speaking majority, its culture and its tradition of civil law, is fundamental to the well being of Canada. Consequently, the legislature and Government of Quebec have a role to protect and develop the unique character of Quebec society within Canada.
>
> 6. If any future constitutional amendment confers powers on one province, these powers must be available to all provinces.
>
> 7. Canada is a federal system where federal, provincial, and territorial governments work in partnership while respecting each others' jurisdictions. Canadians want their governments to work cooperatively and with flexibility to ensure the efficiency and effectiveness of the federation. Canadians want their governments to work together particularly in the delivery of their social programs. Provinces and territories renew their commitment to work in partnership with the Government of Canada to best serve the needs of Canadians.

In more detail, Article 5 represents a formal recognition on the part of the provinces that Quebec is a distinct society. Moreover it is entirely fitting that this proclamation of Quebec's specificity took place in Calgary, the erstwhile capital of "symmetric federalism". Article 6 allows Ottawa to make bilateral deals with any province (but clearly this was written with Quebec in mind) which could then become multilateral should the provinces so wish. Ron Watts (1999, 4-5) notes that Article 7 has "acknowledged the interdependence of governments and called for more cooperation between the different orders of government in their respective jurisdictions, pointing implicitly to the significance of the federal spending power". However, care must be taken in interpreting this quotation. Specifically, while the nine signatory provinces are speaking about and to Quebec in articles 5 and 6, they are obviously *not speaking for Quebec in article 7* since Quebec is not a signatory.

From my perspective, the *Calgary Declaration* is more significant than is generally assumed. First, it is wholly consistent with the spirit of s.94. This is so because i) from article 7, the common law provinces want to work more closely with Ottawa, ii) from article 5 Quebec is distinct in terms of its language, culture and legal traditions and it may need to go its own way in terms of "national" programs in order to promote its distinctiveness; and iii) from article 6, Ottawa can make special bilateral deals with Quebec, with the other provinces coming on board if they wish. Second, a good case can be made that the 2004 COF pharmacare proposal built upon the principles/conception of the Calgary Declaration. And arguably so did Ottawa in the context of the bilateral asymmetric side deal for Quebec in the 2004 First Ministers' healthcare agreement, when it agreed that the other provinces could have the side-deal apply to them (along the lines of article 6). As already noted, this is a clever compromise – *de jure* symmetry, but *de facto* asymmetry. Finally, and here I am probably going way too far, the fact that all common-law provinces agreed to article 5 may have emboldened the Harper Conservatives to go the further step within the open federalism framework of declaring that the Québécois form a nation within a united Canada.

Pan-Canadian Provincialism and National Programs

In roughly the same time frame as the *Calgary Declaration*, the Annual Premiers' Conferences were wrestling with the possibility of having the provinces collectively play a more important role in designing and monitoring pan-Canadian principles and standards for Canada's social envelope. The motivating factor here was the arbitrary and unilateral federal actions that characterized the dramatic 1995 cuts in transfers to the provinces. It was in this context that the province of Ontario commissioned my 1996 ACCESS paper (Courchene 1996) which fed directly, albeit controversially, into the 1996 Jasper APC as well as the 1997 APC in St. Andrews. Part of the ACCESS analysis had to do with whether and how interprovincial agreements (e.g., mutual recognition across provinces of provincial credentials) or federal-provincial agreements (e.g., the Agreement on Internal Trade) could be made binding on the parties. As pointed out in the ACCESS paper, the Australian federation has found a solution to this problem. This is because their Constitution contains a provision for delegating powers upward. Specifically, s.51(xxxvii) of the Australian Constitution reads:

> 51. The Parliament shall, subject to the Constitution, have power to make laws for the peace, order and good government of the Commonwealth with respect to
>
> ...
>
> (xxxvii) Matters referred to the Parliament of the Commonwealth by the Parliament or Parliaments or any State or States, but so that the law shall extend only to States by whose Parliaments the matter is referred, or which afterwards adopt the law.

The best example of the workings of this provision relates to the early 1990s Mutual Recognition Agreement among the Australian states pertaining to regulations and standards with respect to cross-border sales of goods and services and the transferability of credentials. The states designed the appropriate legislation, but then realized that it might be difficult to make the agreement binding on themselves. The solution took the form of requesting that the Commonwealth also pass the identical template legislation, after which the individual states would follow suit. Because of federal paramountcy provision in the Australian Constitution, the agreement became binding on the states – in effect, constitutionalized.

Sturgess (1993, 10) elaborates on this process as follows:

> … the Commonwealth is obtaining no power from the States under this very limited reference, other than to pass a single Act of Parliament once-for-all. It cannot pass further legislation in the same area, nor can it establish a bureaucracy through which to regulate the States. In that sense, there is no reference to powers at all.
>
> In effect, the States are using the Commonwealth to jointly make an amendment to each of their constitutions ... In practice, what the States are doing is ceding sovereignty to each other [and not to the Commonwealth government – TJC].

Unfortunately, Canada does not have access to this sort of option under its constitution, although one of the rationales for the paper by Adam (2008) is to ascertain whether s.94 could be re-activated to serve this purpose, among others. In the interim, one fall-back position might be to draw in part from Australian practice and combine this with "manner and form" legislation. Specifically, the governments would design the accord or convention to their liking. Template legislation would then be drafted and passed in the legislatures of all signing parties. Embedded in this legislation would be manner and form requirements for amendment procedures relating both to the legislation itself and any future amendments. This may not be constitutionally binding, but derogations from it would become very difficult, particularly if the convention itself embodied citizen rights and, as a result, garnered considerable popular support. The Alberta-BC Trade, Investment and Labour Market Agreement (TILMA 2006) is a variant of this approach, including passage in the legislatures of the two participating governments.

The rationale for including the foregoing analysis under the umbrella of the spending power is that if the provinces can find ways to make binding pan-Canadian agreements the door is then open for enhancing their policy manoeuvrability in the federation. For example, any future cash transfers from Ottawa could presumably be more unconditional since the provinces themselves will now be able to ensure the preservation and promotion of the economic and social unions. Alternatively, Canadians would arguably be more willing for the provinces to embark on creative programs if the provinces will be bound by pan-Canadian principles.

The Social Union Framework Agreement (SUFA)

The 1999 Social Union Framework Agreement was a natural follow-up to the *Report to Premiers* and the flexible approach to the implementation of the Canada Child Tax Benefit. While SUFA is a wide-ranging document that has implications for many aspects of the social union, the focus here will only be on the two sections that are directly relevant to the spending power issue. The first of these relates to new Canada-wide programs involving federal-provincial cash transfers and the second focuses on the federal spending power at it relates to individuals and organizations. From SUFA:

New Canada-wide initiatives supported by transfers to Provinces and Territories

With respect to any new Canada-wide initiatives in health care, post-secondary education, social assistance and social services that are funded through the intergovernmental transfers, whether block-funded or cost-shared, the Government of Canada will:

36. Work collaboratively with all provincial and territorial governments to identify Canada-wide priorities and objectives.

37. Not introduce such new initiatives without the agreement of a majority of provincial governments.

38. Each provincial and territorial government will determine the detailed program design and mix best suited to its own needs and circumstances to meet the agreed objectives.

39. A provincial/territorial government which, because of its existing programming, does not require the total transfer to fulfill the agreed objectives would be able to reinvest any funds not required for those objectives in the same or a related priority area.

40. The Government of Canada and the provincial/territorial governments will agree on accountability framework for such new social initiatives and investments.

41. All provincial and territorial governments that meet or commit to meet the agreed Canada-wide objectives and agree to respect the accountability framework will receive their share of available funding.

Direct federal spending

42.a. Another use of the federal spending power is making transfers to individuals and to organizations in order to promote equality of opportunity, mobility, and other Canada-wide objectives.

42.b. When the federal government introduces new Canada-wide initiatives funded through direct transfers to individuals or organizations for health care, post-secondary education, social assistance and social services, it will, prior to implementation, give at least three months' notice and offer to consult. Governments participating in these consultations will have the opportunity to identify potential duplication and to propose alternative approaches to achieve flexible and effective implementation.

Focusing first on the traditional spending power area (Sections 36-41), these are very flexible and province-friendly principles at virtually every stage of the process – initiation, design and delivery, opting out with compensation, accountability, etc. However, some social policy analysts have raised concerns with respect to section 37 above. Indeed Tom Kent (2008) notes that it is likely that we will never see another major shared cost program because Ottawa would have little incentive to spend federal money on a presumed pan-Canadian program that would allow opting out by the four largest provinces. In an important sense, therefore, the SUFA approach to the traditional spending power may have gone *too far* in accommodating opting out of federal programs, especially for those provinces that are interested in working more closely with Ottawa. This is so because Ottawa, not the provinces, would balk at engaging in future shared-cost provinces where provinces comprising a majority of the population (although not a majority of the provinces) could opt out with compensation.

Quite different concerns are associated with article 42 of SUFA, which relates to the exercise of what is termed "direct federal spending", i.e., federal spending going *directly* to citizens and institutions as distinct from going *indirectly* "through the provinces". At one level, this can be viewed as a rather straightforward attempt to make operational some of the spending power principles contained in s.36(1) of the *Constitution Act, 1982*. Indeed, Kent (2008) has, as already noted, labeled SUFA as signaling the end of shared-cost programs, he sees it as breathing life into the spending power as it relates to individuals. And in anticipation of this he recommends new federal programs relating to family support, to human capital investment (for both training and PSE), to parents for day care, and to child health.

What is missing from the above analysis is the reality that Quebec was not a signatory of SUFA. Much of the rationale for this is that SUFA formally recognizes the existence of the federal spending power as it relates to individuals and institutions (s.42). Quebec's refusal to be part of SUFA is hardly surprising given that it was the exercise of this direct spending power in the form of grants to universities that triggered the Quebec PIT in the first place. Arguably, however, the over-arching political reality is that Quebec views the social envelope as the essence of s.92(13) so that any SUFA-like agreement would be viewed as encroaching on s.92(13) and, therefore, would be unacceptable.

To round out this section on spending power principles, attention is directed to a rather dramatic political initiative that has expanded Quebec's political and policy space.

Open Federalism, the Spending Power, and the Québécois Nation

The major features of Prime Minister Harper's open-federalism policy were elaborated in the earlier section on Canadian policies/practices. What is appropriate to add in the present context is Harper's surprising declaration that "the Québécois form a nation within a united Canada". Harper introduced this resolution in the House of Commons on November 22, 2006 and it received unanimous House of Commons support on November 27, 2006. High politics aside for the moment, I believe that this is a most welcome initiative. Canadians have for a long time been willing to confer the "nation" designation on our first peoples. As far back as my appearance as an expert witness before Quebec's *Commission sur l'avenir politique et constitutionnel du Québec* (normally referred to and the Bélanger-Campeau Commission after its joint chairs, Michel Bélanger and Jean Campeau) my expressed view was that, for Quebecers, Quebec will always be their nation and Canada will always be their state (Courchene, 1991). For the rest of Canadians, Canada is typically viewed as the embodiment of *both* nation and state. In terms of high politics, the formal recognition of this reality may be of significant help in creating an institutional, even constitutional, approach to the spending power, one that will allow both "nations" to achieve their goals. Intriguingly, if the rest of Canada wants to work closely with Ottawa in defining the ROC nation, then Quebecers will need to be given the flexibility to define their own nation, and vice versa.

Having thus surveyed Canadian practice as it relates to the federal spending power in the previous section and some of the institutional and even constitutional principles underpinning its exercise in the current section, attention will now be focused on the manner in which this body of analysis might inform the range of options and even proposals for addressing the spending power. However, the march of events (globalization, access to information technology, etc.) has resulted in the appearance of several fresh perspectives that were neglected in the analysis to this point and that ought to play some role in terms of informing the approaches to the spending power. Hence, the following section will begin with these emerging perspectives.

PERSPECTIVES AND OPTIONS

Information Age Perspectives

While the foregoing analysis was framed in the context of the traditional spending power parameters (e.g., fiscal imbalances, "watertight compartments" and the division of powers, the evolution of the social envelope, the variety of proposals and agreements that have conditioned the operation of the federal spending power, and so on), this needs to be supplemented, even augmented, from the vantage point of the new global order, that is, from the perspective of the emergence of the Information Age. Among the generally agreed features of this era are the following (adapted from Courchene 2001):

- As befits this knowledge/information paradigm, human capital is taking its rightful place alongside physical and financial capital as an engine of economic prosperity;
- Accordingly, citizens are emerging the principal beneficiaries of the Information Age;
- Partly because cities (especially what are called global city regions) are the repositories of dense concentrations of human capital needed to generate growth, trade and innovation, they have become the key institutional drivers in the Information Age, even though Canadian cities are jurisdictionally constitutionless;
- The "network" has become the pre-eminent and pervasive organizational form of the Information Age.

The bottom line here is rather straightforward. The information era has privileged a new set of policies (human capital), a new set of players (citizens and NGOs), a resurgent set of institutions (cities), and a new set of organizational forms (networks, including global supply chains), all of which represent dramatic shifts in the power structures of 21st century societies. But while societal power may have shifted, the division of powers remains in its 19th century structure.

The national-interest/provincial-jurisdiction nexus

One consequence of the Information Age is that several policy areas that lie within provincial jurisdiction have become essential to the national interest. Cities, day care, human capital and health care fall into this national-interest/provincial-jurisdiction (NI/PJ) category. It is this NI/PJ nexus that has typically been ignored in the foregoing analysis. To see this, consider the role of cities and their designation as the new economic drivers of the new global order. While there may be ways of integrating cities more fully and more formally in the operations of political and fiscal federalism without altering the formal division of powers (Courchene 2008), the Conference Board's Anne Golden argues that Ottawa should not defer from focusing on cities just because the *Constitution Act, 1867* made them the creatures of their respective provinces. In more detail (Golden 2009, 260):

> It would be paradoxical to expect Ottawa to restrict itself to indirect ways of helping cities out of deference to constitutional roles prescribed in 1867, an era when conditions were entirely different. All intelligent human arrangements must evolve in response to changing conditions. No observer of Canadian and global trends would today design a constitution that forbade federal government involvement in the engines of national prosperity. It is, after all, a two way street: flourishing cities help Ottawa achieve its overall economic and social objectives for the country.

Networked federalism

A second set of considerations relates to the nature of governance in the Information Age. In *Networked Federalism* Janice Stein (2009) argues that governance in a decentralized federation is not about disentangling overlapping jurisdictions. Rather it is about accommodating and managing complexity, and for this "the model of a network embedded in a grid ... is a more useful metaphor than that of parallel lines of government neatly separated from one another" (ibid., 355-356). From Stein's perspective, the most serious obstacles to the renewal of federalism are the jurisdictional squabbles and silo arrangements and, more generally, "the deeply embedded political culture of rights and entitlements of both orders of government and their emphasis on control" (365). In a sense, networked federalism may well be the Information Age version of Carl Freidrich's (1968, 7) vision of federalism:

> ... federalism should not be seen only as a static pattern of design, characterized by a particular and precisely fixed division of powers between government levels. Federalism is also and perhaps primarily the process ... of adopting joint policies and making joint decisions on joint problems.

These Information Age perspectives are not intended to undermine attempts, where appropriate, to circumscribe the federal spending power. However, they are intended to ensure that limiting the spending power does not serve to rigidify federal governance. Indeed in terms of the options that follow, some fall into the "restricting" camp and some in the "enabling" camp in terms of the relationship between the spending power and jurisdictional assignment of competences.

Options for Limiting the Federal Spending Power

The good news is that there is a wealth of Canadian practice and principle that can be drawn upon in addressing the federal spending power challenge. Moreover, over the years Canada and Canadians have proven to be masters at the "art" of federalism. Through alterations in the magnitude of and incentives within the federal-provincial transfer system, through "opting in" and/or "opting out", through downward delegation (e.g., Quebec's GST collection), through creative arrangements/agreements to secure the internal social and economic unions, and through *de facto* asymmetry within *de jure* symmetry, Canadians have been able to alter the effective division of powers in response to internal and external forces, and all of this without changing the written constitutional word. The time to call on our innate collective creativity is again at hand.

A generic approach to the federal spending power and new shared-cost programs

Toward this end, the obvious option is to distill a workable model from the various spending power provisions that have surfaced over the years. Arguably the most acceptable of these is the wording of the Meech Lake Accord:

> The Government of Canada shall provide reasonable compensation to the government of a province that chooses not to participate in a new national shared-cost program that is established by the Government of Canada in an area of exclusive provincial jurisdiction, if the province carries on a program or initiative that is compatible with the national objectives.

This wording would satisfy the Throne Speech commitment. And it does so in a manner that is generic, i.e., it applies equally to all provinces. One would presume that it would also satisfy Quebec, and for the same reason that Premier Bourassa found Meech acceptable, i.e., it does not formally mention, let alone recognize, the federal spending power.

This approach could be supplemented in various ways:

- Adding a set of commitments that governments work together to determine priorities, objectives, accountability, etc;
- Allowing provinces flexibility over the actual program design;
- Third party dispute resolution procedures;
- Addressing mechanisms to ensure temporal stability of the program and its funding. This may be achieved via legislative ratification by all participating governments, i.e., a version of "manner and form" legislation alluded to earlier.

A deux-nations approach to new shared-cost programs

Given our experience with the CPP/QPP, with the PIT, and more recently with the pharmacare proposal and the 2004 health accord, there appears to be a revealed preference for selected programs falling under "property and civil rights" to be pursued at the respective "national" levels, where national in this context means Quebec City for Quebec and Ottawa for the rest of the provinces. To the extent that the legislated proclamation that the Québécois form a nation within a united Canada has some substantive implications, this also would seem to point in the direction of a deux-nations approach to shared-cost programs.

The most straightforward approach here may be to convert the earlier spending power provision into a *deux-nations* variant. For example,

> The Government of Canada shall provide reasonable compensation to the government of Quebec should it choose not to participate with the rest of the provinces in a new pan-Canadian shared-cost program that is established by the Government of Canada in an area of exclusive provincial jurisdiction, if Quebec carries on a program or initiative that is compatible with the pan-Canadian objectives.

This would be a non-constitutional version of s.94. It would allow the common-law provinces to petition Ottawa for new shared-cost programs, without the ability of Quebec to cast a veto. In turn, however, Quebec could receive compensation commensurate with the per capita value of the new program to the nine opting-in provinces.

These are dueling visions of the way to limit the federal spending power. Quebec would presumably view the generic option as falling short, substantively and symbolically, whereas the other provinces would not likely accept the *deux-nations* version in isolation without the generic version. While we will return to this later, the recent emergence of "bilateral federalism" needs to be addressed.

Generalizing bilateral federalism

The two proposals above coincide with the two issues identified in the forgoing analysis relating to the FSP, namely sheltering provinces from unwanted federal intrusion into areas of exclusive provincial jurisdiction on the one hand and allowing like-minded provinces to work with each other and with Ottawa to develop pan-provincial, perhaps pan-Canadian, approaches to selected areas of provincial jurisdiction on the other. However, because of the free-wheeling spending of the Paul Martin government, there is another spending power issue that needs to be confronted, namely the reining-in of what was earlier referred to as "bilateral federalism", namely the signing of one-on-one agreements between Ottawa and selected provinces in areas like day care, cities and the 2004 offshore agreements with Nova Scotia and Newfoundland and Labrador. While the earlier analysis was concerned with preserving and promoting the social union and the economic union, bilateral federalism threatens to undermine or fragment what might be termed the "federal union". Why not draw on article 6 of the Calgary Declaration to turn this problem into a solution?

Article 6 of the Calgary Declaration (with appropriate modification for the issue at hand) would read as follows:

> If any future federal-provincial agreement confers powers or privileges on a province or a set of provinces, these powers or privileges must be available to all provinces.

While this is intended to prevent fragmentation of the interprovincial and provincial-federal relationships, there is also an upside to this proposal. Ottawa would be free to enter into an agreement with a given province in full knowledge that other provinces can request similar treatment. This represents an opportunity for Ottawa to work with selected provinces to introduce new policies or programs that may eventually become pan-provincial. This could be an add-on to the previous two approaches.

Limiting the direct federal spending power

Assuming that Kent (2008) is correct in predicting that more intensive use of the FSP will likely be related to *direct* federal spending to individuals and institutions, might not this mean that this area also needs to be subject to some FSP limits? To be sure, s.36(1) of the *Constitution Act 1982* commits Canada's governments, *inter alia*, to promote equal opportunities for, and the provision of public services of reasonable quality to, all Canadians so that initiatives in these areas might not fall under exclusive provincial jurisdiction. If constraining the exercise of the direct federal spending power is deemed desirable, then the slightly reworked wording of Meech may be appropriate:

> The Government of Canada shall provide reasonable compensation to the government of a province if it chooses not to participate in Canada-wide initiatives directed to individuals or institutions that are established by the Government of Canada in areas of provincial jurisdiction, if the province carries on initiatives that are compatible with the pan-Canadian objectives.

Because all provinces except Quebec were signatories to SUFA, which included its own approach to direct federal spending, this limiting of the direct FSP may be an issue primarily for Quebec, in which case the *deux-nations* version of the above direct spending power proposal would replace "province" by "Quebec".

Intriguingly, these dueling visions (generic vs deux nations) for both the shared-cost and direct FSP may well be simplified were the "nation" status of Quebec to be enshrined. To this issue I now turn.

Constitutionalizing the Spending Power Options

The analysis of options to this point has taken its cue from the 2007 Speech from the Throne which refers to the commitment to "introduce *legislation* to place formal limits on the use of the federal spending power" (emphasis added). As this is being written (March 2008), there are musings from the Harper

Conservatives that "step by step" and "when the ground is fertile" open federalism will be extended to constitutionally enshrining the recognition of Quebec as a "nation". How might this affect the preceding analysis?

A case can be made that the enshrining "the Québécois form a nation within a united Canada" will, of and by itself, serve to condition or limit the exercise of the federal spending power in Quebec. That is, such a constitutionalized declaration will deliver much of what was intended under the above *deux-nations* proposals. Moreover, it will recognize the specificity and special status of Quebec within Canada in a much more wide-ranging and symbolic way than the "distinct society" clause of Meech.

But while it may address Quebec's spending-power concerns, it may do little for the rest of Canada. Specifically, it would be important to breathe life into a version of s.94, so that the common-law provinces have the ability to "opt-in" to pan-Canadian programs in the social envelope and beyond. Yet even this will likely fall short, especially if some of the common law provinces want to follow Quebec's lead and run their own versions of pan-Canadian programs. So something along the Meech wording, but applying to the exercise of the direct federal-spending power as well as to new shared-cost programs, would likely be in order. Indeed, demands for asymmetry are sure to arise in the energy producing provinces in the context of the climate change challenge where, intriguingly, the designation ROC (rest of Canada) for energy initiatives will likely include Quebec as a member.

This aside, the essential point here is that if the status of Quebec as a nation were enshrined, provisions must be put in place to allow the rest of the provinces, should they so wish, to work with each other and with Ottawa in a networking fashion to be able to create "national" programs for ROC. To be sure, this will likely give rise to "West Lothian" issues (i.e., whether Quebec MPs can vote on programs that will apply only to ROC), but it is instructive to remind readers that we are already finessing this issue with the CPP/QPP.

This leads to two concluding comments. The earlier survey of Canadian practices and principles as it relates to the federal spending power, and the social envelope more generally, clearly demonstrates that Quebec has been able to carve out for itself a remarkable degree of political and policy space, so much so that it is the envy of sub-national governments everywhere. And for the most part, this has been accomplished through political rather than constitutional channels. While the time may well be ripe for some legislative and even constitutional approaches to limiting the exercise of the federal spending power and to increasing Quebec's power and symbolism in the federation, these initiatives must not be at the expense of the existing and creative process dimension of Canadian federalism. Indeed, the key assumption underlying the above analysis is that addressing the federal spending power should also serve to increase, not decrease, the flexibility of the process (or networking) dimension of both Canadian federalism and federal-provincial relations. In other words, successfully addressing the FSP issue requires both a restraining and an enabling component.

The final comment is that the ongoing motivation for rethinking the FSP relates largely to Quebec. Specifically, the combination of open federalism, of recognizing and addressing the fiscal imbalance, and of proclaiming Quebec as a nation led to substantial emphasis in the foregoing analysis being placed on *deux nations* perspectives. Going forward, however, the focus will increasingly be on western Canada and energy-environmental nexus, where these *deux nations* approaches will fall short of the mark. But the FSP issues (including the federal regulatory and treaty making powers) in the context of what might be referred to as "environmental federalism" are best left for another time and place.

REFERENCES

Adam, M.-A. 2008. "Fiscal Federalism and the Future of Canada: Can Section 94 of the Constitution Act, 1867 be an Alternate to the Spending Power?" in J.R. Allan and T.J. Courchene (eds.), *Transitions: Economic and Political Federalism in an Era of Change* (the 2006-07 volume in the series *Canada: The State of the Federation*). Kingston and Montreal: Queen's Institute of Intergovernmental Relations and McGill-Queen's University Press, 295-322.

Calgary Declaration. 1997. At www.exec.gov.nl.ca/currentevents/unity/unityr1.htm.

Canada 1991. *Shaping Canada's Future Together.*

— 2004. *Asymetrical Federalism That Respects Quebec's Jurisdiction*. Ottawa: Canadian Intergovernmental Conference Secretariat. At www.scics.gc.ca/cinfo04/800042012_e.pdf.

Castells, M. 2004. "Informationalism, Networks and Society: A Theoretical Blueprint", in M. Castells (ed.), *Network Society: A Cross Cultural Perspective*. Cheltenham, UK: Edward Elgar, 3-25.

Courchene, T.J. 1979. *Refinancing the Canadian Federation: A Survey of the 1997 Fiscal Arrangements Act*. Toronto: C.D. Howe Institute.

— 1991. *The Community of the Canadas.* Reflections/Réflexions #8. Kingston: Institute of Intergovernmental Relations, Queen's University. (The French version is in the background papers to the Bélanger-Campeau Commission.)

— 1996. *ACCESS: A Convention on the Canadian Economic and Social Systems.* Toronto: Ministry of Intergovernmental Affairs. Reprinted in *Assessing Access: Towards a New Social Union 1997*. Kingston: Institute of Intergovernmental Relations, Queen's University, 77-112.

— 2001. *A State of Minds: Towards a Human Capital Future for Canadians*. Montreal: Institute for Research on Public Policy.

— 2006. "Variations on the Federalism Theme", *Policy Options/Options politiques.* Montreal: Institute for Research on Public Policy, 46-54.

— 2008. "Global Future for Canada's Global Cities", *Policy Matters* 8(2). Montreal: Institute for Research on Public Policy.

Courchene, T.J. and J.R. Allan. 2010. "Carbon Pricing and Federalism" in T.J. Courchene and J.R. Allan (eds.), *Carbon Pricing and Environmental Federalism.* Kingston and Montreal: Queen's Institute of Intergovernmental Relations and McGill-Queen's University Press, 75-94.

Craven, G. 1993. "Federal Constitutions and External Relations", in B. Hocking (ed.), *Foreign Relations and Federal States*. London and New York: Leicester University Press, 9-27.

DiGiacomo, G. 2008. *The Government of Canada's Contradictory Approach to the Spending Power: The UI/EI Case*, in J.R. Allan and T.J. Courchene (eds.), *Transitions: Economic and Political Federalism in an Era of Change* (the 2006-07 volume in the series *Canada: The State of the Federation*). Kingston and Montreal: Queen's Institute of Intergovernmental Relations and McGill-Queen's University Press, 323-345.

Forget, C. 1984. "Quebec's Experience with the Personal Income Tax", in D.W. Conklin (ed.), *A Separate Personal Income Tax for Ontario: Background Studies.* Toronto: Ontario Economic Council, 187-212.

Friedrich, C. 1968. *Trends of Federalism in Theory and Practice.* New York: Praeger.

Golden, A. 2009. "Major Cities as a National Priority", in J.R. Allan, T.J. Courchene, and C. Leuprecht (eds.), *Canada: The State of the Federation 2006-07 – Transitions: Fiscal and Political Federalism in an Era of Change.* Kingston and Montreal: Queen's Institute of Intergovernmental Relations and McGill-Queen's University Press.

Hogg, P. 1985. *Constitutional Law of Canada,* 2nd ed. Toronto: Carswells, 123-127.

Kellock, B.H. and S. Leroy. 2007. "Questioning the Legality of the Federal 'Spending Power'", a Fraser Institute Occasional Paper Number 89. Vancouver: The Fraser Institute.

Kent, T. 2008. "The Federal Spending Power is Chiefly for People, not Provinces", Spending Power Working Papers Series, 2008-2. Kingston: Queen's Institute of Intergovernmental Relations, at www.queensu.ca/iigr/working/spendingPower.html.

Kwavnick, D. 1973. *The Tremblay Report.* Toronto: McClelland and Stewart.

LaSelva, S. 1983. "Federalism and Unanimity: The Supreme and the Constitutional Amendment", *Canadian Journal of Political Science* XVI (4) (December), 757-770.

Ministerial Council in Social Policy Reform and Renewal. 2006. *A Report to the Premier.* This report can be accessed from the intergovernmental secretariat of any province.

Ontario Economic Council. 1983. *A Separate Personal Income Tax for Ontario: An Ontario Economic Council Position Paper.* Toronto: Ontario Economic Council.

Petter, A. 1989. "Federalism and the Myth of the Federal Spending Power", *Canadian Bar Review* 68: 448-479. At www.mondopolitico.com/library/myth/mprinto.htm.

Scott, F.R. 1977. *Essays on the Constitution.* Toronto: University of Toronto Press.

Social Union Framework Agreement. 1999. At socialunion.gc.ca/news/020499_e.html.

Stein, J. 2009. "Networked Federalism", in J.R. Allan, T.J. Courchene, and C. Leuprecht (eds.), *Canada: The State of the Federation 2006-07 – Transitions: Fiscal and Political Federalism in an Era of Change.* Kingston and Montreal: Queen's Institute of Intergovernmental Relations and McGill-Queen's University Press.

Sturgess, G.L. 1993. "Fuzzy Law and Low Maintenance Regulation: The Birth of Mutual Recognition in Australia". Paper prepared for "A Conference on Mutual Recognition" sponsored by the Royal Institute of Public Administration, Brisbane, February 12, mimeo.

Telford, H. 2003. "The Federal Spending Power in Canada: Nation-Building or Nation-Destroying", *Publius: The Journal of Federalism* 33(1): 23-45.

The Economist. 2005. "Mr. Dithers and His Distracting 'Fiscal Cafeteria'" (February 19).

TILMA 2006. Trade, Investment and Labour Market Agreement, Alberta and British Columbia. April 28. At www.tilma.ca/agreement/files/pdf/AB-BC_MOU-TILMA_Agreement-Apr-06.pdf.

Watts, R.L. 1999. *The Spending Power in Federal Systems: A Comparative Study.* Kingston: Institute of Intergovernmental Relations, Queen's University.

5

The Spending Power and the Harper Government

Harvey Lazar

Dans ce texte complémentaire au chapitre de Thomas Courchene, l'auteur s'intéresse à la conception du gouvernement de Stephen Harper du pouvoir fédéral de dépenser. Un gouvernement dont le bilan indique qu'en se désengageant des transferts majeurs affectés de longue date aux programmes sociaux et de santé, les conservateurs n'ont pas privilégié une approche de ce pouvoir vraiment différente de leurs prédécesseurs. Leur approche s'en démarque toutefois par des mesures financières et des engagements politiques qui dénotent l'ambition de restreindre les initiatives d'envergure fondées sur le pouvoir de dépenser. Dans l'ensemble, conclut l'auteur, le gouvernement Harper a su établir entre des idées, des identités et des intérêts concurrents un équilibre reposant sur une approche prudente et limitée du pouvoir fédéral de dépenser.

INTRODUCTION

In the preceding chapter, Thomas Courchene has taken us on a tour of the policies, practices, and principles associated with the federal spending power. My intention is to complement Courchene's work by viewing the spending power through a different lens. First, I contribute a way of thinking about the spending power. For ease of communication, I refer to this conceptualization as a framework, although it is probably insufficiently developed to qualify as such. I then apply this framework to the record of the Harper government based on its fiscal actions through to Budget 2008.

My framework is based on the idea that the spending power serves two distinct but overlapping purposes. One purpose is to act as an instrument of public policy. In its public-policy formulation, the spending power is a tool that can be used by the federal government, ideally with provincial-territorial support, to advance a particular policy objective. This power may be exercised either by transferring money to provinces and territories conditionally or by transferring money to persons and organizations directly. Federal agreements with provinces and territories are usually concluded before intergovernmental fiscal transfers are made. In the case of federal transfers to persons or organizations, federal-provincial-territorial agreement may also be required if Ottawa wants to ensure that the provinces and territories do not reduce their expenditures on those targeted persons or organizations, since the net effect of such reductions would be to thwart the federal government's original policy intent and simply enrich provincial and territorial treasuries. Use of the federal spending power as an instrument of public policy is the basis of many programs, including medicare, child benefits, economic development programs, and the Canada Research Chairs Program, among others.

There are theoretical and practical arguments for and against this instrumental role for the exercise of the federal spending power. From a *theoretical* perspective, proponents of the spending power see it mainly as an instrument for redistribution from higher-income provinces or taxpayers to lower-income provinces or taxpayers, thus helping to create a Canada-wide sharing community. This, proponents argue, makes the federation more equitable. They may also argue that, if structured appropriately, such redistribution can also serve economic efficiency objectives. There need not be an equity-efficiency trade-off. To the contrary, they point out that it is economically more efficient to centralize revenues rather than expenditures and to use intergovernmental transfers to fill the resultant vertical fiscal gap between the provinces and territories and the federal government.

Still from the theoretical perspective, others argue the opposite, rejecting the idea that a purposefully designed, vertical fiscal gap can be economically efficient. They point to the theory of fiscal responsibility, which states simply that in order to ensure clear lines of accountability, the government that spends should also be the one that taxes.

At the level of *practical* politics, governments of less affluent provinces outside of central Canada tend to support the exercise of the spending power because the programs it funds invariably entail redistribution in their favour. Others outside of central Canada – particularly in Alberta – worry that the demographic preponderance of Ontario and Quebec will swamp their interests and dictate whether and how the spending power will be used. They therefore wish to limit Ottawa's discretion in using the power. As for Quebec, although it has historically had per capita incomes below the national average, the province has not traditionally viewed the spending power as the appropriate way to secure redistribution in its favour. Nonetheless, when Ottawa has proceeded with a spending power initiative, Quebec has ensured that it receives its appropriate share of the federal tax room or money being transferred.[1] (Quebec's position is discussed further below.) With regard to Ontario, since the early 1990s its governments, regardless of party stripe, have argued that too many of the Canada-wide federal-provincial programs have had a redistributive component. Further, they argue that these equalizing elements are an unreasonably heavy

[1]This was not entirely the case in the years immediately following the Second World War.

burden on Ontario's federal taxpayers. In the main, Ontario governments have not been calling for a reduced role for the spending power, but rather for its use at the program level to be fairer to the province's residents. In short, with the partial exception of Quebec, at the policy level, provincial stances toward the federal spending power are heavily influenced by their economic and financial interests.

The spending power, however, is more than a mere instrument of public policy. The power is also a symbol: it signals the kind of federation that the federal government desires for Canada. Individual provinces also have views about the nature of the federal pact, and these vary from province to province and over time. Some provinces have long been strong supporters of a strong government in Ottawa, while others are firmly positioned in the opposite camp. But provincial views may also change when the government in power changes or provincial circumstances are altered. For example, at different points in history, Ontario has been an adamant opponent of a strong federal government, while at other times it has been a close ally of Ottawa. There are also different opinions among language groups regarding the kind of federation Canada is and should be. In a nutshell, attachments to Canada relative to provincial attachments are stronger in the primarily English-speaking provinces than in Quebec. In other words, issues of identity play a big role in shaping the federation.

It follows from this contest of ideas, interests, and identities that there are also competing views on whether, to what extent, and in what ways Ottawa should use the spending power to construct and maintain the federation. Most of these views have been around in one guise or another for a long time. Some are primordial in the sense of being fundamental to Canada's future as a federation of ten provinces and three territories (and three founding nations?). For a substantial majority of Quebec francophones, Canada-wide nation-building must not be at the expense of Quebec nation-building. Conversely, many anglophones consider it entirely appropriate for the federal government to play a Canada-wide nation-building role. In recent decades, aboriginal peoples have been pressing their claims to justice through the idea of nationhood, and they look to federal transfers as a way of breathing economic life into their aspirations.[2] Primordial views may not be based exclusively on identity, but typically involve a substantial identity dimension.

On the last point, the position of Quebec governments is especially relevant. Quebec's typical response to Canada-wide initiatives based on the federal spending power is to express solidarity with the values attached to the initiative, but to argue that Ottawa's proposals belong within provincial jurisdiction. Quebec subscribes to the classical view of federalism in which each order of government stays largely within its own area of constitutional authority, safeguarding its sovereignty. The Quebec authorities see the spending power as unconstitutional or at least politically illegitimate. They tend to argue, therefore, that if other provinces and territories hold a different view about the legitimacy of the federal spending power, then the appropriate solutions are asymmetrical

---

[2]Such transfers may not involve the spending power in a formal way.

arrangements. For example, when Ottawa seeks to exercise its spending power, more often than not Quebec negotiates an opting-out agreement with the federal government which allows it to design and deliver its piece of the Canada-wide program more or less independently of Ottawa. Alternatively, Quebec works within the federal-provincial framework but secures an explicit understanding that nothing in the agreement will derogate from Quebec's constitutional authority. No matter which route it follows, Quebec secures its appropriate share of federal dollars or tax room. The key point here is that Quebec protects its constitutional autonomy with great determination.

There is one further point to be added on the contest over the nature of the federation. The voices in this contest are by and large as old as the federation itself. Almost every position around the bargaining table today, except for the aboriginal voice, was heard in the events leading up to 1867. Voices that have survived so long clearly have resonance with some significant part of the citizenry – that is to say, they have political legitimacy.

Tom Courchene argues that many of the major challenges Canada now faces, such as human capital formation, the knowledge economy and the environment, are all large enough and important enough to require a national strategy. If that argument is accepted, the question then arises as to how to advance those agendas, given that the relevant program areas fall largely under provincial jurisdiction. In some cases, a traditional, collaborative federal-provincial Canada-wide strategy may be the best approach. The Social Union Framework Agreement (SUFA) (Canada 1999), which Mr. Harper's government has explicitly endorsed, sets out the procedures that Ottawa is expected to follow when involved in such collaboration. If a new federal initiative is to be supported by federal transfers to the provinces, SUFA calls on the federal government to work collaboratively with the provinces and not to introduce such an initiative without the agreement of a majority of the provincial governments. If the new federal initiative is to be funded through direct transfers to individuals or organizations, the federal government is to give the provinces at least three months' notice and to offer to consult prior to implementation (ibid.).

In other cases, it may make sense for the federal government to invite to the table any party that brings useful assets, not just the provinces and territories. These assets might be jurisdiction (which governments have), knowledge (which might rest in interest groups, universities, think tanks), delivery systems (voluntary organizations, municipal governments), land rights (First Nations), relevant links to experience in other countries (which might be found in individuals as well as in organizations), and so on. Courchene's focus on environmental issues might readily fit within this broader, networked approach.[3]

Whether the more traditional collaborative approach is taken, or the wider and less formal networked approach is adopted, there is nevertheless a need for flexibility. There has to be room for asymmetry given the competing views about the federation and the fact that Quebec and other provinces and territories

---

[3]Theoretically, the possibility exists for provincial leadership on these national issues. This presumably would not involve the federal spending power; therefore, that possibility is not pursued further here.

may, from time to time, wish to stand outside of a national strategy that engages their constitutional jurisdiction. This approach recognizes more of an opt-in than an opt-out strategy as the appropriate means of bridging the gap between more pan-Canadian visions of the federation and those that focus on provincial autonomy or minority protection. In fact, the "six province rule" under SUFA is an example of an opt-in approach (ibid.).

From all of the above, it follows that we are unlikely to find a tidy approach to the federal spending power, given that it serves as both instrument and symbol, and given the diversity of opinion on whether and how it should be used. This assessment suggests the use of a multiplicity of governance models, each designed for a particular challenge. Seen in this way, there is lots of room for the creative use of ambiguity. Let us go back to the case of Quebec and to my assertion that the policy perspectives Quebec governments are often similar to those of Ottawa or other jurisdictions. The result of this process is that a common national policy will be produced, but where Quebec legislates and implements its part of the policy on its own. The process is not neat, but it can and does work. It creates the desired policy outcomes while recognizing competing views within the federation. There are numerous examples, from place-specific approaches to dealing with the social and economic development of First Nations to the different federal-provincial model agreements for labour market development.[4]

THE FEDERAL SPENDING POWER UNDER THE HARPER GOVERNMENT

Let me move now to a few thoughts about how the Harper government is managing the spending power issue, bearing in mind its 2007 Speech from the Throne. In that speech, the Harper government committed to bringing forward legislation "to place formal limits on the use of the federal spending power for new shared-cost programs in areas of exclusive provincial jurisdiction".[5] This commitment included opt-out provisions. Since then, however, the federal government has not clarified what approach it would take to meet this commitment.[6] Enacting a version of the relevant SUFA provisions seemed, for a while, the most likely course since the government had announced in its budget documents that it intended to play by those rules.[7] In its 2008 election platform,

---

[4]See, for example, the Trade, Investment and Labour Mobility Agreement, Alberta and British Columbia, 28 April 2006, online: TILMA at www.tilma.ca/ageement/files/pdf/AB-BC_MOU-TILMA_Agreement-Apr-06.pdf.

[5]*Debates of the Senate*, vol. 144, No. 1 (16 October 2007) at 4 (Rt. Hon. Michaëlle Jean), online: Government of Canada at www.sft-ddt.gc.ca/grfx/docs/sftddt-e.pdf, at 8.

[6]This announcement was made in the budget documents: see Department of Finance (2008) and "The Budget Plan 2008: Responsible Leadership", online: Department of Finance at www.budget.gc.ca/2008/pdf/plan-eng.pdf, at 70.

[7]Department of Finance (2006) and "The Budget Plan 2006: Focusing on Priorities", online: Department of Finance at www.fin.gc.ca/budget06/pdf/bp2006e.pdf.

the Conservative Party continued with its SUFA-like undertakings but dropped its explicit reference to new legislation, apparently substituting a "Charter of Open Federalism" in its place.[8] Whether the government follows the legislative or Charter approach, the action will have symbolic implications, with the legislative approach likely to be better received in Quebec than a non-legislative federal Charter.

Whether the legislative or Charter approach is pursued, the actions of the government would also have functional implications in that it would make it harder for the federal government to achieve functional goals without some measure of provincial support. At the same time, the SUFA path would set out a procedure for Ottawa to follow when attempting to secure that support.

If the Harper government does adopt a SUFA-like approach (legislative or Charter), what might the impact be on the Conservatives' ability to meet their own agenda and on future governments' room to manoeuvre? In the years leading up to the election of the Conservatives in 2006, there was considerable debate about whether the Harper government would create a firewall between federal and provincial governments and move Ottawa out of that part of its social policy business that relies on the spending power. In response to the fears expressed by critics and political opponents, the Conservatives pointed to policy statements and an election platform that said otherwise.

At the time of writing, the Conservatives have been in office for two and a half years and have delivered three budgets. So there is a track record by which the Harper government can be judged, always remembering that it has been a minority government and remained so after the 2008 election. In the earliest days of the Harper government, it discontinued the Dryden child-care federal-provincial agreements and replaced them with what can only be viewed as minimal cash transfers. This move helped to keep the firewall debate alive. Was the government's child-care decision a harbinger of things to come or a one-off decision? The evidence suggests that it was neither the first of many decisions that would eventually extricate the government from social programs that rely on the spending power, nor an entirely random event. The Harper government has its own lens through which it views both social programs and the spending power, and its lens is different than that of the Liberal governments that preceded it. But it is not a firewall lens if only because a national government cannot adopt such a view and remain a national government: a national government cannot ignore the competing views of the federation. These assertions are even more relevant when that government is in a minority position.

Whatever the explanations, the Harper government's 2006,[9] 2007,[10] and 2008[11] budgets showed considerable continuity with the policies of previous governments. In these documents, the federal government

---

[8]*The True North Strong and Free: Stephen Harper's Plan for Canadians*, online: Conservative Party of Canada at www.conservative.ca/media/20081007-Platform-e.pdf, at 28.

[9]*Supra* note 7.

- proclaimed its adherence to SUFA rules;
- identified health care, post-secondary education and training, and infrastructure as shared priorities;
- endorsed the 2004 federal-provincial First Ministers' Health Accord, which runs to 2013-14;
- extended the Canada Social Transfer to 2013-14 and enlarged it;
- put equalization and territorial formula financing on the same timetable as the Liberals, with extensions to 2013-14;
- respected (arguably) the special offshore deals with Newfoundland and Labrador and Nova Scotia, inherited from the Martin Liberals, which effectively shelter their equalization payments against reductions from offshore resource revenues; and
- made permanent the Gas Tax Fund to help finance municipal infrastructure.

As for the direct spending power, the government appears not to be planning any major changes to the National Child Benefit or to the Canada Foundation for Innovation, and it seems to accept the idea of maintaining the Canada Student Loans Program, promising to streamline and modernize it. The 2008 Budget also announced a new consolidated Canada Student Grant Program to maintain the level of student aid when the funds of the Canada Millennium Scholarship Program run out. The government further committed to a number of additional programmatic initiatives relating to graduate students and international study, as well as enhanced support for research through the direct spending power. In short, the Harper government has made no significant departures from the approach to the *direct* spending power taken by previous governments.

To be sure, there have been significant symbolical and functional differences between the Harper government and its predecessors. Not only did the Conservatives terminate the Liberal child-care initiative, but, importantly, they also, did away with the Kelowna Accord. It may (or may not) be noteworthy that social assistance and social services were not included in this list of shared priorities, even though the Canada Social Transfer is nominally intended in part for these purposes and the federal government has a long history of supporting people with disabilities.

Yet at the same time, the government increased the Canada Social Transfer by $2 billion annually and intruded deeply into provincial jurisdiction with its stated priority regarding patient wait times (more below). Based on the above considerations alone, it would be difficult to argue that the record to date supports the "harbinger of things to come" concern.

---

[10]Department of Finance (2007) and "The Budget Plan 2007: Aspire to a Stronger, Safer, Better Canada", online: Department of Finance at www.budget.gc.ca/2007/pdf/bp2007e.pdf.

[11]*Supra* note 6. It is unclear whether much significance should be attached to this omission since the budget documents refer to both social assistance and social services in their discussion of the Canada Social Transfer.

Further evidence against the firewall scenario is provided by the government's major overhaul of equalization and territorial formula financing.[12] While these two programs do not rely on the spending power for their constitutional support, they involve similar kinds of trade-offs (balancing incentives and equity considerations, balancing the interests of the more affluent and the less affluent provinces) as other transfer programs that do rest on the spending power. The equalization decisions are clear evidence of the government trying to balance competing claims on the federal treasury in a way that would be familiar to earlier governments. The Harper government accepted the advice of an expert panel appointed by the Liberal government and, in so doing, abandoned an explicit election promise not to include any resource revenues in the equalization formula. This suggests that the Harper government struggled with the same trade-offs that all federal governments must reflect on and manage.[13] Overall, relative to preceding Liberal governments there is more continuity than change in the government's current approach to the spending power. This suggests that fears of the firewall scenario are at best overstated as is the idea that the government has plans to decimate the social sector. Whether these conclusions would apply in the case of a majority Conservative government is a matter for conjecture. There was nothing in the Conservative 2008 election platform to suggest that the government planned a sharp turn in this direction, and the election result left the government in a minority position again.

Although I have just argued that there is considerable continuity between the approaches taken by the Harper government (2006-08) and previous governments, this does not mean that the Conservatives' approach to the spending power is the same as that of the Liberals. On the revenue side of its agenda, Parliament enacted the government's promised cuts to the Goods and

---

[12]In its 2007 budget plan, *supra* note 10, and acting on the advice of the Expert Panel on Equalization and Territorial Formula Financing that was established by the Martin government in 2005, the federal government amended the equalization formula in several key respects. In establishing the equalization standard, the government included the fiscal capacity of all ten provinces; previously, the standard had included only five, the Province of Alberta not among them. Although the government also reduced the rate of resource revenue inclusion from 100 to 50 percent, this was more than offset by the inclusion of one-half of Alberta's resource revenues. Taken together, these modifications significantly enriched the equalization standard. A fiscal capacity cap was also implemented to ensure that equalization payments did not bring the overall fiscal capacity of any equalization-receiving province to a level higher than that of the non-equalization-receiving province with the lowest fiscal capacity (in 2008 this position was held by Ontario). As for its special arrangements with Newfoundland and Labrador and Nova Scotia, Ottawa offered these provinces two options. The first was that they could receive the same benefits as before Budget 2007, with no fiscal capacity cap on either equalization or the Offshore Accords payments. Alternatively, each province could accept the new, strengthened equalization formula and continue to receive payments under the Offshore Accords subject to the cap.

[13]This view is reinforced by statements by the federal Finance Minister in the immediate aftermath of the 2008 election suggesting that equalization needed to be amended because it was proving too costly for the federal government.

Services Tax. This action purposefully narrowed in a very substantial way the government's fiscal room for introducing new programs through the spending power. Moreover, to the extent that Ottawa continues to enjoy fiscally significant surpluses in 2009 and beyond (not likely at the time of writing), the government has explicitly undertaken to give priority to further tax cuts, not to introducing new programs in provincial jurisdiction.

What about the $33 billion in annual cash transfers under the Canada Health Transfer and the Canada Social Transfer, both implemented using the spending power? Has the federal government been imposing additional requirements on provinces and territories as a condition of receiving these funds "in the name of accountability", which is a government priority? Or has Ottawa been easing up on existing conditions "in the name of accountability"? In other words, there are different ways of tackling accountability. Under one approach, the government could take the position that it is inappropriate to ask Parliament to vote $33 billion annually without having an accountability framework to evaluate the use of these expenditures. While there is a substantial Canada Health Transfer accountability framework, no counterpart exists for the Canada Social Transfer. Alternatively, the government could take the view that conditional transfers confuse which level of government is responsible for health and social programs, and thus detract from the clarity of roles and responsibilities as well as from accountability. Liberal governments in the 1990s had juggled these competing views. The 1995 federal budget celebrated the second view, but after the federal fiscal position improved, arguably the Liberals were leaning more toward the first view.

Is the government showing evidence of breaking from the status quo it inherited from the Liberals regarding these two views on accountability? Part of the answer was provided when the patient wait-times guarantee disappeared from the public agenda. The guarantee was one of five priorities identified in the Harper government's first Speech from the Throne, and the Conservatives pursued it quietly with the provinces, some of which considered it not only intrusive but also bad policy. However, the federal pedal has been removed from the metal on this issue – a victory for the second view of accountability, with its focus on clarifying roles and responsibilities.

With regard to the Canada Social Transfer, the government has declared a notional $800 million increase for national post-secondary education beginning in 2008-09. Intriguingly, in Budget 2007, the government stated that this increase would take effect following discussions with provinces and territories on how best to make use of those new investments and ensure appropriate reporting and accountability to Canadians. These discussions were to build on the valuable work already undertaken by the Council of the Federation. This suggests that, with respect to the national post-secondary component of the Canada Social Transfer, the Conservatives were again opening up the possibility of some form of the first kind of accountability regime described above. Budget 2008 did not, however, indicate what had happened on this issue, and at the time of writing this idea of some form of public accountability for the federal post-secondary transfer to provinces, like the patient wait-time guarantee, is reportedly not on any substantial federal-provincial agenda and seems to have disappeared from public view. How does all of the above fit with the federal government's commitment to place limits on the spending power? One result of all these considerations is that the commitment articulated in the 2007 Speech from the Throne, and reiterated in a different form in the 2008 election platform, has not been much of a constraint on the Harper government's freedom of action. That commitment applies to new shared-cost programs, but arguably not to renewals of existing programs. If this interpretation is correct, then, when the various federal-provincial and federal-territorial transfer programs come up for renewal in 2013-14, the government will not be legally constrained by the new statute – assuming that it follows the precise wording of either the Speech from the Throne or the election platform.

Implementing the commitment in either way could make the introduction of new, joint federal-provincial programs somewhat more difficult. The public record, however, does not suggest that the Harper government has plans to introduce any large new programs like pharmacare or home care. If Parliament were to enact relevant SUFA-like restrictions, or if the government were to unilaterally promulgate a non-legislative Charter, this would not interfere with the government's functional plans; however, such measures might satisfy to some modest degree a symbolic priority for the provinces that oppose the spending power in principle, like Quebec and Alberta. It is also noteworthy that the actual SUFA text appears to be broader in scope than the words of the Throne Speech. SUFA does not refer to "new programs"; rather, it refers to "new initiatives". The latter expression could well cover new components in an existing program. Importantly, SUFA also touches the direct spending power, whereas the 2007 Speech from the Throne and the 2008 election platform were silent on it. For a future activist non-Conservative federal government, SUFA-like legislation could well slow down its social agenda, although ultimately it could not block it, nor would a Conservative Charter necessarily bind a future non-Conservative government. But such legislative or political limitations on the federal spending power fit well with current Conservative priorities, including a vision of accountability for federal transfers to provinces that emphasizes the clarification of roles and responsibilities.

CONCLUSION

Competing ideas and interests and diverse identities have led to competing visions of the kind of federation Canada is and should be. It follows that there are competing views on the spending power. The spending power has both functional and symbolic roles, and the contest applies to both. With respect to the functional role, there are competing theories about whether the spending power is economically efficient, at least as it applies to intergovernmental transfers. These theoretical differences are reflected in competing political claims. The symbolic role of the spending power is also the subject of differences. The disparity in opinion on these issues has existed since Confederation, which indicates that the differences have deep roots and are unlikely to go away – any political opinion that has the staying power to survive 140 years presumably has considerable political legitimacy.

It is therefore politically difficult for the federal government to dismiss any of the contending views lightly. Indeed, any federal government that privileges one position too heavily to the exclusion of others is unlikely to remain in office very long. This is not to argue that Ottawa does not, and should not, have its own agenda, but it does suggest that any government must weigh carefully this range of diverse opinion in formulating that agenda.

As for the broader record of the Harper government, it has balanced the competition of ideas, interests, and identities in its approach to the spending power. In so doing, it has asserted forcefully and explicitly that program areas covered by the Canada Health Transfer and the Canada Social Transfer are areas of shared responsibility, and has extended their legislative lives. The Conservative government initially attempted to improve provincial accountability for these programs by substantial intervention. But it has since been leaning toward an accountability regime for these two large transfers that focuses on clarity of roles and responsibilities. At the same time, the federal government does not appear to have any major new social policy initiatives in mind, and it has very significantly reduced its fiscal room for launching any such initiative.

For that reason, if the Harper government acts on its Throne Speech commitment and asks Parliament to legislate controls on the spending power along the lines set out in the Social Union Framework Agreement, it will not be significantly restricting its own functional agenda. This would be even more the case were it to proceed through the Charter route.

Whether a more socially activist federal government would be constrained by such hypothetical legislation or hypothetical Charter in the future depends in part on two considerations. The first is whether that new action would render decision-making more administratively complex than under the current SUFA. The answer would almost certainly be yes, but the degree of additional complexity is an open question. If it were a big problem, the federal government could amend the legislation or Charter to meet its needs, assuming the political costs of such amendments in federal-provincial relations were tolerable to Ottawa. The second consideration is whether a more activist government could rely mainly on the direct spending power to advance its agenda or would have to make substantial use of intergovernmental transfers. If the federal government could rely on the direct power, its freedom of action would obviously be less constrained than if it had to rely mainly on intergovernmental transfers.

REFERENCES

Canada. 1999. *Framework to Improve the Social Union for Canadians: An Agreement between the Government of Canada and the Governments of the Provinces and Territories*, 4 February 1999 [SUFA].

Department of Finance. 2006. *2006 Budget.* Ottawa: Public Works and Government Services Canada.

— 2007. *2007 Budget.* Ottawa: Public Works and Government Services Canada.

— 2008. *2008 Budget.* Ottawa: Public Works and Government Services Canada.

III

The Spending Power: Legal Considerations

6

Imperium in imperio? Des déséquilibres, du pouvoir fédéral de dépenser et du constitutionnalisme au Canada

Marc Chevrier

This chapter examines Canada's federal spending power from both a historical and political perspective. The analysis of the origins of federalism suggests that the spending power is at odds with the spirit of federalism itself, to the extent that it takes the form of an asymmetrical pact between an imperial power and small nations with restricted autonomy. Modern federalism, as exemplified by the American experience, is not all that far from the imperial federalism of ancient Rome, which imposed the empire's hegemony on conquered cities while leaving them with a degree of internal autonomy. The juridical idea of federal equilibrium fails to capture the fact that in practice, disequilibria are common, including financial asymmetry in favour of the central government.

In Canada, understanding the constitutional regime founded in 1867 requires attention to the often neglected political dimension of federalism, as distinct from its constitutional aspect. The author argues that modern political federalism in Canada grew out of the evolutionary British Constitution and England's tradition of accommodating historical nations. The founding fathers, aware of this tradition, believed that the Canadian Constitution would carry forward the progress of the Glorious Revolution of 1688 and, to that end, wanted to grant Quebec a status similar to that of Scotland in the United Kingdom. Political and intellectual actors in Lower Canada saw Confederation as an act of retrocession that would free Quebec from the overarching union of 1840. Understood this way, the context surrounding the Constitution's implementation is favourable to Quebec nationalist discourse. In Quebec the claim for autonomy is seen as having precedence over the claims of interdependence, but the opposite is true in English Canada.

From the 1950s onward, the federal government committed itself to using the spending power to build the Canadian nation, and gradually embraced the idea that it had general responsibility for the well-being of its citizens. The constitutional reform of 1982 transformed this vision into constitutional dogma, and implicitly gave the federal government a central role in conceiving and shaping the country's social policies. From an analysis of the systems of other countries, the author concludes that Canada has a choice to make. It could become an imperial federation, where the rule of law is applied with full stringency only to relations between governments and individuals, and where the federal government's dominium *over its property extends to its relations with societies and nations within the country. Alternatively, this* dominium *could be limited by a constitutional amendment prohibiting or limiting conditional use of the spending power. It remains unclear which of these two outcomes will prevail in Canada's future federal dynamic.*

INTRODUCTION

Après l'échec des grandes réformes constitutionnelles du Lac Meech (Bibliothèque du Parlement 1987) et de Charlottetown,[1] le pouvoir fédéral de dépenser s'est imposé comme le thème dominant des relations intergouvernementales au Canada. Bien que ce pouvoir controversé fît partie des amendements constitutionnels envisagés en 1987 et en 1992, la discussion politique s'est transportée du forum constitutionnel au forum politique, avec la volonté affichée de plusieurs acteurs politiques de corriger le « déséquilibre fiscal » canadien par la conclusion d'ententes intergouvernementales. Le pouvoir fédéral de dépenser a suscité depuis longtemps un double débat. Le premier, animé par les économistes et les spécialistes des politiques publiques, a surtout porté sur les avantages économiques et sociaux que l'on peut escompter de l'utilisation de ce pouvoir pour orienter les politiques sociales et optimiser l'union économique canadienne. Le deuxième a touché principalement à la légitimité même de ce pouvoir, que d'aucuns ont jugé contraire à la constitution canadienne et aux principes du fédéralisme.

Le but du présent article est de revenir sur ce dernier débat doctrinal, sans toutefois prétendre le trancher, loin s'en faut. Je n'entends pas non plus ajouter au débat juridique qui a opposé les tenants de la légalité de ce pouvoir aux partisans de son inconstitutionnalité, encore qu'il sera utile d'y faire allusion. Deux questions seront ici étudiées, l'une théorique et l'autre analytique. La première vise à déterminer si les principes mêmes du fédéralisme interdisent le déploiement de ce pouvoir. La deuxième consiste à tirer les conséquences de la constatation du fait qu'en dépit de la controverse doctrinale sur la légitimité du pouvoir fédéral de dépenser, celui-ci est courant dans la plupart des régimes fédéraux. Au fond, il s'agit de savoir ce que l'usage généralisé de ce pouvoir révèle de la dynamique et de la nature des régimes fédératifs contemporains. Pour répondre à ces deux questions, il sera utile de remonter aux origines historiques du fédéralisme ainsi que de rappeler certaines propriétés des régimes fédératifs modernes. Dans un deuxième temps, j'examinerai en quoi le débat sur le pouvoir fédéral de dépenser découle, pour une bonne part, de la culture politique et de la tradition constitutionnelle canadiennes, et notamment, de la conception particulière qu'ont les Québécois de l'autonomie. Finalement, nous verrons comment au Canada, sous l'influence d'un nationalisme pancanadien et d'une vision strictement libérale de la société, les relations entre collectivités ne suivent pas les mêmes principes que ceux qui régissent les rapports entre l'individu et l'État. Cette disparité de traitement montre que le Canada se

---

[1]Comité mixte spécial sur le renouvellement du Canada (1992).

considère de plus en plus comme un empire moderne, lui-même conçu à l'origine comme un dominion.

L'AMBIGUÏTÉ ORIGINELLE DU FÉDÉRALISME

Les théoriciens du fédéralisme traitent généralement de ce régime d'État en partant des mêmes observations étymologiques. Le terme « fédéralisme » est dérivé du latin « *fœdus* » qui signifie un pacte ou une forme de traité (Elazar 1987 à la p. 5; Groppi 2004 à la p. 6; Saint-Ouen 2005 à la p. 15). S'agissant du fédéralisme du temps de l'antiquité romaine, Ronald Watts se contente d'observer, en une seule ligne, que la République romaine pratiquait des arrangements asymétriques en vertu desquels elle exerçait la puissance fédérale à l'égard des villes partenaires plus faibles (Watts 1999 aux pp. 2-3). Watts évoque sans doute, sans la nommer, la ligue latine ou ce que le grand historien du droit romain Theodore Mommsen a appelé la « ligue nationale latine » (Mommsen 1985 aux pp. 226, 231). Du 5e siècle avant J.-C. jusqu'à l'an 338 avant J.-C., la ville de Rome et une trentaine d'autres villes de l'Italie centrale qui partageaient la même langue (le *nomen latinum*) ont vécu sous le régime d'une confédération, que la guerre entre Rome et les villes confédérées rompit à l'avantage de la première. Cette confédération avait une capitale, Aricia, où était célébrée la fête fédérale, ainsi qu'une assemblée, le *consilium*, où les représentants réunis des diverses cités délibéraient de politique étrangère, de défense et de la fondation de nouvelles colonies. Dans cette ligue, Rome avait un rôle prépondérant, du fait de son ascendant militaire et de sa puissance législative, puisque les lois adoptées par les comices romaines pouvaient s'appliquer à l'ensemble des villes confédérées. Cependant, ces dernières conservaient une assez grande autonomie interne et la liberté de conclure des traités avec des villes non-membres de la ligue ou de leur faire la guerre (Plancherel-Bongard 1998).

À la suite de la rivalité des cités latines qui se liguèrent contre Rome entre 340-338 avant J.-C., la ligue latine fut dissoute. Victorieuse, Rome recomposa les termes de ses relations avec les villes soumises, dont certaines entrèrent dans une nouvelle confédération, dite « italique ». Les rapports de subordination entre Rome et les villes vaincues variaient considérablement. Quand Rome décidait d'exercer sa domination, la ville vaincue, privée de tout droit, entrait dans le domaine public romain, par un acte unilatéral nommé la *deditio*. Lorsque toutefois Rome ne voyait pas d'intérêt à soumettre totalement la cité vaincue, il passait alors un *foedus*, que l'on pouvait assimiler à un acte unilatéral de complaisance. Certaines villes incorporées au domaine romain recevaient un traitement de faveur en étant considérées comme fédérées, ce qui leur conférait le droit à l'autonomie interne. Ces villes favorisées demeuraient toutefois assujetties, par la vertu d'un *foedus iniquuum*, à de lourdes obligations. Comme l'a observé Carole Plancherel-Bongard :

> Ces villes n'avaient pas le droit de déclarer la guerre, ni de conclure des traités : elles étaient donc entièrement soumises à Rome pour la politique extérieure. Elles avaient l'obligation de fournir magistrats, soldats, navires et céréales,

mais n'avaient pas à payer leur tribut. Elles avaient aussi le droit de battre leur propre monnaie et un droit de regard sur leurs douanes (ibid. à la p. 284).

Avec les cités vaincues maintenues hors du domaine public romain, Rome concluait des actes bilatéraux, appelés aussi *foedus* ou *foedera*, qui avaient pour but soit d'établir des rapports de bon voisinage (*amicitia*), soit un engagement perpétuel de non-agression et d'assistance mutuelle. Ces *foedera* accablaient les villes ainsi alliées, notamment dans le cas de la confédération italique, de lourdes charges, équivalentes à celles qu'imposait un *foedus iniquum*. En somme, le statut de villes fédérées liées à Rome par un *foedus* signifiait le droit à une souveraineté limitée, soumise à la puissance impériale de Rome. Ces villes jouissant d'une « autonomie à la fois restreinte et assurée » étaient nommées *foederati* (Mommsen 1985 à la p. 278). En somme, le *foedus* est un pacte foncièrement inégalitaire qui, bien qu'il eût été désigné comme une alliance égale (ibid. à la p. 238), consacrait l'hégémonie de Rome. En parlant des diverses ligues ou associations qui lièrent Rome aux Latins, de la royauté jusqu'au principat, Mommsen fit les observations suivantes:

> Mais il y a deux caractères qui se sont maintenus à travers les siècles et leurs variations ; ce sont : d'une part, l'inégalité de l'alliance qui . . . implique, non seulement en fait, mais en droit, l'hégémonie de Rome et ; d'autre part, le maintien d'une certaine souveraineté, sans doute restreinte, mais jamais complètement supprimée, des cités soumises à cette hégémonie. L'État romain n'a été, pendant tout ce laps de temps, rien d'autre chose qu'une confédération de cités principalement urbaines placées sous la direction de la cité romaine . . . . Au reste, l'alliance inégale contient nécessairement en elle une tendance à l'absorption dans le sein de la cité dirigeante. (ibid. à la p. 227)

Mommsen identifie plusieurs caractéristiques du fédéralisme romain, qui ne sont pas sans intérêt pour la compréhension du fédéralisme moderne. Premièrement, il instaure un rapport de domination en faveur d'une puissance hégémonique. Deuxièmement, ce rapport inégalitaire maintient la souveraineté résiduelle des cités fédérées. C'est, dit Mommsen dans un extraordinaire oxymore, « une sujétion autonome » qui accorde une indépendance politique limitée, « mais garantie par la puissance protectrice » (ibid. à la p. 290). Le fondement de cette autonomie limitée est « l'autorité exercée par la cité fédérée ou libre sur son propre territoire, c'est-à-dire, selon la conception des Romains, l'existence à son profit de la propriété publique – ou de la propriété privée dérivée de la propriété publique – sur le sol enfermé dans ses limites » (ibid. à la p. 317). Enfin, cette alliance inégalitaire est dynamique et laisse place à un processus d'unification qui conforte la puissance dirigeante.

Cette courte incursion dans l'histoire romaine est riche en enseignements, en ce qu'elle met au jour l'ambiguïté constitutive du fédéralisme en tant que régime d'État. Si l'on s'en tient à l'étymologie du concept, le fédéralisme connote l'idée de la fondation d'une entité politique nouvelle sur la base d'un pacte conclu entre des partenaires déjà existants. Mais quels devraient être les principes gouvernant les rapports entre ces partenaires ? Un partenariat égalitaire, l'amitié, l'équilibre entre des souverainetés coordonnées et multiples ? Ou la domination, l'expansion d'une souveraineté hégémonique et le jeu inégal des forces ? Ce sont là des possibilités contenues dans l'idée même d'un régime fédéral, qu'on ne peut exclure *a priori* si l'enjeu de la réflexion est la compréhension de la dynamique effective d'un tel régime, dans la variété de ses manifestations.[2] Le fédéralisme, ancien et moderne, est une réalité aux facettes multiples qui mêle inextricablement autonomie, puissance et subordination.

L'AMBIGUÏTÉ DU FÉDÉRALISME MODERNE OU LE NOUVEAU RÉGIME MIXTE

L'ambiguïté constitutive du fédéralisme n'a pas échappé à certains penseurs politiques. Montesquieu, le premier, voit dans le fédéralisme une forme de régime mixte combinant les avantages extérieurs du gouvernement monarchique aux avantages intérieurs du gouvernement républicain (Montesquieu 1961 aux p. 137). Montesquieu était tributaire de la pensée politique classique qui n'envisageait que des républiques de petite taille. L'agrandissement de l'État et la puissance se trouvaient seulement combinés dans la monarchie. Donc, si une république veut se défendre, elle doit s'unir à ses semblables pour opposer à la menace une défense équivalente à celle d'un monarque. Or, selon Montesquieu, la république fédérative est une forme d'alliance forcée qui fait cohabiter deux genres de gouvernements contradictoires en principe : l'un recherche la guerre et l'agrandissement, l'autre la paix et la modération. Cependant, la république fédérative trouve sa stabilité par l'esprit de démocratie qui anime les républiques fédérées, qui aliènent cependant une partie de leur souveraineté au profit d'un directoire commun.

Alexis de Tocqueville suivra les traces de Montesquieu dans l'analyse du fédéralisme américain, quoiqu'en lui donnant toutefois une nouvelle ampleur. À l'instar de Montesquieu, Tocqueville considère le système fédéral comme la combinaison de deux types de société ou d'État. D'un côté, les petites nations paisibles et libres, et de l'autre côté, l'empire ou les grandes nations qui accroissent la puissance et les passions.[3] Les avantages que Tocqueville associe à l'un et à l'autre de ces types vont au-delà de ceux que Montesquieu avait considérés pour la république et la monarchie. En réalité, Tocqueville dresse une espèce de portrait-type de deux sociétés, qui ont chacune leur dynamique et leur culture propres. Des petites nations, il tire un portrait semblable à celui qu'a fait Montesquieu des républiques : une société restreinte où règnent l'égalité des conditions, la simplicité des mœurs, la tranquillité sociale, l'étroitesse des ambitions et des intérêts, ainsi que le conformisme. Quant à l'empire ou la grande nation, elle est agitée, en proie aux passions démultipliées par la force des ambitions et des partis ; les sentiments humains étant plus exacerbés, ils

---

[2]Ce type de compréhension se distingue de l'approche purement normative qui dérive sa compréhension des ressorts du fédéralisme d'une vision formelle du bien et de la justice. Voir également Weinstock (2001).

[3]Les références à la pensée de Tocqueville sur le fédéralisme américain sont tirées de son maître livre (Tocqueville 1981).

atteignent à la grandeur ou à la dépravation. L'empire accélère les forces productives et les inventions de même qu'il accroît les inégalités. La force du nombre devient en elle-même d'autant plus redoutable qu'elle fait éprouver à des millions d'hommes les mêmes sentiments au même moment. Bien que Tocqueville admette que l'humanité serait plus heureuse « s'il n'y avait que de petites nations et point de grandes », « on ne peut faire qu'il n'y ait pas de grandes nations » (ibid. à la p. 238). Tocqueville semble postuler une loi des sociétés qui les conduit vers l'acquisition de la force, qui est le propre des grandes nations. La force, qu'elle soit militaire ou commerciale, devient la condition d'existence des grandes nations.

Plusieurs observations découlent des analyses de Tocqueville. En premier lieu, le système fédératif est pour lui une forme atténuée ou contrainte d'empire, en ce qu'il instaure une forme d'État et une société de type impérial, mues par la recherche de la puissance, mais entravées dans leur développement par la dynamique concurrente de petits États tournés vers la préservation de leur liberté. Cette combinaison des contraires suppose qu'au lieu de s'annuler jusqu'à l'autodestruction du système, ces dynamiques rivales inhérentes au fédéralisme américain auraient un effet stabilisateur, par l'addition des avantages associés à l'empire et aux petites républiques et par la mitigation des faiblesses propres à ces deux régimes pris isolément. En deuxième lieu, contrairement à Montesquieu, Tocqueville ne réduit pas le système fédératif à une société de sociétés ; ce dernier juxtapose aux sociétés de base une société nouvelle, plus étendue, capable d'absorber les ambitions et les passions contenues dans les petites nations et de former une nouvelle nationalité. De plus, le fédéralisme moderne instaure une spécialisation des tâches politiques et sociales : les petites sociétés tournent la puissance publique et l'énergie individuelle « du côté des améliorations intérieures » (ibid. à la p. 239) ; l'amour du bien-être y supplante la recherche de la gloire et de la puissance. Dégagé des soucis et des vicissitudes de la vie locale, le gouvernement de l'Union peut ainsi se consacrer à la cohésion de l'ensemble et au renforcement de la puissance commerciale et extérieure. Cette spécialisation met en place au sein même de la collectivité deux dynamiques sociétales qui se complètent. Enfin, le système fédératif, selon Tocqueville, crée des attaches graduées entre le citoyen et l'État ; le premier porte son amour de la patrie d'abord sur la petite nation, puis le dirige sur l'Union elle-même, par prolongement de son patriotisme provincial. Tocqueville semble croire que l'allégeance en « étagement » est propre à renforcer « l'esprit public » de l'union, puisque s'appuyant sur son attachement viscéral à sa première patrie, le citoyen transporte ce même affect à la patrie commune tout entière.

Que Tocqueville utilisât le concept d'empire pour penser le fédéralisme américain n'a rien de surprenant ; plusieurs pères fondateurs de la république de 1787 le firent eux-mêmes (Ferguson 2004 aux pp. 33-35), dont notamment Hamilton qui écrivait dans le Fédéraliste no 22 : « L'édifice de l'Empire américain doit reposer sur la base solide du consentement du peuple » (Hamilton 1787 à la p. 177). John Pocock note qu'au dix-neuvième siècle, les Américains n'eurent de cesse d'employer le terme *empire* pour désigner leur république continentale (Pocock 1990 à la p. 69). Il est certain qu'en rompant avec la doctrine qui ne distinguait pas le fédéralisme du confédéralisme, ils voulaient établir une nouvelle forme d'État qui, contrairement aux États-Unis nés de la confédération d'États de 1777, aurait des moyens constitutionnels et financiers de se dédier à la puissance. Dans le vocabulaire des anti-fédéralistes, la référence à l'Empire, posé comme l'équivalent de l'État national ou unitaire, était omniprésente (Chopin 2002 aux pp. 103-121). Pour plusieurs anti-fédéralistes, l'établissement d'un nouvel empire américain sous la forme d'un gouvernement fédéral déboucherait sur l'usurpation des droits des États et ultimement sur la tyrannie « d'une autorité absolue, suprême et illimitée, qui détruirait en dernier ressort la souveraineté des États » (ibid. à la p. 113).

Par ailleurs, les pères fondateurs américains, s'ils invoquèrent la république fédérative de Montesquieu, n'envisageaient pas tous vraiment le fédéralisme comme base d'un État continental élargi. Comme le faisait remarquer David F. Epstein, Madison, dans le célèbre texte où il préconise l'élargissement de la sphère politique comme moyen de neutraliser les factions, ne recommande là pas véritablement la solution fédérale. Ni la multiplication des factions ni l'agrandissement des circonscriptions électorales n'impliquent nécessairement un gouvernement fédéral fondé sur la division de la souveraineté. Le raisonnement déployé par Madison suppose plutôt que l'arène politique de l'Union se place au centre de la vie politique (Epstein 1984 à la p. 102). C'est pourquoi, selon Epstein, Madison, lors de la Convention de Philadelphie, proposa que le Congrès possédât un veto à l'encontre des lois étatiques et invoqua à l'appui de sa proposition une argumentation semblable à celle du Fédéraliste no 10.

Le concept d'empire a connu, au cours des dernières années, une certaine faveur dans l'étude du régime politique américain ; cependant, les analyses qui ont renoué avec ce concept s'en sont servies pour appréhender essentiellement la puissance extérieure américaine (voir notamment Nexon et Wright 2007), et non point pour rendre compte de la dynamique fédérale interne des États-Unis. Plusieurs ouvrages d'histoire politique et juridique des États-Unis témoignent toutefois d'un intérêt accru pour le concept (voir Bilder 2004; voir également Hulscboch 2005), engouement que Lauren Benton a qualifié de « tournant impérial » (Benton 2006). Le concept d'édification d'empire (*empire-building*) est demeuré un thème récurrent de la critique des dérives bureaucratiques et autocratiques du régime présidentiel américain, critique dont l'origine remonte à la hantise qu'avaient les anti-fédéralistes du Léviathan qui émergerait de la constitution de 1787.[4]

ÉQUILIBRE ET DÉSÉQUILIBRE EN RÉGIME FÉDÉRATIF

Les régimes de fédération sont pour une large part des créatures juridiques, dans la mesure où la forme de l'État et de ses institutions découle de conceptions juridiques du pouvoir et de la souveraineté. La littérature sur le fédéralisme part généralement de la doctrine juridique de l'État fédéral pour élaborer sa

---

[4]Sur cette problématique, voir Levinson (2004).

définition du concept. Cette omniprésence du discours juridique est inévitable, puisque les fédérations comptent sur la constitution et les tribunaux pour prendre forme. De plus, les innombrables conflits de compétence que les fédérations suscitent mobilisent les ressources du droit constitutionnel, que ce soit dans l'arène politique ou au prétoire. Les conceptions de la fédération varient d'un régime fédéral à l'autre, ainsi que d'une tradition juridique à l'autre. Les juristes civilistes de culture européenne aiment déduire de l'organisation d'un État fédéral un nombre limité de principes ou de « lois », généralement la séparation, l'autonomie et la participation, auxquels certains ajoutent les principes de subsidiarité ou d'adéquation. Les juristes anglo-saxons, influencés par les travaux de K.C. Wheare, ont tendance à concevoir la fédération comme la juxtaposition de deux ordres de gouvernement tous deux souverains, indépendants l'un de l'autre, mais coordonnés.[5]

L'une des idées sous-jacentes à ces diverses conceptions juridiques de la fédération est celle de l'équilibre fédéral. Puisque la fédération est définie en tant que régime de division de la souveraineté entre deux ordres de gouvernement séparés ou de fragmentation de la puissance publique, la souveraineté ultime étant laissée au peuple, le maintien du caractère fédéral du régime dépend donc de l'institutionnalisation de cette division et d'une séparation entre deux ordres de gouvernement qui, sans être nécessairement symétrique, connaît un certain point d'équilibre. On trouve ce souci d'équilibre dans l'idée que chaque ordre de gouvernement forme un État institutionnellement complet, dans le principe de l'arbitrage judiciaire des conflits de pouvoirs et dans la participation des deux ordres de gouvernement dans la procédure de réforme de la constitution.

L'idée d'équilibre fédéral semble avoir présupposé la pensée des pères fondateurs de la république fédérale américaine. En concevant un nouvel ordre politique qui fasse coexister en son sein une pluralité d'organes souverains dont aucun ne possède la souveraineté ultime, les fédéralistes américains conçurent un État composé (ou mixte) fondé sur « [l]'équilibre des pouvoirs entre la fédération et les États » (Chopin 2002 à la p. 279). Cette vision équilibriste de la fédération a conduit, dans les décennies qui ont suivi la convention de Philadelphie de 1787, à l'essor du fédéralisme dualiste (Kincaid 1996). De la même manière use-t-on depuis quelques années aux États-Unis de la notion de souveraineté dualiste (*dual sovereignty*) pour désigner le regain du contrôle judiciaire des lois basé sur les prescriptions du fédéralisme.[6]

La notion d'équilibre est particulièrement présente dans la littérature des juristes et politologues québécois. C'est le critère à partir duquel Henri Brun et Guy Tremblay évaluent la répartition constitutionnelle des pouvoirs et des ressources au Canada, en postulant que « [l]'équilibre des forces entre les gouvernements dans un régime fédératif n'est pas une panacée, mais il peut servir à assurer à long terme le maintien de ce qui constitue l'essence même d'un tel régime, l'autonomie respective des deux ordres de gouvernement »

[5]Sur ces différences d'approche, voir Chevrier (2007).

[6]Voir notamment Prélot et Rogoff (1996) ; Brisbin (1998) ; Conlan et Vergniolle de Chantal (2001) à la p. 253.

(Brun et Tremblay 2002 à la p. 425). Eugénie Brouillet semble distinguer deux critères d'équilibre. Le premier, formel, résulte de l'égalité juridique entre les niveaux de gouvernement. Le deuxième, dynamique, est le produit des forces de centralisation et de décentralisation, et englobe notamment la distribution des ressources et des compétences legislatives (Brouillet 2005 aux pp. 85-87). On observe le même souci d'équilibre dynamique dans les écrits de Nicole Duplé (2004 à la p. 247) ou dans ceux de Réjean Pelletier (2005). W.R. Lederman a fait aussi de la recherche de l'équilibre entre la centralisation fédérale et l'autonomie provinciale un principe d'interprétation du partage des compétences legislatives (Lederman 1965).

La même défense de l'équilibre fédéral traverse les rapports de commissions d'enquête québécoise sur le fédéralisme canadien. S'inspirant des travaux de K.C. Wheare, le rapport de la Commission royale d'enquête sur les problèmes constitutionnels de 1956 (« le rapport Tremblay ») définit le régime fédératif comme un régime d'État maintenant en équilibre deux tendances opposées, l'unité centralisatrice et l'indépendance des unités politiques préexistantes à l'union. Le rapport de la Commission sur le déséquilibre fiscal de 2002 (« le rapport Séguin ») s'appuie sur la définition du régime fédératif donnée par le rapport Tremblay, elle-même empruntée à la définition de Wheare, pour en déduire un principe d'équilibre fiscal dont l'existence est subordonnée à trois conditions : (1) la suffisance des champs fiscaux ; chaque ordre de gouvernement doit pouvoir prélever par lui-même les ressources financières nécessaires à l'exercice de ses responsabilités ; (2) la complétude, la somme des revenus autonomes et des transferts doit couvrir les dépenses totales de chaque ordre de gouvernement ; (3) l'inconditionnalité, les paiements de transferts versés aux États fédérés doivent être inconditionnels. Selon André Tremblay, les demandes constitutionnelles des gouvernements québécois ont porté essentiellement sur la préservation de l'équilibre fiscal « ou l'adéquation des ressources fiscales aux compétences législatives » (Tremblay 2000 à la p. 189).

Or, la notion d'équilibre fédéral, si présente dans la littérature sur le fédéralisme, risque d'embrouiller la compréhension de la dynamique politique et sociale des régimes fédératifs. Il ne s'agit pas de nier ici le fait que cette vision du fédéralisme ait une valeur normative structurante et qu'elle pèse sur la définition que le droit constitutionnel donne du régime fédératif. Cependant, elle comporte plusieurs limitations qui occultent plusieurs dimensions des régimes fédératifs que ne saisit pas une conception strictement juridique du pouvoir. Cette conception, foncièrement abstraite, n'assigne à la souveraineté aucune finalité particulière et la réduit à une quantité finie et uniforme d'un pouvoir normatif ultime. Elle met de côté les conditions socio-économiques de production du pouvoir étatique et isole le régime constitutionnel du système politique global. Le pouvoir étant vu comme une quantité finie, elle croit pouvoir le répartir de façon symétrique et étanche, par une simple répartition constitutionnelle des pouvoirs.

Toutefois, si l'on envisage la dynamique d'un régime fédératif autrement que par l'approche formelle de la souveraineté ou du pouvoir gouvernemental, l'appréciation que l'on se fera d'un tel régime sera tout autre. Par exemple, si l'on s'en tient à la vision hobbesienne de la souveraineté, qui la lie à la capacité d'un pouvoir de commander l'ordre et de prévenir la violence dans la société, le régime fédératif paraîtra déséquilibré, puisque la défense, le pouvoir d'urgence, la répression criminelle sont souvent les prérogatives du seul pouvoir fédéral. Si l'on préfère la notion foucaldienne de biopouvoir, axée sur le contrôle du corps et de la vie, à la notion juridique et institutionnelle de la souveraineté, la distribution des forces et des pouvoirs dans un régime fédératif paraîtra également autre. On verra plutôt plusieurs niveaux de gouvernement entrer en concurrence dans le contrôle de l'environnement, de la santé publique, de la technologie et de la reproduction culturelle et sociale. Bref, l'étude des régimes fédératifs gagne à aller au-delà de la définition formaliste du pouvoir.

On a reproché à Tocqueville de ne pas avoir compris la vraie nature du fédéralisme américain parce qu'il a comparé le gouvernement américain à un « gouvernement national incomplet » et trahi par le fait même sa lecture « nationaliste » du régime (Feldman 2006). Pourtant, Tocqueville a parfaitement saisi que le fédéralisme américain juxtapose deux ordres de souveraineté dans le même État. Il a de même illustré les nombreuses innovations apportées par les Américains en 1787 à la doctrine et aux pratiques fédérales antérieures. Tocqueville ne dit pas que le gouvernement américain est un État unitaire auquel les États confédérés de 1777 furent subordonnés. Il constate plutôt qu'en raison des circonstances dans lesquelles sont nés les États-Unis, du profil des élites politiques, des disparités entre la constitution fédérale et les constitutions des États, ainsi que les dynamiques sociales contrastées qui existent dans les États et au sein de l'Union toute entière, le gouvernement de l'Union a « l'apparence et, jusqu'à un certain point, la force d'un gouvernement national » (Tocqueville 1981 à la p. 244). En réalité, ce que constate Tocqueville, c'est que si la constitution américaine donne l'impression d'équilibrer les souverainetés, c'est en contrepoids à de nombreux déséquilibres qui achèvent de conférer la prépondérance au gouvernement de l'Union. Ce gouvernement, note Tocqueville, jouit d'une constitution accordant au pouvoir exécutif plus de liberté et de pouvoir qu'en octroient à leur propre exécutif les constitutions étatiques. Il évolue dans une orbite agrandie qui mobilise de grands intérêts et de grandes ambitions ; il a tous les pouvoirs nécessaires pour exécuter ses plans et ainsi se projeter à l'intérieur comme à l'extérieur du pays.

Si l'on prolonge la pensée de Tocqueville on s'aperçoit aisément que les régimes fédératifs contemporains érigent de nombreux déséquilibres, plusieurs d'entre eux étant parties prenantes du régime constitutionnel. Sur le plan territorial, le régime fédératif institue une asymétrie entre le gouvernement fédéral, qui est le seul dont l'autorité couvre l'ensemble du territoire fédératif, et les États fédérés, dont l'autorité est confinée à une portion seulement du territoire. Dans plusieurs régimes fédératifs, tels le Canada et l'Australie, le gouvernement fédéral exerce en outre sa compétence sur de vastes territoires qui n'ont pas été constitués en États fédérés et qui ont, partant, un statut équivalent à celui de dépendances néo-coloniales. Au déséquilibre territorial se greffe le déséquilibre démographique, le gouvernement fédéral étant le seul à administrer l'ensemble de la population. Dans plusieurs États fédéraux, il existe une telle variation de population entre les États fédérés que plusieurs d'entre eux sont d'une taille trop modeste pour pouvoir entretenir une panoplie de services publics ou tenir tête aux grandes entreprises. Ces asymétries démographiques font souvent coexister des États faibles et peu viables avec d'autres qui ont les moyens de leur autonomie. Même sur le plan constitutionnel, de nombreux dispositifs donnent au gouvernement fédéral un net avantage : la prépondérance fédérale en cas de conflits de lois, la reconnaissance au parlement fédéral de compétences implicites ou accessoires, l'existence de pouvoirs exécutifs ou législatifs unilatéraux (pouvoirs de désaveu et de réserve, expropriation pour fins de défense, la nomination des juges, sénateurs et représentants de la Couronne, pouvoir déclaratoire, le *President's Rule* et le pouvoir d'urgence en Inde, etc.), les prérogatives internationales de l'État fédéral, le contrôle de l'initiative constitutionnelle (en Australie, notamment, et *de facto* aux États-Unis). Sur le plan politique, la carrière dans l'arène politique fédérale est souvent considérée comme plus prestigieuse et rapporte plus que la carrière à l'échelon étatique. Le Parlement fédéral jouit souvent d'un surcroît de légitimité, grâce au bicaméralisme, alors que les législatures étatiques, d'une députation plus modeste, sont souvent monocamérales comme au Canada et en Allemagne. De plus, la médiatisation de la vie politique contribue à mettre continuellement à l'avant-scène des grands diffuseurs les acteurs politiques fédéraux au détriment des acteurs des États.

À ces déséquilibres se greffent les nombreux déséquilibres financiers propres au régime fédératif, dont le déséquilibre vertical entre l'État fédéral et les États fédérés et le déséquilibre horizontal entre ces derniers. La littérature que nous venons de citer sur la notion d'équilibre fiscal donne à penser que cette exigence est une réalité universelle du fédéralisme contemporain. À vrai dire, on connaît peu d'exemples de régimes dits fédératifs où les États fédérés détiendraient la plus grande partie des ressources fiscales. On peut certes citer le cas historique de la Suisse qui, après le passage de la confédération à la fédération, a connu une période pendant laquelle le gouvernement fédéral suisse se bornait à prélever les droits de douanes.[7] Mais aujourd'hui, en Suisse, comme dans la plupart des régimes fédératifs, la prépondérance fiscale du gouvernement fédéral semble être la norme. Ce déséquilibre vertical s'explique notamment par des raisons d'économie politique ; les impôts fédéraux étant jugés plus neutres et plus efficaces, alors que la coexistence de champs fiscaux séparés engendrerait des effets pervers ou des débordements qui entravent l'efficacité de la collecte fiscale et de l'économie. De plus, fort de moyens fiscaux excédant la réalité de ses responsabilités propres, le gouvernement fédéral peut ainsi corriger, par le versement de transferts, les déséquilibres de richesse existant entre les États.

La question du déséquilibre fiscal vertical devrait être distinguée de celle de l'adéquation des moyens fiscaux aux responsabilités constitutionnelles. Parmi les principes fondamentaux du fédéralisme, le théoricien suisse Guy Héraud range celui d'exacte adéquation. Suivant ce principe, chaque niveau de gouvernement devrait posséder des pouvoirs juridiques adéquats aux tâches à remplir, y compris les moyens matériels (Héraud 1968 à la p. 50). Cela n'implique pas nécessairement que chaque niveau de gouvernement jouisse d'une autonomie absolue, équivalente à l'indépendance financière, sans recevoir

[7]Confédération helvétique, Commission d'information et de formation, *Le système fiscal suisse*, Berne, 2001 à la p. 7, en ligne : www.estv.admin.ch/f/dokumentation/publikationen/dok/ch_steuersystem/ganz.pdf.

aucun transfert de l'autre palier de gouvernement. D'autres auteurs, sans parler d'adéquation, déduisent du principe d'autonomie l'exigence selon laquelle chaque ordre de gouvernement devrait avoir les moyens de ses dépenses, comme l'écrit Maurice Croisat : « [d]ans la conception du dualisme, les finances fédérales doivent permettre à chaque niveau de gouvernement de bénéficier de revenus suffisants pour financer ses dépenses, l'autonomie financière étant une condition nécessaire à l'exercice de l'autonomie politique » (Croisat 1995 à la p. 83). En Italie, pays qui s'est quasi-fédéralisé depuis 2001, l'expression « fédéralisme fiscal » (*federalismo fiscale*) est synonyme de dévolution financière. *Federalismo fiscale* signifie le principe en vertu duquel chaque ordre de gouvernement devrait être en mesure de développer ses activités grâce à ses ressources financières propres.[8] Tania Groppi soutient qu'il existe deux principaux modèles de dévolution financière dans les États décentralisés : celui fondé sur une séparation des ressources financières et celui basé sur l'intégration des ressources. Dans le premier modèle, chaque niveau de gouvernement prélève lui-même les ressources financières requises par ses activités grâce à ses pouvoirs fiscaux propres. Dans le deuxième modèle, les entités décentralisées reçoivent une quote-part des revenus fiscaux, prélevés dans leur totalité par l'État central ou fédéral. Le régime fédératif qui semble s'approcher le plus du premier modèle est la confédération suisse, alors que la Belgique, l'Autriche et l'Australie tendent vers l'intégration du système fiscal. Le Canada, l'Allemagne et les États-Unis combinent les deux modèles. D'autres auteurs opposent au modèle suisse de la séparation des sources de revenus le modèle allemand, qui comptabilise l'ensemble des recettes publiques disponibles et redistribue une quote-part aux États et aux municipalités en fonction de certains critères (Bird *et al.* 2003 à la p. 357).

Le classement des systèmes fiscaux proposé par Tania Groppi demeure un modèle théorique et il n'est pas facile de concevoir qu'il reflète parfaitement la répartition effective des finances dans les régimes fédératifs. Ce classement ne permet pas d'établir qu'il existe de tels régimes où, en raison d'une parfaite adéquation et séparation des pouvoirs fiscaux, il ne surviendrait aucun déséquilibre fiscal dans la répartition des finances publiques. Si l'on se fie aux données recueillies par Ronald Watts, il semble plutôt que les principales fédérations ou quasi-fédérations connues connaissent généralement un déséquilibre vertical de leurs finances, d'une ampleur certes variable d'un pays à l'autre. Qui plus est, constate Watts, même si le constituant avait prévu une correspondance étroite entre les recettes autonomes et les dépenses de chaque palier de gouvernement, les coûts des dépenses et les changements apportés au système fiscal finissent toujours par briser l'équilibre initial (Watts 1999 à la p. 48). Les études commandées par la Commission sur le déséquilibre fiscal à des experts en matière de fédéralisme fiscal et publiées en 2001 montrent que parmi les pays étudiés (Suisse, Australie, Allemagne et États-Unis), la prépondérance fédérale dans le champ fiscal est assez répandue.[9] Dans tous ces pays, les

---

[8]Groppi (2004 à la p. 71). Voir aussi Wheare (1963 à la p. 93). Voir aussi Noël (2006).

[9]Voir les études recueillies dans une des annexes du rapport Séguin (Québec 2002a).

déséquilibres financiers verticaux sont corrigés par des mécanismes de transfert. De plus, une étude de l'OCDE indique que peu importe qu'on envisage des États unitaires ou fédéraux, l'écart entre les dépenses et les revenus semble être généralisé pour les collectivités décentralisées et s'est accru entre 1985 et 2001 (Journard et Kongsrud 2003).

Ce bref survol de la distribution des ressources fiscales dans les régimes fédéraux indique qu'aucun ne pratique une parfaite adéquation entre les ressources fiscales autonomes et les dépenses de chaque palier gouvernemental. Par ailleurs, plusieurs, mais pas tous, tendent vers l'adéquation des ressources totales, prélevées et reçues, de chaque niveau de gouvernement à ses responsabilités, bien que l'idée d'une telle adéquation appartienne au registre des notions floues dont les acteurs politiques sont appelés à débattre continuellement. Sans être des anomalies, les déséquilibres financiers verticaux observés dans divers régimes fédératifs s'ajoutent aux nombreux autres déséquilibres qui achèvent de conférer au gouvernement fédéral une nette prépondérance dans l'économie des pouvoirs, des ressources, du prestige, dans l'accès aux personnes et au territoire. N'étant pas dépossédés de leurs ressources ni de leurs pouvoirs, les États fédérés se trouvent néanmoins placés dans une situation de relative dépendance et de confinement constitutionnel.

Ce dernier constat n'a en soi rien de surprenant puisque les inventeurs du fédéralisme moderne eurent l'ambition d'inventer une nouvelle forme d'association entre États qui renverserait les rapports de subordination observés dans les associations fédérales jusqu'alors connues, qui s'apparentaient alors plutôt à des ligues confédérales de défense possédant un pouvoir commun aux attributions limitées. Les fédéralistes américains avaient conscience que leur invention prenait la forme d'un régime mixte, combinant les traits du confédéralisme pré-moderne et celui d'un État national ou unitaire. Les juristes et les théoriciens du fédéralisme se sont emparés de l'invention américaine pour en faire un régime d'équilibre des pouvoirs réglementé par la constitution et tempéré par certaines vertus politiques. Il n'est pas faux de dire que le régime fédératif cherche à maintenir un certain équilibre entre deux ordres de gouvernement, mais ce n'est pas nécessairement rendre compte de son fonctionnement réel ni de certains de ses présupposés véritables. Il serait plus à propos de dire, en reprenant les analyses de Tocqueville, que l'État fédéral est une forme d'empire interne, contraint notamment par une forte normativité constitutionnelle posant des limites à la centralisation, qui maintient toutefois de nombreux déséquilibres érigés par la forme fédérative de l'État. Souvent dépouillés des principaux attributs de la souveraineté, les États fédérés ont le statut de puissances publiques résiduelles, aptes à exercer l'autorité d'un État à l'égard de certaines responsabilités qui leur échoient en raison de leur proximité avec les citoyens ou avec la culture d'un territoire donné. Mais les inégalités entre les États fédérés sont si grandes qu'il n'est pas rare de trouver, dans un même État fédéral, des États fédérés sans ressources maintenus en vie par l'assistance fédérale et d'autres, riches en moyens et peuplés, aptes à disputer au gouvernement fédéral sa prééminence, mus aussi par une dynamique impériale d'expansion et d'emballement des ambitions. Or, ce ne sont pas tous les groupes humains qui acceptent d'être gouvernés par une puissance publique diminuée ;

d'où les conflits et le mécontentement que suscitent à l'ordinaire les régimes fédératifs où coexistent une diversité de cultures et de nations.

LE FÉDÉRALISME, LE CONSTITUTIONNALISME CANADIEN ET LA NOTION QUÉBECOISE D'AUTONOMIE

Résumant les positions traditionnelles du Québec relativement au pouvoir fédéral de dépenser, le rapport de la Commission sur le déséquilibre fiscal écrit :

> Le gouvernement du Québec a toujours affirmé que le "pouvoir fédéral de dépenser" invoqué par le gouvernement fédéral remettait en cause le partage des compétences tel qu'établi par la Constitution, et que pour cette raison, il était contraire à l'esprit même du fédéralisme. (Québec 2002b à la p. 127)

Quelques années auparavant, la Commission royale sur les problèmes constitutionnels, c'est-à-dire la Commission Tremblay, s'était elle aussi réclamée de l'esprit même du fédéralisme, voire de celui du fédéralisme canadien lui-même, pour rejeter les prétentions du gouvernement fédéral canadien à un pouvoir fiscal illimité. En vertu de la doctrine du fédéralisme, selon la Commission Tremblay, les deux niveaux de gouvernement doivent non seulement détenir toutes les ressources financières nécessaires à leurs responsabilités législatives, mais leur politique fiscale respective doit respecter la distribution constitutionnelle des pouvoirs et ne pas tendre à « la rendre stérile ou inefficace » (Québec 1956 à la p. 209). Bien que les deux commissions renvoient toutes deux aux principes mêmes du fédéralisme, il est apparent que leur interprétation de ce qu'est le fédéralisme est largement tributaire de leur conception du fédéralisme canadien. La discussion théorique du fédéralisme est certes présente dans le rapport Tremblay de 1956 qui, influencé par la doctrine sociale de l'Église et le pluralisme du théoricien anglais Harold Laski, a érigé le fédéralisme en principe d'organisation sociale servant de rempart à la centralisation politique et à l'individualisme (Chevrier 1994, aux pp. 45-57). Cette discussion théorique brille néanmoins par son absence dans les autres rapports de commission d'enquête ou extraordinaire qui ont étudié le fédéralisme canadien à l'aube des revendications québécoises, pensons à la Commission sur l'avenir politique du Québec (Commission Bélanger-Campeau) ou à la Commission Séguin. Ces dernières commissions présupposent une interprétation partagée du fédéralisme canadien sur les origines et les fondements auxquels on ne sent pas le besoin de revenir.

Dans un article incisif publié en 1965, J.R. Mallory prétend que le Canada français s'est trompé sur la nature la constitution canadienne. Il a cru, à tort, qu'elle lui fournirait toutes les garanties nécessaires à sa survivance, alors qu'elle se borne à répartir les responsabilités législatives. Selon Mallory, le Canada français a davantage survécu en raison du mythe de la nation qu'il a entretenu et du pouvoir politique qu'il a exercé sur la constitution.[10] Il ajoute que la constitution canadienne n'envisage aucun autre type de droit que celui des assemblées legislatives.[11] Il est curieux de voir Mallory reprendre le vieux préjugé français contre la constitution britannique, qui n'en serait pas une, parce que non écrite et purement coutumière. Plus significatif encore est le fait que Mallory n'accorde aucune importance à l'aspect proprement britannique de la constitution canadienne dans la compréhension de sa dimension fédérale. À vrai dire, il n'est pas le seul à évacuer ce qu'il y a de non-écrit dans le fédéralisme canadien ; beaucoup de juristes et de politologues l'ont fait avant lui et après lui, dans les deux communautés linguistiques d'ailleurs. Même les Québécois qui promeuvent une interprétation décentralisée de l'*Acte de l'Amérique du Nord Britannique*, aujourd'hui la *Loi constitutionnelle de 1867*,[12] considèrent cette loi constitutionnelle à la manière d'un code complet du fédéralisme et tirent peu de leçons, sinon aucune, de l'histoire constitutionnelle et de la tradition politique britanniques.

L'entreprise constituante canadienne de 1867 se démarque à plusieurs égards de la démarche américaine en 1787. Elle se distingue, notamment, par le fait qu'elle combine deux visions du constitutionnalisme : d'une part, la tradition non-écrite, évolutive et *whig* anglaise et, d'autre part, la tradition écrite et républicaine américaine. Robert Vipond exprime autrement cette distinction en soutenant que la constitution canadienne de 1867 renferme deux conceptions du fédéralisme : le fédéralisme politique britannique, fondé sur la souveraineté d'un parlement impérial accordant à des entités déléguées des marges d'autonomie dont il est le maître, et le fédéralisme constitutionnel américain, basé sur un partage des pouvoirs constitutionnalisés (Vipond 1991 aux pp. 25 et 156). En créant une structure quasi-fédérale dotée d'un régime parlementaire, les pères fondateurs et les légistes britanniques n'eurent pas d'autre choix que de faire exception à la tradition anglaise et de codifier ainsi un partage des pouvoirs qui scellerait les termes d'une entente intercoloniale. Cette dimension codifiée du fédéralisme canadien s'inscrit dans la logique du fédéralisme constitutionnel américain. La dimension proprement politique et britannique du fédéralisme canadien demeure cependant encore mal comprise.

Comme j'ai eu l'occasion de le montrer dans un autre texte, les pères fondateurs canadiens étaient persuadés que leur entreprise constituante perpétuerait la transplantation en Amérique des acquis de la Glorieuse Révolution de 1688 (Chevrier 2006). En s'assurant que la constitution du

---

[10]Mallory 1965 à la p. 11 : « The survival of French Canada as a fact has depended more on a sustaining national myth and on political power than it has on constitutional guarantees. »

[11]Ibid. à la p. 12 : « In this respect, it is indeed a constitution "similar in Principle to that of the United Kingdom". As de Tocqueville said of the British constitution, "*elle n'existe point*" ». À cet effet, voir de Tocqueville 1981 à la p. 82 : « En Angleterre, on reconnaît au parlement le droit de modifier la constitution. En Angleterre, la constitution peut donc changer sans cesse, ou plutôt elle n'existe point. Le parlement, en même temps qu'il est corps législatif, est corps constituant. »

[12](R.-U.), 30 & 31 Vict., c. 3, reproduit dans L.R.C. 1985, app. II, n° 5.

Dominion canadien soit en principe similaire à celle du Royaume-Uni, ils redéployaient la conception *whig* du pouvoir et de la légitimité dans un nouvel espace colonial appelé à concurrencer la république américaine, en se constituant lui-même en empire dans l'empire britannique.

La naissance de la démocratie parlementaire au Royaume-Uni remonte, comme les pères fondateurs le célébrèrent à l'envi, à la Seconde Révolution anglaise de 1688. Après avoir connu successivement l'absolutisme des Stuarts et la tyrannie de Cromwell, une nouvelle élite politique prit les rênes du pouvoir en Grande-Bretagne et réussit à établir une démocratie constitutionnelle qui conserverait les formes monarchiques du pouvoir. Le célèbre *Bill of Rights* de 1689 n'était pas en lui-même une constitution codifiant l'organisation politique ; il s'agissait plutôt d'un contrat qui reflétait les aspirations d'une nouvelle élite, en fait très restreinte. À l'époque, sur les neuf millions d'habitants que comptait le royaume, seul un quart de millions d'hommes avaient le droit de vote et, à peine 2000 familles contrôlaient la vie économique et sociale (Mougel 2005 à la p. 16). Bien que les *Whigs* et les *Tories* fussent des ennemis politiques et voués à la défense d'intérêts opposés – le monde de l'argent et la petite noblesse terrienne (*the gentry*) – ils savaient faire cause commune les uns avec les autres quand il s'agissait de défendre la patrie. Cette élite divisée mais capable de faire bloc autour de certains acquis communs se croyait investie d'une mission spéciale : gouverner au nom d'un peuple absent. Avec le temps, l'élite gouvernante britannique a ouvert ses rangs à de nouvelles tranches de la population, par élargissement progressif du suffrage, et les partis conservateur et libéral éclipsèrent les vieux clubs aristocratiques d'antan. Seulement, la lutte pour le pouvoir continua d'opposer deux équipes politiques partageant en fait la même compréhension des règles fondamentales de la démocratie parlementaire.[13] Ainsi, la constitution anglaise n'avait pas besoin d'être écrite puisqu'elle s'incarnait dans les acteurs politiques eux-mêmes.

La constitution canadienne de 1867 est *whig* de diverses façons. Elle ne s'attache pas à décrire la réalité du pouvoir ; elle reproduit le spectacle du pouvoir (*the theatrical show of society*, pour reprendre les mots célèbres de Bagehot). Elle ne constituait pas un manuel civique fait pour l'éducation du citoyen, qui de toute façon restait loin de l'entreprise constituante. C'est avant tout une loi statutaire au style technique écrite par des avocats pour l'usage de la profession juridique et des juges. Elle est silencieuse sur plusieurs points essentiels ; ces silences constitutionnels renvoient toutefois à la compréhension partagée de l'élite gouvernante de ce que sont les règles de l'éthique politique et de la coexistence entre les communautés. En somme, elle recelait une normativité politique et fluide, faite d'usages, de conventions et de silences convenus – ce que David M. Thomas (1997) a appelé les *abeyances* – qui devait compléter la normativité écrite inscrite dans la loi impériale par concession au fédéralisme.

---

[13]Bogdanor 1988 aux pp. 56-57: « Whatever other differences there have been between the political parties, they did not seek to dispute the fundamental rules through which political activity was regulated. »

Un bel exemple de cette normativité politique fluide comblant les silences du droit écrit constitutionnel est l'importance qu'a joué dans les débats constituants de 1865 l'exemple de l'union anglo-écossaise de 1707.[14] Cette union, qui a scellé l'incorporation de l'Écosse au royaume anglais par la disparition du parlement d'Édimbourg et de la couronne écossaise, était remarquable par plusieurs de ses caractéristiques. Il s'agissait d'un arrangement entre deux élites, les aristocraties écossaise et anglaise, toutes les deux gagnées à la conception *Court Whig* du pouvoir. Cet arrangement convenait d'une entente inégalitaire et asymétrique entre une nation dominante et une nation affaiblie qui enlevait à cette dernière sa liberté politique en échange de garanties pour son Église établie (presbytérienne), son droit et ses universités, complétées de garanties de représentation à Westminster et du libre-échange économique. L'union de 1707 mettait en place une union politique par laquelle l'Écosse intégrée politiquement dans l'État unitaire britannique, survivait en tant que société civile, délivrée du souci du politique. Cette entente asymétrique a promu la classe juridique écossaise, du moins jusqu'au milieu du XIXe siècle, au rang de classe gouvernante locale, faisant le lien entre la population écossaise et Londres.

Plusieurs pères fondateurs ont vu un parallèle entre l'union canadienne et l'union anglo-écossaise. Ce fut John A. Macdonald qui a donné à l'analogie la plus grande portée. Convaincu que l'union anglo-écossaise constituait une forme d'entente fédérale qui conférait à l'Écosse un droit de veto sur les lois de Westminster la concernant, il estimait que l'union canadienne proposée par les résolutions de Québec reproduirait une union fédérale du même type entre le Canada français et le Canada britannique. C'est en référant au précédent écossais que Macdonald et George-Étienne Cartier ont défendu la codification du droit civil du Canada-est. Beaucoup des dispositions de l'*Acte de l'Amérique du Nord britannique* relatives à l'éducation, à la religion et au droit sont la cristallisation juridique de cette vision politique de l'union canadienne, qui met en scène plusieurs Écossais immigrés au Canada ou leurs descendants et un bon nombre d'avocats du Canada français, qui promeuvent leurs intérêts professionnels à travers une union politique qui redonne au Canada français son assemblée et son autonomie – à la différence certes de l'Écosse – quoique amoindrie par de nombreuses concessions à la puissance fédérale.

Ainsi, la théorie du pacte entre deux peuples fondateurs, dont on a maintes fois tenté de démontrer l'absence de validité en droit constitutionnel canadien,[15] aurait une certaine vraisemblance, dans la mesure où elle renvoie à une forme d'union politique asymétrique et inégalitaire entre deux élites gouvernantes agissant au nom de leur nation ou communauté. Cette union s'inscrit dans la tradition britannique du fédéralisme politique qui a institué des arrangements politiques – régis par des usages et des conventions – entre la nation anglaise et les nations historiques qu'elle a incorporées. Ce fédéralisme politique sous-tend le fédéralisme constitutionnel institué par la *Loi constitutionnelle de 1867*

---

[14]Les développements qui suivent sont tirés du texte que j'ai publié sur la question : Chevrier (2008).

[15]Sur ces débats, voir notamment Stanley (1956).

(*supra* note 12), bien que l'interaction entre les deux n'ait pas vraiment été bien comprise. Si la constitution britannique, historique et non écrite, a supposé que les élites politiques, divisées en deux clans opposés, s'unissent dans la défense d'une même patrie et d'une même conception du jeu parlementaire, cette compréhension commune a souvent fait défaut au Canada, étant donné les lignes de partage linguistique et religieuse entre les deux communautés nationales. Le fédéralisme constitutionnel, renforcé par l'interprétation judiciaire, a fini par prendre le dessus sur le fédéralisme politique d'inspiration britannique sans que celui-ci disparaisse pour autant.

L'idée de l'autonomie constitutionnelle sans interférence fédérale, si présente dans le discours politique québécois, prend sa source dans la conjonction de ces deux fédéralismes, pas toujours bien distingués, et dans le contexte historique de l'émergence de l'identité constitutionnelle de l'État du Québec, né en 1867. Les promoteurs bas-canadiens de l'union fédérale se félicitèrent de ce que le Québec ait accédé à une pleine autonomie et que l'union fût le fruit d'une réunion de nationalités et de provinces qui n'ont pas abdiqué leur autonomie (Rumilly 1948 aux pp. 7-12). L'un des aspects de ce contexte qui a marqué la vision de l'autonomie québécoise est le régime d'union de 1840, si bien qu'à l'époque, les acteurs politiques du Canada français saluèrent dans l'union de 1867 avant tout une « séparation ». En effet, cette union était vue comme une rétrocession de l'autonomie perdue par l'union de 1840 et comme la séparation constitutionnelle de deux collectivités qui, devant coexister dans le même parlement et le même gouvernement, avaient déjà commencé à vivre séparées à plusieurs égards. Selon Arthur Silver, la propagande des conservateurs bas-canadiens en faveur de l'union insistait sur le caractère séparé et souverain des nouveaux États provinciaux (Silver 1982 à la p. 218).

Il est utile ici de rappeler l'influence qu'a exercée une figure oubliée de l'histoire politique canadienne et québécoise, soit Joseph-Charles Taché, que son biographe présente comme le véritable père fondateur intellectuel du Canada français (Bossé 1971 à la p. 162). Il est le premier à avoir conçu un plan détaillé d'union fédérale des colonies de l'Amérique du Nord Britannique, qui préfigure les résolutions de Québec. En parlant de la nouvelle « confédération », Taché écrivit : « Posons de suite que, dans notre opinion, il faudrait de toute nécessité faire aux législatures la part la plus large possible » (Taché 1858 à la p. 147). S'agissant de l'union de 1840, il ajoute :

> Il va sans dire que toujours, lorsque nous parlons des diverses provinces, nous séparons le Haut-Canada du Bas-Canada et que nous les comptons comme deux provinces entièrement distinctes : dans la question actuelle il est évident que l'Union des deux Canadas est et demeure comme non avenue. (ibid. à la p. 148)

Ainsi, « Par la distribution des pouvoirs que nous avons proposée, les législatures séparées seraient du coup aussi indépendantes que si elles faisaient parties [*sic*] d'un état constitué à part » (ibid. à la p. 155)·

Taché a une conception limitative des pouvoirs du gouvernement fédéral ; ses attributions touchent essentiellement au commerce et à la monnaie, aux douanes, aux grands travaux publics, à la milice (défense) et à la justice criminelle. Ses pouvoirs sont le résultat d'une « cession de droits spécialement désignés » faite par les « provinces » constituantes, qui possèdent le pouvoir de légiférer à l'égard du reste, le « droit inhérent » (ibid. à la p. 148). La répartition des pouvoirs préconisée par Taché repose sur deux dichotomies ; la première, entre l'ordre matériel et l'ordre moral ou spirituel, la deuxième, entre les droits civils et les droits politiques. Pour ce qui est de la première, « tout ce qui a trait aux pouvoirs comme aux avantages du gouvernement général que nous proposons aux provinces, tient exclusivement à l'ordre matériel » (ibid. à la p. 151). Par contre, « C'est aux gouvernements séparés des provinces, c'est aux nationalités que nous laissons le soin de ces choses, supérieures en importance aux plus grands progrès » (ibid.). Quant à la deuxième dichotomie, l'opposition entre les droits civils et les droits politiques, Taché postule que les premiers sont supérieurs aux deuxièmes, si bien qu'il « vaudrait mille fois pour un peuple renoncer à ses droits politiques que de laisser attenter au libre exercice de ses droits civils » (ibid. à la p. 178). Les droits civils selon Taché incluent la liberté de religion, l'inviolabilité du domicile et de la propriété, la liberté d'opinion, la liberté d'enseignement, le droit d'association, le droit de pétition, l'égalité devant la loi, le droit d'être jugé par ses pairs, le droit de puissance paternelle et le droit de contracter. À l'inverse, les droits politiques reçoivent une portée limitée ; ce sont « ceux en vertu desquels les citoyens d'un état sont admis à participer au gouvernement de leur pays dans les attributions d'électeurs ou de fonctionnaires publics » (ibid. à la p. 179). On comprend dès lors que les « provinces » recevant l'exclusivité sur l'essentiel des droits civils, le gouvernement fédéral voit son action limitée à la projection extérieure de l'État, à l'ordre criminel et au progrès matériel. C'est ainsi, écrit Taché, que le pouvoir fédéral n'aurait rien à faire avec les nationalités, avec les intérêts particuliers des provinces, avec les divers éléments qui composent les populations ; toutes ces choses tombant sous le contrôle exclusif des gouvernements locaux, sur les attributions desquelles le pouvoir fédéral ne pourrait empiéter et avec lesquelles il ne doit point pouvoir entrer en conflits (ibid. à la p. 182).

Bien que conservateur ultramontain, Taché formule un plan d'union fédérale empreint d'un républicanisme latent. Il compare le conservatisme frugal et égalitaire du peuple canadien-français à la vertu du peuple romain. Il critique le parlementarisme britannique comme un régime dominé par les aristocraties terrienne et monétaire et fustige les ambitions impériales des États-Unis, dont le régime accorde une trop grande importance à l'électivité des fonctions judiciaires et administratives. C'est pourquoi il propose que la nouvelle union canadienne combine les avantages de la monarchie constitutionnelle britannique et ceux du républicanisme présidentiel américain. Alors que le gouvernement fédéral, par nécessité de lui conférer puissance et unité à l'extérieur, adopterait la forme anglaise, les provinces suivraient le modèle américain, avec un président et deux chambres législatives, et posséderaient une constitution écrite, sanctionnée par un tribunal *ad hoc* (ibid. aux pp. 187-188).

Il est clair, toutefois, que les résolutions de Québec de 1864 s'écarteront de l'ambitieux plan formulé en 1857 par Taché. Selon P.B. Waite, Taché, en publiant une série d'articles anonymes dans le *Courrier du Canada* après la conférence de Québec, aurait néanmoins grandement contribué à rendre acceptable le contenu de ces résolutions auprès des conservateurs de l'ancien

Bas-Canada (Waite 1959 aux pp. 297-298). L'auteur de ces chroniques anonymes reconnaît dans les résolutions de Québec un compromis raisonnable entre les visions française et anglaise, entre le fédéralisme et l'union législative, bien que celles-ci renversent la logique prévue par le plan de Taché de 1857 : au parlement fédéral la compétence générale, aux législatures provinciales des compétences spécifiques. Somme toute, les résolutions de Québec offraient des « garanties suffisantes » aux gouvernements locaux « pour les protéger contre toute tentative d'empiètement de la part du gouvernement central » et accordaient au « gouvernement central une somme de pouvoirs suffisante pour lui permettre de travailler sans être gêné, au bien matériel et à l'agrandissement des différents états de la confédération pris collectivement et séparément ».[16] Taché n'était pas vexé que les lois provinciales soient soumises au pouvoir de réserve et de désaveu ; les États provinciaux seraient ni plus ni moins assujettis au même pouvoir que Londres détenait à cette époque, et la présence de ministres canadiens-français dans le cabinet fédéral formerait à vrai dire la sauvegarde ultime de l'autonomie provincial (Waite 1959 à la p. 301).

La conception de l'autonomie que dessine Joseph-Charles Taché et que semblent reprendre – à ses yeux – les résolutions de Québec s'apparente à ce qu'on pourrait appeler l'*autonomie impériale*. Le gouvernement fédéral de l'union est vu comme un gouvernement lointain garant de l'ordre, de la paix et de la prospérité, qui n'interfère nullement dans la vie civile, politique et culturelle de ses composantes fédérées. C'est un gouvernement tourné vers l'extérieur, vers l'accroissement de l'empire matériel, territorial et militaire de l'union dans lequel le Canada français croit avoir une part, dans la mesure où ce gouvernement est source de prestige et d'influence, et que le Canada français considère néanmoins comme un recours ultime, ses libertés civiles et culturelles devraient-elles être menacées. L'autonomie impériale sépare l'empire en expansion des autonomies fédérées, lesquelles s'investissent dans leur espace culturel et civil, exempt d'ingérence fédérale, sans chercher à avoir l'emprise sur le gouvernement supérieur par l'entremise d'une seconde chambre fédérale ou d'autres mécanismes de participation. Taché favorisa certes l'élection des sénateurs fédéraux, mais ni dans le texte de Taché, ni dans le discours autonomiste québécois, cette question n'a revêtu de grande importance.

Selon François Rocher, le discours autonomiste québécois se caractérise par son insistance systématique sur l'idée du pacte fédéral et d'une autonomie sans subordination, ainsi que par l'absence d'importance accordée à l'interdépendance, aux mécanismes de solidarité entre les partenaires de la fédération et à la participation des États fédérés dans les institutions fédérales (Rocher 2006). En ce sens, ce discours ne tiendrait compte que d'une partie des exigences normatives du fédéralisme ; du rapport de la commission Tremblay jusqu'aux plus récentes réclamations constitutionnelles des gouvernements québécois, l'autonomie revendiquée postule dans les faits « la non-participation du Québec à l'édification de la communauté politique canadienne » (ibid. à la p. 122). Depuis les années 1960, elle ambitionne de créer une société globale

[16] « La Confédération : X » *Le Courrier du Canada* (26 décembre 1864), tel que cité dans Waite (1959 à la p. 301).

québécoise, dotée de son propre État-providence, quoique en marge de la société politique canadienne, avec la garantie d'une immunité contre toute immixtion fédérale ou décloisonnement des compétences fait au nom du pragmatisme ou de l'efficacité.

LE NATIONALISME CANADIEN ET LA DYNAMIQUE IMPÉRIALE DU FÉDÉRALISME CANADIEN CONTEMPORAIN

À l'inverse, constate Rocher, le discours fédéraliste au Canada anglais tend à mettre systématiquement en avant les exigences découlant de l'interdépendance et à minimiser, voire à ignorer, celles qu'implique l'autonomie. Il voit le système fédéral comme un régime de division du pouvoir politique dont la valeur est jugée à l'aune de critères fonctionnels, telles que la performance, l'efficacité et la légitimité, ou démocratiques, telles que la transparence et l'imputabilité. À partir des années 1950, le gouvernement fédéral s'est donné la mission d'édifier la « nation » canadienne par ses interventions. Peu à peu s'est dessinée l'idée que ce gouvernement est investi de la responsabilité générale de voir au bien-être de tous les citoyens du pays et de mobiliser à cette fin tous les pouvoirs constitutionnels et financiers mis à sa disposition. Promoteur d'une citoyenneté canadienne englobant aussi bien les dimensions économique que sociale, le gouvernement fédéral s'est posé de cette façon en garant d'un système de couverture sociale régi par des normes nationales vouées à l'uniformité et à la cohérence de l'union économique canadienne. L'étanchéité des compétences constitutionnelles, si chère au Québec, devenait dès lors un obstacle au processus d'édification d'un État national canadien fondé sur le lien direct entre le gouvernement fédéral et les citoyens que tisse une vision unitaire, universaliste et individualiste de la nation. La réforme de 1982 a érigé cette vision en dogme constitutionnel dont les tribunaux sont les gardiens et a accordé, implicitement, un rôle prépondérant au gouvernement fédéral dans la conception et l'orientation des politiques sociales du pays. De plus, les programmes sociaux, ayant acquis avec le temps une grande valeur symbolique, participant de l'identité canadienne, ne pouvaient être abandonnés aux seuls États provinciaux. Le pouvoir fédéral de dépenser est ainsi devenu l'instrument par lequel l'intérêt national s'exprime dans les champs de compétence provinciale, trouvant sa légitimité dans l'expression du vote populaire au Parlement federal (Telford 2003 à la p. 35). Comme l'a observé Louis Balthazar, l'exercice de ce pouvoir, qui invoque généralement l'existence d'un « consensus national », présuppose que le Canada se pense comme une seule nation, au point que les adjectifs « fédéral » et « national » deviennent synonymes.[17] L'affirmation du rôle prépondérant du gouvernement fédéral dans les politiques sociales avait pour corollaire l'idée que les gouvernements des États provinciaux

[17]Balthazar 1998 aux pp. 107-108 : « The very tendency to use the word "national" to refer to a federal government reflects a trend toward a kind of federation in which federated states are hardly more than junior governments or administrative units. »

sont incapables de gérer efficacement et équitablement leurs propres politiques et que le gouvernement fédéral doit voler à leur secours ou les contraindre à traiter équitablement leurs minorités de langue officielle (Lachapelle et Bernier 1998 à la p. 82).

Cette évolution des choses soulève deux problèmes. Premièrement, quel est le statut des États provinciaux au Canada en dehors du Québec ? Deuxièmement, que signifie le fait que les relations entre l'État et l'individu soient traitées différemment de celles entre les deux ordres de gouvernement ou les diverses « sociétés » composant le Canada ? Examinons rapidement ces deux questions en cherchant à mettre en lumière ce qu'elles révèlent de la dynamique fédérale au Canada.

Il va sans dire que la querelle autour du pouvoir fédéral de dépenser est l'un des griefs permanents des gouvernements du Québec et des intellectuels québécois contre le régime fédéral, bien que des voix se soient élevées au Canada anglais pour critiquer la légitimité ou les modalités d'exercice de ce pouvoir. S'il est vrai que le Canada en dehors du Québec se voit comme formant une seule nation et mandate à ce titre le gouvernement fédéral, devenu « national », du soin d'édicter des normes uniformes et de prendre l'initiative des politiques sociales, que sont devenus alors les États provinciaux ? Quelle est la nature de la communauté politique qu'ils représentent, si elle n'est qu'un fragment d'une nation ? Dans leur introduction à la version française des *Débats sur la fondation du Canada,* Guy Laforest et Stéphane Kelly constatent que la réforme constitutionnelle a été le lieu d'une révolution au Canada anglais, qu'ils illustrent par le fait qu'en 1981, aucune des assemblées législatives provinciales, à part l'Assemblée nationale du Québec, n'a jugé bon de tenir un débat parlementaire sur le projet de réforme mis en avant par le gouvernement Trudeau. Ce silence était d'autant plus étonnant qu'au XIXe siècle, au moment de la fondation du Dominion canadien, les assemblées des colonies des Maritimes et de la Colombie-Britannique furent le théâtre d'âpres débats, dont le principal enjeu était la préservation de la liberté des colonies en tant que « *self-governing political community* » (Laforest et Kelly 2004 à la p. xvii). Le silence de neuf législatures provinciales en 1981-1982 était-il le signe que la préservation de cette liberté politique n'était plus leur souci et qu'elles s'en remettaient désormais au gouvernement « national » d'Ottawa ? Pour rendre compte des différentes conceptions du fédéralisme existant au Canada, Will Kymlicka distingue ce qu'il appelle le fédéralisme territorial du fédéralisme multinational. Alors que les Québécois et les peuples autochtones se considèrent comme membres d'une nation spécifique parmi plusieurs autres au sein du pays, le Canada anglais a tendance à voir le pays tout entier comme une seule et même nation, dont les États provinciaux seraient les subdivisions régionales. Le fédéralisme territorial, que l'on retrouve dans plusieurs fédérations, les États-Unis, le Brésil et l'Australie, « sert non pas à satisfaire le désir d'autonomie de minorités nationales, mais plutôt à faciliter la répartition et l'étalement du pouvoir à l'intérieur d'une collectivité nationale unique ».[18]

---

[18]Kymlicka 1998 à la p. 24. Voir également Smith 2004 à la p. 53.

La distinction établie par Kymlicka est intéressante mais insatisfaisante. En effet, elle semble suggérer que la différence entre les deux types de conception du fédéralisme tient dans l'attachement au territoire ; un Ontarien, un Albertain serait un individu qui ne verrait dans cette qualité qu'une appartenance à un territoire intégré dans un ensemble national. Cependant, les revendications nationales des autochtones et des Québécois ont aussi un volet territorial très important, pour ne pas dire essentiel. Leur identité est donc aussi territorialisée. La difficulté d'établir une distinction entre ces deux formes de fédéralisme sur la base du territoire révèle une difficulté plus générale, qui est de comprendre le statut des États fédérés dans les fédérations uninationales.

La république fédérative est, pour reprendre la célèbre définition de Montesquieu, une « société de sociétés ». Peut-on considérer les États provinciaux en dehors du Québec comme autant de « sociétés » incluses au sein d'une nation pancanadienne ? David J. Elkins et Richard Simeon (1980 à la p. XV) ont déjà utilisé le concept de « provincial societies ». Parler de telles sociétés supposerait que ces collectivités aient un statut intermédiaire entre la nation et les entités régionales et municipales, qu'elles soient conçues par leurs habitants comme un espace de solidarité et de responsabilité collective à l'intérieur duquel certaines questions sont tranchées, telles que l'éducation, l'organisation des soins de santé, la gestion des ressources naturelles, etc. Les réactions négatives qu'a suscitées au Canada anglais la tentative de reconnaissance du Québec en tant que société distincte entre les années 1987 et 1990 peuvent notamment s'expliquer par le fait que la clause projetée à l'époque laissait entendre que le reste du Canada n'était pas fait lui-même de sociétés ou que s'il en avait, elles étaient d'un rang inférieur. Par contre, la réforme constitutionnelle de 1982, mue par une conception unitaire de la nation, a aussi consacré une vision unitaire de la société, tel que l'illustre la clause limitative de l'article 1 de la *Charte canadienne des droits et libertés,*[19] qui met en avant l'idée d'une « société libre et démocratique » canadienne, et non celle d'une « fédération libre et démocratique ». La consécration d'une société canadienne unifiée par le droit constitutionnel laisse peu de place à une pluralité de nations ou de sociétés au sein d'une même nation. On voit ici la difficulté de penser le statut des entités fédérées quand celles-ci ne sont en elles-mêmes ni des nations, ni des sociétés à part entière et quand elles sont investies, comme c'est le cas au Canada, du pouvoir de réglementer l'autorité locale. Les États provinciaux jouissent à l'égard des municipalités d'un pouvoir équivalent à celui d'un État unitaire à l'égard des siennes. Il est clair, tel que l'ont rappelé Keith Brownsey et Michael Howlett, que les provinces sont devenues beaucoup plus importantes que de simples gouvernements municipaux.[20] De plus, ce sont les États provinciaux qui légifèrent relativement aux droits des personnes, à tout le champ du droit civil, et qui voient à la reproduction de la culture et de la société par l'éducation, la santé, etc. En ce sens, ce sont les instances qui instituent la

---

[19]Partie I de la *Loi constitutionnelle de 1982*, constituant l'annexe B de la *Loi de 1982 sur le Canada* (R.-U.), 1982, c. 11.

[20]Brownsey et Howlett 2001 à la p. 13: « the provinces have become much more than municipal governments. »

société civile, en ce qu'elle est instituée par des rapports de droit (Brunelle 1997 aux pp. 22-33). On remarquera qu'en dépit de l'existence d'un pouvoir d'uniformisation du droit civil et de la *common law*, le Parlement fédéral s'est gardé de recourir à ce pouvoir ; sans doute a-t-on compté davantage sur l'interprétation judiciaire pour assurer cette uniformisation que sur une loi fédérale. Cependant, l'absence de recours à ce pouvoir est indicative de ce que les États provinciaux, même unis par une même vision unitaire de la nation canadienne à part le Québec, continuent de se considérer, du moins minimalement, comme autant de sociétés civiles. S'ils ont adhéré à l'Union sociale canadienne en 1999 – sans le Québec – ce n'est point pour disparaître en tant qu'ordre de gouvernement ou société, quand bien grand serait le rôle reconnu au gouvernement fédéral. Entre la société libre et démocratique canadienne et les individus nantis de droits constitutionnels qui la composent, il existe un moyen terme, que perpétue le régime fédéral canadien, qui reste toutefois encore à penser.

L'autre problème soulevé tient au fait que les relations entre sociétés ou nations au sein du régime fédéral canadien ne soient pas soumises aux mêmes exigences qu'à celles qui s'appliquent aux relations entre l'État et les individus. La réforme constitutionnelle de 1982 a substantiellement modifié les rapports entre la puissance publique et les personnes ; le Canada est passé d'un régime de suprématie parlementaire à celui de démocratie constitutionnelle qui impose aux deux ordres de gouvernement des limites permanentes à l'exercice de leurs prérogatives. Ainsi, aucune atteinte aux droits et libertés de la personne n'est valide à moins qu'elle ne soit le fait d'une règle de droit qui se justifie dans le cadre d'une société libre et démocratique. Les États provinciaux ont également adopté leur propre charte ou déclaration des droits auxquelles les tribunaux ont reconnu une portée quasi-constitutionnelle. S'est donc développé au Canada un nouveau régime de normativité constitutionnelle, très contraignant pour les titulaires de la puissance publique, qui a rééquilibré les rapports entre les différents pouvoirs et transformé la culture politique bien au-delà des forums parlementaire et judiciaire.

Par contre, lorsqu'on observe la manière dont sont traités les rapports entre les sociétés ou les nations qui composent le Canada, on s'aperçoit aisément que les exigences normatives ne sont pas les mêmes. Parmi les attributions qui leur sont reconnues, les tribunaux ont certes celle d'arbitrer les litiges intergouvernementaux ; en ce sens, ils ont mis en œuvre la dimension constitutionnelle du fédéralisme canadien, sa variante politique, continuant certes d'exister, sans être vraiment reconnue comme telle ou explicitée dans le langage du droit constitutionnel. Cependant, l'arbitrage judiciaire des conflits de compétence n'a pas réussi jusqu'ici à normaliser l'ensemble des relations entre les deux ordres de gouvernement. Le reproche principal qui est fait au pouvoir fédéral de dépenser, on le sait, est qu'il est un instrument par lequel un palier de gouvernement parvient à contourner le partage constitutionnel des compétences aux fins de réglementer les compétences de l'autre palier de gouvernement. C'est donc dire qu'une bonne partie des rapports entre les deux ordres de gouvernement n'est pas tout à fait assujettie aux prescriptions du droit constitutionnel ; ils dépendent de l'équilibre des forces politiques, des alliances possibles, des partis au pouvoir, du choc des idéologies, etc.

Si l'on regarde la pratique du fédéralisme, il n'apparaît pas d'emblée que l'existence d'un pouvoir fédéral de dépenser illimité est en soi contraire à l'esprit même du fédéralisme, pour la simple raison qu'un tel pouvoir existe dans plusieurs fédérations reconnues pour telles ; pensons aux États-Unis et à l'Australie. À moins de juger que ces fédérations n'en sont pas et forment plutôt une autre forme d'État dont la catégorie reste à définir, on est obligé d'admettre qu'aucun modèle universel du pouvoir fédéral de dépenser ne s'impose. L'étude réalisée par Andrée Lajoie pour le compte de la Commission sur le déséquilibre fiscal le montre bien ; on peut en effet distinguer les fédérations anglo-saxonnes où ce pouvoir est reconnu dans sa forme illimitée – par la constitution ou les tribunaux – des fédérations européennes dont le droit constitutionnel tend à limiter ce pouvoir (Québec 2001). Aux États-Unis, le débat sur la légitimité du pouvoir fédéral de dépenser est aussi ancien que l'origine même de la fédération américaine. Les Antifédéralistes craignaient que le Congrès, par son pouvoir de lever des taxes pour la défense commune et le bien-être général de l'Union, n'abusât de ce pouvoir au détriment de la liberté des États et des individus.[21] Au début de la république américaine, Jefferson et Hamilton se sont opposés sur le sens à donner aux pouvoirs du congrès ; selon Hamilton, le Congrès devrait avoir la liberté de remplir les missions qui lui sont confiées par tous les moyens qui ne sont pas immoraux ou contraires à la société politique (voir Elkins et McKitrick 1993 aux pp. 232-233). Cependant, comme l'a noté Anthony Birch dans une étude comparative faite sur le fédéralisme fiscal au Canada, aux États-Unis et en Australie, la vision hamiltonnienne du pouvoir, favorable à l'élargissement des prérogatives du Congrès, l'a emporté aux États-Unis à partir de 1865, et l'idée que le Congrès puisse user des subventions qu'il verse aux États pour y attacher des conditions est devenue communément acceptée (Birch 1955 à la p. 151).

Le Canada pourrait, à l'instar des exemples américain et australien, opter pour la voie hamiltonnienne, soit en laissant les choses en état, par le maintien du flou constitutionnel actuel entourant la validité et la légitimité du pouvoir de dépenser, soit en comptant sur la Cour suprême pour valider un tel pouvoir sans qu'elle lui fixe de limites véritables. On verrait ainsi émerger un gouvernement fédéral qui, en vertu de ses droits de propriétaire sur ses fonds propres, aurait carte blanche pour encadrer les politiques publiques des États provinciaux, au nom de l'efficacité, de l'intégration et de la justice sociale, dans une dynamique unificatrice, créatrice d'une société canadienne globale en expansion, grâce à l'immigration, à l'exploitation des ressources et au peuplement vers le grand nord, aux conquêtes incessantes de la technologie qui repoussent les horizons humains. La dynamique impériale sous-jacente au fédéralisme américain qu'avait repéré Tocqueville s'épanouirait sans frein au Canada, en tant qu'empire d'opportunités, qui tire partie de l'économie mondialisée et repousse les limites du biopouvoir, à l'instar de l'américain. Cette trajectoire sociopolitique n'est pas en soi improbable. Elle correspond à l'un des desseins peu connus des pères fondateurs, qui rêvaient de fonder, avec le *Dominion of Canada*, un empire qui rivaliserait avec la république du sud. Au vrai, il est

[21] Voir Brutus, texte 1, 18 octobre 1787 dans Ketham (2003 aux pp. 280-281).

possible de soutenir que cette ambition est déjà grandement réalisée. Ainsi que l'a montré Stéphane Kelly dans son ouvrage *Les fins du Canada*, la tradition politique canadienne, lorsqu'on envisage la philosophie et la pratique du pouvoir des premiers ministres Macdonald, Laurier, MacKenzie et Trudeau, s'est distinguée par une étonnante continuité, en ce qu'elle est restée fidèle à la conception hamiltonnienne du pouvoir et du fédéralisme (Kelly 2001 à la p. 241).

La reconnaissance d'un pouvoir fédéral illimité de dépenser marquerait aussi la nature du constitutionnalisme et la théorie de l'État au Canada. Dans un ouvrage consacré à la théorie de l'État en Europe, la philosophe Blandine Kriegel (2002) oppose la république à l'empire. Elle montre que la théorie de la république, qui remonte aux écrits de publicistes tels que Jean Bodin et s'est construite, en France, contre le droit impérial romain, conçoit la souveraineté de l'État comme la bonne puissance, la puissance légitime, c'est-à-dire, une puissance soumise à des limites ou lois fondamentales. Ainsi la république ou l'État de droit est fondé sur la législation, non sur la force. Le commandement de l'armée, l'usage de la puissance militaire comme outil de domination de la vie civile n'est pas le principal attribut de la république. Celle-ci s'oppose de même aux seigneuries, c'est-à-dire aux régimes où l'État et la société civile sont vues par le prince comme étant sa propriété. Le seigneur, écrit Kriegel, « confond les relations publiques avec les relations individuelles. Il amalgame les liens privés des hommes entre eux avec les rapports qu'ils entretiennent avec les choses. Il traite les personnes comme des biens, il exerce le pouvoir comme on use du droit de propriété » (ibid. à la p. 93). La distinction entre *imperium* et *dominium*, en tant qu'attributs de la puissance publique, a traversé le temps depuis la Rome antique[22] et sous-tendu la pensée politique moderne, notamment chez Locke (Spitz 1995) et Rousseau (Larrère 1995). Selon François Chevrette, cette distinction est également présente dans le droit constitutionnel canadien, qui fait la part entre l'État propriétaire et l'État puissance publique (Chevrette 2003).

À la lumière de cette distinction établie par Kriegel, il apparaît que l'un des enjeux de la reconnaissance d'un pouvoir fédéral de dépenser est le rôle du *dominium* fédéral, la puissance qu'il exerce par son droit de propriétaire sur ses actifs meubles et immeubles, dans la régulation des rapports de type fédératif entre les sociétés et les nations qui coexistent dans l'ensemble canadien. L'affirmation d'un pouvoir fédéral sans limite véritable reviendrait à ériger ce *dominium* en principe d'arbitrage de la répartition effective des responsabilités gouvernementales. En contournant le partage formel des compétences législatives – répartiteur de la souveraineté étatique canadienne – et prescrivant ses propres règles attachées aux subventions versées aux États provinciaux ou aux personnes physiques et morales, le gouvernement fédéral s'affirmerait *de facto* comme le propriétaire ultime du pacte fédératif ; il devient sa chose, son bien, ses rapports avec les États fédérés étant déterminés par la prééminence de son *dominium*. En d'autres termes, on sort de la logique de la république pour entrer dans celle de la seigneurie. Ainsi que l'écrit Chevrette:

[22]Sur l'origine romaine des concepts, voir Gaudemet (1995).

> Quand l'État, fédéral ou provincial, agit en sa qualité de propriétaire, il est . . . comme une personne privée, physique ou morale. D'où il résulte que, de même qu'à cette dernière, le partage des compétences législatives ne lui est point opposable et qu'il peut poser des actes et mener des activités qu'il serait incompétent à autoriser législativement. À ce titre, on a quelque raison de parler de la prééminence du *dominium*. (ibid. aux pp. 669-670)

Certes, les États provinciaux possèdent aussi un *dominium*, en tant que propriétaire de leurs fonds et des terres publiques ; seulement, il n'a pas l'ampleur qu'aurait le *dominium* généralisé du parlement fédéral à l'égard des attributions constitutionnelles des États provinciaux.

Les dangers qu'occasionnerait la reconnaissance d'un *dominium* illimité sur le régime fédéral canadien formaient l'un des arguments que Pierre-Elliott Trudeau invoqua en 1957 contre le pouvoir fédéral de dépenser. Les défenseurs de ce pouvoir prétendaient que le gouvernement fédéral, collectant beaucoup de revenus autres que les taxes prélevées des contribuables, pouvait librement disposer de ces fonds privés et en faire « don » à qui il veut. Trudeau rétorqua : « si un gouvernement fédéral ou des gouvernements provinciaux décidaient de se prévaloir avec excès de leur droit constitutionnel de donner des "dons privés" en dehors de leur juridiction, ils ruineraient à coup sûr et le système fédéral, et le citoyen » (Trudeau 1967 à la p. 99). Andrew Petter a également constaté que plusieurs juristes favorables au pouvoir fédéral de dépenser assimilent le gouvernement fédéral à une personne privée, et lui reconnaissent donc le pouvoir, au même titre que tout individu, de disposer à guise de sa propriété et d'en faire « don » à qui il veut (Petter 1989 à la p. 461).

Dans une entrevue donnée à la revue *Options politiques* au lendemain du dépôt du budget 2007 par le ministre des Finances Jim Flaherty, celui-ci déclarait, en réponse à une question portant sur ses intentions de limiter le pouvoir fédéral de dépenser: « Well, I have noted a tendency toward expansionism in Ottawa that is really quite remarkable. We really have to be careful, we have to be good stewards together to make sure that we don't empire-build here ».[23]

Si le ministre Flaherty est sérieux dans son intention de réfréner la propension à l'empire du gouvernement fédéral, il devra alors songer à restreindre son *dominium*. Divers scénarios sont possibles. On pourrait éliminer carrément le pouvoir fédéral de dépenser, comme l'a proposé Andrew Petter, en accompagnant cette interdiction d'une réforme du partage des ressources fiscales et d'une bonification de la péréquation (Petter 1989 à la p. 475). On pourrait également assortir l'exercice du pouvoir fédéral de dépenser de conditions, ce qui suppose la reconnaissance de sa légitimité constitutionnelle. Il est également possible de donner une nouvelle vie à l'article 94 de la *Loi*

---

[23]Entrevue de Jim Flaherty, « Respecting Responsibilities under the Constitution» *Options politiques* (avril 2007) 6 à la p. 7, en ligne: www.irpp.org/po/archive/apr07/flaherty.pdf.

constitutionnelle de 1867,[24] de manière à établir deux régimes d'exercice de ce pouvoir, l'un pour le Québec, l'autre pour le reste du Canada (Adam 2007 aux pp. 30-34). Alain Noël a préconisé une combinaison de la première option et de coopérations renforcées entre les États provinciaux – à part le Québec – et Ottawa sous le régime de l'article 94 (Noël 2008).

Il se peut cependant qu'aucune de ces options ne se réalise et que l'édification d'empire (*empire-building*) poursuive son chemin. Comme l'a rappelé Will Kymlicka, le pouvoir fédéral de dépenser a été jusqu'ici l'un des instruments par lequel la majorité anglophone du Canada a promu sa vision pancanadienne du nationalisme et ainsi favorisé ses propres intérêts. La standardisation des services publics obtenue par l'exercice de ce pouvoir constitue « le fondement même de l'identité canadienne » (Kymlicka 1998 à la p. 40). Ce centralisme s'impose aux Québécois et aux Autochtones qui, eux aussi, veulent agir en tant que nation et pas seulement en tant qu'individus citoyens du Canada. Il reconduirait ce que Vincent Di Norcia a nommé la forme culturelle de l'empire : « [T]he empire structure of Canada has a cultural form. This is implicit in the fact that empire is constituted by one society's dominion over another society . . . . Culture is not an institution but a deep collective structure which determines the whole of social life » (Di Norcia 1979 à la p. 218).

Or, selon Carl Friedrich, si l'on tient pour acquis que la fédération est une solution de rechange à l'empire, c'est que la première aurait pour base le consensus, et l'autre, la coercition (Friedrich 1963 à la p. 586).

CONCLUSION

De prime abord, la problématique du pouvoir fédéral de dépenser paraît un sujet technique, qui intéresse les spécialistes des finances publiques et les économistes, et non point les théoriciens du fédéralisme ou du politique. Or, à bien examiner la question, on s'aperçoit qu'elle est intimement liée à la nature du fédéralisme, que la théorie politique et la doctrine juridique tendent à concevoir comme un régime d'équilibre des puissances et d'adéquation des ressources aux tâches constitutionnelles. Cependant, l'étude des origines historiques du fédéralisme – antique et moderne – révèle qu'on ne peut exclure l'hypothèse selon laquelle le fédéralisme prend la forme d'un pacte inégal entre

---

[24] *Supra* note 12. L'article 94 se lit comme suit :

> Nonobstant toute disposition contraire énoncée dans la présente loi, le parlement du Canada pourra adopter des mesures à l'effet de pourvoir à l'uniformité de toutes les lois ou de parties des lois relatives à la propriété et aux droits civils dans Ontario, la Nouvelle-Écosse et le Nouveau-Brunswick, et de la procédure dans tous les tribunaux ou aucun des tribunaux de ces trois provinces; et depuis et après la passation de toute loi à cet effet, le pouvoir du parlement du Canada de décréter des lois relatives aux sujets énoncés dans telles lois, sera illimité, nonobstant toute chose au contraire dans la présente loi; mais toute loi du parlement du Canada pourvoyant à cette uniformité n'aura d'effet dans une province qu'après avoir été adoptée et décrétée par la législature de cette province.

une puissance impériale et des collectivités à l'autonomie restreinte. Ce qu'a saisi Tocqueville en étudiant le cas américain, c'est que la dynamique impériale d'une grande nation en expansion peut se combiner avec la liberté de petites collectivités, qui se maintiennent notamment grâce aux contraintes du droit constitutionnel contre les multiples déséquilibres qui avantagent le gouvernement fédéral américain.

Dans le cas canadien, la compréhension du fédéralisme constitutionnel instauré en 1867 doit se doubler de celle du fédéralisme politique, négligé ou oublié, qui s'est nourri de la constitution évolutive britannique et de la tradition d'accommodement entre la nation anglaise et les nations historiques par des arrangements asymétriques. De même, il convient de comprendre la spécificité du discours autonomiste québécois, prompt à revendiquer une autonomie inconditionnée et séparée, qui s'explique en partie par le contexte historique de la naissance de l'État du Québec en 1867. Toutes ces dimensions du constitutionnalisme et de la culture politique canadienne nous aident à comprendre pourquoi beaucoup d'acteurs politiques et d'intellectuels, en particulier au Québec, ont vu dans le pouvoir fédéral de dépenser une atteinte au caractère fédéral du pays.

Si le Canada décide de consacrer un pouvoir fédéral illimité de dépenser, il ne cessera probablement pas d'être pour autant un régime fédératif en raison de ce seul fait : il ne fera qu'actualiser un fédéralisme impérial, qui a été l'une des formes socio-historiques de ce régime d'État. Cela voudra dire que les rapports entre sociétés et les nations d'un pays multinational ne seront pas soumis au même régime de normativité constitutionnelle que celui s'imposant aux rapports entre l'État et les personnes depuis 1982. Décrivant l'ambition poursuivie par l'œuvre de Harold Innis, Arthur Kroker a posé ce dilemme : « How to obtain "balance and proportion" between claims of empire (power) and culture (history) » (Kroker 1985 à la p. 15). Créé en tant que dominion, c'est-à-dire, étymologiquement, la propriété d'un souverain, le Canada se proclame depuis 1982 fondé sur la primauté du droit. L'avenir nous dira lequel de ces deux pôles l'emportera dans la dynamique fédérale canadienne : ou bien l'expansion de l'empire domanial fédéral dans la grande nation canadienne – *imperium in imperio* – ou bien l'extension du règne du droit à la coexistence des communautés dans un État multinational.

REFERENCES

Adam, M.-A. 2007. « Federalism and the Spending Power: Section 94 to the Rescue » *Options politiques* (mars).

Balthazar, L. 1998. « Global Integration and the Sovereignty of States » dans Hugh Johnston et John R. Wood, dir., *Managing Change in the 21st Century: Indian and Canadian Perspectives*. Calgary: Shastri-Indo Canadian Institute.

Benton, L. 2006. « Constitutions and Empires » 31 *Law & Soc. Inquiry* 177.

Bibliothèque du Parlement, Direction de la recherche parlementaire. 1987. *Modification constitutionnelle de 1987*, Ottawa, Ministre des Approvisionnements et Services Canada [Accord du Lac Meech].

Bilder, M.S. 2004. *The Transatlantic Constitution: Colonial Legal Culture and the Empire*. Cambridge: Harvard University Press.

Birch, A.H. 1955. *Federalism, Finance, and Social Legislation in Canada, Australia, and the United States.* Oxford: Oxford University Press.

Bird, R. *et al.* 2003. « Assignment of Responsibilities and Fiscal Federalism » dans Raoul Blindenbacher et Arnold Koller, dir., *Federalism in a Changing World – Learning from Each Other: Scientific Background, Proceedings and Plenary Speeches of the International Conference on Federalism 2002.* Montréal: McGill-Queen's University Press.

Bogdanor, V. 1988. « Britain: The Political Constitution » dans Vernon Bogdanor, dir., *Constitutions in Democratic Politics.* Aldershot: Gower.

Bossé, E. 1971. *Joseph-Charles Taché (1820–1894), un grand représentant de l'élite canadienne-française.* Québec: Garneau.

Brisbin, R.A. 1998. « The Reconstitution of American Federalism: The Rehnquist Court and Federal-States Relations, 1991-1997 » 28(1) *Publius: The Journal of Federalism* 189-216.

Brouillet, E. 2005. *La négation de la nation : l'identité culturelle québécoise et le fédéralisme canadien.* Sillery (Qc) : Septentrion.

Brownsey, K. et M. Howlett. 2001. *The Provincial State in Canada.* Peterborough: Broadview Press.

Brun, H. et G. Tremblay. 2002. *Droit constitutionnel*, 4e éd. Cowansville (Qc) : Yvon Blais.

Brunelle, D. 1997. *Droit & exclusion : critique de l'ordre libéral.* Paris : L'harmattan.

Canada. 1992. *Rapport du consensus sur la constitution*, Charlottetown [Accord de Charlottetown].

Chevrette, F. 2003. « Dominium et Imperium: L'État propriétaire et l'État puissance publique en droit constitutionnel canadien » dans Benoît Moore, dir., *Mélanges Jean Pineau.* Montréal : Thémis.

Chevrier, M. 1994. « La conception pluraliste et subsidiaire de l'État dans le rapport Tremblay de 1956 : entre l'utopie et la clairvoyance » dans *Les cahiers d'histoire du Québec au XXe siècle*, n° 2.

— 2006. « La genèse de l'idée fédérale chez les pères fondateurs américains et canadiens » dans Alain-G. Gagnon, dir., *Le fédéralisme canadien contemporain : fondements, traditions, institutions.* Montréal : Presses de l'Université de Montréal.

— 2007. « Federalism in Canada: A World of Competing Definitions and Views » dans Stephen Tierney, dir., *Multiculturalism and the Canadian Constitution.* Vancouver: UBC Press.

— 2008. « Le Québec, une Écosse française ? Asymétries et rôle des juristes dans les unions anglo-écossaise (1707) et canadienne (1867) » dans Linda Cardinal, dir., *Le fédéralisme asymétrique les minorités linguistiques et nationales.* Sudbury : Prise de Parole.

Chopin, T. 2002. *La république « une et divisible » : les fondements de la Fédération américaine.* Paris : Commentaire Plon.

Conlan, T.J. et F. Vergniolle de Chantal. 2001. « The Rehnquist Court and Contemporary American Federalism » *Political Science Quartely* 116.

Croisat, M. 1995. *Le fédéralisme dans les démocraties contemporaines*, 2e éd. Paris : Montchrestien.

Di Norcia, V. 1979. « The Empire Structures of the Canadian State » dans Stanley G. French, dir., *La confédération canadienne : qu'en pensent les philosophes?* Montréal : Association canadienne de philosophie.

Duplé, N. 2004. *Droit constitutionnel : principes fondamentaux*, 2e éd. Montréal : Wilson & Lafleur.

Elazar, D.J. 1987. *Exploring Federalism.* Tuscaloosa: University of Alabama Press.

Elkins, S. et E. McKitrick. 1993. *The Age of Federalism: The Early American Republic, 1788–1800.* New York: Oxford University Press.

Elkins, D.J. et R. Simeon. 1980. *Small Worlds: Provinces and Parties in Canadian Political Life.* Toronto: Methuen Publications.

Epstein, D.F. 1984. *The Political Theory of the Federalist.* Chicago: University of Chicago Press.

Feldman, J.-P. 2006. « Alexis de Tocqueville et le fédéralisme américain » 4 *Revue du droit public et de la science politique en France et à l'étranger* 881.

Ferguson, N. 2004. *Colossus: The Rise and Fall of the American Empire.* Londres: Penguin Books.

Friedrich, C.J. 1963. *Man and His Government: An Empirical Theory of Politics.* NewYork: McGraw-Hill.

Gaudemet, J. 1995. « Dominium-Imperium : Les deux pouvoirs dans la Rome ancienne » 22 *Droits* 3.

Groppi, T. 2004. *Il federalismo.* Editori Laterza.

Hamilton, A. 1787. « Le fédéraliste no 22 » dans Alexander Hamilton, John Jay et James Madison, *Le fédéraliste*, trad. par Gaston Jèse. Paris : Economica.

Héraud, G. 1968. *Les principes du fédéralisme et de la fédération européenne : contribution à la théorie juridique du fédéralisme.* Paris : Presse d'Europe.

Hulscboch, D.J. 2005. *Constituting Empire: New York and the Transformation of Constitutionalism in the Atlantic World 1664-1830.* Chapel Hill: University of North Carolina Press.

Journard, I. et P.M. Kongsrud. 2003. *Fiscal Relations Across Government Levels.* OECD Economic Studies No 36.

Kelly, S. 2001. *Les fins du Canada.* Montréal : Boréal.

Ketham, R., dir. 2003. *The Anti-Federalist Papers and the Constitutional Convention Debates.* New York: Signet Classic.

Kincaid, J. 1996. « From Dual to Coercive Federalism in American Intergovernmental Relations » dans Jong S. Jun et Deil S. Wright, dir., *Globalization & Decentralization: Institutional Context, Policy Issues, and Intergovernmental Relations in Japan and the United States.* Washington: Georgetown University Press.

Kriegel, B. 2002. *État de droit ou Empire*? Paris : Bayard.

Kroker, A. 1985. *Technology and the Canadian Mind.* Montreal: New World Perspectives.

Kymlicka, W. 1998. « Le fédéralisme multinational au Canada : un partenariat à repenser » dans Guy Laforest et Roger Gibbins, dir., *Sortir de l'impasse : les voies de la réconciliation.* Montréal : Institut de recherche en politiques publiques.

Lachapelle, G. et L. Bernier. 1998. « Le fédéralisme fiscal : le Canada peut-il devenir une démocratie d'accommodation? » dans Manon Tremblay, dir., *Les politiques publiques canadiennes.* Québec : Presses de l'Université Laval.

Laforest, G. et S. Kelly. 2004. « Introduction de l'édition en langue française » dans Janet Ajzenstat et al., dir., *Débats sur la fondation du Canada.* Québec : Presses de l'Université Laval.

Larrère, C. 1995. « Propriété et souveraineté chez Rousseau » 22 *Droits* 39.

Lederman, W.R. 1965. « The Balanced Interpretation of the Federal Distribution of Legislative Powers in Canada » dans P.-A. Crépeau et C.B. Macpherson, dir., *L'avenir du fédéralisme canadien.* Toronto: University of Toronto Press; Montréal : Presses de l'Université de Montréal.

Levinson, D.L. 2004. « Empire-Building Government in Constitutional Law » 118 *Harv. L. Rev.* 915.

Mallory, J.R. 1965. « The Five Faces of Federalism » dans P.-A. Crépeau et C.B. Macpherson, dir., *L'avenir du fédéralisme canadien.* Toronto: University of Toronto Press; Montréal : Presses de l'Université de Montréal.

Mommsen, T. 1985. *Manuel des antiquités romaines*, trad. par Joachim Marquardt. Paris : Diffusion du Raccord.

Montesquieu, C. de. 1961. *De l'esprit des lois.* Paris : Librairie Garnier Frères, Deuxième partie, Livre IX, c. 1.

Mougel, F.-C. 2005. *Les élites britanniques de la Glorieuse Révolution à Tony Blair (1688-2005).* Paris : Ellipses.

Nexon, D.H. et T. Wright. 2007. « What's at Stake in the American Empire Debate » 101 *American Political Science Review* 253.

Noël, A. 2008. « Éliminer le pouvoir de dépenser » *Options politiques* (mars).

— 2006. « Équilibres et déséquilibres dans le partage des ressources financières » dans Alain-G. Gagnon, dir., *Le fédéralisme canadien contemporain : fondements, traditions, institutions.* Montréal : Presses de l'Université de Montréal.

Pelletier, R. 2005. « Fédéralisme et fédérations : approches et pratiques » dans Louis Imbeau, dir., *Politiques publiques comparées dans les États fédérés : l'Allemagne, l'Australie, le Canada, les États-Unis et la Suisse.* Saint-Nicolas (Qc) : Presses de l'Université Laval.

Petter, A. 1989. « Federalism and the Myth of the Federal Spending Power » 68 *R. du B. can.* 448.

Plancherel-Bongard, C. 1998. « Les rapports de subordination entre Rome et les confédérations latine et italique » 66 *Rev. hist. dr.* 279.

Pocock, J.G.A. 1990. « States, Republics, and Empires: The American Founding in Early Modern Perspective » dans Terence Ball et John G.A. Pocock, dir., *Conceptual Change and the Constitution.* Kansas City: University of Kansas.

Prélot, P.-H. et M. Rogoff. 1996. « Le fédéralisme devant la Cour suprême des États-Unis » 3 *Revue du droit public et de la science politique en France et à l'étranger* 759.

Québec. 1956. *Rapport de la Commission royale d'enquête sur les problèmes constitutionnels*, vol. 2.

Québec, Commission sur le déséquilibre fiscal. 2001. *Le « pouvoir fédéral de dépenser »*, annexe 1, Bibliothèque nationale du Québec.

— 2002a. *Recueil des textes soumis au Symposium international sur le déséquilibre fiscal*, annexe.

— 2002b. *Pour un nouveau partage des moyens financiers au Canada.* Québec : Publications du Québec.

Rocher, F. 2006. « La dynamique Québec-Canada ou le refus de l'idéal fédéral » dans Alain-G. Gagnon, dir., *Le fédéralisme canadien contemporain : fondements, traditions, institutions.* Montréal : Presses de l'Université de Montréal.

Rumilly, R. 1948. *L'autonomie provinciale.* Montréal : Éditions de l'arbre.

Saint-Ouen, F. 2005. *Le fédéralisme.* CH-Gollion, Infolio.

Silver, A.I. 1982. *The French-Canadian Idea of Confederation, 1864-1900.* Toronto: University of Toronto Press.

Smith, J. 2004. *Federalism.* Vancouver: UBC Press.

Spitz, J.-F. 1995. « Imperium et Dominium chez Locke » 22 *Droits* 27.

Stanley, G.F.C. 1956. « Act or Pact: Another Look at Confederation » Société historique du Canada, Rapport de l'assemblée annuelle 1.

Taché, J.-C. 1858. *Des provinces de l'Amérique du Nord et d'une union fédérale.* Québec : Brousseau frères.

Telford, H. 2003. « The Federal Spending Power in Canada: Nation-Building or Nation-Destroying? » 33 *Publius: The Journal of Federalism* 23.

Thomas, D.M. 1997. *Whistling Past the Graveyard: Constitutional Abeyances, Quebec, and the Future of Canada.* Don Mills: Oxford University Press.

Tocqueville, A. de. 1981. *De la démocratie en Amérique.* Paris : Garnier-Flammarion.

Tremblay, A. 2000. « Pouvoir fédéral de dépenser » dans Alain-G. Gagnon, dir., *L'union sociale canadienne sans le Québec.* Montréal : Saint-Martin.

Trudeau, P.-E. 1967. « Les octrois fédéraux aux universités » *Cité libre* (février 1957), reproduit dans *Le fédéralisme et la société canadienne-française.* Montréal : HMH.

Vipond, R.C. 1991. *Liberty and Community: Canadian Federalism and the Failure of the Constitution.* Albany: State University of New York Press.

Waite, P.B. 1959. « The Quebec Resolutions and *Le Courrier du Canada*, 1864-1865 » 40 *Canadian Historical Review* 294.

Watts, R.L. 1999. *Comparaison des régimes fédéraux*, 2e éd. Montréal: McGill-Queen's University Press.

Weinstock, D. 2001. « Vers une théorie normative du fédéralisme » 167 *Revue internationale de sciences sociales* 79.

Wheare, K.C. 1963. *Federal Government*, 4e éd. London: Oxford Paperbacks.

7

How Do You Limit a Power That Does Not Exist?

Alain Noël

Examinant les enjeux constitutionnels liés aux accords intergouvernementaux sur le pouvoir fédéral de dépenser, pouvoir qu'il juge inexistant, l'auteur retrace d'abord les contextes historiques où il a fait l'objet d'une reconnaissance constitutionnelle explicite, tant au Canada que dans certaines fédérations. Il revient ensuite sur les premiers développements politiques ayant favorisé l'exercice d'un supposé pouvoir fédéral de dépenser, avant d'aborder la période récente en analysant la proposition sur le fédéralisme faite en 2007 par le gouvernement Harper, dont il critique la priorité anachronique accordée aux programmes à coûts partagés. Puis il décortique les insuffisances des solutions négociées antérieurement, de l'Accord du lac Meech à l'Entente-cadre sur l'union sociale. Il juge d'ailleurs indésirable ce genre de solutions qui, en limitant le pouvoir fédéral de dépenser, en reconnaissent implicitement l'existence. Du point de vue constitutionnel, la meilleure option serait donc de supprimer les dépenses et les transferts fédéraux conditionnels dans les domaines de compétence provinciale, tout en compensant directement les provinces pour les pertes de recettes que cela leur occasionnerait. Face à la résistance politique qu'une telle mesure ne manquerait pas de susciter, il conclut que la solution au problème du pouvoir de dépenser sera de nature politique et non juridique.

INTRODUCTION

In 1867, when Britain's Parliament adopted the *British North America Act*, no mention was made of a federal power to spend in areas of provincial jurisdiction. This omission was not an oversight. In many countries, including the Australian federation, which was created by that same Parliament thirty-three years later, this power was attributed explicitly to the federal government (Quebec, Commission on Fiscal Imbalance 2002a, 114). Elsewhere, as in the United States, the courts settled the matter early and confirmed unambiguously the existence of a similar power (ibid. 2002b, 25-26; Telford 2003, 26-27). Not so in Canada. On the contrary, in its 1937 ruling on unemployment insurance, the Judicial Committee of the Privy Council made clear that federal spending legislation remained covered by the division of powers. "Assuming the

Dominion has collected by means of taxation a fund", wrote Lord Atkin for the Committee, "it by no means follows that any legislation which disposes of it is necessarily within Dominion competence. It may still be legislation affecting the classes of subjects enumerated in s.92, and, if so, would be *ultra vires*".[1]

This ruling did not prevent Ottawa from regularly invoking a federal spending power in the following decades, with the support of numerous legal scholars who proved adept at "intellectual gymnastics, first to skirt around the decision of the Privy Council and second to skirt around the distribution of powers" (Adam 2007, 4). Still, as Andrée Lajoie demonstrates in her contribution to this volume, Canadian courts have never confirmed the existence of a federal spending power (see also Kellock and LeRoy 2007, 19).

Australia and the United States had no qualms about the idea of a federal spending power, and in fact few had worries about the division of powers itself, because these federations were territorial, not multinational. They opted for federal institutions not to accommodate linguistic or cultural diversity but to manage their large territories with flexibility, maintain vigorous local governments, and establish counterweights to majority rule. In Canada, as in Switzerland and Belgium, these motives were not absent, but the critical factor behind the adoption of federal arrangements was the recognition that the country could be sustained only if its constituent peoples were able to preserve their autonomy.[2] A unitary government, explained John A. Macdonald in a famous 1865 speech to the Legislative Assembly, would be the most satisfying option, but "it would not meet the assent of the people of Lower Canada ... a minority, with a different language, nationality, and religion from the majority".[3]

Territorial federations centralized with little resistance because they did not have a national minority bent on preserving its distinctiveness and autonomy. In multinational federations, in contrast, the initial division of powers and financial resources became paramount, as a protection against the unmitigated rule of the majority. Where the constitution did not explicitly acknowledge the existence of distinct internal nations, as in Canada, federal institutions appeared all the more critical, as the sole instruments designed to preserve a long-standing, implicit understanding of the country (Asch 1984, 83).

This political reality explains why a federal spending power was never included in the Canadian Constitution. In a multinational federation, people who constitute the minority necessarily worry about the propensity of the majority to override the division of powers in the name of national priorities, and they seek an arrangement that is as clear and as watertight as possible. As summarized by historian Arthur Silver, in 1867 the people of Quebec sought "an autonomous French-Canadian country under the control of French Canadians" and "the greatest possible amount of provincial *sovereignty* ... combined with a modicum

---

[1]*Canada (A.G.) v. Ontario (A.G.)*, [1937] A.C. 355 at 366-367 (P.C.).

[2]See Lijphart (1999, 195) (where the author makes the distinction between two types of federations). See also Kymlicka (1998, 2); McGarry (2002, 417, 421, 428); Gagnon (2007, 14-15).

[3]Speech of the Hon. John A. Macdonald to the Legislative Assembly of the United Province of Canada, 6 February 1865, reprinted in Waite (1963, 40-41).

of federal *association*" (Silver 1997, 218-219 [emphasis in original]). In this context, it would have made no sense to introduce an override provision that would allow the majority to have its way in spite of the division of powers (Brouillet 2005, 194-197).

This, however, was precisely the purpose of the federal spending power. As Andrew Petter put it:

> The *raison d'être* of the federal spending power (and of conditional grants in particular) is to permit the federal government to use fiscal means to influence decision-making at the provincial level. In other words, it allows national majorities to set priorities and to determine policy within spheres of influence allocated under the Constitution to regional majorities. Thus, both by design and effect, the spending power runs counter to the political purpose of a federal system. (Petter 1989, 465)

Not surprisingly, the most consistent and forceful opposition to the federal spending power has come from Quebec. Elsewhere in Canada, the attitudes and positions of citizens, experts, and governments have ranged from lukewarm acquiescence to enthusiastic endorsement. The 1999 Social Union Framework Agreement (SUFA), for instance, which was signed by all governments except Quebec, was well received across the country, even though it stated unreservedly that "the use of the federal spending power under the constitution has been essential to the development of Canada's social union" and has "enabled governments to introduce new and innovative social programs" (Canada 1999).

Given the balance of political forces, Quebec's opposition has never been sufficient to prevent the federal government from using the spending power to do indirectly what it cannot do directly. In theory, a court challenge would have been possible. The range and magnitude of federal recourse to the spending power, however, made a Quebec victory in court highly unlikely. Judges, explained Andrew Petter, simply would not "undo forty years of political development" and "dismantle the structure of modern government" (Petter 1989, 473). The only avenue left open to contest the federal spending power was political. An agreement had to be found to counter or limit the use of this non-constitutional instrument.

Numerous attempts have been made since the 1960s to craft an acceptable set of rules to govern the exercise of this power. Usually these arrangements have included a requirement for some form of provincial consent before the introduction of a new program, and the opportunity for a provincial government to opt out of the newly created program with financial compensation. Unanimity on such rules, however, has proved elusive, and in practice the federal spending power has survived unchecked.

This chapter revisits some of these attempts. It starts with the latest reform proposal, articulated in the October 2007 Speech from the Throne, to assess the possibility of attaining an unlikely objective: agreeing on limits to a power that, constitutionally, does not exist. The first section discusses the October 2007 federal offer to limit the spending power, and its unenthusiastic reception, in Quebec in particular. The second section steps back in time to consider an alternative proposal, inspired by the efforts that led to the social union negotiations of the late 1990s. The third section introduces a proposal that is at once simpler and more radical – a proposal that would eliminate any reference to a spending power that has never been constitutional. Such a solution would resolve the contradiction associated with any attempt to limit a power that the Quebec government does not want to recognize, even indirectly. Finally, the concluding section acknowledges the formidable political obstacles that such a reform would face in a country that has yet to reconcile itself with its history and destiny as a multinational federation.

THE HARPER PROPOSAL: REGULATING BLACK-AND-WHITE TV SETS

In a December 2005 Quebec City campaign speech, Stephen Harper explained his vision of "a new style of open federalism" (Noël 2006a, 26). He promised to break with the "domineering and paternalistic federalism" of the Liberals, and better respect the autonomy of the provinces and the division of powers established in the Constitution. In particular, a Conservative government would initiate a collaborative process with the provinces to eliminate the fiscal imbalance in the federation, and limit the use of the federal spending power. Harper did not say so explicitly in Quebec, but his party's platform was quite specific (Conservative Party of Canada 2006, 42-43): a majority of provinces would need to agree to any new shared-cost program in an area of provincial jurisdiction, and any province could opt out of such a program with financial compensation. This same commitment was reiterated in the 2006 and 2007 budget speeches. In the 16 October 2007 Speech from the Throne, it was given priority in the following terms:

> Our Government believes that the constitutional jurisdiction of each order of government should be respected. To this end, guided by our federalism of openness, our Government will introduce legislation to place formal limits on the use of the federal spending power for new shared-cost programs in areas of exclusive provincial jurisdiction. This legislation will allow provinces and territories to opt out with reasonable compensation if they offer compatible programs.[4]

As long as it had remained a remote idea, this proposal had been received politely, but once the Speech from the Throne announced a firm commitment to legislate, it was roundly criticized, and for good reason.

Indeed, the Conservative proposal as formulated was in practice beside the point, because it was confined to shared-cost programs. Ottawa has not introduced or modified a major shared-cost program in more than ten years, and it is unlikely to do so in the future. With the introduction of Established Programs Financing in the late 1970s, most such programs were transformed

[4]*Debates of the Senate*, Vol. 144, No. 1 (16 October 2007) at 4 (Rt. Hon. Michaëlle Jean).

into block grants. The last shared-cost program of any significance, the Canada Assistance Plan, was eliminated in 1995 with the introduction of the Canada Health and Social Transfer (CHST), a large block transfer distributed more or less on a per capita basis. Since then, far from looking back, federal finance ministers have stayed away from any commitment that would leave a part of their budget determined by the decisions of other governments (Noël 2003). Stricter rules circumscribing the introduction of new shared-cost programs would thus be irrelevant. After the Speech from the Throne, in an editorial, I compared this promise to an offer to give provincial governments full control over the regulation of standards for black-and-white TV sets (Noël 2007a). The Harper solution may have been appropriate for the 1960s, but it stood as a sort of Maginot line, conceived for an earlier war.

This proposal to limit the federal spending power failed to address its actual and very diverse manifestations: block transfers with conditions (as in the case of the Canada Health Transfer and Canada Social Transfer, which had replaced the CHST in 2004); direct transfers to institutions and persons (research grants, scholarships, funds earmarked for health care); and fiscal expenditures for social purposes (to support child care or post-secondary education, for instance). It is difficult, admittedly, to conceive of a framework that would encompass all these forms of interventions. Without such a solution, however, the federal spending power cannot be effectively limited. Restraining a single type of instrument would simply displace the problem. Transfers to provinces, for instance, could become transfers to persons, and these transfers could themselves be replaced by tax credits.

Narrow in scope to the point of being meaningless, the Throne Speech proposal was also superficial. It overlooked the fact that to obtain this illusory limitation on a non-constitutional practice, Quebec would have to make the major concession of recognizing the legitimacy of that practice. The 1992 Charlottetown Accord had stumbled over this question of recognition, and so had the 1999 Social Union Framework Agreement (Rocher 1992, 89-92; Noël 2001, 12-13, 19-20).

Recognizing the spending power has implications that are not only symbolic or legal. Because this instrument is used, by definition, in areas of provincial jurisdiction, its deployment often requires intergovernmental negotiations. In health care, for instance, Ottawa can reduce wait times only if provincial governments agree to use improved transfers to this end. Even when funds are transferred to institutions or individuals – through research grants, scholarships, or personal benefits – provincial governments are likely to have a say. This was the case, for example, with the Millennium Scholarships Fund (Noël 2001, 20). In such a context, marked more by political coordination and bargaining than by the unfolding of constitutional law, a formal recognition of the federal spending power could become significant. As Keith Banting explained in his analysis of the Meech Lake debate, in a policy environment characterized by uncertainty and extensive negotiations, a broad agreement to recognize and circumscribe the federal spending power "would strengthen the spending power far more than a favourable ruling of the Supreme Court ever could" (Banting 1988, S85).

In other words, to limit the spending power is also to recognize it. Any limits must be strong and encompassing, because the spending power can take multiple and interchangeable forms. Taken together, these two considerations – recognition of the spending power and its multifaceted character – imply that there is no incremental road toward a satisfying solution. A partial limitation would be worse than the status quo, because it would entrench the spending power. At the same time, given the reach of the spending power and its multifaceted character, a comprehensive framework remains difficult to devise and implement.

Here lies the knot: the federal spending power is difficult to limit effectively because of the range and the extent of its use; yet without an encompassing and enforceable limitation, no agreement is possible because it would involve some form of recognition and consent. Seen in this light, the issue appears to be less legal than political. A settlement requires a genuine federal commitment and a high level of intergovernmental trust, as well as a willingness to address an existential question, clearly tied to the country's original federal and multinational pact.

This perilous road has been traveled before, without much success. Thirty years of constitutional debates, and the failure to reach a settlement satisfying to all, have convinced citizens, politicians, and experts that ambitious institutional propositions are better left dormant. One should not underestimate, however, the democratic potential of broad and open public deliberations on fundamental issues. Indeed, the Canadian constitutional debates of the 1980s and 1990s, for all their limitations, did contribute to enhanced citizen participation, and they allowed women, aboriginal peoples, and various minorities to affirm their rights (Noël 2006b, 424-425, 434). At the very least, some lessons may be drawn from these past debates over the country's federal arrangements.

INTERGOVERNMENTAL LESSONS

On 14 October 1964, all first ministers agreed on a formula to amend the Constitution: the Fulton-Favreau formula. Over the following year, however, public debates raised sufficient doubts about this compromise to convince the Quebec government of Jean Lesage to withdraw its support for the formula. It did so on 20 January 1966, to the dismay of Prime Minister Lester B. Pearson (Russell 1993, 72-73; Québec 2003, 256-261). Other attempts followed, but none obtained the clear support of all governments, even temporarily, until the 1987 Meech Lake Accord.

Designed to meet conditions laid down by the Quebec government for its approval of the *Constitution Act, 1982*, the Meech Lake Accord included what would have been the first legislated limit on the federal spending power. The proposed new section 106(A) of the *Constitution Act, 1867* guaranteed "reasonable compensation to the government of a province that chooses not to participate in a national shared-cost program that is established by the Government of Canada ... in an area of exclusive provincial jurisdiction, if the province carries on a program or initiative that is compatible with the national objectives". The provision also stated that "nothing in this section extends the legislative powers of the Parliament of Canada or of the legislatures of the provinces" (Library of Parliament 1987).

Even though shared-cost programs were still relevant at the time, the Meech Lake Accord was immediately faulted for neglecting the many other forms through which the federal spending power was exercised (Petter 1989, 475). More importantly, as many Quebec legal scholars noted at the time, the proposed new section would have effectively recognized a federal spending power by granting Ottawa the capacity to establish "national objectives" in "fields of exclusive provincial legislative jurisdiction" (Lajoie 1988, 183; Arbour *et al.* 1987). Quebec premier Robert Bourassa took satisfaction from the fact that "section 106(A) is drafted so that it speaks solely of the right to opt out, without either ... [recognizing] or defining the federal spending power.... So Québec keeps the right to contest before the courts any unconstitutional use of the spending power" (Robert Bourassa to the Quebec National Assembly 1987). That the section was silent on recognition and definition did not, however, preclude it from effectively consolidating the spending power or, in the prudent words of Peter Hogg, from clarifying its "breadth" (Hogg 1988, 157). Bourassa's notion that not naming the spending power might counter its use was as likely to be effectual as the intimation, for those who know their Harry Potter, that the evil and invincible Lord Voldemort be referred to only as "He-Who-Must-Not-Be-Named". Comforting perhaps, but not convincing.

The Meech Lake Accord nevertheless marked a first step in addressing the issue of the spending power and seeking an intergovernmental compromise. The 1992 Charlottetown Accord followed suit, but was more ambitious. It invoked a framework, to be negotiated later, that would "guide the use of the federal spending power in all areas of provincial jurisdiction" (Russell 1993, 249). In Quebec, this clause was criticized for recognizing an almost unlimited federal power to spend in areas of provincial jurisdiction (Pelletier 1992, 77-85; Turp and Gagnon 1992, 38-40). The very notion of exclusive provincial jurisdiction, observed François Rocher, was practically emptied of its content (Rocher 1992, 92). For all these shortcomings, however, the Charlottetown Accord at least acknowledged that the problem of the spending power did not begin and end with shared-cost programs. Any negotiated solution had to be encompassing, and, obviously, no such solution, ever came.

The other constituents of this intergovernmental saga have been non-constitutional. Following the February 1995 budget, which restructured and radically reduced federal social transfers, provincial and territorial governments initiated a joint process for social policy renewal that soon evolved into a federal/provincial/territorial discussion on the social union. At first, the Quebec government remained on the sidelines, convinced that the process was nothing more than "another pan-Canadian exercise that the provinces welcome with open arms" that could lead only "to the abandonment of Québec's fundamental demands and to their gradual erosion via intergovernmental and administrative means" (Bouchard 1996). Weakened by the referendum defeat and faced with an increasingly interventionist federal government, however, the Quebec government of Lucien Bouchard finally decided that it was better to take part in the process. As explained by Joseph Facal, who was Quebec minister for Intergovernmental Affairs from 1998 to 2002, the new politics of federal surpluses did not yield restored transfers but rather a multiplication of direct initiatives in areas of provincial jurisdiction:

> The 1997 federal budget gave birth for instance to the Canada Millennium Scholarship Fund, the Canadian Foundation for Innovation, the National Child Benefit and the Health Transition Fund. Others were to follow. In other words, the federal government decided to make itself more visible and influential through programs of direct funding to individuals and institutions in areas of provincial jurisdiction, instead of simply restoring funding to pre-1995 levels or vacating room through tax-point transfers to allow provincial governments to raise more revenues through tax increases. (Facal 2007, 157)

The Quebec government offered to join with other provincial governments in a consensus proposal if they would accept genuine limits on the use of the federal spending power. Quebec demanded, in particular, "an unconditional right to opt out with full financial compensation in respect of any new initiative or new federal program, whether jointly funded or not, in the sectors of social programs within the jurisdiction of the provinces". The Bouchard government insisted, as well, that its proposal "must in no way be interpreted as direct or indirect recognition of federal spending power or any federal role whatsoever in the realm of social policy".[5] This position took into account the two key aspects of the problem: Quebec did not recognize a federal power to spend in areas of provincial jurisdiction, and it demanded a right to opt out of all new or modified programs, cofunded or not.

For all its apparent radicalism, this position was itself a compromise because it accepted the status quo for existing programs – probably a realistic concession, given the programs' weight and the extent of their institutionalization. Despite its emphasis on not recognizing a federal spending power, this stance (like Bourassa's at the time of Meech Lake) in fact acknowledged that power by indirectly accepting the legitimacy of federal spending programs that offered an opt-out. In subsequent discussions with other provinces, Quebec made a further concession and accepted that funds obtained through opting out had to be invested in the same area (Warriner and Peach 2007, 148).

Interestingly, all provincial governments accepted Quebec's conditions. A new consensus emerged at the Annual Premiers' Conference in Saskatoon in August 1998, and it was reaffirmed and elaborated upon on 29 January 1999 in Victoria, British Columbia. On the spending power, the Victoria proposal stated that the federal government would seek "the consent of a majority of provinces" before introducing "any new or modified Canada-wide program in areas of provincial jurisdiction"; that it would "provide full financial compensation to any provincial or territorial government that chooses not to participate in any new or modified Canada-wide program, providing it carries on a program or initiative that addresses the priority areas of the new or modified Canada-wide program"; and that "federal spending in an area of provincial jurisdiction which

---

[5]Statement by Jacques Brassard (1998, 11); Press Release by Lucien Bouchard (12 December 1997), reprinted in Facal (2007).

occurs in a province or territory must have the consent of the province or territory involved".[6]

This proposal was innovative and without precedent. For the first time, a formulation succeeded in covering all potential manifestations of the spending power without formally recognizing its legitimacy. Although a form of indirect recognition was involved, since provinces would be allowed to opt out only if federal spending initiatives fell within their areas of jurisdiction, this was balanced by the requirement that a provincial government had to consent before any new federal initiative could apply on its territory. Together with the comprehensive character of the opting-out formula, this requirement for consent would secure provincial governments against encroachments of which they did not approve. These provisions would apply only to new or modified programs, but over time their reach was guaranteed to expand, to make them increasingly effective.

The Victoria Proposal lasted less than a week. Within days, on 4 February 1999, all provinces but Quebec accepted a counter-proposal put forward by the federal government, the Social Union Framework Agreement (SUFA), which embodied a radically different understanding of the federal spending power. In the words of André Tremblay, SUFA was nothing less than a "tribute to the federal spending power" (Tremblay 2001, 170). As mentioned earlier, this intergovernmental agreement treated the spending power as a constitutional attribute of the federal government and as an essential tool for the country, and no meaningful consent and opting-out formula counterbalanced this very explicit recognition (ibid., 175-177; Noël 2001, 12). The Quebec government simply could not approve it.

In any event, SUFA rapidly became irrelevant. Having undermined the provinces' joint effort to devise new rules for the social union, the federal government no longer needed the resulting framework and seldom mentioned its rules in subsequent intergovernmental discussions. Having made practically no gains, provincial governments soon found that they had little incentive to refer to it either. SUFA and its rules more or less vanished from the intergovernmental landscape (Noël, St-Hilaire, and Fortin 2003, 3-4).

This episode in intergovernmental relations nevertheless holds a lesson for any discussion on the spending power: there does exist a formula – the 1999 Victoria formula – that can reconcile the Quebec government with the governments of all the other provinces. This formula involves an encompassing understanding of the spending power, in all its manifestations, along with a strong consent requirement and an opting-out provision that would allow a dissenting province to devise its own alternative to a new federal initiative in an area of provincial jurisdiction.

The institutional arrangements and intergovernmental dynamics generated by such a formula would not be without tensions and contradictions. Deciding at what point a program would be sufficiently modified to require provincial consent, for instance, might not be easy. As well, determining whether a

---

[6] *Securing Canada's Social Union into the 21st Century (The Victoria Proposal)*, reprinted in Gagnon and Segal, 2001, 236-237.

particular federal intervention involved the spending power could be difficult. Tax expenditures could be particularly hard to pin down in this respect. Finally, of course, managing the asymmetry that could result from the uneven use of opting-out possibilities could cause political difficulties. These uncertainties and problems, however, would stem less from the proposed formula than from the use of the federal spending power, which would remain contrary to both the spirit and the letter of the Constitution. If a strong formula succeeded in keeping the federal government within its jurisdiction, thus neutralizing the spending power, there would be less uncertainty, no opting out, and little asymmetry.

These considerations lead to a second option, which is too rarely considered.

ELIMINATING THE SPENDING POWER

In his seminal 1989 article on the myth of the federal spending power, Andrew Petter argued that the Meech Lake Accord did not go far enough to resolve the issue. The limits it placed on new shared-cost programs did nothing, he wrote, to constrain established shared-cost programs, direct expenditures, and tax expenditures. These were all connected. To use a prosaic metaphor, the situation was akin to a tube of toothpaste: if you squeezed in one place, the bulge simply moved somewhere else. To avoid this problem, Petter suggested a four-point approach aimed not at limiting, or squeezing, the federal spending power, but rather at eliminating it. His proposal, which went to the root of the problem, also resolved the difficulties associated with any strong opting-out formula.

First, proposed Petter, "conditional transfers between governments should be constitutionally prohibited, and the tax room currently required to fund such transfers given over to the government with legislative jurisdiction". Second, governments should agree to eliminate all "other conditional grants, loans and tax expenditures for the promotion of policies that fall outside their respective legislative jurisdiction". Third, the federal government should reaffirm and reinforce its commitment to equalize revenues across provinces. Fourth, "formal procedures for constitutional amendment should be made more flexible" (Petter 1989, 475).

If we leave aside the last of these four propositions, Petter's suggestions stood very close to the recommendations made in 2002 by Quebec's Séguin Commission on fiscal imbalance, even though that commission did not suggest the outright elimination of the federal spending power. Nor were Petter's views far from the proposal that had been put forward in 1956 by the Tremblay Commission on constitutional problems.[7]

Petter's main idea was to eliminate federal transfers and expenditures in areas of provincial jurisdiction, and adjust the allocation of revenues to compensate for the budgetary consequences of these lost transfers. In this scenario, which the Séguin Commission found perfectly feasible, an improved equalization program would help fill the gap left by the elimination of social

[7]For more on the Tremblay Commission, see Noël (2007b).

transfers (Quebec, Commission on Fiscal Imbalance 2002). The constitutional division of powers would then be respected, the allocation of financial resources would roughly match the division of powers and, with strong and autonomous provincial governments, there would be little need for opting out and asymmetry, except perhaps on a symbolic level or on certain matters where specific provinces might choose forms of enhanced cooperation with the federal government.

This possibility of enhanced cooperation would usefully address a concern that had led Petter to his fourth proposition, namely, that constitutional amendment should be made easier. If "governments are to be deprived of spending as an informal means of constitutional adjustment", he wrote, "it is essential that formal amendment procedures be made more flexible" (Petter 1989, 477). Without a doubt, the Canadian Constitution is difficult to amend. The *Constitution Act, 1982* was designed that way, seemingly to prevent future politicians from proceeding like those of 1981, who did not respect the very rules they were instituting for future changes (Russell 1993, 121). In subsequent years, governments made the amending process more daunting by adding regional vetoes and provincial referenda as prerequisites for any constitutional modification (Taillon 2007). In this context, Petter's proposal for flexible amendment procedures is a non-starter. Flexibility could be obtained, however, by allowing provincial governments that wished to participate in new federal or federal-provincial programs to do so, possibly in accordance with section 94 of the *Constitution Act, 1867*.[8] As Thomas Courchene notes (this volume), such an "opting-in" formula would make more sense than the current "opting-out" approach since *a province is not "opting out" when it chooses to operate a program that is within its own constitutional jurisdiction* (see page 98, [emphasis in original]).

The solution advanced by Petter would succeed in re-establishing the federal principle by reaffirming the centrality of the constitutional division of powers and the importance of distributing financial resources accordingly. It would settle the question of the spending power without recognizing that power, even indirectly, and it would prevent excessive reliance on the opting-out mechanism. In a country that values clarity, the elimination of the spending power would also offer a clear, transparent, and simple solution. It would indeed be easier to stop speaking of a non-existent power than to devise complex, arcane procedures to constrain and limit it.

Outside Quebec, there would obviously be strong political resistance to such a reform. We have seen how lame the proposal put forward in the 2007 Speech from the Throne was. Nevertheless, Liberal Member of Parliament Bob Rae described it as being nothing less than an "emasculation" of the federal government, inspired by "a fundamentalist misreading of our history and Constitution". Confederation, he argued, "was not a compact between two peoples or a carve-out by a few principalities", but was meant to provide "effective" governance in the service of a "pan-Canadian vision led by federal governments with the support of Parliament and people. ... Thirteen fiefs putting

[8] Adam (2007). See also Marc-Antoine Adam, this volume.

up more walls and moats between themselves and their neighbours does not make a country", Rae added. Canadians "want their federal government to support early childhood education, decent housing, cities that work, a healthy environment, new initiatives in health care, more mobility for students, better research and stronger universities", and this "requires a federal government that dares to speak its name and exercise its powers" (Rae 2007).

In Rae's understanding of "a vigorous and progressive federalism", it is unclear what would remain of the federal principle and the constitutional division of powers. In any event, he obviously overstates the implications of a return to basic constitutional principles. If we leave aside equalization – a program that does not involve the spending power, as it is unconditional and rests fully within federal jurisdiction – the bulk of federal transfers to the provinces are now block transfers, simply distributed on a per capita basis, with few conditions (Godbout 2008, 53). The elimination of these transfers, combined with a new division of financial resources between Ottawa and the provinces, would yield fairly similar results, with more autonomous governments and enhanced accountability. And again, provinces willing to seek enhanced cooperation could always do so.

The true obstacle, as is suggested by Rae's rhetoric of "principalities", "fiefs", and "emasculation", is symbolic and political. Canadians who have difficulties with the federal idea of sharing sovereignty between two autonomous orders of government – let alone with the idea of a genuinely multinational federation – will not reconcile themselves easily to the elimination of a policy instrument that, in effect, allows the federal government to change the division of powers without seeking a constitutional amendment, or even the consent of the provinces (Courchene, this volume, p. 115; Kellock and LeRoy 2007, 13). Given the country's contemporary evolution away from the federal principle, this reluctance may be understandable. That does not mean it is right.

CONCLUSION

The federal government defines the spending power as "the power of parliament to make payments to people or institutions or governments for purposes on which it [Parliament] does not necessarily have the power to legislate" (Trudeau 1969, 4). This definition leaves little doubt about the dubious constitutionality of the manoeuvre, which is intended precisely to circumvent the division of powers. As Marc-Antoine Adam notes, "taken to its logical conclusion, the unlimited spending power thesis would imply that the provision of public services of any kind would largely be excluded from the purview of the distribution of power, for it is essentially spending" (Adam 2007, 4).

The main arguments in favour of the spending power, observes Adam, remain its "massive practice ... over the past half century" and the broad support it has received outside Quebec (ibid., 5). Canadian governments have used the spending power to make the country more centralized and uniform, in line with the preferences of the majority. The Canadian federation, in other words, has become less multinational and more territorial. This trend, of course, is in tune with the constitutional evolution of the country, which culminated with the *Constitution Act, 1982*, a fundamental transformation adopted without the approval of the Quebec government (Brouillet 2005, 380-381). It is reflected, as well, in the growing fiscal imbalance between the two orders of government, which has left Ottawa with more capacity than ever to intervene in areas of provincial jurisdiction.

Nationalist rhetoric notwithstanding, a more centralized federation is not necessarily a more generous and just one. In federations, the relationship between centralization and social justice remains indeterminate. In Canada, one would be hard pressed to prove that Ottawa alone was able to promote equity and justice. In addition, in a multinational federation, social justice demands respect for the consent and autonomy of the constituents (Simeon 2006, 41; Noel 2006c, 57-72).

The reform announced in the 2007 Speech from the Throne would not alter these majoritarian trends, because the limitations it would put on the federal spending power would be ineffective. Worse, the reform would help to consolidate an instrument that remains non-constitutional. In a recent essay on the question, Peter Russell underlines the difficulty of reaching any satisfactory solution through the judicial or political process, and suggests instead that modest intergovernmental accommodations should be sought, on an informal and incremental basis (Russell 2006, 183). There are, however, other alternatives. As explained above, one option is to tie a strong consent and opting-out mechanism to any use of the federal spending power, and a second is simply to renounce the use of this non-constitutional power and to allocate revenues in a manner consistent with the division of powers. The first option remains plausible, given that it once formed the basis of a consensus among provincial governments, though admittedly in a negotiation context. The second option is consistent with the conclusions of the Séguin Commission on fiscal imbalance, and in accord with the country's basic constitutional order.

In the end, the spending power problem is a political one. Over the years, Canada has distanced itself from its history and destiny as a multinational federation, and has reconstructed its institutions and practices from a more territorial, monochromatic perspective – so much so that some scholars are comfortable concluding that the country is indeed a territorial and not a multinational federation (Smith 2004, 33-35). True enough, institutions have been shaped largely along the lines favoured by the majority, with too little attention to the federal principle and to its requirement of recognition, consent, and autonomy (Gagnon 2007, 159). This does not mean, however, that no other option is possible. In the 2005-2006 electoral campaign, the simple mention by Stephen Harper of a new style of open federalism was sufficient to generate interest and good will in Quebec (Noël 2006a). In the two years that followed, Quebecers were recognized as a nation within Canada, and some efforts were made to improve federal transfers to the provinces. Addressing the spending power issue adequately remains on the agenda, and doing so would go a long way toward giving meaning to this new style of open federalism. Half-measures, however, will not do. A workable solution must encompass all dimensions of the spending power, and must ensure that it is either tightly limited by strong rules on consent and opting-out, or effectively eliminated.

REFERENCES

Adam, M.-A. 2007. *Fiscal Federalism and the Future of Canada: Can Section 94 of the Constitution Act, 1867 Be an Alternative to the Spending Power?* Online: Institute of Intergovernmental Relations at: www.queensu.ca/iigr/working/spendingPower/ AdamFinal. pdf.

Arbour, J.M. *et al.* 1987."Le projet d'accord du lac Meech", *Le Devoir* (27 May).

Asch, M. 1984. *Home and Native Land: Aboriginal Rights and the Canadian Constitution.* Toronto: Methuen.

Banting, K.G. 1988. "Federalism, Social Reform and the Spending Power", *Canadian Public Policy* 14.

Bouchard, L. 1996. "The Re-balancing of the Roles and Responsibilities of Ottawa and the Provinces: Another Road to Centralization" (Press Release, 23 August), reprinted in *Québec's Positions on Constitutional and Intergovernmental Issues from 1936 to March 2001.* Quebec: Secrétariat aux affaires intergouvernementales canadiennes, 2004, p. 103. At www.saic.gouv.qc.ca/institutionnelles_constitution nelles/table_matieres_en.htm.

Bourassa, Robert, to the Quebec National Assembly, 18 June 1987, reprinted in Donald Johnston, ed., *With a Bang, Not a Whimper: Pierre Trudeau Speaks Out.* Toronto: Stoddart (1988), 139-140.

Brassard, Jacques, 17 April 1998, reprinted in *Québec's Positions on Constitutional and Intergovernmental Issues from 1936 to March 2001.* Quebec: Secrétariat aux affaires intergouvernementales canadiennes, 2004, p. 111. At www.saic.gouv.qc.ca/ institutionnelles_constitutionnelles/table_matieres_en.htm.

Brouillet, E. 2005. *La négation de la nation: l'identité culturelle québécoise et le fédéralisme canadien.* Québec: Éditions de Septentrion.

Canada. 1999. *Framework to Improve the Social Union for Canadians: An Agreement between the Government of Canada and the Governments of the Provinces and Territories,* 4 February [SUFA].

Conservative Party of Canada. 2006. *Stand Up for Canada: Federal Election Platform 2006.* N.p.

Facal, J. 2007. "Reflections", in W.E. Warriner and I. Peach (eds.), *Canadian Social Policy Renewal, 1994–2000.* Halifax: Fernwood.

Gagnon, A.-G. 2007. *Au-delà de la nation unificatrice: Plaidoyer pour le fédéralisme multinational.* Barcelona: Institut d'Estudis Autonòmics.

Gagnon, A.-G. and H. Segal, eds. 2001. *The Canadian Social Union without Québec: 8 Critical Analyses.* Montreal: Institute for Research in Public Policy.

Godbout, L. 2008. "Budget fédéral 2008: une occasion ratée de stimuler notre productivité", *Policy Options* (April).

Hogg, H. 1988. "Analysis of the New Spending Provision (Section 106A)", in K.E. Swinton and C.J. Rogerson (eds.), *Competing Constitutional Visions: The Meech Lake Accord.* Toronto: Carswell.

Kellock, B.H. and S. LeRoy. 2007. "Questioning the Legality of the Federal 'Spending Power'", *Public Policy Sources* 89. At www.fraserinstitute.org/commerce.web/ product_files/LegalityofSpendingPower.pdf.

Kymlicka, W. 1998. *Finding Our Way: Rethinking Ethnocultural Relations in Canada.* Toronto: Oxford University Press Canada.

Lajoie, A. 1988. "The Federal Spending Power and Meech Lake", in K.E. Swinton and C.J. Rogerson (eds.), *Competing Constitutional Visions: The Meech Lake Accord.* Toronto: Carswell.

Library of Parliament, Research Branch, Law and Government Division. 1987. *The 1987 Constitutional Accord.* Ottawa: Minister of Supply and Services Canada.

Lijphart, A. 1999. *Patterns of Democracy: Government Forms and Performance in Thirty-Six Countries.* New Haven: Yale University Press.

McGarry, J. 2002. "Federal Political Systems and the Accommodation of National Minorities", in A.I. Griffiths and K. Nerenberg (eds.), *Handbook of Federal Countries 2002.* Montreal: McGill-Queen's University Press.

Noël, A. 2001. "General Study of the Framework Agreement". in A.-G. Gagnon and H. Segal (eds.), *The Canadian Social Union without Québec: 8 Critical Analyses.* Montreal: Institute for Research in Public Policy.

— 2003. "Power and Purpose in Intergovernmental Relations", in S. Fortin, A. Noël, and F. St-Hilaire (eds.), *Forging the Canadian Social Union: SUFA and Beyond.* Montreal: Institute for Research on Public Policy.

— 2006a. "Il suffisait de presque rien: Promises and Pitfalls of Open Federalism", in R. Simeon *et al.* (eds.), *Open Federalism: Interpretations, Significance.* Kingston: Institute of Intergovernmental Relations, Queen's University.

— 2006b. "Democratic Deliberation in a Multinational Federation", *Critical Review of International Social and Political Philosophy* 9.

— 2006c. "Social Justice in Overlapping Sharing Communities", in S. Choudhry, J.-F. Gaudreault-DesBiens, and L. Sossin (eds.), *Dilemmas of Solidarity: Rethinking Redistribution in the Canadian Federation.* Toronto: University of Toronto Press.

— 2007a. "Pouvoir fédéral de dépenser: gain majeur ou illusion?" *La Presse* (20 October).

— 2007b. "L'héritage de la Commission Tremblay: penser l'autonomie dans un cadre fédéral rigide", *Bulletin d'histoire politique* 16(1).

Noël, A., F. St-Hilaire, and S. Fortin. 2003. "Learning from the SUFA Experience", in S. Fortin, A. Noël, and F. St-Hilaire (eds.), *Forging the Canadian Social Union: SUFA and Beyond.* Montreal: Institute for Research on Public Policy.

Pelletier, B. 1992. "Le partage constitutionnel des pouvoirs, selon l'entente de Charlottetown" in *Référendum, 26 octobre 1992: Les objections de 20 spécialistes aux offres fédérales.* Montréal: Saint-Martin.

Petter, A. 1989. "Federalism and the Myth of the Federal Spending Power", *Canadian Bar Review* 68.

Quebec, Commission on Fiscal Imbalance. 2002a. *A New Division of Canada's Financial Resources: Report.* Quebec: The Commission. At: www.desequilibrefiscal.gouv.qc.ca/en/pdf/rapport_final_en.pdf.

— 2002b. *The "Federal Spending Power"*. Quebec: The Commission.

Québec, Secrétariat aux affaires intergouvernementales canadiennes. 2003. *Correspondence from January to February 1966 between the Prime Minister of Québec, Jean Lesage, and the Prime Minister of Canada, Lester B. Pearson, regarding the Fulton-Favreau formula* at 251-261, online: Québec's Positions on Constitutional and Intergovernmental Issues from 1936 to March 2001, www.saic.gouv.qc.ca/publications/Positions/Part3/Document8_en.pdf.

Rae, B. 2007. "Why Something Called the Spending Power Matters", *Globe and Mail* (1 October) A17.

Rocher, F. 1992. "La consécration du fédéralisme centralisateur", in *Référendum, 26 octobre 1992: Les objections de 20 spécialistes aux offres fédérales.* Montréal: Saint-Martin.

Russell, P.H. 1993. *Constitutional Odyssey: Can Canadians Become a Sovereign People?* 2d ed. Toronto: University of Toronto Press.

— 2006. "Fiscal Federalism: Not Resolvable by Constitutional Law", in S. Choudhry, J.-F. Gaudreault-DesBiens, and L. Sossin (eds.), *Dilemmas of Solidarity: Rethinking Redistribution in the Canadian Federation.* Toronto: University of Toronto Press.

Silver, A.I. 1997. *The French-Canadian Idea of Confederation, 1864-1900*, 2d ed. Toronto: University of Toronto Press.

Simeon, R. 2006. "Social Justice: Does Federalism Make a Difference?", in S. Choudhry, J.-F. Gaudreault-DesBiens, and L. Sossin (eds.), *Dilemmas of Solidarity: Rethinking Redistribution in the Canadian Federation.* Toronto: University of Toronto Press.

Smith, J. 2004. *Federalism.* Vancouver: UBC Press.

Taillon, P. 2007. "Les obstacles juridiques à une réforme du fédéralisme". Montréal: Institut de recherche sur le Québec. At: www.irq.qc.ca/PDF/IRQ-obstacles_juridiques_reforme_federalisme-PT-etude_complete_7.pdf.

Telford, H. 2003. "The Federal Spending Power in Canada: Nation-Building or Nation-Destroying?" *Publius: The Journal of Federalism* 33.

Tremblay, A. 2001. "Federal Spending Power", in A.-G. Gagnon and H. Segal (eds.), *The Canadian Social Union without Québec: 8 Critical Analyses.* Montreal: Institute for Research in Public Policy.

Trudeau, P.E. 1969. *Federal-Provincial Grants and the Spending Power of Parliament.* Ottawa: Government of Canada.

Turp, D. and A.-G. Gagnon. 1992. "Le *Rapport du consensus de 1992 sur la Constitution* ou l'extinction de l'Entente du lac Meech", in *Référendum, 26 octobre 1992: Les objections de 20 spécialistes aux offres fédérales.* Montréal: Saint-Martin.

Waite, P.B., ed. 1963. *The Confederation Debates in the Province of Canada/1865.* Toronto: McClelland & Stewart.

Warriner, W.E. and I. Peach, ed. 2007. *Canadian Social Policy Renewal, 1994–2000.* Halifax: Fernwood.

8

The Myth of the Federal Spending Power Revisited

Andrew Petter

L'auteur reprend en l'actualisant son analyse de 1989, selon laquelle le pouvoir fédéral de dépenser est inconstitutionnel et ne saurait être légitimé par aucune des justifications politiques en usage. Estimant que ce pouvoir pouvait être contesté au nom de la doctrine juridique, des valeurs constitutionnelles et de la realpolitik, il proposait alors un programme de réforme constitutionnelle en quatre points qui interdirait les transferts conditionnels entre gouvernements, supprimerait l'utilisation de toute forme de subventions conditionnelles par les gouvernements fédéral et provinciaux, établirait une formule constitutionnelle garantissant le maintien ou le relèvement des niveaux de péréquation existants, et assouplirait les procédures officielles de révision de la Constitution.

Toujours aussi préoccupé des risques que fait courir le pouvoir de dépenser aux valeurs fédérales et démocratiques, l'auteur estime que la doctrine juridique a été modifiée ces dernières années par une jurisprudence légitimant ce pouvoir. Il note aussi qu'on a amoindri durant cette même période les possibilités de réforme constitutionnelle en rigidifiant la Constitution. Suivant l'évolution des réalités politiques, conclut-il, ce blocage produira des variations à la hausse ou à la baisse du pouvoir de dépenser.

The life of the law has not been logic, it has been experience.
– Oliver Wendell Holmes

I am indebted to Marc-Antoine Adam for his encouragement, and to Maureen Maloney, Ally McKay, and Murray Rankin for their helpful comments and suggestions.

INTRODUCTION

Some 20 years ago, I published an essay arguing that the federal spending power – the power asserted by the federal government to spend funds on programs within provincial legislative jurisdiction – was inconsistent with Canadian constitutional doctrine and values, and that the political justifications offered in its support did not withstand close scrutiny (Petter 1989). At the same time, I maintained that the extent of governmental reliance upon the spending power precluded the courts from curtailing its use. I therefore urged a program of political reform going beyond the modest limitations on the spending power then being proposed in the Meech Lake Constitutional Accord (Library of Parliament 1987).

By challenging the orthodox view of constitutional scholars outside Quebec,[1] my essay caused a momentary stir in English Canada at the time it was published. I was therefore surprised to learn recently that this essay has been the subject of ongoing interest in Quebec, where constitutional scholars continue to question the legitimacy of the federal spending power, despite judicial statements supporting its use.

As an academic, I have grown accustomed to my ideas being ignored or, where they do gain notice, quickly forgotten. The fact that an essay I wrote two decades ago continues to command attention, therefore, is as flattering as it is unfamiliar. Thus while I initially resisted requests from the editors of this book to update my views on the federal spending power, I have succumbed to their overtures. When it comes to expressing my constitutional opinions, it turns out that, like Oscar Wilde, I can resist everything except temptation.

THE CASE AGAINST THE FEDERAL SPENDING POWER

The case I made against the federal spending power some twenty years ago was based on legal doctrine, constitutional values, and *realpolitik*. With respect to legal doctrine, I argued that the spending power was justified neither by the text of the Constitution nor by decisions of the courts. The language of the Constitution suggested to me that, for the purposes of division of powers analysis, legislation authorizing spending should be characterized no differently than legislation authorizing regulation. I could see "no basis in language or in logic for suggesting that when Parliament authorizes expenditures of funds with respect to some matter it acts any less 'in relation' to that matter than when it regulates with respect to the same matter" (ibid., 456). This view was supported by judicial authority. In the *Reference Re Employment and Social Insurance Act*,[2] the only case on the federal spending power that had been decided at the

---

[1]For a review of these scholars and their views, see Petter (1989, 454).

[2][1937] 1 D.L.R. 684 (P.C.), (*sub nom. Canada (A.G.) v. Ontario (A.G.)*) [1937] A.C. 326 [*Unemployment Insurance Reference*]. At the time, this was the only case

time by either the Supreme Court or the Privy Council, Lord Atkin held that money raised by means of taxation could not be disposed of by federal legislation where it was found that "in pith and substance the legislation invades civil rights within the Province.... To hold otherwise", he noted, "would afford the Dominion an easy passage into the provincial domain".[3]

Entering the arena of constitutional values, I maintained that the spending power threatened both the federal nature and the democratic character of the Canadian state. The spending power, I argued, not only allowed political responsibility to be shifted from one order of government to the other but, by causing responsibility to become interspersed, made it "virtually impossible for citizens to determine which order of government to hold accountable for policies that fail or, for that matter, for ones that succeed" (Petter 1989, 467). The result was to reduce the influence of ordinary citizens over the policy-making process and to increase the influence of governmental elites. Moreover, this consequence was not limited to areas in which the spending power was actually exercised. Once it was accepted that the federal government could spend where it pleased, electors and their representatives could attribute responsibility for almost any failure in provincial policy to an absence of federal support:

> In sum, reliance upon the spending power to overcome legislative limitations in a federal system of responsible government creates the worst of all possible worlds. It imposes upon citizens the costs and inconvenience of supporting two orders of government while denying them the benefits of local control. In addition, it creates a situation in which political power is so diffused that citizens possess less ability to influence and control government decision-making than they would even in a unitary state. (ibid., 467-468)

My evaluation of the federal spending power from the perspective of *realpolitik* cut in two directions. On the one hand, I argued that defenders of the power were wrong to suggest that it was required to counter regional disparities, compensate for provincial fiscal incapacities, or maintain progressive politics in Canada. The first two concerns could be better addressed by means of a robust equalization program involving unconditional fiscal transfers and federal relinquishment of the tax room used to fund programs falling within provincial jurisdiction. The third concern reflected mistaken assumptions that national politics are inherently more progressive than provincial politics, and that the spending power is an effective mechanism for realigning jurisdictional responsibilities. On the other hand, I argued that, after four decades of political development based on the spending power, it was beyond the capacity of the courts to invalidate the power itself or the structures of government to which it had given rise. Moreover, given the dynamic nature of social conditions and

---

concerning the federal spending power that had been decided by either the Supreme Court or the Privy Council. The decision of the Supreme Court of Canada in *YMHA Jewish Community Centre of Winnipeg Inc. v. Brown*, [1989] 1 S.C.R. 1532 [*YMHA*] was released after the article had been completed but prior to publication, and was referred to in a postscript.

[3] *Unemployment Insurance Reference*, ibid. at 687.

political circumstances in Canada, I maintained that, if the spending power were now to be taken away, it should be replaced with more flexible procedures for constitutional amendment.

Based on the above, I contended that the best hope for addressing the problems with the spending power lay in a program of constitutional reform consisting of four parts. The first would prohibit conditional transfers between governments, with the tax room required to fund existing transfers being given over to the government with legislative jurisdiction. The second would end the federal and provincial governments' use of other conditional grants, loans, and tax expenditures to promote policies falling outside their respective legislative jurisdictions. The third would spell out in the Constitution a formula guaranteeing that current levels of equalization, including those encased within existing conditional grant programs, would be maintained and enhanced. The fourth would make formal procedures for constitutional amendment more flexible. While I conceded that the chances of achieving such a program of reform were not great, I saw a glimmer of hope in the more limited proposals that had been agreed to at the time in the Meech Lake Accord.

THE FEDERAL SPENDING POWER REVISITED

My critique of the federal spending power was given a cool reception by constitutional scholars in English Canada; however, it received a warmer welcome from academics in Quebec where it has lately gained renewed interest. Indeed, Professor Alain Noël recently went so far as to urge implementation of the four proposals for reform that I proposed two decades ago.[4] This has encouraged me to revisit the issue with fresh eyes. Although I participated in discussions on the federal spending power in the late 1990s as the British Columbia minister responsible for the Social Union Framework Agreement negotiations, I have not broached the topic as a scholar since I penned my previous essay.

So how have two decades of wear and tear affected my thinking on the subject of the spending power? First, my concern about the danger it poses to federal and democratic values persists. This concern is not diminished by the fact that the federal government's actual use of the spending power has become less prevalent over the past 20 years. On the contrary, the huge cuts in federal transfers to the provinces in the 1990s, and the resulting intergovernmental recriminations and finger-pointing, strengthen my view that the spending power undermines provincial autonomy and political accountability. I find it hard to believe that Canadian governments would have dared to contemplate such massive cuts to health-care spending had political authority over health care, or clearly delineated components of the healthcare system, been confined to a single order of government. Moreover, if political authority had been so confined, I believe that any government proposing such cuts would have been

[4]In addition to Noël's chapter in this volume, see Noël (2008).

severely punished at the polls. As it happened, the federal and provincial governments were able to obscure and minimize their respective responsibilities for damaging the health-care system by attributing such damage to each other's policies.

My views on legal doctrine, on the other hand, have been modified by recent case authority. While I continue to believe that the spending power is not authorized by the constitutional text, there can be no doubt in my view that this power has now been authorized by the courts. A constitution is, as Charles Evans Hughes once remarked, "what the judges say it is",[5] and Canadian judges have gone out of their way in the past 20 years to say that the Canadian Constitution supports the federal spending power. Andrée Lajoie's chapter documents numerous recent cases in which the Supreme Court of Canada has voiced support for that power.[6] While Professor Lajoie valiantly tries to characterize these pronouncements as non-binding *obiter dicta,* this characterization is a bit too strained and formalistic for me. Indeed, the fact that judges of the Supreme Court have so freely and frequently offered their support for the federal spending power, when arguably not required to do so, to my mind only reinforces how convinced they are that the matter is not controversial. This opinion is bolstered by my continuing belief that, as a matter of *realpolitik*, the courts lack the ability to invalidate the spending power. As I put it in my original essay, "It is simply beyond the capacity of courts to undo forty [now sixty] years of political development" (Petter 1989, 473).

My views on other elements of the *realpolitik* of the federal spending power have also remained relatively constant. I continue to believe that, given a robust system of unconditional regional equalization payments, the spending power is not required to address regional disparities, to compensate for provincial fiscal incapacities, or to advance progressive politics in Canada. With respect to the issue of constitutional adaptation, I am more convinced than ever that we need a constitution that is easier to amend in order to meet changing social circumstances and political needs. It is fanciful to think that a document crafted to address the conditions of the 19th century can, without modification, meet those of the 21st century. Indeed, the extensive use of the federal spending power to overcome constitutional limitations over the past 60 years is evidence that it cannot.

Unfortunately, the Constitution has become even less flexible since my original essay was written. A number of developments have further restricted the possibilities for constitutional amendment: the political fallout from the Meech Lake and Charlottetown Accords (Library of Parliament 1987; Special Joint Committee on a Renewed Canada 1992); the emerging political expectations

---

[5]Hughes (1908, 139). Hughes went on to become Chief Justice of the United States Supreme Court.

[6]These cases include *YMHA*, *supra* note 2; *Reference Re Canada Assistance Plan,* [1991] 2 S.C.R. 525; *Eldridge v. British Columbia (A.G.)*, [1997] 3 S.C.R. 624; *Auton (Guardian ad litem of) v. British Columbia (A.G.)*, 2004 SCC 78, [2004] 3 S.C.R. 657; and *Chaoulli v. Quebec (A.G.)*, 2005 SCC 35, [2005] 1 S.C.R. 791.

(and, in some provinces, the legislative requirements)[7] that constitutional amendments be approved by referenda; and the enactment of federal legislation requiring constitutional amendments to command the support of provinces representing a majority of the population in five regions.[8] This degree of inflexibility is a serious deficiency that does not bode well for the future of the country at a time when we are experiencing major changes and political challenges both at home and abroad. Indeed, in my view, this deficiency surpasses those of the spending power.

PROSPECTS FOR CONSTITUTIONAL REFORM

What are the prospects for constitutional reform with respect to the spending power? There are two related facets to this question: one concerns the nature of the reform required; the other, the likelihood of it being adopted. A number of strategies are proposed by authors whose work appears in this volume. They range from simple invalidation of the federal spending power by the judiciary, as advocated by Andrée Lajoie, to resort to section 94 of the *Constitution Act, 1867*, as advocated by Marc-Antoine Adam (2009), to the adoption of my own constitutional reform proposals of 20 years ago, as advocated by Alain Noël.

Having already explained why I do not regard simple judicial invalidation as being either likely or feasible, I will turn to the innovative suggestion by Marc-Antoine Adam that an answer may lie in section 94.[9] This unused provision allows the federal Parliament to enact uniform laws in relation to property and civil rights in Ontario, Nova Scotia, and New Brunswick, though it provides that such laws do not take effect unless they are also enacted by the legislature of the affected province. Adam believes that section 94 should now be read as applying to all common law provinces, and he urges that it be embraced by the courts as a constitutional alternative to an unconstitutional federal spending power. To facilitate this, he suggests that the courts infer from section 94 (when read together with section 36 of the *Constitution Act, 1982*)[10] a

---

[7]See *Constitutional Referendum Act*, R.S.A. 2000, c. C-25; *Constitutional Amendment Approval Act*, R.S.B.C. 1996, c. 67.

[8]*An Act Respecting Constitutional Amendments*, S.C. 1996, c. 1, s. 1(1).

[9]*Constitution Act, 1867* (U.K.), 30 & 31 Vict., c. 3, s. 94 reprinted in R.S.C. 1985, App. II, No. 5. The text of s. 94 reads:

> Notwithstanding anything in this Act, the Parliament of Canada may make Provision for the Uniformity of all or any of the Laws relative to Property and Civil Rights in Ontario, Nova Scotia, and New Brunswick, and of the Procedure of all or any of the Courts in those Three Provinces, and from and after the passing of any Act in that Behalf the Power of the Parliament of Canada to make Laws in relation to any Matter comprised in any such Act shall, notwithstanding anything in this Act, be unrestricted; but any Act of the Parliament of Canada making Provision for such Uniformity shall not have effect in any Province unless and until it is adopted and enacted as Law by the Legislature thereof.

[10]*Constitution Act, 1982*, s. 36, being Schedule B to the *Canada Act 1982* (U.K.), 1982, c. 11. The text of s. 36 reads:

right of compensation for those provinces that do not participate in federal programs initiated under this provision. He further suggests that the courts allow participating provinces to back out of such federal programs should they later wish to do so.

This is all very creative, but no more likely in my view to win judicial favour than simple invalidation of the federal spending power. In addition to asking courts to ignore their jurisprudence of the past 20 years, Adam asks them to bring into play a provision of the Constitution that has never been used, and to transform it in three significant ways. This would be more an act of political invention than constitutional interpretation, and it is surely beyond the creative capacities even of judges schooled in the inventive age of the Charter. Moreover, even if section 94 could be resurrected and reshaped in this way, the section 94 cure could be worse than the spending power disease. A revitalized section 94, with full rights of compensation for provinces that did not participate in federal legislative schemes, could lead to a dangerous and destabilizing degree of asymmetry in federal arrangements, with Parliament exercising varying degrees of authority over social policy in different provinces. Such asymmetrical responsibilities could prove more destructive of political accountability than the diffusion of responsibilities that occurs with the federal spending power, as federal politicians from non-participating provinces set policies for participating provinces whose voters have no means of holding those politicians accountable (except by urging provincial governments to back out of such schemes at huge cost).

This brings me to my proposals for constitutional reform, which Alain Noël has so kindly revived. Do they appeal to me today as they did when I first put them forward? In the abstract, they do. The vision of a flexible federal constitution with clear spheres of federal and political responsibility, combined with an equalization program that guarantees provinces the fiscal capacity to provide their residents with an adequate level of social services, attracts me as much now as it did then. But life, unfortunately, does not play itself out in the abstract. While I continue to favour a constitution with these attributes, the extent of our current constitutional rigidity makes this goal increasingly unattainable. Ironically, our growing need for a more flexible Constitution has become the reason that we are unlikely to get one.

---

(1) Without altering the legislative authority of Parliament or of the provincial legislatures, or the rights of any of them with respect to the exercise of their legislative authority, Parliament and the legislatures, together with the government of Canada and the provincial governments, are committed to

(a) promoting equal opportunities for the well-being of Canadians;

(b) furthering economic development to reduce disparity in opportunities; and

(c) providing essential public services of reasonable quality to all Canadians.

(2) Parliament and the government of Canada are committed to the principle of making equalization payments to ensure that provincial governments have sufficient revenues to provide reasonably comparable levels of public services at reasonably comparable levels of taxation.

CONCLUSION

In light of current conditions, I fear that we will be stuck with the status quo for the foreseeable future. The Constitution will remain in a state of stasis and the exercise of the spending power will expand and contract over time, based on political exigencies. I deeply lament this fact. I believe that resort to the federal spending power is a poor alternative to a flexible Constitution that can facilitate realignments of regulatory as well as fiscal powers in order to better address the needs of Canadians. It should realistically be within our capacity to entertain new systems and configurations of governance, including proposals to expand federal powers where this reflects Canadian values and promotes better policy outcomes. For example, given Canadians' common commitment to medicare, the international market pressures being placed on provincial health-care systems, and the nexus between health-care costs and federal policies on patent medicines, it should be possible for Canadians to contemplate shifting legislative responsibilities for some or all health-care services to the federal Parliament. It should similarly be possible to contemplate giving Parliament constitutional authority to create a comprehensive income-based tuition system for post-secondary education.[11] A flexible Constitution that offered Canadians realistic opportunities to make jurisdictional changes such as these, where they commanded substantial public support, would provide a more effective and accountable instrument for policy-making and nation-building in the 21st century.

Unfortunately, lamentation does not qualify as a practical response. I wish that it did, given our current constitutional rigidity, for I have difficulty seeing how Canada could function without a federal spending power. Limitations, to be sure, can be placed on that power from time to time by way of inter-governmental agreement, as was done with the Social Union Framework Agreement,[12] or by way of federal legislation, as the government of Prime Minister Harper has proposed. However, without an alternative means of constitutional adaptation, such limitations will invariably be transitory and will inevitably succumb to changing societal pressures and fresh public demands. Thus, while some of us may continue to regard the federal spending power as a constitutional myth, we would do well to remember that it is a myth perpetuated by a political reality – the reality that the only thing worse than a Constitution that can be compromised is a Constitution that cannot be changed.

---

[11]Given the degree of labour mobility within Canada, such a plan, whether provided in the form of deferred tuition or loan repayments, would be delivered most efficiently and effectively by means of national administration linked to the federal tax system.

[12]*Framework to Improve the Social Union for Canadians: An Agreement between the Government of Canada and the Governments of the Provinces and Territories*, 4 February [SUFA].

REFERENCES

Adam, M.-A. 2009. "Fiscal Federalism and the Future of Canada: Can Section 94 of the *Constitution Act, 1867* be an Alternative to the Spending Power?" in J.R. Allan, T.J. Courchene, and C. Leuprecht (eds.), *Transitions: Fiscal and Political Federalism in an Era of Change.* Kingston: Institute of Intergovernmental Relations, Queen's University.

Hughes, C.E. 1908. *Addresses and Papers of Charles Evans Hughes: Governor of New York 1906-1908.* New York: Knickerbocker.

Library of Parliament, Research Branch, Law and Government Division. 1987. *The 1987 Constitutional Accord.* Ottawa: Minister of Supply and Services Canada [Meech Lake Accord].

Noël, A. 2008. "Éliminer le pouvoir de dépenser", *Policy Options* (March) 80.

Petter, A. 1989. "Federalism and the Myth of the Federal Spending Power", *Canadian Bar Review* 68 (September), 448-479.

Special Joint Committee on a Renewed Canada. 1992. *Consensus Report on the Constitution.* Charlottetown [Charlottetown Accord].

9

Section 36(1), New Governance Theory, and the Spending Power

Hoi Kong

Examinant deux enjeux de longue date de la théorie constitutionnelle, à savoir l'indétermination juridique et la compétence institutionnelle, l'auteur circonscrit l'actuel débat canadien sur le pouvoir fédéral de dépenser, justifie la surveillance judiciaire et soutient que la section 36(1) offre le cadre constitutionnel le plus valable pour évaluer l'exercice controversé du pouvoir de dépenser. Puisant dans la recherche sur la théorie du minimalisme judiciaire et de la nouvelle gouvernance, il propose une règle doctrinale qui crée un mince consensus sur la signification de la section 36(1) tout en tenant compte des limites institutionnelles de la magistrature. Pour appliquer cette règle, il préconise la mise sur pied d'un organisme administratif mixte, puis défend cette proposition face aux objections qu'elle pourrait susciter.

INTRODUCTION

Constitutional theorists have long struggled with two questions.[1] The first concerns the problem of legal indeterminacy: how should courts resolve cases in the face of reasonable disagreement about what the law requires? The second raises the issue of limited judicial competence: how should courts respond to cases that strain their institutional capacities? These questions do not, of course, arise only in debates about constitutional theory. They are often pertinent to disputes about the constitutionality of specific government action, and in Canada

---

This chapter substantially revises a previously published article, "The Spending Power, Constitutional Interpretation and Legal Pragmatism" (2008) *Queen's Law Journal* 34. In the process of revision, I greatly benefited from the challenging questions posed at a February 2009 McGill University Faculty of Law seminar by Frédéric Bachand, François Crépeau, Evan Fox-Decent, Daniel Jutras, Nicholas Kasirer, Robert Leckey, René Provost, Shauna Van Praagh, and Lionel Smith. I also thank Hugo Choquette for excellent research assistance.

[1]For an overview of these debates, see Dorf (2003). Professor Dorf labels cases that raise these two kinds of questions, respectively, "hard cases" and "big cases".

they have particular force in debates about the federal spending power. Authors disagree about the constitutionality of some exercises of the federal spending power, and the complexity of fiscal federalism poses institutional challenges for courts that would oversee the power.

In this chapter, I address the theoretical debates about legal indeterminacy and institutional competence by proposing a doctrinal rule, grounded in section 36(1) of the *Constitution Act, 1982*,[2] that if adopted would enable the judiciary to effectively oversee controversial exercises of the spending power. The argument proceeds in three sections. In the first section, I define the contours of the contemporary Canadian debate over the spending power, justify judicial oversight of the spending power, and argue that section 36(1) is the appropriate locus of constitutional authority for some controversial exercises of the spending power. In the second section, I offer an interpretation of section 36(1) that draws upon the literature on judicial minimalism and responds to critiques of that literature. Finally, I propose a doctrinal rule that draws on New Governance theory, argue for that theory's application to the controversies that surround the spending power, and defend my proposal against a range of objections.

THE SPENDING POWER AND CONSTITUTIONAL AUTHORIZATION

In Canada, federal exercises of the spending power are controversial when they have coercive effects and when those effects lack clear constitutional authorization. In the first subsection, I will assess what coercion means in the federalism context and provide an overview of how the spending power can be exercised coercively. I argue that, unlike some other instances of coercion in Canadian federalism, current doctrine and theory do not provide clear authorization for coercive exercises of the spending power.

Coercion, the Spending Power, and Constitutional Authorization

Coercion can be defined generally as activity that prevents an agent from acting autonomously, where infringements on autonomy are measured against some normative standard.[3] Understanding what coercion means in the federalism

---

[2]*Constitution Act, 1982*, s.36(1), being schedule B to the *Canada Act 1982* (U.K.), 1982, c. 11. Section 36(1) states:

> Without altering the legislative authority of Parliament or of the provincial legislatures, or the rights of any of them with respect to the exercise of their legislative authority, Parliament and the legislatures, together with the government of Canada and the provincial governments, are committed to (a) promoting equal opportunities for the well-being of Canadians; (b) furthering economic development to reduce disparity in opportunities; and (c) providing essential public services of reasonable quality to all Canadians.

[3]See the summary of the philosophical literature on coercion in Berman (2001, 13-19). I advance in this chapter a conception of legal coercion that emphasizes the degree

context requires an initial inquiry into what autonomy means in that context. The constitutional allocation of legislative responsibilities in a federation constitutes individuals as federal and provincial citizens, and provides forums in which they can exercise their democratic agency.[4] One way in which citizens of a federal state exercise this form of agency is by electing and monitoring legislatures, the scope of whose authority has been defined by the constitution.[5] When a legislative body in a federation is prevented from acting freely within the scope of its constitutional authority, the autonomy of citizens who exercise their democratic agency through that legislature is compromised. The allocation of legislative authority in the constitution sets a baseline against which to measure infringements on the autonomy of citizens *qua* citizens of a federal state. In the federalism context, coercion occurs when (a) a government is compelled to act in a way in which it is constitutionally authorized to refuse to act, or (b) it is prevented from acting in a way in which it is otherwise constitutionally authorized to act. Exercises of the spending power can result in either kind of coercion.

An exercise of the spending power is coercive if a recipient (typically provincial) government has no choice but to accept conditions attached to a funding grant (from, typically, the federal government).[6] Under these circumstances, the recipient government needs the resources to fulfill its constitutionally authorized role, and the political cost of leaving that role unfulfilled is prohibitive.[7] The recipient government is, as a result, *forced to act* in a way in which it has constitutionally valid reasons for refusing to act.

There is another way that a government can act coercively through its taxing and spending power. The federal government, because of its access to more diverse sources of tax revenues and its less extensive spheres of constitutional authority, or its capacity to resist pressure from competitor

---

and quality of the pressure brought to bear upon the coerced party. To be coercive, the pressure exerted by law must be sufficiently intense to function as a sufficient reason for the coerced party to act (see Lamond 2000, 52). In addition, activity is only coercive if it places a burden of justification on the agent who exerts this kind of pressure. Such a burden arises only against a background of assumptions about when law can legitimately exert pressure sufficient to constitute a reason for acting (see Edmundson 1995, 99).

[4]For this conception of federal citizenship, see Levy (2007) and Weinstock (2001).

[5]For this understanding of citizen oversight within a federation, see LaPierre (1985, 635).

[6]That provinces are authorized to spend outside of their jurisdictions is controversial, under the terms of the argument here presented, only if that authorization purports to extend to exercises of the spending power that amount to coercion. For judicial authorization of extra-territorial spending by provinces, see *Dunbar v. Saskatchewan (A.G.)* (1985), 11 D.L.R. (4th) 374 (Sask. Q.B.). Such spending occurred in the decades following Confederation when Quebec empowered school boards to directly fund French language schools in Ontario (see Cook 1969, 60).

[7]This is the concern about coercion articulated by the United States Supreme Court in *Dole v. South Dakota*, 483 U.S. 203 (1987). See also Gaudreault-DesBiens (2006 and 2004).

jurisdictions, or both, can occupy tax room far in excess of what is required to fulfill its constitutionally authorized role within the federation. In so doing, the federal government can deprive provincial governments of resources necessary to fulfill their constitutionally authorized roles.[8] Under these conditions, a provincial government is *prevented from acting* in ways in which it is constitutionally authorized to act.[9]

With this conception of coercion and these examples of it in view, we can now turn our attention to the significance of coercion in the context of federalism, more generally. Under current constitutional doctrine, Parliament is not absolutely proscribed from legislating in areas that fall within provincial jurisdiction. Double aspect doctrine presupposes the possibility of jurisdictional overlap: a single area of social and economic life can be validly regulated by both the federal and provincial legislatures.[10] Paramountcy doctrine regulates cases of conflict in these areas of overlap, and judicial application of the doctrine renders provincial legislation inoperative to the extent of the conflict:[11] the province is in effect commanded not to achieve legislative objectives that the division of powers authorizes it to pursue.[12] In such a case, paramountcy doctrine authorizes the federal government to act coercively.[13]

---

[8]This concern is articulated in Quebec, Commission on Fiscal Imbalance (2002, 16). The concern about the fiscal capacity of provinces is not new. It arose as early as the 1880s when Quebec requested more federal transfers (see Cook 1969, 28), and it came to the fore of public consciousness in the post-war period when the provinces entered into tax rental agreements with the federal government (La Forest 1967, 27-35).

[9]These are not the only two possible examples of coercion. There is a range of means by which governments can influence one another's legislative and governance priorities. For example, the federal government can direct spending at individuals or organizations, provincial tax rates can have extra-territorial effects, and the federal government can own property that benefits from property tax exemptions and can thereby impact municipal and provincial budgets and, ultimately, governing priorities. For the range of means by which governments can deploy legislation and resources in a manner that influences other governments, see Roderick A. Macdonald, this volume. For a general catalogue of ways in which federal and provincial legislation can interact, see Brisson and Morel (1997). This chapter does not aim to catalogue all possible instances of mutual influence, but rather to isolate instances that are clearly coercive. The line between coercion and influence is a matter of degree, and if any means of fiscal influence other than those in the main text cross the line, they too are constitutionally suspect.

[10]For canonical statements of the doctrine, see *Hodge v. R.* (1883), 9 A.C. 117 (P.C.); *Multiple Access v. McCutcheon,* [1982] 2 S.C.R. 161.

[11]For a recent statement of these doctrines, see *Canadian Western Bank v. Alberta,* 2007 SCC 22, [2007] 2 S.C.R. 3 [*Canadian Western*]. Of course, conflict rules in a federation need not exclusively favour the federal order of government. See for instance the provincial paramountcy rule in s.94A. Moreover, federal paramountcy rules in Canada are entirely judicially generated. Unlike in the United States and Australia, there is no express supremacy clause in the Canadian Constitution. On this point, see Hogg (2007 s.16.2, fn. 10, 11).

[12]A province can choose to legislate even if it recognizes that its legislation will be rendered inoperable by federal law. There may be political advantages in signalling to the provincial electorate that such legislation is a political priority. Paramountcy doctrine

By contrast, the federal government is constitutionally prohibited from regulating in areas of provincial jurisdiction in which it does not also have jurisdiction. In addition, a violation of the division of powers occurs when the federal government has an arguable case that it does also have jurisdiction, but intrinsic and extrinsic evidence show that it intends to regulate in a subject-matter area that falls within provincial jurisdiction.[14] In both cases, the federal government is acting ultra vires. Parliament lacks constitutional authority to legislate and, as a consequence, paramountcy doctrine cannot authorize the federal government effectively to command provincial legislatures to refrain from achieving their legislative objectives. The contrast between paramountcy cases and cases where the federal government acts ultra vires reveals that in the federalism context, coercion is not objectionable in itself; rather, only coercion that lacks constitutional authorization is objectionable.

Current theories do not provide convincing accounts of when coercive exercises of the spending power are or are not authorized. Much of the contemporary debate about the spending power has focused on the "gift theory", and analysis of that debate enables us to see that no existing theory provides a convincing account for when and whether coercive spending is authorized by the Constitution. Professor Peter Hogg is the contemporary scholar most closely associated with the gift theory (see, e.g., Hogg 2007, s.6.8(a)). He argues that because spending is a private act of government, and thus distinct from legislating, federalism considerations cannot limit federal exercises of the spending power. He argues further that a judicial and academic consensus supports his position (ibid.).

Professor Andrée Lajoie challenges the existence of any such consensus: she argues that the Supreme Court of Canada has not made an authoritative

---

does not prevent provinces from passing such legislation, nor does it render the legislation invalid. Yet if there is a conflict, paramountcy doctrine has the effect of precluding a provincial legislature from achieving legislative objectives that are within that province's constitutional authority.

[13]Application of interjurisdictional immunity doctrine has a similar effect on a province, but there is an important distinction to be drawn between the doctrines. Under interjurisdictional immunity doctrine, a federal undertaking or an area of federal jurisdiction is constitutionally immunized from provincial legislation, but not because of any positive action by the federal government. In such a case, it is difficult to conceive of the federal government as acting coercively. For a recent restatement and narrowing of interjurisdictional immunity doctrine, see *Canadian Western*, *supra* note 11; *British Columbia (A.G.) v. Lafarge Canada Inc.*, 2007 SCC 23, [2007] 2 S.C.R. 86.

[14]For both of these possibilities and a paradigmatic application of pith and substance doctrine, see *R. v. Morgentaler*, [1988] 1 S.C.R. 30 [*Morgentaler*]. For a scholarly articulation of colourability doctrine, which is underexplored in *Morgentaler*, see Abel (1969, 494). I am concerned in the main text with legislative acts, rather than specific provisions of such acts. Ancillary doctrine does permit the federal government to regulate in provincial jurisdiction if a legislative provision that so regulates is sufficiently integrated within an otherwise valid federal regulatory scheme and the intrusion satisfies a means-ends test (see *General Motors of Canada Ltd. v. City National Leasing*, [1989] 1 S.C.R. 641 at 666-67 [*General Motors*]).

decision about the constitutionality of conditional grants, which, from the perspective of one concerned about the impact of the spending power on the provinces, are particularly controversial when they amount to coercive commands.[15] She argues that, at the time of her writing, the only judicial support for such grants was expressed in *obiter dicta* of Supreme Court decisions, not in *ratio decidendi*. She notes further that there is a diversity of academic opinion on the constitutionality of the spending power (see Lajoie 2006, 158-159).

Although the Court has affirmed the constitutionality of conditional exercises of the spending power in several cases,[16] it has not made a clear ruling about the constitutionality of such an exercise in a case where that was an issue presented.[17] The absence of a clear doctrinal statement provides a strong but not decisive response to the gift theory: the case law does not authoritatively resolve the issue of whether conditional exercises of the spending power are constitutional. The fact that the Supreme Court has not authoritatively held that conditional exercises of the spending power are unconstitutional is similarly not a decisive argument against recognizing such a power.[18] This fact merely points to uncertainty in the case law.

Moreover, as others have noted, the analogy between the federal government and a private actor upon which the gift theory depends ignores the political costs of permitting the federal government to act with the impunity of a private actor (Gaudreault-DesBiens 2006, 190-192). Allowing the federal government, without limits, effectively to regulate in areas of provincial jurisdiction by attaching conditions on spending undermines democratic values. It confuses lines of authority, as even the best informed citizens will not be able

---

[15]See *supra* notes 8, 9, and accompanying text for a discussion of why conditional grants are controversial.

[16]The Supreme Court of Canada has in several cases reasoned that conditional federal spending is constitutional. See *YMWA Jewish Community Centre v. Brown*, [1989] 1 S.C.R. 1532 at 1549; *Reference Re Canada Assistance Plan*, [1991] 2 S.C.R. 525; *Eldridge v. British Columbia*, [1997] 3 S.C.R. 624 at para. 24; *Auton (Guardian ad litem of) v. British Columbia (A.G.)*, [2004] 3 S.C.R. 657 at App. B.

[17]*Confédération des syndicats nationaux v. Canada (Attorney General)*, 2008 SCC 68 at paras. 39, 49, 95.

[18]*Reference Re Employment and Social Insurance Act (Can.)*, [1937] 1 D.L.R. 684 (P.C.), (*sub nom. Canada (A.G.) v. Ontario (A.G.)*) [1937] A.C. 326 [*Unemployment Insurance Reference*] stands for the proposition that exercises of the federal spending power can be held to be ultra vires if in their purpose they invade areas of exclusive provincial jurisdiction. (See also *Liquidators of Maritime Bank v. Receiver General of New Brunswick,* [1892] A.C. 437. The arguments against *Unemployment Insurance* being considered authoritative apply a fortiori to it.) But there are problems with appealing to this case as valid contemporary authority. The doctrinal and policy world in which it was decided differs greatly from our own. To the extent that *Unemployment Insurance* is necessarily tied to the watertight compartments theory of federalism, it has been overtaken by developments in cognate areas of doctrine and intergovernmental practice. In my view, proponents and opponents of the gift theory disagree about the relative weight of *Unemployment Insurance* and the Court's statements about conditional spending in the cases cited in *supra* note 16.

to determine who is ultimately responsible for governmental action, and it permits the federal government to distort the legislative priorities of provincial governments (Petter 1989, 467-468). Ultimately, the attempt to ground coercive exercises of the spending power in the federal government's power to make decisions as a private actor fails, because the costs of such an extension of that power are too high to be imposed without clear constitutional authorization.

The Case for Judicial Oversight of the Spending Power

Before setting out the affirmative case for judicial oversight of the spending power under section 36(1), I will justify such oversight, and rule out alternative approaches to authorizing and regulating the spending power. Let us consider first the argument for judicial oversight. A critic of such oversight might argue that regulation of the spending power should be left exclusively to the political branches. Professor Sujit Choudhry has argued that the federal and provincial governments have tactically decided not to seek from the courts clear guidelines about when the federal government is authorized to spend in areas of provincial jurisdiction (Choudhry 2000, fn. 17). Moreover, when the Supreme Court of Canada was recently presented with a question about the constitutionality of conditional exercises of the spending power, it declined to answer, deciding the case on other grounds.[19] One might argue that this apparent reticence on the part of political actors to seek guidance, and courts to provide it, indicate that there are good reasons to avoid judicial oversight of the spending power. After all, constitutional interpretation does not lie in the exclusive purview of the judiciary,[20] and perhaps in the context of the spending power, there are good reasons for the judiciary to be excluded from offering an opinion about the constitutionality of controversial exercises of the spending power.

A response to this argument can begin by noting that judicial review of federalism disputes is an established part of our constitutional tradition. Judicial review did not always enjoy this place in Canadian federalism. Until the mid-1880s, it was an open question whether courts would engage in judicial review of federalism issues. Opponents of judicial review argued that the federal government could, through exercise of its power of disallowance, adequately regulate the relations between the orders of government (Saywell 2002, c.1). The courts rejected that argument, and the power of disallowance has long fallen into desuetude (Vipond 1991, 54-59, 116-131). Our constitutional tradition has firmly entrenched judicial oversight of federalism and has rejected a constitutionally enshrined form of regulating federalism disputes, which denies a role for judicial review.

---

[19] *Confédération des syndicats nationaux v. Canada (Attorney General)*, 2008 SCC 68.

[20] The other branches of government are generally assumed to engage in constitutional interpretation when they undertake constitutionally significant action. See on this point, Fox-Decent (2007).

One might argue that whatever our constitutional traditions, there are good reasons for courts to refrain from engaging in federalism review, either in general or in the particular context of disputes over the spending power. Consider first the argument that courts should in general avoid judicial review of federalism disputes. Professor Paul Weiler has presented perhaps the strongest Canadian version of this argument.[21] According to Weiler, the balance of power between the federal and provincial governments should be determined by bargaining between the orders of governments. To my knowledge, no one has offered a convincing response to Professor Katherine Swinton's criticism of Weiler's argument. Absent such a counter-argument, Swinton's claim that there are no political institutions in Canada capable of overcoming imbalances in power between the federal and provincial governments remains decisive. As Swinton notes, without such institutions, Weiler's arguments in favour of political bargaining are unconvincing because they would permit the federal government to dictate its terms to the provinces and thereby undercut the federal principle, which underwrites the constitutional division of powers.[22] Weiler's arguments would enable the federal government to achieve the result forbidden by the constitutional convention against exercises of the power of disallowance.

Even if general arguments against judicial review of federalism fail, perhaps there are good reasons to argue against judicial review in the specific context of the spending power. There may be good reasons to favour non-judicial constitutional interpretations in a variety of contexts.[23] Indeed, courts have limited institutional competence to adjudicate spending power disputes, given the regulatory complexity of fiscal federalism,[24] and any doctrinal rule will have to account for that limited competence. Nonetheless, where constitutional interests are at stake, the value of legality requires that resolutions of federalism

---

[21]Weiler (1973). In the United States, this argument is most closely associated with process theories of federalism (see, e.g., Wechsler 1959; and Choper 1980).

[22]Swinton (1990). By contrast, U.S. proponents of process theories of federalism claim that the states have sufficient influence within federal institutions to counterbalance any tendencies toward federal dominance (Wechsler 1959; and Choper 1980). These American theories have come under criticism on a variety of grounds. For a summary of those criticisms, see Prakash and Yoo (2001). For an articulation of the federal principle, and the claim that the expansive powers granted to the federal government in the *Constitution Act, 1867* undercut it, see Wheare (1963). Wheare's interpretation of the provisions of the *Constitution Act, 1867* focuses on the text but pays insufficient attention to constitutional history and doctrinal developments. Historians have noted that some provincial delegations to the constitutional convention sought to enshrine in the *Constitution Act, 1867* express protections for provincial interests, which counter-balanced the document's centralizing provisions (see Moore 1998; and Vipond 1989). In addition, the principle of "mutual modification", which is an expression of the federal principle, has been an organizing constitutional principle for courts since the *Parsons* case was decided (*Citizens Insurance Co. of Canada v. Parsons* (1881), 7 App. Cas. 96).

[23]There is an extensive literature that argues for the primacy of non-judicial constitutional interpretation. For a recent American contribution, see Kramer (2004); for a Canadian summary of the literature and contribution to it, see Kelly (2005).

[24]For a recent assertion of this claim, see Macdonald (this volume).

disputes appeal to reasons framed in terms of constitutional law and principle.[25] One problem of leaving constitutional issues exclusively to the political branches is that they are under no obligation to articulate constitutional, as opposed to purely political, reasons for their actions.[26] By contrast, courts deciding controversial cases involving constitutional provisions give constitutional reasons for their decisions.[27] Any proponent of non-judicial resolutions of spending power disputes bears the burden of showing that, under current conditions, the political branches are in a better institutional position

---

[25]See below p. 202.

[26]By "purely political reasoning", I intend reasoning that does not engage constitutional values. Although admittedly vague, this formulation excludes reasons that are not public-regarding and aim only at partisan political advantage; one essential attribute of constitutional reasoning is that it is public-regarding. For the distinction between public-regarding reasons and other forms of reasoning, see Elster (1997). For the contrast between political and judicial decision-making drawn in the text and for the claim that political decision-makers are not required to offer constitutionally relevant reasons for their actions, see Eisgruber (2001, 59-62); and for a claim that courts are "exemplars of public reason", see Rawls (1996, chapter 6, section 6). Dean Larry Kramer has recently argued that the political branches do give reasons, and typically give better reasons that are unconstrained by the requirements of legal convention, through institutions such as senate committees (Kramer 2004). Of course, the importance of committees varies by jurisdiction. In Canada, legislative committees can have relatively little influence on the executive-dominated legislative process (see Freeman and Forcese 2005). Moreover, it is unclear whether deliberation sufficient to safeguard important constitutional interests occurs when interests of greater salience to constituents and interest groups are at stake in a piece of legislation, see Lyons (2005). We presume that the political branches do engage in constitutional reasoning (see *infra* note 42; for a cognate point about the reasoning of juries, see Raz (2009, 236, fn. 10), but where constitutionally controversial action is at issue, we require express constitutional justifications and assessments. Under current constitutional conditions, in Canada, political actors do not consistently provide such reasons. Courts do.

[27]This is a statement about what is generally expected of courts within constitutional democracies that have judicial review. It represents a convention, shared among legal officials, and this convention is part of the criteria for the validity of legal rules within such democracies. See on this point, Himma (2003, 186, 188-189). Professor Himma frames the rule of recognition for constitutional democracies in this way: "A duly enacted norm is legally valid if and only if it conforms to what the Supreme Court takes to be the morally best interpretation of the substantive protections of the Constitution." I should introduce two caveats here. It is true that the Supreme Court often dismisses cases, typically as-of-right criminal appeals, from the bench. But the Court in such cases refers to reasons of the courts below; it does not issue the judgment as ukase. In addition, it is true that courts in some civil law jurisdictions offer terse reasons. But those courts do offer some reasons and the assumption is that these are good reasons, even if from the perspective of common law reasoning, they are insufficiently robust. Moreover, in the civilian tradition judicial reasoning is supplemented by doctrinal writing. Both have a recognized place in the legal order and both give reasoned content to the law. For an influential discussion of the role of judicial and academic writing in one civilian jurisdiction see Planiol (1904, 959).

than courts to arbitrate disputes over the spending power and to offer constitutional reasons in support of their resolutions.

No participant in current debates over the spending power has discharged that burden. Recurring charges of political opportunism levied against government actors suggest that these actors are not perceived to be providing good-faith constitutional reasons for their actions.[28] Even if these charges mischaracterize the motivations of political actors, it remains the case that in federalism disputes, the judiciary is the branch most likely to be viewed as an impartial arbiter and as the authoritative source of public-regarding, constitutional reasons.[29] These perceptions provide strong reasons for courts to be involved in the regulation of the spending power, even if their institutional capacity to oversee controversial exercises of the spending power is limited.

This chapter proposes a rule that places the main burden of resolving issues that lie beyond the institutional competence of courts on political actors, and imposes a duty on those actors to generate constitutional reasons for their actions. The role of the judiciary, in this proposal, is to articulate the rule that sets these conditions, and once the political branches have agreed to assume the main burden of regulation, to evaluate their reasons against a deferential constitutional standard.[30] With such a rule, the judiciary would acknowledge its limited institutional competence, while preserving its role as ultimate constitutional arbiter and ensuring that constitutional reasons are enunciated to justify constitutionally controversial practices. Before turning to that rule, let us consider the question of where to locate constitutional authorization for controversial exercises of the spending power.

---

[28]For a standard instance of such recrimination, see the recent comments by Pauline Marois at www.radio-canada.ca/nouvelles/Politique/2009/06/13/002-PQ-Marois-souverainete.shtml.

[29]Some authors have challenged the Court's role as an impartial arbiter in the federalism disputes. For an overview of the debates, see Greschner (2000). These criticisms share or respond to a widely accepted assumption that courts are *expected to act* impartially. One does not attack the metaphor of courts as umpires unless significant numbers of people believe the metaphor to be apt. By contrast, this background assumption finds no place in the sometimes intemperate criticisms that are levelled against the motivations of the political branches. There is, for instance, no debate over whether the metaphor of an umpire accurately captures the federalism decision-making of Parliament.

[30]As we shall see below, the advantage of the judiciary, relative to the political branches, lies in its unique obligation to engage in constitutional reason-giving. Of course, the political branches have the *option* of offering such reasons, but they are not obliged to do so and because in federalism disputes, the political branches are themselves involved in the relevant disputes, the judiciary is in a better place to discharge the settlement function of law. On the settlement function of courts in federalism disputes, see Stone (2008, 27-30). On the capacity of courts to perform the settlement function of courts, in constitutional disputes generally, see Alexander and Schauer (1997).

Ruling Out Alternatives to Section 36(1)

In the previous section, we cleared away several objections to judicial oversight of the spending power, and we can now consider what source of constitutional law is the relevant object of judicial interpretation. Some authors argue that the division-of-powers provisions of the *Constitution Act, 1867*[31] and a particular set of judicial interpretations of those provisions are the correct source of constitutional authority. Professor Andrée Lajoie, the most prominent proponent of this position, argues that if under current constitutional doctrine the federal government does not have section 91 jurisdiction to legislate in an area, it cannot spend in that area. An initial problem with this position, as we have noted above, is that the Supreme Court has not issued a clear ruling against federal spending – including conditional spending – in areas of provincial jurisdiction. The Supreme Court has acknowledged the validity of such spending in several cases, and authors have noted that it seems strained to insist upon a distinction between *obiter dicta* and *ratio decidendi* to support the claim that such spending is constitutionally prohibited (see, e.g., Andrew Petter, this volume). It is unclear why one should disregard the Court's decision to characterize a practice as constitutional particularly since implicit in this decision is a choice not to remain silent on the issue or not to declare that practice unconstitutional. Finally, against this backdrop of decisions affirmatively recognizing the constitutionality of the spending power, the Court recently decided not to speak to the constitutionality of the federal spending power in areas of provincial jurisdiction, when that was one of the constitutional questions posed.[32]

Let us accept for the sake of argument the claim that according to the current division of powers doctrine, most instances of federal spending in areas of provincial jurisdiction are unconstitutional because they are unauthorized by the division of powers. Such a claim cannot be dispositive of a disagreement in constitutional scholarship. Constitutional scholarship does not primarily entail simple descriptions of current constitutional doctrine. Constitutional law is a normative endeavour, and constitutional law scholarship, properly understood, involves evaluations and prescriptions.[33] For instance, Choudhry has argued that even if Privy Council cases excluded Parliament from legislating in areas of social policy and those cases continued to be valid constitutional authority, that restriction should be eliminated. The consequent expansion of federal jurisdiction, he argues, would be consistent with contemporary federalism doctrine.[34] One might respond to Choudhry's arguments by challenging the

---

[31]*Constitution Act, 1867* (U.K.), 30 & 31 Vict., c. 3, reprinted in R.S.C. 1985, App. II, No. 5.

[32]*Confédération des syndicats nationaux v. Canada, supra* note 19.

[33]For the normative quality of constitutional scholarship, see e.g., Friedman (2005, 257). For the general claim that constitutional law is a normative practice, see Fallon (2007-08).

[34]Choudhry has articulated a rationale, grounded in the provincial inability step of the *Crown Zellerbach* test (see *Crown Zellerbach*, [1988] 1 S.C.R. 401), that would sustain federal legislation over social policy, and might therefore provide support for

wisdom of such an expansion of federal powers, or one might criticize current trends in federalism doctrine.[35] Such arguments are properly normative. By contrast, writing on constitutional law is unconvincing when it describes decided cases and presents such descriptions as argument-stoppers.[36]

Before I turn to argue that section 36(1) is the most plausible source of constitutional authorization for exercises of the spending power, I will rule out an argument that extends Choudhry's division of powers arguments to cover currently controversial exercises of the spending power. An interpretive approach to this power, such as the one for which Choudhry argues, does not authorize encroachments on provincial jurisdiction. It rather redefines the scope of federal legislative authority to incorporate areas of provincial regulation currently understood to fall within exclusive provincial jurisdiction. One might claim that under this argument, any federal exercises of the spending power that currently encroach upon areas of provincial jurisdiction, including coercive exercises, would no longer do so.[37]

We can approach this claim by considering a hypothetical. Imagine that Parliament passes a statute directly commanding a provincial legislature to legislate or refrain from legislating in an area in which double aspect doctrine authorizes both orders of government to legislate. The central problem with such a statute is that the federal government is not constitutionally authorized to issue such a command. This problem has nothing to do with the scope of federal legislative jurisdiction. In our hypothetical, Parliament has authority to legislate in the subject-matter area and, as we have seen above, under certain circumstances it can exercise that authority coercively.[38] What Parliament lacks in our hypothetical is specific constitutional authorization to severely

---

exercises of the spending power that have the effect of regulating in social policy domains (Choudhry 2002, 174-175). The provincial inability branch is one of four elements of a test to determine whether federal legislation satisfies the national dimensions branch of the peace, order and good government power.

[35]See for such criticisms, Brouillet (2005) and Leclair (2003).

[36]It is rare for scholars to be thoroughgoing in their assertions about the capacity of precedents to decide a debate. For instance, Lajoie claims that the Supreme Court has never expressly overruled the Privy Council's *Unemployment Insurance* case, *supra* note 18. At the same time that she invokes these precedents to support her arguments about the spending power, she criticizes the general centralizing tendencies of the Supreme Court's federalism decisions (ibid.). It is unclear why the existence of precedents *in favour of* a position she supports in one debate should be sufficient to decide that debate, while the existence of another set of precedents *contrary to* her position in another debate serve only as occasions to criticize the Court and, ultimately, Canadian federalism. To avoid the impression that she is strategically using precedents to advocate for a policy outcome that she prefers, Lajoie might provide explicitly normative arguments that engage and credit views of federalism that diverge from her own.

[37]Invocation of the peace, order and good government power to justify and limit the federal spending power has a long pedigree. See *Angers v. M.N.R.*, [1957] Ex. C.R. 83.

[38]*Supra* note 13 and accompanying text.

compromise the sovereignty of the provincial legislature and, ultimately, the democratic agency of the provincial electorate.[39]

Coercive exercises of the spending power are similar in form and substance to the hypothetical commands that we have just considered, and we have seen that, for good reasons, current constitutional law does not authorize the federal government to issue such commands. If the judiciary were to expand the scope of the federal government's jurisdiction, it would not authorize coercive federal spending, nor would it override the reasons for prohibiting the federal government from issuing direct commands to the provinces. No clear source of constitutional authority analogous to paramountcy doctrine would authorize such action.[40]

From this discussion one might conclude that all coercive exercises of the spending power, even long-standing ones that have been expressly recognized by the Supreme Court of Canada, are necessarily unconstitutional. However, such a response would forego the benefits that attend presuming long-standing governmental practices to be constitutional. An analogy may illustrate these benefits. Where there are two plausible readings of a statute, one of which renders it constitutional and the other unconstitutional, courts will adopt the former.[41] The benefits of such a presumption in favour of existing governmental action are systemic. We presume that government actors are good-faith interpreters of the Constitution, because to do otherwise would overextend the judiciary and undermine the effective operation of legislatures and executives.[42]

---

[39]The hypothetical is, of course, a variant of the one that the Privy Council raised in *Ontario (A.G.) v. Canada (A.G.)*, [1896] A.C. 348 (P.C.). This concern about compromised provincial legislative sovereignty and the resulting diminished capacity of provincial electorates to hold their legislators accountable motivates some objections to inter-legislative delegations, see *e.g.*, the reasons of Justice Rand in *Nova Scotia (A.G.) v. Canada (A.G.)* (1950), [1951] S.C.R. 31 at 49 [*N.S. (A.G.) v. Can. (A.G.)*]. Professor Gerard La Forest (as he then was) argued for the existence of conditional legislation and incorporations by reference on the grounds that these kinds of devices do not compromise legislative sovereignty of the provinces (see La Forest 1975, 137-140). Similar concerns about the legislative autonomy of sub-federal units motivate American anti-commandeering doctrine, see, e.g., *United States v. Printz*, 521 U.S. 898 (1997). The *Constitution Act, 1867* (U.K.), 30 & 31 Vict., c. 3, reprinted in R.S.C. 1985, App. II, No. 5, does provide the federal government with the powers of disallowance and reservation, which have the effect of enabling it to prevent provinces from legislating. For an examination of how these powers have fallen into desuetude (see Vipond 1991). That these powers are by constitutional convention no longer valid supports the claim in the main text: the federal government cannot directly command the provinces to refrain from acting within their spheres of constitutional authority.

[40]See *supra* note 11 and accompanying text for the discussion of paramountcy doctrine and coercion.

[41]See, e.g., *McKay v. R.*, [1965] S.C.R. 798.

[42]See Thayer (1893), for a classic statement of these reasons for deference, and Tushnet (1995, 300-301), for a recent argument for them. For a recent overview of the debate about the presumption of constitutionality in Canadian constitutional law, and an argument in favour of that presumption, see Lambert (2007, 57-60).

In the context of coercive exercises of the spending power, these reasons have additional force. The Court has expressly acknowledged the constitutionality of such exercises and government actors and citizens can reasonably have acted in reliance upon those statements.[43] There may be good reasons for defeating this presumption, even if reliance interests are frustrated as a result.[44] However, section 36(1) provides a normative framework for assessing particular instances of a long-standing practice and balancing the relevant interests. Such an approach to the spending power is more sensitive to the range of interests at stake and, absent arguments against adopting this approach, it is superior to one that requires courts to engage in a wholesale override of the presumption of constitutionality. I turn now to consider how precisely section 36(1) can function as the locus of constitutional authority for exercises of the spending power.

SECTION 36(1) AND PRAGMATIC MINIMALISM

In a previous article, I argued that the meaning of section 36(1) is deeply indeterminate (Kong 2008). I will not restate those arguments here. I only note that there are two substantive sources of controversy.[45] A first dispute about the meaning of section 36(1) reveals a deep disagreement between two normative visions of federalism.[46] One vision focuses on federalism as an institutional means of affording protections to minority populations via constitutional safeguards for subfederal units. The alternative vision focuses on federalism as a means of fashioning national identity and of cultivating cross-cutting affiliations that palliate tendencies toward majoritarianism within subfederal units. This debate has persisted throughout Canadian constitutional history.[47] A second

[43]In other contexts, reliance interests provide strong reasons against overturning established constitutional rules. See *Planned Parenthood v. Casey*, 505 U.S. 833 (1992). For a similar argument, in the spending power context, that considers the legitimacy costs attending effective judicial overruling of long-established political practices, see Andrew Petter, this volume.

[44]The argument may be that precedent rested on a flawed political or moral understanding or that political or moral understandings have shifted, such that the precedent no longer tracks an existing social consensus. For the former, see the extensive arguments about the constitutional significance of *Brown v. Board of Education*, 347 U.S. 483 (1954) in Balkin (2004). For the latter, see the reasons in *Reference Re Same-Sex Marriage*, 2004 SCC 79, [2004] 3 S.C.R. 698. Such reasons for overruling precedent in the present context would need to be balanced against the costs of overruling. For a recent consideration by the Supreme Court of Canada of *stare decisis*, see *R. v. Henry*, 2005 SCC 76, [2005] 3 S.C.R. 609 at paras. 41-46.

[45]Ibid. In that article, I presented these substantive disputes in the context of a methodological discussion about how to interpret section 36(1).

[46]For a recent description of these contrasts in federalism theory, see Norman (2006, c. 5).

[47]For analyses of these perennial debates, see La Forest (2004, c. 11); Hogg and Wright (2005).

source of disagreement about the content of section 36(1) can be traced to concerns about institutional capacity. Even if a first-best normative interpretation of section 36(1) were available to all reasonable interpreters, there might be limits on the judiciary's capacity to apply that interpretation. Where such limits exist, interpreters should not always attempt to approximate that first-best interpretation. Where the costs of such an attempt at approximation overwhelm any benefits, interpreters should opt for second-best readings.[48] In the context of section 36(1), given courts' limited institutional capacity, they should at least strongly consider refraining from approximating first-best interpretations.

My interpretation of section 36(1), and the doctrinal rule that I propose to implement that interpretation, respond to these two controversies. I offer a minimalist interpretation of section 36(1), which I suggest will accommodate reasonable disagreements about the normative significance of federalism in Canada, and I propose a doctrinal rule that responds to the institutional limits of the judiciary, while safeguarding its role as a privileged locus of constitutional settlements. Before I turn to these arguments, I will respond to two general objections to invoking section 36(1) as a source of constitutional authorization for the spending power.

A first objection challenges the justiciability of section 36(1). It is true that section 36(1) uses open-ended language, which suggests that it is not binding on governments. The hortatory nature of the section is evident in the phrase "committed to".[49] However, although the section does not *require* that governments fulfill its objectives, it does *authorize* governments to pursue those objectives and sets out the conditions under which governments are justified in acting pursuant to it. Although section 36(1) does not impose a positive obligation on governments to act, it does set out the constitutional limits on what governments can do when they are acting in ways that only section 36(1) can

[48]For an argument in favour of second-best approaches to judicial doctrine, see Vermeule (2006, 80-82).

[49]Aymen Nader argues that the phrase "committed to" is not merely hortatory. He points to the dictionary definition of being committed and notes that commitment implies obligation (see Nader 1996, 351-352). Nader's claim is favourable to my general argument that section 36(1) should be enforced; I can concede it and still advance my argument. Nonetheless, it is worth noting that the phrasing of section 36(1) is different from the phrasing of other sections in the *Constitution Act, 1982* that clearly do impose obligations. No duty-imposing section allows governments to satisfy its requirements by simply manifesting a commitment to them. For instance, where an individual can claim that she falls within the scope of the rights provisions, the government owes a prima facie duty not to violate that right, unless it is justified in doing otherwise under section 1. With those provisions, the government does not have available to itself an argument that it was committed to not violating that right but failed to do so. It is this difference in language which suggests that section 36(1) places a lower burden on governments that they can satisfy without meeting the section's objectives, and it is this lower burden that leads commentators to conclude that section 36(1) is merely hortatory. For an example of this analysis of the verb "to commit" in section 36, see Gibson (1996, 28-29).

authorize.[50] At a minimum, the text of the section does not authorize governments to act contrary to its objectives when they fall within its scope, and any actions that arguably have this effect are appropriately subject to judicial review under section 36(1).

There is a second objection to invoking section 36(1) to authorize the spending power. This objection claims that any such invocation would concede that before the *Constitution Act, 1982* came into force, controversial exercises of the spending power were unconstitutional.[51] The legislative history of section 36(1) suggests that this objection is overdrawn. According to Nader's careful examination of the relevant legislative history of section 36, the specific federal purpose behind this section was to provide a constitutional grounding for federal exercises of the spending power in areas of provincial jurisdiction and, in particular, for conditional exercises of that power.[52] Nader has convincingly argued that Prime Minister Trudeau sought to enshrine conditional exercises of the spending power in the text of the constitution, from the time he was Minister of Justice presiding over the 1969 Committee on Federalism until the time of the drafting of the *Constitution Act, 1982*.[53] This history suggests that one motivation behind the drafting of section 36(1) was to clarify the constitutional status of a controversial practice. I should be clear that I do not claim that this argument about intentions *can determine the meaning* of section 36(1).[54] I point to the legislative history for the limited purpose of showing that invoking section 36(1) as a source of constitutional authority does not necessarily imply a concession that controversial exercises of the spending power were

[50]An analogy might assist here. Under s.15(1) of the Canadian Charter of Rights and Freedoms, *supra* note 2, governments are not obliged to provide goods and services, whereas under s.23, provincial governments are so obliged (once a set of conditions is satisfied). However, when governments do provide goods and services, they are obliged by s.15(1) to allocate them in a non-discriminatory manner. In the s.36(1) context, I argue that the constitution does not oblige governments to engage in the activities specified. Governments are not subject to s.23-type positive obligations under s.36(1). But once governments do engage in the activities specified, they are under an obligation to adhere to the limits of s.36(1), because that section is the source of constitutional authorization for those activities and there is no other plausible source.

[51]For this criticism, see Marc-Antoine Adam, this volume. Adam prescribes s.94 as an alternative source of authorization for federal spending in areas of provincial jurisdiction. A full consideration of his position is beyond the scope of this chapter; I note only that in my view, Petter's criticisms of this argument are decisive (Petter, this volume).

[52]*Supra* note 49 at 320-347, 354-355.

[53]*Ibid.* For the clearest exposition of this position, see Government of Canada (1989).

[54]Legislation generally and constitutions in particular are the result of divergent interests coming together. The compromises arrived at are not, in any meaningful sense, intended by the participants, but are simply the result of their actions (see Brest 1980, 209-222; Farber and Frickey 1997, 41-42).

unconstitutional before the coming into force of the *Constitution Act, 1982*.[55] That history simply offers a plausible alternative account of the constitutional status of controversial pre-1982 exercises of the spending power.

Having cleared away these preliminary objections to invoking section 36(1) as a source of constitutional authority for the spending power, I turn now to a minimalist interpretation of that section and to a pragmatic defence of minimalism.

Minimalist Interpretation of Section 36(1)

Let us begin our discussion by setting out again the express constitutional text. Section 36(1) states:

> Without altering the legislative authority of Parliament or of the provincial legislatures, or the rights of any of them with respect to the exercise of their legislative authority, Parliament and the legislatures, together with the government of Canada and the provincial governments, are committed to (a) promoting equal opportunities for the well-being of Canadians; (b) furthering economic development to reduce disparity in opportunities; and (c) providing essential public services of reasonable quality to all Canadians.

I noted above that this section is open to a set of rival interpretations, each of which carries an implicit judgment about the nature of Canadian federalism and about the institutional capacity of courts. One response to this level of indeterminacy would be to claim that one interpretation is correct and the other incorrect. Yet the disagreements about the meaning of section 36(1) reflect underlying persistent debates in our constitutional history, and the alternative positions reflect positions that fall within a reasonable spectrum.[56] It is conceivable that by offering more evidence or by further refining arguments, we will arrive finally at a just or correct resolution of these debates that all reasonable observers would accept. Given our constitutional history, this is unlikely. But to say that there is persistent disagreement is not the same thing as to say that there are no areas of consensus. Whatever disagreements there may be about the scope of section 36(1)'s authorization, there are some exercises of the spending power that are clearly not authorized by that section.

---

[55]On a more general note, it is unclear why such a concession should be considered a strong argument against invoking section 36(1). Imagine a similar argument in the *Charter* context. A constitutional claim about governmental action that only raised issues about discrimination would have been met with indifference prior to the coming into force of section 15. The obvious effect of the *Charter* was to subject such activity to explicit constitutional scrutiny. Similarly, one might concede that prior to 1982, conditional exercises of the spending power were unconstitutional, but with the coming into force of section 36(1), those exercises benefitted from clear constitutional authorization.

[56]For a general treatment of debates in which contending positions fall within the range of reasonable disagreement and for the claim that such debates are persistent, see Waldron (1999a, 176-180).

There are two ways in which governmental action can uncontroversially be considered to be unauthorized by section 36(1).[57] First, although some federal influence on provincial legislative priorities by federal government spending pursuant to the objectives of the section is permissible, federal action that is disproportionate to or unnecessary for the obtaining of those objectives amounts to unjustifiable coercion.[58] Second, provincial action that undermines those objectives cannot be justified by the section. Provincial action in pursuit of legitimate autonomy interests that justify departure from section 36(1)'s standards cannot unnecessarily or disproportionately undermine those standards. Let us consider each of these claims in turn.

Unjustified Federal Government Action under Section 36(1)

It is generally accepted that a vertical fiscal gap between the federal and provincial governments is necessary to facilitate the pursuit of redistributive objectives within a federation (see, e.g., Lazar 2000, 12). At a certain point, however, the gap can become disproportionate to and unnecessary for the pursuit of section 36(1)'s redistributive objectives. Imagine that the federal government could occupy an amount of tax room far in excess of its own budgetary needs and its section 36(1) obligations. Imagine also that it could occupy that tax room at the expense of the provincial governments, and that the federal government was not subject to the kinds of political or economic constraints faced by the provinces. Imagine further that if the federal government expanded its taxing activity, the provinces' capacity to tax would necessarily be reduced. Finally, imagine that the provinces' constitutional obligations were much more costly than those of the federal government and that the provincial governments, as a result, would rely upon the federal government for support.[59]

Under these hypothetical conditions, provincial autonomy would be severely compromised because the provinces would not have the resources to pursue independent policy directions within their areas of competence. This degree of incapacity would be unjustified because, on the hypothetical facts I have set out, it would be the result of federal action that was disproportionate to

---

[57]I take it to be axiomatic and therefore uncontroversial that s.36(1) does not justify government action that is unnecessary for, or disproportionate to, the goals of that section, since such action bears no rational relationship to the section. It is important that the contents of a claim be considered uncontroversial, given that I am trying to define what all reasonable observers would accept to be the minimum content of s.36(1).

[58]For the claim that these requirements provide a normative structure for reasoning in Canadian constitutional law generally and in Canadian federalism more specifically, see Beatty (1995). As with all such means-ends tests, the degree of scrutiny applied to government action can determine the outcome of a given case, and all attempts to make wholesale-level judgments about the degree of deference owed to species of government action require complex assessments (see Roosevelt III 2006, c.2).

[59]Some commentators argue that this is the state of affairs in Canada today (see Noël 2006).

and unnecessary for the pursuit of the legitimate federal objective of equal provision of social services. The federal action would not be authorized by section 36(1).

From this hypothetical, we can infer two clear conditions under which federal governmental action exceeds the grant of authority in section 36(1). First, because that section only authorizes federal influence in areas of provincial jurisdiction for specific purposes, any federal action that is not *necessary* for the achievement of those purposes or any other constitutionally recognized purposes is unconstitutional. Second, federal governmental action that is necessary to the achievement of section 36(1)'s objectives must be *proportional* to those objectives. Federal influence within provincial spheres of constitutional authority is clearly unconstitutional when it removes from a province, without authorization, its capacity to self-regulate, and as a result deprives its citizens of the capacity to effectively select and oversee provincial policy.

Unjustified Provincial Action under Section 36(1), Substantive Federal Equality

If we accept this account of unconstitutional action under section 36(1), we might ask at this stage in the argument whether there are any exercises of the spending power that will satisfy section 36(1)'s proportionality and necessity requirements but would nonetheless be unconstitutional. A province might have a unique and constitutionally significant autonomy interest that was not captured by those requirements, and its citizens might as a result understand their interests in social service delivery in ways that are different from the rest of the country. This notion of a unique autonomy interest raises questions about what degree of provincial autonomy is consistent with the objectives of section 36(1).

As a general matter, provincial regulation that subverts the three goals of section 36(1) cannot be constitutionally authorized by that section. A province that legislated in a manner which had clearly destructive effects on the capacity of residents in other provinces to receive a baseline level of social services would be acting contrary to section 36(1)'s requirements.[60] In addition, a province that adopted policies that triggered a "race to the bottom" would violate section 36(1).[61] But this restriction on provincial autonomy may not be absolute. To understand why not, let us consider a hypothetical that involves a province with a unique and constitutionally significant autonomy interest.

Imagine that it was impossible for the goals of section 36(1) to be achieved without eliminating the capacity of the provinces to regulate their own affairs. In this hypothetical situation, the sphere of provincial autonomy would be reduced to a negligible size, because there would be an imbalance between the spending

---

[60]Recall that s.36(1) expressly mentions provincial and federal legislatures and states that they should both be committed to its objectives. For a classic application of public choice theory to federalism that raises the issue of externalities referred to in the main text, see Macey (1990).

[61]For recent work on such races to the bottom in Canada, see Harrison (2006). See especially Boychuk (2006).

and taxing responsibilities of the two orders of government and that imbalance would be necessary and proportionate to the goal of providing a baseline level of services across the country. Imagine further that under these conditions, a province that acted in pursuit of its unique and constitutionally significant autonomy interest would necessarily impose costs on other provinces that would be contrary to section 36(1)'s objectives.

Because our hypothetical province would, on the facts I have stipulated, have a constitutionally significant and unique position within the federation, it should have a correspondingly larger margin of appreciation than other provinces. Any choice by that province to defect from the national scheme in defence of its constitutionally unique position would be entitled to greater deference than another province's choice to defect. And section 36(1)'s necessity and proportionality requirements would impose limits on the province with the unique autonomy interest. This province could only undermine the section's objectives if such action was needed to protect that interest, and only to an extent proportional to its protection.

A Pragmatic Defence of Minimalism

The above interpretation of section 36(1) shares attributes with Professor Cass Sunstein's description of "minimalist" judicial decisions.[62] Sunstein has argued that a minimalist court produces "incompletely theorized agreements."[63] In these, interested parties to a conflict can agree on outcomes without necessarily agreeing on the reasons for arriving at those outcomes. Minimalist decisions aim to be *shallow*, in that they do not attempt to resolve persistent normative debates, and *narrow*, in that their precedential value is typically limited (ibid.). The necessity and proportionality requirements that I have read into section 36(1) are similarly shallow and narrow. My interpretation of section 36(1) is shallow in that it does not stake out a position in a controversial normative debate, but rather seeks areas of consensus, and it is narrow in that it does not establish a bright-line rule, but rather calls for incremental developments of the law.

Proponents of judicial minimalism claim that it has several virtues. First, it is said to facilitate liberal discourse, as it enables disputants to deliberate within the terms of an overlapping consensus (ibid., 50). Under conditions of intense disagreement, such deliberation enables individuals to start from points of agreement and exchange reasons from that common ground, in a spirit of reciprocity and mutual respect (ibid., 50-51). The conditions for clear section 36(1) violations that I have identified above aim to establish the same kind of ground. I claim that all reasonable participants in the debate about the spending power acknowledge that section 36(1) is violated under the clear conditions

---

[62]For an argument that the Supreme Court of Canada has articulated a defence of judicial minimalism in a recent federalism case (see Kong 2008, 353ff).

[63]Sunstein (1999, 11). In addition to the agreement identified in the text, agreement can also be at the high level of principle, where arguments converge about the value of an abstract principle but diverge about its concrete expression.

specified. From that point of agreement, participants can aim to resolve particular conflicts.

Second, proponents argue that judicial minimalism reduces the error costs of constitutional judgment.[64] By reducing the breadth and depth of judicial decision-making, judicial minimalism can limit the possibility that a court will err in its decisions. There are two kinds of errors that can arise from constitutional decision-making. The first kind is normative, and the second empirical. The normative case for leaving constitutional judgments to the political branches is well known. Perhaps its strongest articulation is by Professor Jeremy Waldron.[65] According to Waldron, legislative bodies represent the considered moral judgments of constituents. The process of democratic deliberation, followed by voting, allows all viewpoints to be expressed, considered, and then accepted or rejected. By contrast, judicial review truncates this deliberative process, and entrusts it to a small unrepresentative body that is often constrained by legal conventions from openly debating the relevant moral issues. Proponents of minimalism claim that in cases which attract extensive and contentious democratic debate, minimalism reduces the scope of a judgment's effects and thereby expands the reach of democratic bodies' deliberative domain (Sunstein 1999, 59).

The arguments for deference to elected or delegated decision-making bodies on empirical issues are similarly well established. Adjudication is best suited to bilateral disputes over private claims of rights; it is least well suited to disputes that implicate polycentric issues requiring a weighing of multiple interests and the capacity to seek out and evaluate complex data.[66] By limiting the reach of a constitutional decision's effects, minimalism entrusts most empirical assessments to the legislative and executive branches.

Critics of minimalism have focused on Sunstein's account of how minimalist decisions are extended to novel fact situations. They have charged

---

[64]For the notion of error costs, see Vermeule 2006, 77, 256-257. When courts err, they can impose social and legal costs (see Sunstein 1999, 49). An interpretive approach that reduces the likelihood of errors tends to reduce the costs of errors, since, as a matter of probability, it will produce fewer errors. When evaluating the error costs of a doctrinal test, one should also assess the potential magnitude of an error (ibid., 4).

[65]Waldron (1999b). For an overview of this debate and its significance in the federalism review context, see Stone (2008, 27-30). Professor Stone argues that the strongest arguments for federalism review address the settlement function of courts in federalism disputes, but she further notes that even this settlement function can be fulfilled by more democratic bodies. We will see below that the possibility to which Professor Stone adverts is salient to the doctrinal rule advanced in this paper.

[66]Fuller (1978). See also Chayes (1976). For recent arguments that the relative institutional competence arguments in Fuller's work, and in the work of legal process scholars more generally, should be supplemented by empirical analysis, see Sunstein and Vermeule (2003, 900-902); Fallon (1994, 977-978). For a recent attempt to cabin and structure the scope of institutional competence arguments in judicial decisions, see King (2008). I will offer below a more nuanced version of the polycentricity argument and trace out the implications of this more nuanced account for judicial interpretations of section 36(1).

minimalism with being under-theorized and with distorting the nature of legal reasoning.[67] For instance, Professor David Brinks argues that Sunstein inaccurately distinguishes analogical from philosophical reasoning. According to Brinks, in Sunsteinian minimalism, reasoning by analogy permits courts to make incremental, fact-specific advances in the law, without appeal to general theories or principles (Brinks 2001, 50). But, Brinks notes, when courts engage in analogical reasoning, they are necessarily guided by theories that allow courts to generalize beyond specific facts and that provide guidance to those who are subject to the authority of judicial decisions.[68] Finally, Brinks argues that because the minimalist rejects theory, he cannot defend any particular decision that instantiates an incompletely theorized agreement (Brinks 2001, 52). The value of legality requires courts to offer public justifications for their actions, and minimalism fails to satisfy this requirement.

In order to respond to this criticism, let us first flesh out this conception of legality. Professor Ronald Dworkin in *Law's Empire* famously argues that constitutional interpretation entails the requirements of "fit" and "justification". In hard cases, he says, courts should aim to interpret existing constitutional materials in the best possible political or moral light, keeping in view the purposes of those materials (Dworkin 1986, 90 and generally at chapter 6). Such a process of interpretation contributes to a "genuine political community" in which "people are governed by common principles, not just by rules hammered out in political compromise" (ibid., 211). On this account of constitutional interpretation, citizens are participants in a society-wide process of responsive reason-giving and part of a community characterized by the mutual regard of its members (ibid., 211-215). In *Justice in Robes*, Dworkin frames these claims in terms of legality. He argues that legality requires that "governments govern under a set of principles applicable in principle to all"[69] and notes that the process of identifying what these principles require in particular cases involves

---

[67]For a claim that minimalism requires a fully worked at normative theory that chooses from among substantive alternatives, see Siegel (2005, at 2003). For the claim that the Rawlsian defense of minimalism is a justificatory theory like any other, see Dorf (2005, 1262). For the claim that Sunstein's minimalism distorts the nature of legal reasoning, see Brinks (2001, 50-54) and Dorf (1998-1999, 30-33).

[68]Ibid. Dorf makes the same point when he writes of Sunstein's treatment of public forum doctrine: "Common law reasoning contains considerably more theory than Sunstein and other minimalists seem to admit. The pattern of decided cases crystallizes in doctrines that both exemplify and justify the underlying pattern. In defining the contours of the public forum doctrine, the Court did not simply *state* that a public debate is more like one forum or another: it explained why this was so by reference to principles, values and policies the public forum doctrine purports to serve." [citations omitted] Dorf (1998-1999, 32).

[69]Dworkin (2006, 176). Professor Frederick Schauer has noted that because of the generality of reasons, the act of reason-giving implies a commitment to making future decisions that fall within the scope of those reasons' application (Schauer 1995, 644). This feature of reason-giving sees intrinsic value in consistency and further restricts the capacity of those who participate in a reason-giving enterprise to act in self-serving ways (ibid., 653).

publicly defending and articulating particular conceptions of these principles.[70] I understand him to be arguing that government action is grounded in legality when a constitutional concern for government by common principles is instantiated in the *substance* of constitutional law and the *process* of articulating to citizens the reasons for judicial decisions. Sunstein's critics seem to argue that because minimalist decisions deny the possibility of principled reason-giving, they do not meet these substantive and procedural requirements of legality.

My defence of minimalism is partial and begins with a distinction between constitutional interpretation, on the one hand, and extensions of a case interpreting the constitution to novel situations, on the other. Although according to Sunstein's account of analogical reasoning, extensions of constitutional precedents are not justified in terms of a single normative theory, it does not follow that *the interpretation of the constitution* which grounds a precedent also lacks such justification. We have seen above one general justification for such interpretations: they economize on disagreements.[71] Consider a federalism example that Sunstein cites. He gives as an example of minimalism the United States Supreme Court's reasoning in *United States v. Lopez*.[72] There, he argues, the Court did not provide a comprehensive theory of federalism (Sunstein 1999, 16–17). The shallowness of the decision, he suggests, permits people with widely divergent views of federalism to support an interpretation of the constitution they all understood to be plausible.

Critics of minimalism might argue that although minimalist interpretations can be so justified, this kind of justification does not meet the requirements of legality. According to this criticism, legal justification requires a commitment to objectivity, and in this context objectivity entails the requirement that courts argue for the *correctness* of their interpretations.[73] Minimalists do not argue for

---

[70]Dworkin (2006, 184). Professor Matthew Adler has recently argued that Dworkin is a kind of popular constitutionalist. He writes: "Dworkin's recognitional community must be the community of all citizens, not merely lawyers, judges, legislators, or officials – for otherwise his claim that law can express the responsibility of equal concern that *citizens* have for each other, thereby creating genuine associative moral obligations *for citizens*, and justifying the coercion *of citizens* would be ungrounded" (see Adler 2006).

[71]Deliberative democratic theorists also argue that economizing on disagreements has democratic value (see Guttman and Thompson 1996, 55).

[72]514 U.S. 549 (1995) [*Lopez*]. The majority reasoned in *Lopez* that Congress can legislate pursuant to the Commerce clause only when it regulates the channels and instrumentalities of inter-state commerce, or intra-state commercial activity that has a substantial effect on inter-state commerce. The details of the decision or the resulting doctrine are not relevant here. What is significant is that the Court opted for this multifactored test, which requires case-by-case assessments, rather than for a bright-line rule that instantiates a particular and comprehensive understanding of federalism.

[73]Professor Gerald Postema describes three attributes of objectivity: (a) Independence – "if a judgment is objective its claim on our regard transcends the judging subject". (b) Correctness or validity of judgments – "the independence secured by objectivity must secure the basis for a distinction between something's *seeming* to be so (someone's *thinking, believing, taking* it to be so) and its *being so*". (c) Invariance across judging subjects – "objectivity is the possibility in principle of other subjects taking up

the correctness of their interpretations, the critics continue, but merely that their interpretations are accepted by a range of participants in a particular debate.

The critics are mistaken. Minimalist constitutional interpretations have available to them a justification that includes a claim about their correctness. Moreover, the relevant conception of correctness reflects the values that underwrite the principle of legality. This justification for minimalist interpretations finds its roots in American pragmatism.[74] According to the pragmatist, a consensus among the members of a community facilitates pragmatist deliberation, and such deliberation is regulated by a particular definition of truth.[75] Professor Cheryl Misak notes that for Peirce "a true belief is a belief that could not be improved upon, a belief that would forever meet the challenge of reasons, argument and evidence" (ibid., 49). As Misak notes, such a belief was for Peirce a regulative ideal and set the norms by which inquiry proceeds (ibid., 98-99). Inquiries begin against a stable background of set beliefs and assumptions, which are then put into question as they are tested against experience and reason, in a social and cooperative process of deliberation.[76] Recall that the minimalist interpretation I offered for section 36(1) was one that I claimed all reasonable observers would accept. Such an interpretation satisfies the pragmatist's conception of truth.[77] A minimalist interpretation is correct, where "correctness" means that it is currently immune to challenge.

---

the position and confirming them (positional judgments). Where such confirmation (or disconfirmation) is ruled out, so too is objectivity" (Postema 2001, 105, 107, 108-109).

[74]In this chapter, I adopt insights from the pragmatic tradition that finds its roots in the work of Peirce (1997) and Dewey (1944). I also draw on legal authors whose work is deeply influenced by the pragmatist movement (see, e.g., Fuller 2001; Dorf and Sabel 1998). I specifically reject the version of pragmatism that understands the ends against which legal acts are measured to be fixed in advance. See for the distinction Garrett and Liebman (2004, 281).

[75]For the distinction between this approach to deliberation and disagreement, and the Rawlsian project of bracketing comprehensive worldviews, see Misak (2000, 20-24, 29-30).

[76]As Hilary Putnam has noted, this version of pragmatism, which finds its roots in Peirce and Dewey, is inhospitable to either thoroughgoing skepticism or relativism. Although the pragmatist accepts the fallibility of his present beliefs, he does not deny the possibility of true beliefs. The pragmatist may doubt the truth of *any given* belief but he does not doubt the truth of *all* beliefs. He is a fallibilist but not a skeptic (see Putnam 1995, 21). Peirce famously described thoroughgoing skepticism as "paper doubt" (Levi 1998, 177-178). Such doubt deprives human beings of the capacity to deliberate in ways necessary to distinguish between truth and falsity. "True doubt" and its corollary, true deliberation, can only proceed from a present framework of beliefs that are accepted as true, but open to contestation. The pragmatist similarly rejects relativism because it denies the possibility of intersubjective deliberation about truth. For a statement of the Peircean arguments for rejecting a Rortian, relativist version of pragmatism (see Putnam 1995, 74-75). This conception of reasoning also captures civic republican approaches to constitutional interpretation (see, e.g., Michelman 1988).

[77]Although the full argument is beyond the scope of this chapter, I claim that pragmatic theories of legal meaning are better than the main alternatives. According to

We can go further in our defence of minimalist constitutional interpretation. Not only do such interpretations entail a claim of correctness, they facilitate deliberative reason-giving, and are thus consistent with the value of legality. Because minimalist interpretations are widely accepted, they permit those who occupy positions across a normative spectrum to *reason together* about how to resolve particular disputes. Sunstein's critics are correct to note that when courts extend precedents, they appeal to principles and that such appeals require courts to stake out positions in normative debates. Although this fact about legal reasoning is fatal to Sunstein's description of analogical reasoning, it highlights the value of minimalist interpretations. To understand the nature of this value, we can contrast minimalist interpretations with their opposite, namely, interpretations that enshrine a particular, controversial normative vision.

Consider an interpretation of the peace, order and good government power that limits its application to emergency situations. This limitative interpretation seeks to safeguard the values associated with provincial autonomy, while excluding those values associated with national coordination.[78] When judges who hold firmly to the excluded values are faced with such an interpretation, they are reduced to strategically limiting its scope[79] or they are consigned to

---

one alternative, the meaning of constitutional texts is radically indeterminate. This alternative overstates the degree of indeterminacy in constitutional interpretation. At certain moments and among some communities of interpreters, texts have clear meanings. That texts are open to challenge, either as a result of changed shared understandings within the interpretive group or as a result of changes in the composition of the relevant interpretive community, does not undercut this fact. For a debate about the extent and meaning of indeterminacy in law, see Langille (1988), and Hutchinson (1989). Another alternative to pragmatist interpretation claims that the meaning of any constitutional text can be fixed by application of a particular constitutional theory. Given persistent interpretive debates in constitutional law, this cannot be a descriptive claim. If it is to be defended at all, it must be on normative grounds. In this space, I cannot answer all the normative arguments in favour of the main theories of constitutional interpretation. Instead, I note that each interpretive approach instantiates a *particular value* and that claims about the strength of particular values tend to be *relative*: participants in debates about constitutional theory typically decline to claim that the value for which they advocate should trump in every instance. As defenders of these theories concede, their validity is contingent, and they are contingent in precisely the ways that a pragmatic theory of interpretation would predict: under certain circumstances, theory is tested against experience, found wanting and subject to revision (see Dorf 1997). Finally, I suggest that a pragmatist theory of interpretation has a strong claim to allegiance because of its respect for the agency of citizens and interpreters, and its consequent grounding in the value of legality. For this agency-focused conception of legality, see Fuller (1965, 162).

[78]English Canadian criticisms of the Privy Council's federalism decisions made this argument (see, e.g., Laskin 1947).

[79]For the charge that Chief Justice Roberts and Justice Alito apply precedent with which they disagree in a way that tightly (and disingenuously) constrains the scope of its application, see Stone (2008). Such uses of precedent are objectionable because they are unresponsive to the logic of the cases upon which they purport to rely.

repeatedly writing dissents.[80] By contrast, when applying a minimalist interpretation such as the one I propose for section 36(1), judges who hold positions across a normative spectrum can exchange reasons with their opponents and respect the authority of precedent.[81] They engage in *responsive reason-giving* which, as we have seen above, legality requires of state actors.[82]

Thus far in this section, I have articulated a minimalist interpretation of section 36(1) and defended that interpretation and minimalism itself against a range of criticisms. There remains one serious criticism of minimalism in the section 36(1) context. To introduce this final criticism of minimalism, I will draw in the next section on Professor Mitchell Berman's distinction between constitutional meaning and constitutional doctrine;[83] and I will generate a doctrinal rule that implements the minimalist interpretation of section 36(1) identified above. Berman's distinction reveals that even when, by drawing upon the full range of interpretive techniques available in constitutional law, we can discern with relative ease the meaning of a constitutional provision, that meaning cannot be directly enforced by the courts. In enforcing a constitution, courts generate and apply doctrinal rules that have embedded within them a set of judgments about the effects of doctrine and the institutional limits of courts.[84]

---

[80]See L'Heureux-Dubé (2000) for a defense of such dissents.

[81]Consider the *Oakes* Test, which is minimalist in the way that my proposed interpretation of section 36(1) is. *R. v. Oakes* [1986] 1 S.C.R. 103. All reasonable observers accept that a legal rule that is not rationally connected or proportionate to a legitimate government objective cannot satisfy section 1 of the Charter. When judges disagree about applications of the *Oakes* test, they exchange principled reasons about that test; they do not attack the test itself nor do they engage in strategic reasoning that seeks to undermine the test. See, e.g., the range of opinions about the application of section 1 in *Irwin Toy Ltd. v. Quebec (Attorney General),* [1989] 1 S.C.R. 927.

[82]Cooperative processes of deliberation are favoured by deliberative theories of democracy, and some link pragmatism to these theories (see, e.g., Westbrook 2005). We shall see in the third section below that the doctrinal rule I propose extends deliberation beyond courts and their members and includes the political branches, as well as citizens.

[83]Berman (2004, 3). No interpretation of a constitutional provision's meaning is self-executing. At a minimum, courts will specify the onus of proof that a claimant bears in establishing a violation. Imagine, for instance, that it is clear that a constitutional provision protecting freedom of expression prohibits all government action that restricts speech. At the very least, a court will set out a doctrinal rule that sets the onus a claimant bears in establishing whether government action has this effect (ibid., 10). Most doctrinal rules in constitutional law are more complex than this. See Fallon (2001, c.5), for a typology of doctrinal rules.

[84]Berman (2004) identifies six concerns that a court will consider when formulating a doctrinal rule: *adjudicatory* (how will this rule minimize adjudicatory errors?); *deterrent* (how will this rule help ensure compliance with the meaning of the constitution?); *protective* (how will this rule avoid any chilling effects?); *fiscal* (how will this rule allow for reduced litigation costs?); *institutional* (how will this rule reduce interbranch friction and preserve the courts' authority?); and *substantive* (how will this rule help effectuate a given constitutional norm?).

Berman's distinction helps us to see the importance of distinguishing between a minimalist interpretation and a doctrinal rule that gives effect to that interpretation. A minimalist interpretation reflects the shallow reasons for a shared consensus on a controversial matter. By contrast, a mimimalist doctrinal rule gives effect to or enforces that shared consensus.[85] While the conditions identified above for clear section 36(1) violations constitute a minimalist interpretation of the section, they are not themselves a doctrinal rule. A doctrinal rule would enable a court to identify when these conditions are satisfied. A court might adopt a *Lopez*-style multifactor test that would require courts to engage in case-by-case assessments of exercises of the spending power. But this is precisely the kind of analysis that courts are incapable of undertaking in the fiscal federalism context. Although such an approach has the merit of not enshrining a particular vision of federalism, it comes with the cost of burdening the judiciary with a task that it cannot carry out. If courts had ideal capacities, then case-by-case analyses of whether federal and provincial action was necessary and proportionate to the goals of section 36(1) would be the first-best solution.

But courts do not have these capacities, and requiring them to engage in such analyses would yield at least three foreseeable negative consequences. First, courts would lose a measure of credibility, as they would consistently show themselves to be incompetent to oversee the spending power.[86] Second, because the outcomes of judicial decisions would lack the relevant kinds of justifications, it would be difficult for the courts to craft consistent judgments that would guide government actors.[87] Third, because courts lack the relevant

---

[85]Professor Sunstein in his analysis of *Lopez* seems to conflate minimalist grounds with minimalist doctrinal rules (Sunstein 1999). For an argument that because courts operate under institutional limits that themselves yield minimalist outcomes, judges should incorporate normative justifications in their reasons, see Molot (2004). For an argument that minimalism can in some instances be harmful because it under-protects fundamental values, see Fiss (2008).

[86]For the credibility costs of undertaking such review, see Choper (1980, 201-202, 258). Authors have castigated the Supreme Court of Canada for exhibiting just such incompetence in *Chaoulli v. Quebec (A.G.)*, 2005 SCC 35, [2005] 1 S.C.R. 791. See, *e.g.*, Flood, Stabile, and Kontic (2005, 307). The debate over judicial oversight of the health care system turns on what observers believe the limits of judicial deference to government action to be. Governmental delivery of health services can at some point and under some circumstances yield arbitrary infringements of section 7 interests. The question is how or whether courts should define those limits and critics should be cognizant of the fact that unlike academics, courts are obliged to resolve concrete cases, often with limited information and often under conditions of intense disagreement. For this recognition of the conditions under which courts make decisions, of the implications these conditions have for judicial doctrine, and of the difference between writing by academic experts and that of courts (see Vermeule and Sunstein 2003).

[87]This charge of arbitrariness is typically levelled against judicial adoption of standards (see, e.g., Alexander 1999). I assume without argument the truth of the generally accepted claim that the reason-giving function of judicial doctrine lends legitimacy to the results of judicial decisions (see, e.g., Wechsler 1959).

expertise, those outcomes may be worse, by any relevant measure, than either the admittedly imperfect status quo or a doctrine that required less of the courts.[88]

The challenge for the remainder of this chapter is to develop a rule that avoids these pitfalls of *minimalist doctrine* while capturing the benefits of a *minimalist interpretation* of section 36(1). The proposed rule would build on the minimalist judicial interpretation set out above, would primarily leave the case-by-case assessments of whether a particular case satisfies the requirements of that interpretation to political actors better positioned to undertake such assessments, and would subject these assessments to *ex post* judicial review in order to preserve the place of Canadian courts as arbiters of constitutional reasoning in federalism matters. New Governance theory provides the foundation for such a doctrinal rule, and it is to a consideration of that theory that I now turn.

NEW GOVERNANCE THEORY AND SECTION 36(1)

New Governance theory has seen multiple iterations;[89] what follows is an encapsulation. The theory has two facets, one epistemological and the other institutional. The epistemological facet rests on a particular assumption about the capacity of actors within a legal system to know or understand what is relevant to their governance projects. In developing this epistemological argument, the New Governance theorist draws on the pragmatic tradition of Peirce (1997) and Dewey (1944). In legal theory, this understanding of knowledge has been articulated by Fuller (2001). In this conception of knowledge, principles that are currently held, and objectives that are currently aspired to, are inevitably recast and reshaped as individuals and groups implement means to give them effect (ibid.). In turn, the means chosen and put into play will be reconceived and altered as the ends are recast (ibid.). This process of continuous responsive learning does not only describe how individuals cognize phenomena and act in the world. It provides a norm that can guide collective action and shape institutions.

Dorf and Sabel (1998, 314) find some evidence of pragmatic institutions in the United States' federal arrangements, and they argue that these should set the norm for further development of American federalism. In the Sabel-Dorf model of federalism, Congress funds and authorizes reform programs in subnational jurisdictions and sets broad policy objectives, but makes the authorization and funding conditional on good faith participation in a regime of public reporting and on constant mutual corroboration, which generates rolling best practice standards (ibid., 288, 341-343). Federal administrative agencies assist in setting best practice standards and assess compliance by looking at activities across

[88]For an argument in favour of second best approaches to judicial doctrine, see Vermeule (2006, 80-82).

[89]For a succinct account, see Simon (2006, 37). For a comprehensive summary of the literature, see Lobel (2004).

diverse jurisdictions (ibid., 345). The courts in the New Governance federal state adopt the terms of participants in this system of accountability to assess whether policies satisfy the standards defined by the participants themselves (ibid., 288). Any given violation is defined by reference to what is revealed as possible according to standards adopted and generated by the members of the federation (ibid.). Accountability is assured as citizens of particular jurisdictions measure their policies against those of other jurisdictions, and express their reasoned disagreement either at the ballot box or through litigation (ibid.).

The New Governance theorist prescribes for subnational units a continuing process of learning and experimentation that is coordinated by the national government and that gives citizens opportunities to engage actively in their own governance. Moreover, according to New Governance theorists, this model of federalism is not only normatively desirable; it offers an effective response to the fluid and complex regulatory environments of modern federal states. They argue that neither centralized command-and-control structures (which are insufficiently sensitive to local variation) (see Lobel 2004, 381-385; Dorb and Sabel 1998, 316), nor completely decentralized ones (which are susceptible to self-interested localism that is indifferent to the coordination needs of the national community) (Sabel 2001, 129), can respond adequately to this complexity.

This brief summary of New Governance theory reveals a set of policy concerns that also animate section 36(1). Section 36(1) requires comparisons among the provinces, and given the vertical fiscal gap, the federal government is in the best position to act as the focal point of policy coordination aimed at meeting the section's objectives.[90] As we have just seen, interjurisdictional comparisons and federal coordination are hallmarks of New Governance federalism. In addition, the object of section 36(1)'s regulation — fiscal federalism — is extraordinarily complex, and the underlying economic conditions are ever-changing.[91] These are the very conditions to which New Governance institutions are responsive. Finally, as do New Governance theories of federalism, the text of section 36(1) seems to require policy cooperation between the federal and provincial governments, and seems therefore to reject either federal command and control measures or purely decentralized decision-making.

Before articulating a doctrinal rule for section 36(1) that incorporates the above principles of New Governance institutional design, I will address in more detail the role of courts in New Governance theory. I begin by nuancing the distinction drawn above between cases raising polycentric issues and those

[90]For the claim that vertical fiscal imbalances typically cast federal governments in this role, see Watts (2005).

[91]For a recent statement that notes both the complexity and fluidity of the conditions that fiscal federalism policies aim to regulate, see Council of the Federation (2006, 12-13). Other jurisdictions' attempts to regulate fiscal federalism and, in particular, to achieve the kind of equalization among subfederal units required by section 36(1), have come under sustained criticism for their complexity and abstruseness. For a summary of these critiques of the formulas used by an independent agency charged with setting equalization levels in Australia, see Williams (2005); and Warren (2008).

raising bilateral claims of rights.[92] Professors Sabel and Simon have noted that even in instances of classic private law litigation, courts often articulate rules that have unforeseen systemic effects.[93] Consider a court articulating a standard of care in tort law. Such standards tend to be framed at a high level of generality, and those potentially subject to a standard will, to varying degrees, be uncertain about what a violation of it entails. They will organize their activities to manage that risk, either by factoring into the cost of operations the value of potential damages or by altering their behaviours to fall within the range of activity that clearly falls within the scope of the standard. Actors who fall within the scope of the standard will respond to actions taken by others, and the costs of such mutually responsive activity will be distributed across the system. The systemic and polycentric effects of judicial rule-making in paradigmatic private law cases are not sharply distinguishable from those of public law cases, and courts formulating rules in private law cases are thrust in the position of considering those effects as they render judgment.

Despite these points of continuity, litigation that aims to restructure public institutions gives rise to particular challenges for courts. Public law litigation arises when there is a dispute about whether a public authority has met some standard of conduct. Resistance to meeting standards tends to result from various forms of political blockage, and it is the *political nature* of this blockage that sharply distinguishes private from public litigation (Sable and Simon 2003-04, 1062). There are at least three sources of such political blockage: majoritarian resistance to compliance with a constitutional standard, political capture of public institutions by a highly motivated and well-resourced minority, and coordination failures, in which all parties share an interest in meeting a particular standard but the configuration of incentives leads parties to settle for suboptimal outcomes.[94] Sabel and Simon note the emergent tendency in public law for courts to address these blockages, not through highly specific command-and-control remedies, but rather through remedies that are open-ended,

---

[92]*Supra* note *66* and accompanying text.

[93]Sabel and Simon (2003-04, 1056-1062). For another instance of courts engaging in these kinds of innovative activities, see Dorf and Sabel (2000). For a proposed application of New Governance theory to federalism jurisprudence, see Dorf (1998-99). Dorf offers a variety of means by which courts can foster deliberation: First, he echoes Judge Calabresi's notion of a constitutional remand: when an old law potentially conflicts with a constitutional norm, the courts will remand the legislation to the legislature to determine whether the law reflects public policy, and if the legislature re-enacts the law, courts will be reluctant to strike it down (ibid., 69-70). Second, he argues for prophylactic rules in which the court articulates a norm that over-enforces the constitution, for the purpose of deterring unconstitutional governmental action, while expressly inviting the legislature to articulate an alternative norm (ibid., 70-72). Third, he argues that courts in some circumstances can defer judgment on a novel question of federal law in order to allow the states to pursue diverse approaches and thereby assist the Court in learning from the experiences of the states (ibid., 65).

[94]Ibid., 1064-1065. For an argument that different institutions and processes of social ordering have varying capacities to address these kinds of blockages, see Komesar (2001).

provisional and iterative, and that bring stakeholders together in public processes of deliberation.[95]

Let us consider an example. Sabel and Simon see in the remedies and legislative responses to the *Mount Laurel* litigation evidence of New Governance regulation.[96] In that case, the New Jersey court held that the exclusion of low- and moderate-income housing in a zoning ordinance violated the state constitution's "general welfare" provision. After a long history of litigation, the Court of Appeal held that the legislature's creation of an administrative agency to determine a municipality's fair share of low- and moderate-income housing was constitutional.[97] Sabel and Simon argue that the administrative process established by the New Jersey legislature has been responsive to the plaintiffs' interests by "creating pressures for local accommodation of low income housing and by making the zoning process more transparent".[98] The remedy fashioned by the final decision involved a variety of stakeholders, since the court consulted broadly in constructing the remedy, and crafted a flexible system, administered by selected trial judges, that was designed to convene stakeholders in subsequent constitutional challenges.[99] The *Mount Laurel* remedy responded to the complexity inherent in regulating housing markets and evidenced the features of a New Governance remedy: it

---

[95]Sabel and Simon (2003-04, 1067-1073). Sabel and Simon describe these remedial orders in a variety of contexts, including litigation over education, mental health, prisons, police abuse, and housing. In each area, the authors argue, courts have moved away from highly specific, command-and-control remedies to remedies with the characteristics described in the main text.

[96]*Southern Burlington County NAACP v. Township of Mount Laurel*, 336 A.2d 713 (N.J. 1975) [*Mount Laurel I*], *Southern Burlington County NAACP v. Township of Mount Laurel*, 456 A.2d 390 (N.J. 1983) [*Mount Laurel II*] and *Hills Developments Co. v. Township of Bernards*, 510 A.2d 621 (N.J. 1986) [*Mount Laurel III*]. I intend "*Mount Laurel*" to designate the entirety of the litigation history and events following and surrounding it.

[97]See Haars (1996) for the background and history of the litigation.

[98]Sabel and Simon (2003-04, 1052). Their argument about a shift away from command and control legislation has been echoed by Professor Lohe in his comment on the Massachusetts fair-share methodology (Lohe 2000). The Massachusetts model grants local boards considerable discretion to override restrictive land use regulations, while providing municipalities with an incentive to zone at least ten percent for subsidized housing. Judicious use of these overrides permits these boards to shape responses to local needs. Moreover, where a municipality meets the ten percent threshold, it cannot be compelled to take on more. MASS. GEN. LAWS c. 40B, §§ 30.00, 31.00.

[99]For a description of the process by which the remedy was constructed and delivered, as well as its contents, see Haar (1996, 55-62). For the details of the regime, see *Mount Laurel II, supra* note 96, 438-441, and 459 (for the system of appointed trial judges that would administer subsequent constitutional challenges), and 441-459 (for the range of means by which a municipality can satisfy its fair share obligations and of remedies available to a court that has found a municipality to be in violation of those obligations).

was open-ended, provisional, and iterative, and it brought stakeholders together in public processes of deliberation.

A New Governance Doctrinal Rule

With this example of New Governance judicial oversight in view, I turn now to propose a doctrinal rule that incorporates elements of New Governance theory. This rule states that federal or provincial action will be presumed to be in accordance with section 36(1)'s objectives unless a jointly constituted administrative agency finds that the action is disproportionate to or unnecessary for the achievement of those objectives.[100] If that agency finds that a government has violated section 36(1)'s proportionality and necessity requirements, the agency will issue recommendations on how the government should remedy the violation. If the government decides to depart from those recommendations, it must provide reasons, which a court will review on a reasonableness standard.[101] And if the government's reasons fail on this review, the government will be obliged to provide new reasons or to comply with the agency determination. This doctrinal rule would answer concerns about the institutional capacity of courts to oversee fiscal federalism, and it would have several process-related benefits.

First, because the administrative agency prescribed by the doctrinal rule would be a joint creation of the federal and provincial governments, those governments would be primarily responsible for its institutional design and, by extension, for its outputs.[102] Any problems of agency capture would be the primary responsibility of the political actors who created the agency, although a court could review for bias.

---

[100]Professors Albert Abel and Robin Boadway have proposed similar bodies (see Abel 1978, 313-337; Boadway 2000, 74). Other jurisdictions have fashioned bodies similar to the one proposed in the main text. See the survey of examples in Majeed, Watts, and Brown (2006, 332-335).

[101]For the Court's statement of current judicial review standards, see *Dunsmuir v. New Brunswick*, 2008 SCC 9 [*Dunsmuir*]. The issues addressed by the proposed administrative agency are a hybrid: they require expertise *and* they implicate the constitutional division of powers. The former characteristic attracts deference whereas the latter typically compels close judicial scrutiny: *Dunsmuir*at paras. 51-62. I suggest that the appropriate standard for s.36(1) review is deferential, because one of the reasons for the agency's existence is to make determinations that are beyond the expertise of a court. This level of review is consistent with that articulated in *Reference Re Remuneration of Judges of the Provincial Court (P.E.I.)*, [1997] 3 S.C.R. 3 at paras. 183-84 [*Remuneration Reference*] and *Provincial Court Judges' Assn. of New Brunswick v. New Brunswick (Minister of Justice)*, 2005 SCC 44, [2005] 2 S.C.R. 286 at paras. 28-42 [*Provincial Court Judges' Association*].

[102]Other federations have experiences with constituting such commissions, and they have the effect of palliating the influence of purely political interests in setting fiscal policy (see, e.g., Khemani 2007).

Second, such an agency would provide a forum for governments to come together to discuss differences and arrive at compromises. The New Governance literature suggests that providing such occasions for structured deliberation enables participants in a debate to cast and recast disagreements about policy ends and means, in the course of responding to specific policy problems.[103] An administrative structure such as the one I envision would allow the federal and provincial governments to fashion the grounds of an always provisional overlapping consensus.

Third, such an administrative agency would allow governments to convert substantive debates that generate persistent disagreement into concrete institutional design questions that can be resolved more readily. For instance, if Quebec were concerned about the capacity of Canadian federalism arrangements to accommodate its unique voice, or if Alberta believed that its unique interests with respect to natural resources should be acknowledged, they would structure administrative agency decision-making to reflect those concerns.[104]

Fourth, if appropriately designed, such an administrative agency would bring together intergovernmental and citizen oversight. The agency would permit expert assessments of empirical matters, while ensuring that citizens' own views about social policy delivery were heard. If federalism creates divided citizens, they should have some say in determining how those divisions will be drawn.[105]

Fifth, the proposed agency could serve as an information clearinghouse. It could assess information provided, at regular intervals, by the federal and provincial governments. Drawing on that information, the agency could make cross-jurisdictional comparisons and set standards for evaluating whether government action violated section 36(1)'s proportionality and necessity requirements. Those standards would periodically be reset as new information was gathered and new programs assessed.[106]

---

[103]See, e.g., Dorf and Sabel (2000); Gerstenberg and Sabel (2002); Lobel (2004). In spending power context, the literature suggests that under certain conditions, the existence of deliberative bodies facilitates productive cooperation between orders of government (see Anderson 2008, 504). Professor Anderson writes of the Council of Australian Governments (COAG), an intergovernmental body that brings together federal and state officials: "Both levels of government have found that decisions made in the summit-like atmosphere of the COAG can provide cover for decisions that otherwise might cause political problems if adopted unilaterally."

[104]For the argument that debates about substantive justice that are mediated through institutional design can be less destructive of social peace than direct debates about substantive justice, see Hills (2006, 770). For examples, in the spending power context, of institutional design debates that facilitate cooperation among federal and subfederal units that are otherwise deeply divided on substantive visions of federalism, see Watts (2005).

[105]For this concern about accountability, see Simeon (2006). For a critique of such accountability mechanisms in the complex regulatory environment of federalism, see Phillips (2003); Otis (2000); Simeon and Cameron (2002); DiGiacomo (2005).

[106]For institutional examples of comparative best practices and of public information pooling in Canada, see www.hc-sc.gc.ca/hcs-sss/qual/acces/wait-attente/index-eng.php.

Finally, the existence of a judicially generated constitutional rule would exert pressure on government actors to offer constitutional justifications for their actions and, as a result, judicial review could break through the kinds of blockages I have identified above.[107] To see how, let us consider each form of blockage in the section 36(1) context. First, federal political majorities may frustrate the interest of minorities, concentrated within a province, in receiving the baseline level of services specified by section 36(1); alternatively, national majorities may frustrate the ability of a particular province to provide baseline levels of services to its population. Second, motivated and well-resourced political minorities at either the federal or the provincial levels may dominate the legislative agenda and prevent the pursuit of policies that satisfy section 36(1)'s requirements. Third, all relevant political actors may agree that cooperative policies satisfying section 36(1)'s requirements are optimal, but because each is afraid of the downside risks of pursuing such policies and, in particular, the costs of others' defection from a cooperative policy, the actors collectively accept a suboptimal outcome.

The proposed doctrinal rule aims to break through each of these blockages. The doctrinal rule would, in the first instance, put pressure on political actors to justify a decision not to establish an agency that would facilitate the achievement of section 36(1) objectives and that would permit judicial review of their actions. This kind of pressure provides incentives for legislatures, whether they are dominated by a majority or a motivated minority, to act in ways consistent with a constitutional norm.[108] Absent the proposed doctrinal rule, there is no clear incentive for governments to act in this way. Once the political actors have accepted the constitutional norm and the proposed agency is established, governments would be subject to the standard forms of political pressure that any judicially generated constitutional rule exerts,[109] and these

---

[107]In making this argument, I am invoking instrumental and non-instrumental justifications for judicial review. For a survey of these kinds of reasons, see Harel and Kahana (2008). The central non-instrumental value that I am invoking is the right to justification for a perceived constitutional infringement. The instrumental reasons relate to the effects of judicial decisions on the variety of political blockages identified above. Professors Harel and Kahana are surely correct to note that all instrumental reasons for judicial review will involve some degree of speculation about institutional capacities and consequences, and in the current case, given that what I offer is a proposal rather than an analysis of existing conditions, the degree of speculation involved is particularly high. However, my claims about consequences are relatively modest: I only identify costs that governments will absorb as a result of a decision not to seek judicial review or to ignore judicial decisions. There is a significant literature on those kinds of costs (*supra* note 93), and as such my claims are less controversial than the more standard instrumental claims in judicial review, which tend to make quasi-empirical claims about the quality of judicial versus political branch decision-making (Harel amd Kahana 2008).

[108]As Choudhry has noted, governments have avoided even seeking a determination as to what the constitutional norms in this domain are (Choudhry 2000 and accompanying text).

[109]There is an extensive literature on the extent to which public and judicial opinion influence one another, and authors note that courts enjoy a degree of residual authority that allows them to retain support even in the face of public opposition to the substance of

forms of pressure provide incentives for governments to respect constitutional norms or to offer reasons to justify departures from these norms. Finally, the proposed constitutional rule provides incentives to political actors to overcome coordination problems. Absent such a rule, political actors can, without political cost, ignore the constitutional implications of their actions. Once the judiciary articulates a constitutional rule, that possibility is no longer open and the political branches must factor into their choices the cost of being perceived to act contrary to a constitutional standard. However, even if one accepts these arguments in favour of the proposed doctrinal rule, one might still object that the agency required by that rule is outside the realm of political possibility. According to this objection, political actors in Canada are not motivated to create intergovernmental agencies, and such agencies are politically impractical in the fiscal federalism context. In the following section I will offer some examples that suggest that the doctrinal rule and its attendant agency are politically possible.

Considering Institutional Examples

I conclude this section by describing some institutions that can serve as templates for the kind of agency that the federal and provincial governments might create,[110] and by answering some criticisms of the proposed doctrinal rule. The existence of those model institutions suggests that members of the federation sometimes believe it to be in their interests to create such mechanisms of accountability.[111]

Consider first the 2007 "Building Canada" plan. This plan provides a framework within which the federal government can collaborate with provinces, territories, and municipalities on matters of infrastructure development, and it envisages a federal investment of $33 billion over seven years.[112] While the agency I propose would involve all governments, the Building Canada plan

---

particular decisions (see, e.g., Friedman 2003). In Canada, public esteem for courts is sufficiently high that governments are generally unwilling to provoke public disapprobation by invoking a constitutionally prescribed mechanism to override judicial decisions (see generally, Kahana 2002).

[110]For examination of how one intergovernmental initiative falls short of providing sufficient oversight, see Choudhry (2000).,

[111]New Governance writing generally draws on specific examples to illustrate its claims, and this attempt to test theoretical claims against existing practices is consistent with the theory's pragmatic bent (see, e.g., Dorf and Sabel 2000; Sabel and Zeitlin 2008; de Búrca 2006, 97; Scott and Holder 2006, 211; Hervey 2006, 179). For a survey of emergent trends in policy coordination, public accountability, and continuing, results-based monitoring in Canadian federal institutions, see Fox and Lenihan (2006, 1, 3).

[112]Canada (N.p. 2007, 4). "Over half of the funding under the *Building Canada* plan will be provided as base funding for municipalities. In total, over $17.6 billion will be provided over seven years through the Gas Tax Fund (GTF) and the Goods and Services Tax (GST) Rebate" (ibid., 24).

provides for the signing of framework agreements with each province and territory on a bilateral basis.[113] The first such agreement was signed between the federal Minister of Transport, Infrastructure and Communities and British Columbia's Minister of Transportation on 6 November 2007.[114]

In order to facilitate coordination and cooperation between the levels of government, the framework agreements create an Infrastructure Framework Committee (IFC) (see, e.g., ibid., s.7.1). Each level of government agrees to appoint a co-chair, and the co-chairs are the only voting members of the IFC (see ibid., s.7.2). The first infrastructure framework agreement provides measures for public reporting and accountability. For example, section 2.1 states that "Canada and British Columbia will promote accountability by providing Canadians with regular public reporting on the implementation and outcomes of the Building Canada Plan in British Columbia" (ibid., s.2.1). And section 8.1 states:

> The Parties agree to develop and implement a framework for reporting to the public on the outcomes and results achieved from infrastructure investments in British Columbia across the range of federal infrastructure programs. The reporting framework will be developed within six (6) months of the signing of this Agreement. (ibid., s.8.1)

A second example of the kind of agency I have in mind for addressing section 36(1) disputes can be found in the 2003 Accord on Health Care Renewal. In that Accord, in order to promote accountability and transparency, the First Ministers established the Health Council of Canada as an independent body to inform Canadians about health-care matters (see Health Canada 2006, N.p.). In the 2004 Ten Year Plan, the First Ministers required annual public reports (see ibid.). The 2003 Accord outlined the nature of the Council, and stated:

> The Health Council will publicly report through federal/provincial/ territorial Ministers of Health and will include representatives of both orders of government, experts and the public. To fulfill its mandate, the Council will draw upon consultations and relevant reports, including governments' reports, the work of the Federal/Provincial/Territorial Advisory Committee on

---

[113]"Through Framework Agreements signed with each province and territory, the Government of Canada will work in partnership to address infrastructure issues in a consistent and coherent manner, which takes into account long-term planning" (ibid., 29).

[114]The parties to that agreement also commit to working with municipal governments. For example, the agreement states: "Canada and British Columbia will engage municipal leaders in the delivery of the Building Canada Plan. The Parties fully support the value of municipal participation, and will work with the Union of British Columbia Municipalities and municipalities to address the infrastructure needs in British Columbia" (*Canada – British Columbia: Infrastructure Framework Agreement* (6 November 2007) at 2, online, Building Canada, at www.buildingcanada-chantiers canada.gc.ca/alt-format/pdf/ifa-eci-bc-eng.pdf. In total, five framework agreements have been signed; the most recent between Canada and Nunavut on 8 February 2008.

Governance and Accountability and the Canadian Institute for Health Information (CIHI). (ibid.)

One might concede that these and other forms of accountability institutions exist in Canada[115] and that the requirement to create such institutions, which is imposed by the proposed doctrinal rule, therefore falls within the realm of political possibility. Nonetheless, one might still argue that there is something unique about fiscal federalism that resists the creation of such an administrative agency. To answer this objection, I turn to some comparative examples.

In Australia, South Africa, and India, independent agencies are charged with setting policy to give effect to redistributive objectives similar to those articulated in section 36(1). Since 1933, federal legislation has charged the Commonwealth Grants Commission in Australia with determining how to reduce horizontal fiscal inequity within the Australian federation.[116] Professor Ross Williams notes that "the Australian system of horizontal fiscal equalisation is the most complex and thorough going of all federations. Allowances are made for differences between states in both their revenue-raising capabilities and their costs of delivery of government services" (ibid., 110). The Commission reports to a body comprised of state and federal treasurers, and after deliberations within this body, the federal treasurer makes the ultimate decision as to how revenues are to be distributed (ibid.). This expert agency model has been borrowed by India and South Africa. In India, the Constitution requires a Finance Commission to be appointed every five years. The mandate of each Commission is to pursue equalization objectives by offering proposals that redistribute tax room or revenues from the federal government to the states.[117] Legislation sets out the technical expertise required of the Commission's

---

[115]For an argument that the Social Union Framework Agreement sought to achieve these goals of accountability and to implement these monitoring processes, see Canadian Centre for Management Development, "Implementing the Social Union Framework Agreement: A Learning and Reference Tool", at 35, online: Canada School of Public Service, www.csps-efpc.gc.ca/Research/publications/pdfs/SUFA_e.pdf. For an example of federal-provincial institutional commitment to policy coordination that relies extensively on the ministerial discretion, rather than on compulsory agency reporting, see "About CCME", online: The Canadian Council of Ministers of the Environment, www.ccme.ca/about/index.html#363 ["About CCME"]. For an example of a series of bilateral agreements that impose variable reporting requirements, see "Agreement on the Transfer of Federal Gas Tax Revenues under the New Deal for Cities and Communities: 2005–2015", (14 May 2005) at 3, online: Infrastructure Canada, www.infras tructure.gc.ca/ip-pi/gas-essence_tax/alt_formats/pdf/gt_can_ab_e.pdf; "Gas Tax Agreement: Canada – British Columbia – Union of British Columbia Municipalities" (19 September 2005), 14, 15, online: Infrastructure Canada, www.infrastruc-ture.gc.ca/ip-pi/gas-essence_tax/alt_formats/pdf/gt_can_bc_e.pdf; "Gas Tax/Public Transit Agreement: Canada – Quebec" (28 November 2005) at 6, online: Infrastructure Canada, www.infrastructure.gc.ca/ip-pi/gas-essence_tax/alt_formats/pdf/gt_can_qc-final_e.pdf.

[116]See generally, Williams (2005). In recent years, the primary function of the Commission has been to determine how to distribute federal general sales tax revenues among the states (ibid., 110).

[117]For the current Commission's terms of reference, see fincomindia.nic.in.

members and protects them from political interference. Moreover, its recommendations are binding (Khemani 2007, 468). Stuti Khemani argues that the Indian example provides strong support for the claim that delegating to an independent expert body responsibility for determining the amounts and recipients of federal transfers minimizes the influence of political considerations on fiscal federal policy. Finally, in South Africa part of the mandate of the statutorily created, independent advisory Financial Fiscal Commission is to recommend how the national government should assign revenue to the provincial and local governments and how to do so in ways that account for divergent fiscal needs and capacities.[118]

In this section, I have cited examples of federal-provincial institutions in Canada whose role is to oversee and coordinate policy, and I have described three expert agencies in states where there is a vertical fiscal gap and a constitutional text that at a minimum allows the central government to reduce inequities among the subnational units.[119] With these examples, I hope to suggest that the agency I propose is not outside the realm of political possibility.

Answering Objections

I close this section by turning from these issues of institutional design to answer three objections to the proposed doctrinal rule. A first objection claims that courts are not constitutionally authorized to require governments to set up administrative agencies, and that such a requirement would violate the separation of powers. This objection rests on a misunderstanding of the rule I am proposing. The rule would not require governments to establish an administrative agency, but would merely provide that a court will not engage in

[118]For a brief history of the relationships between national and subnational governments in South Africa, in the pre- and post-Apartheid eras, see Amusa and Mathane (2007). For a description of the Commission's role, mandate, and composition, as well as a summary of the mechanisms by which its independence is safeguarded, see www.ffc.co.za/ffc.asp?main=about/main.asp&menu=about.

[119]Section 96 of the Australian Constitution states: "During a period of ten years after the establishment of the Commonwealth and thereafter until the Parliament otherwise provides, the Parliament may grant financial assistance to any State on such terms and conditions as the Parliament thinks fit." (*Commonwealth of Australia Constitution Act, 1900* (U.K.), 63 & 64 Vict., c. 12, s.96). Part XII, Chapter I of the Indian Constitution empowers the federal government to redistribute tax revenues to the states and expressly contemplates a Finance Commission that prescribes the means of that redistribution (*Constitution of India* (1949), Part XII, c. 1, arts. 264-291). Section 214 of the South African Constitution requires equitable distribution of national revenues among the provincial and local governments and sets out a process of consultation that includes the Financial Fiscal Commission, the provincial and local governments. That section also requires that legislation effecting the equitable distribution can only be passed once a list of considerations enumerated in the Constitution, as well as the recommendations of the Commission, have been considered (*Constitution of the Republic of South Africa, 1996*, c. 13, s.214).

section 36(1) review until they had done so. Such a doctrinal rule would be deferential to the political branches, because it would leave them to decide whether to submit their policy choices to judicial review. It would encourage political negotiation and compromise, and it expressly seeks to avoid usurping the political branches' prerogatives in managing these processes. Moreover, it fits well with the text of section 36(1). That section requires that governments be "committed to" its objectives, and as we have seen above, it sets limits on what governments may do when acting pursuant to it. The proposed doctrinal rule would empower the judiciary to enforce section 36(1)'s limits on governmental action *only after* governments had manifested their commitment to the section's objectives by establishing an oversight body. This doctrinal posture is consistent with a recent statement by the Supreme Court of Canada that "the task of maintaining the balance between federal and provincial powers falls primarily to governments".[120]

In addition, the administrative body that I propose is similar to one the Supreme Court ordered in the *Remuneration Reference* (ibid., paras. 168-185). The proposed administrative body is not excluded by Canadian constitutional law, and a court ordering the creation of such a body would arguably be acting consistently with precedent. In the *Remuneration Reference*, the Court directed that a commission be made responsible for setting provincial court judges' salaries at levels and in a manner that protected the constitutional norm of an independent judiciary.[121] That commission was designed to remove the possibility of improper political influence in a process aimed at resolving a constitutional question, to safeguard the decision-making process from self-dealing, and to ensure that objective information would be considered. The doctrinal rule and administrative oversight body that I have proposed for section 36(1) aim to achieve similar outcomes. The proposed rule allocates responsibility for settling a constitutional question among the branches of government to ensure that their input is constitutionally appropriate; it responds to the risks of self-dealing that would arise from leaving the relevant constitutional questions exclusively to political actors; and it aims to ensure that empirical determinations that are beyond the institutional capacities of the courts will be competently made.

A second criticism of the proposed doctrinal rule claims that it is overly solicitous of political processes. A similar criticism has been levelled against the South Africa Commission: because its recommendations are non-binding, critics argue that the Commission is ineffectual (Watts 2005, 30). A critic might argue that the rule I propose is even more deferential to political actors and therefore would likely be even more ineffectual: the proposed rule would enable governments to frustrate enforcement of section 36(1) by refusing to participate even in the creation of an administrative agency. As a result of such a refusal, the objection continues, section 36(1) would go unenforced. Let us engage this

---

[120] *Reference Re Employment Insurance Act (Can.), ss.22 and 23*2005 SCC 56, [2005] 2 S.C.R. 669 at para. 10.

[121] The reasoning in that case was refined in *Provincial Court Judges' Association*, *supra* note 101 and those refinements are reflected in the doctrinal rule I have proposed.

criticism by considering the ways in which the risks of non-enforcement can be distributed. The risk that a (federal or provincial) government will frustrate enforcement of section 36(1) and undermine the interests of another government may be distributed evenly, so that no government would bear an unequal share of the costs of non-enforcement. Although this may not be an optimal outcome, it is preferable to having the courts directly supervise fiscal federalism under section 36(1)'s auspices. Such supervision, we saw above, would give rise to a host of difficulties. By contrast, reliance on the proposed doctrinal rule would avoid these difficulties. And because, under the hypothetical conditions advanced, the rule would not disproportionately disadvantage any level of government or any province or group of provinces, it would not create perennial losers in federalism disputes.

Alternatively, the risks of non-enforcement may be consistently and disproportionately borne by one government or set of governments. The challenge for a court considering whether to regulate such risks would lie in anticipating where the risks will fall. But this kind of assessment, as well as any more direct form of supervising government action under section 36(1), would require courts to stake out positions in normative debates and engage in empirical assessments that, I have argued above, they should avoid. Courts would have to assess which governments would likely suffer the costs of section 36(1) violations, determine the extent of such costs, and set out and justify normative baselines against which to measure at least some of those costs.

The doctrinal rule that I have argued for would avoid direct judicial assessment of these kinds of costs, and would trade off the risks of non-enforcement against the benefits of promoting democratic deliberation and of acknowledging the limits of judicial capacity. The doctrinal rule would enable the judiciary to function as a constitutional backstop, would put the main burden of regulation of the federation on political actors, would facilitate processes of intergovernmental cooperation and compromise, and would provide forums for democratic deliberation. Even if a more interventionist rule might better protect some set of constitutional values or interests, a more active judiciary bent on enforcing such a rule would risk making decisions that they were incompetent to make and would risk outcomes that were worse, on any relevant measure, than those that would result from implementing the proposed doctrinal rule.[122] Moreover, as we have seen above, the proposed doctrinal rule would mitigate the risk of non-enforcement, by placing governments under political pressure to justify their decisions to depart from constitutional norms or to resist constitutional assessment.[123]

The difficulties of assessment I have described above may be overdrawn. It is possible that a court could issue a stronger form of the proposed doctrinal

---

[122]There is an extensive literature on the unforeseen consequences of judicial decisions that stake out firm positions in socially contentious debates and enforce those positions aggressively in complex policy environments (see, e.g., Klarman 1994; Post and Siegel 2007, Part III). For arguments in favour of judicial under-enforcement of constitutional norms, see Sager (2004, c. 7).

[123]*Supra* note 107 and accompanying text.

rule, while accommodating the judiciary's institutional limits. A court could state that section 36(1) *requires* that the federal and provincial governments jointly create an administrative body of the kind suggested above. We have seen that such a requirement would be consistent with constitutional precedent: in the *Remuneration Reference*, the court stated a *requirement* that provinces create independent agencies. In addition, to mitigate institutional competence concerns, a court might require that the federal and provincial governments create an agency but expressly state that the political branches can satisfy section 36(1)'s requirements in other ways. *Miranda v. Arizona*[124] provides a model for such a rule. The Court in that decision reasoned that the Fourth Amendment exclusionary rule requires that police officers issue a standard warning when arresting a suspect. But, as Dorf notes, "the Court expressly invited Congress and the states to devise 'other procedures which are at least as effective in apprising accused persons of their right to silence'".[125] In the section 36(1) context, a court could similarly reason that there are a variety of ways of satisfying the section's requirement that governments commit to the section's objectives, and that governments would be welcome to generate their own means of satisfying that requirement that were at least as effective as that proposed by the Court. Until the governments did so, however, the proposed agency would be constitutionally required and would set a constitutional minimum.

This stronger version of the doctrinal rule would aim to provide greater protection of constitutional norms than the version I have detailed above, but would come at the cost of placing the judiciary in an active role, in a context where political actors have typically taken the lead in shaping policy and creating institutions. A glance at the comparative examples cited above is instructive: the oversight agencies in Australia, India and South Africa were created at the initiative of the political branches. Given the complexity involved in designing effective fiscal oversight agencies, political resistance to judicial oversight may result in either long delays or ineffective institutions that may undermine the credibility of the courts. The risks of these outcomes are lower when the political branches are given primary responsibility for initiating agency oversight.

A final objection to the doctrinal rule states that review on a reasonableness standard merely defers the moment at which a court would have to act outside of its competence. There are two responses to this objection and each sounds in the language of legality. First, in many cases of judicial review of administrative action, the reviewing court is less competent than the administrative agency being reviewed. We do not abandon the project of judicial review in those cases; we rather believe that the value of legality requires agencies to be held to constitutional account.[126] Second, under the proposed form of reasonableness

[124]384 U.S. 436 (1966).

[125]Dorf (1998-99, 72). On prophylactic rules, generally, see Strauss (1988).

[126]For instance, the test for judicial review under *Pushpanathan v. Canada (Minister of Citizenship and Immigration)*, [1998] 1 S.C.R. 982 expressly contemplates this gap between the institutional competencies of courts and administrative agencies, and

review, governments are required to provide reasons for their actions. As we have seen above, the value of legality requires that governments engaged in constitutionally suspect behaviour offer constitutional reasons for their actions. According to the proposed doctrinal rule, a government that failed to offer reasons for its decision not to abide by an agency determination would fail reasonableness review. Such a requirement represents an advance over a status quo in which government can evade constitutional questions and provide no justifications for constitutionally controversial actions.[127]

CONCLUSIONS

I began this chapter by noting that the spending power gives rise to two long-standing issues in constitutional theory: legal indeterminacy and institutional competence. The interpretation I have offered for section 36(1) and the doctrinal rule that I have proposed aim to address these issues. To conclude, I will retrace my arguments.

In this chapter, I have argued that section 36(1) provides the most plausible constitutional framework for structuring analyses of controversial exercises of the spending power in Canada, and I have argued that New Governance theory is particularly salient to the interpretation and implementation of that section. New Governance federalism theory attempts to resolve concerns about federal and subfederal policy coordination and public accountability, and these concerns underwrite section 36(1). In addition, New Governance theorists have considered how and why courts may be called upon to break through the kinds of political blockages that frustrate attempts to subject the spending power to the discipline of constitutional norms.

One might accept these general points about the significance of New Governance theory to the spending power in Canada but contest the practicability of my proposals. It is worth noting that there may soon be a constitutional reference directly challenging the constitutionality of the spending power.[128] If this happens, the courts will confront the theoretical concerns I have raised in a very concrete form. I have argued that the obvious alternatives to my doctrinal rule are untenable. Courts are incompetent to engage in case-by-case assessments of exercises of the spending power. Moreover, if the judiciary, by enunciating a bright-line rule, were to take one side in the persistent debates about the nature of Canadian federalism, it would lose credibility in the eyes of significant segments of the Canadian public and exclude them from

---

incorporates that concern into the test (at para. 32-35). The gap is not a sufficient reason to abandon judicial review.

[127] *Provincial Court Judges' Association* is instructive in this regard. In that case, Quebec did not provide *constitutional reasons* for its actions and, as such, failed constitutional review (*supra* note 101 at para. 159). At a minimum, the proposed doctrinal rule would capture such cases.

[128] See www.radio-canada.ca/nouvelles/Politique/2009/06/13/002-PQ-Marois-souverainete.shtml.

constitutional discourse. The alternative for which I have argued here expressly engages the concerns about institutional competence and reasonable disagreement to which the spending power gives rise. Finally, it imposes a requirement of reason-giving upon political actors. This requirement is credible because it is enunciated by the judiciary, and it is valuable because it meets the demands of legality.

If we accept the foregoing, then the remaining challenges take the form of separation of powers and political feasibility arguments. We have seen that the proposal is consistent with the *Remuneration Reference*, and any separation of powers objections apply to the doctrinal rule enunciated in that case. I have suggested that any such concerns are misplaced, particularly in the present case, because the responsibility for initiating judicial review and designing the relevant agency would fall primarily on the political branches. Moreover, the political feasibility arguments have been answered by pointing to existing institutions within Canada and abroad. There is nothing in Canadian federalism that precludes the kind of cooperative endeavours that I have proposed, and there is nothing intrinsic to fiscal federalism that resists such oversight.

In short, the proposals I have offered, far from being fanciful, are grounded in constitutional values and in the political experience of our own federation and of others. Ultimately, the value of legality requires governmental accounting to citizens when constitutionally controversial practices are at issue. The proposed rule aims to elicit such reason-giving and to address perennial problems of constitutional theory in the process. Even if my proposals are not adopted, I suggest that the questions I have raised are central to any adequate analysis of the spending power in Canada today.

REFERENCES

Abel, A.S. 1969. "The Neglected Logic of 91 and 92", *The University of Toronto Law Journal* 19(4).

— 1978. "Albert Abel's Constitutional Charter for Canada", *The University of Toronto Law Journal* 28(3).

Adler, M.D. 2006. "Popular Constitutionalism and the Rule of Recognition: Whose Practices Ground U.S. Law?" *Northwestern University Law Review* 100.

Alexander, L. 1999. "'With Me It's All er Nuthin': Formalism in Law and Morality", *University of Chicago Law Review* 66.

Alexander, L. and F. Schauer. 1997. "On Extrajudicial Constitutional Interpretation", *Harvard Law Review* 111.

Amusa, H. and P. Mathane. 2007. "South Africa's Intergovernmental Fiscal Relations: An Evolving System", *South African Journal of Economics* 75(2).

Anderson, G. 2008. "The Council of Australian Governments: A New Institution of Governance for Australia's Conditional Federalism", *University of New South Wales Law Journal* 31.

Balkin, J.M. 2004. "What *Brown* Teaches Us about Constitutional Theory", *Virginia Law Review* 90.

Beatty, D. 1995. *Canadian Constitutional Law in Theory and Practice.* Toronto: University of Toronto Press.

Berman, M.N. 2001. "Coercion without Baselines: Unconstitutional Conditions in Three Dimensions", *Georgetown Law Journal* 90.

— 2004. "Constitutional Decision Rules", *Virginia Law Review* 90.

Boadway, R. 2000. "Recent Developments in the Economics of Federalism", in H. Lazar (ed.), *Toward a New Mission Statement for Canadian Fiscal Federalism.* Montreal: McGill-Queen's University Press.

Boychuk, G.W. 2006. "Slouching toward the Bottom? Provincial Social Assistance Provision in Canada, 1980-2000", in K. Harrison (ed.), *Racing to the Bottom? Provincial Interdependence in the Canadian Federation.* Vancouver: UBC Press.

Brest, P. 1980. "The Misconceived Quest for the Original Understanding", *Boston University Law Review* 60.

Brinks, D.O. 2001. "Legal Interpretation and Morality", in B. Leiter (ed.), *Objectivity in Law and Morals.* Cambridge: Cambridge University Press.

Brisson, J.-M. and A. Morel. 1997. "Droit fédéral et droit civil: complémentarité, dissociation", in *The Harmonization of Federal Legislation with Quebec Civil Law and Canadian Bijuralism: Collection of Studies.* Montreal: Department of Justice.

Brouillet, E. 2005. *La négation de la nation: l'identité québécoise et le fédéralisme canadien.* Sillery, QC: Septentrion.

Canada. 2007. *Building Canada: Modern Infrastructure for a Strong Canada.* At www.buildingcanada-chantierscanada.gc.ca/alt-format/pdf/booklet-livret-eng.pdf?wt.ad=plan-eng>.

Chayes, A. 1976. "The Role of the Judge in Public Law Litigation", *Harvard Law Review* 89.

Choper, J.H. 1980. *Judicial Review and the National Political Process: A Functional Reconsideration of the Role of the Supreme Court.* Chicago: University of Chicago Press.

Choudhry, S. 2000. "Bill 11, The Canada Health Act and the Social Union: The Need for New Institutions", *Osgoode Hall Law Journal* 38.

— 2002. "Recasting Social Canada: A Reconsideration of Federal Jurisdiction over Social Policy", *The University of Toronto Law Journal* 52.

Cook, R. 1969. *Provincial Autonomy, Minority Rights and the Compact Theory.* Ottawa: Queen's Printer for Canada.

Council of the Federation (Canada), Advisory Panel on Fiscal Imbalance. 2006. *Reconciling the Irreconcilable: Addressing Canada's Fiscal Imbalance.* At www.councilofthefederation.ca/pdfs/Report_Fiscalim_Mar3106.pdf.

de Búrca, G. 2006. "EU Race Discrimination Law: A Hybrid Model?" in G.de Búrca and J. Scott (eds.), *Law and New Governance in the EU and the US.* Portland: Hart.

Dewey, J. 1944. *Democracy and Education: An Introduction to the Philosophy of Education.* New York: Free Press.

DiGiacomo, G. 2005. "The Democratic Content of Intergovernmental Agreements in Canada", SIPP Public Policy Paper 38 (December). Online: The Saskatchewan Institute of Public Policy at www.uregina.ca/sipp/documents/pdf/PPP38_%20 DiGiacomo.pdf.

Dorf, M.C. 1997. "Integrating Normative and Descriptive Constitutional Theory: The Case of Original Meaning", *Georgetown Law Journal* 85.

— 1998-99. "Foreword: The Limits of Socratic Deliberation", *Harvard Law Review* 112.

— 2003. "Legal Indeterminacy and Institutional Design", *New York University Law Review* 78.

— 2005. "The Coherentism of Democracy and Distrust", *Yale Law Journal* 114.

Dorf, M.C. and C.F. Sabel. 1998. "A Constitution of Democratic Experimentalism", *Columbia Law Review* 98.

— 2000. "Drug Treatment Courts and Emergent Experimentalist Government", *Vanderbilt Law Review* 53.

Dworkin, R. 1986. *Law's Empire.* Cambridge, MA: Belknap Press.

— 2006. *Justice in Robes.* Cambridge, MA: Belknap Press.

Edmundson, W.A. 1995. "Is Law Coercive?" *Legal Theory* 1.

Eisgruber, C.L. 2001. *Constitutional Self-Government.* Cambridge, MA: Harvard University Press.

Elster, J. 1997. "The Market and the Forum: Three Varieties of Political Theory", in J. Bohman and W. Rehg (eds.), *Essays on Reason and Politics.* Cambridge, MA: MIT Press.

Fallon, R.H., Jr. 1994. "Reflections on the Hart and Wechsler Paradigm", *Vanderbilt Law Review* 47.

— 2001. *Implementing the Constitution.* Cambridge, MA: Harvard University Press.

— 2007-08. "Constitutional Precedent Viewed through the Lens of Hartian Positivist Jurisprudence", *North Carolina Law Review* 86.

Farber, D.A. and P.P. Frickey. 1997. *Law and Public Choice.* Chicago: University of Chicago Press.

Fiss, O. 2008. "The Perils of Minimalism", *Theoretical Inquiries in Law* 9(2).

Flood, C.M., M. Stabile, and S. Kontic. 2005. "Finding Health Policy 'Arbitrary': The Evidence on Waiting, Dying, and Two-Tier Systems", in C.M. Flood, K. Roach, and L. Sossin (eds.), *Access to Care, Access to Justice: The Legal Debate Over Private Health Insurance in Canada.* Toronto: University of Toronto Press.

Fox, G. and D. Lenihan. 2006. "Where Does the Buck Stop? Accountability and Joint Initiatives", *Public Policy Forum.*

Fox-Decent, E. 2007. "Parliamentary Privilege and the Rule of Law", *Canadian Journal of Administrative Law and Practice* 20(2).

Freeman, A. and C. Forcese. 2005. *The Laws of Government: The Legal Foundations of Canadian Democracy.* Toronto: Irwin Law.

Friedman, B. 2003. "Mediated Popular Constitutionalism", *Michigan Law Review* 101.

— 2005. "The Politics of Judicial Review", *Texas Law Review* 84.

Fuller, L.L. 1965. *The Morality of Law.* New Haven: Yale University Press.

— 1978. "The Forms and Limits of Adjudication", *Harvard Law Review* 92.

— 2001. "Means and Ends", in K. Winston (ed.), *The Principles of Social Order: Selected Essays of Lon L. Fuller*, rev. ed. Portland: Hart.

Garrett, B.L. and J.S. Liebman. 2004. "Experimentalist Equal Protection", *Yale Law and Policy Review* 22(2).

Gaudreault-DesBiens, J.-F. 2004. "The Canadian Federal Experiment, or Legalism without Federalism? Toward a Legal Theory of Federalism", in M. Calvo-Garcia and W. Felstiner (eds.), *Federalismo/Federalism.* Madrid: Dyckinson.

— 2006. "The Irreducible Federal Necessity of Jurisdictional Autonomy, and the Irreducibility of Federalism to Jurisdictional Autonomy", in S. Choudhry, J.-F. Gaudreault-DesBiens, and L. Sossin (eds.), *Dilemmas of Solidarity: Rethinking Redistribution in the Canadian Federation.* Toronto: University of Toronto Press.

Gerstenberg, O. and C. Sabel. 2002. "Directly-Deliberative Polyarchy: An Institutional Ideal for Europe?" in C. Joerges and R. Dehousse (eds.), *Good Governance in Europe's Integrated Market.* Oxford: Oxford University Press.

Gibson, D. 1996. "The Canada Health Act and the Constitution", *Health Law Journal* 4.

Government of Canada. 1989. "Federal-Provincial Grants and the Spending Power of Parliament", in A.F. Bayefsky (ed.), *Canada's Constitution Act 1982 & Amendments,* vol. 1. Toronto: McGraw-Hill Ryerson.

Greschner, D. 2000. "The Supreme Court, Federalism, and Metaphors of Moderation", *The Canadian Bar Review* 79.

Guttman, A. and D. Thompson. 1996. *Democracy and Disagreement.* Cambridge, MA: Belknap Press.

Haar, C. 1996. *Suburbs under Siege: Race, Space and Audacious Judges.* Princeton: Princeton University Press.

Harel, A. and T. Kahana. 2008. "The Easy Core Case for Judicial Review". Online: Social Science Research Network at papers.ssrn.com/sol3/papers.cfm?abstract_id=1272493.

Harrison, K., ed. 2006. *Racing to the Bottom? Provincial Interdependence in the Canadian Federation.* Vancouver: UBC Press.

Health Canada. 2006. *First Minister's Meeting on the Future of Health Care 2004: A 10-Year Plan to Strengthen Health Care.* Online: Health Canada at www.hc-sc.gc.ca/hcs-sss/delivery-prestation/fptcollab/2004-fmm-rpm/index_e.html (May 9).

Hervey, T.K. 2006. "The European Union and the Governance of Health Care", in G. de Búrca and J. Scott (eds.), *Law and New Governance in the EU and the US.* Portland: Hart.

Hills, R.M., Jr. 2006. "Federalism as Westphalian Liberalism", *Fordham Law Review* 75.

Himma, K.E. 2003. "Making Sense of Constitutional Disagreement: Legal Positivism, The Bill of Rights, and the Conventional Rule of Recognition in the United States", *Journal of Law in Society* 4(2).

Hogg, P.W. 2007. *Constitutional Law of Canada*, 5th ed., looseleaf. Scarborough: Thomson Carswell.

Hogg, P.W. and W.K. Wright. 2005. "Canadian Federalism, The Privy Council and the Supreme Court: Reflections on the Debate about Canadian Federalism", *University of British Columbia Law Review* 38(2).

Hutchinson, A.C. 1989. "That's Just the Way It Is: Langille on Law", *McGill Law Journal* 34.

Kahana, T. 2002. "Understanding the Notwithstanding Mechanism", *University of Toronto Law Journal* 52.

Kelly, J.B. 2005. *Governing with the Charter.* Vancouver: UBC Press.

Khemani, S. 2007. "Does Delegation of Fiscal Policy to an Independent Agency Make a Difference? Evidence from Intergovernmental Transfers in India", *Journal of Development Economics* 82.

King, J. 2008. "Institutional Approaches to Judicial Restraint", *Oxford Journal of Legal Studies* 28(3).

Klarman, M.J. 1994. "How *Brown* Changed Race Relations: The Backlash Thesis", *Journal of American History* 81.

Komesar, N. 2001. *Law's Limits: The Rule of Law and the Supply and Demand of Rights.* Cambridge, MA: Cambridge University Press.

Kong, H. 2008. "The Spending Power, Constitutional Interpretation and Legal Pragmatism", *Queen's Law Journal* 33.

Kramer, L. 2004. *The People Themselves: Popular Constitutionalism and Judicial Review.* Oxford: Oxford University Press.

La Forest, G.V. 1967. *The Allocation of Taxing Power under the Canadian Constitution.* Toronto: Canadian Tax Foundation.

— 1975. "Delegation of Legislative Power in Canada", *McGill Law Journal* 21.

— 2004. *Pour la liberté d'une société distinct.* Saint-Nicolas, QC: Presses de l'Université Laval.

Lajoie, A. 2006. "The Federal Spending Power and Fiscal Imbalance in Canada", in S. Choudhry, J.-F. Gaudreault-DesBiens, and L. Sossin (eds.), *Dilemmas of Solidarity: Rethinking Redistribution in the Canadian Federation.* Toronto: University of Toronto Press.

Lambert, N. 2007. "The Charter in Administrative Process: Statutory Remedy or Refounding of Administrative Jurisdiction?" *Review of Constitutional Studies* 13(1).

Lamond, G. 2000. "The Coerciveness of Law", *Oxford Journal of Legal Studies* 20.

Langille, B. 1988. "Revolution without Foundation: The Grammar of Scepticism and Law", *McGill Law Journal* 33.

LaPierre, D.B. 1985. "Political Accountability in the National Political Process – The Alternative to Judicial Review of Federalism Issues", *Northwestern University Law Review* 80(3).

Laskin, B. 1947. "'Peace, Order and Good Government' Re-examined", *Canadian Bar Review* 25.

Lazar, H. 2000. "Trust in Intergovernmental Fiscal Relations", in H. Lazar (ed.), *Toward a New Mission Statement for Canadian Fiscal Federalism.* Montreal: McGill-Queen's University Press.

Leclair, J. 2003. "The Supreme Court of Canada's Understanding of Federalism: Efficiency at the Expense of Diversity", *Queen's Law Journal* 28.

Levi, I. 1998. "Pragmatism and Change of View", *Canadian Journal of Philosophy* 24.

Levy, J.T. 2007. "Federalism, Liberalism and the Separation of Loyalties", *American Political Science Review* 101.

L'Heureux-Dubé, C. 2000. "The Dissenting Opinion: Voices of the Future?" *Osgoode Hall Law Journal* 38.

Lohe, W. 2000. "The Massachusetts Comprehensive Permit Law: Collaboration between Affordable Housing Advocates and Environmentalists", *Land Use Law & Zoning Digest* 3 (May).

Lobel, O. 2004. "The Renew Deal: The Fall of Regulation and the Rise of Governance in Contemporary Legal Thought", *Minnesota Law Review* 89.

Lyons, D. 2005. "The Lessons of Lopez: The Political Dynamics of Federalism's Political Safeguards", *Harvard Law Review* 119.

Macey, J.R. 1990. "Federal Deference to Local Regulators and the Economic Theory of Regulation: Towards a Public-Choice Explanation of Federalism", *Virginia Law Review* 76.

Majeed, A., R.L. Watts, and D.M. Brown. 2006. *A Global Dialogue on Federalism: Distribution of Powers and Responsibilities in Federal Countries*, vol. 2. Montreal & Kingston: McGill-Queen's University Press.

Michelman, F. 1988. "Law's Republic", *Yale Law Journal* 97.

Misak, C. 2000. *Truth, Politics and Morality.* Routledge: New York.

Molot, J.T. 2004. "Principled Minimalism: Restriking the Balance Between Judicial Minimalism and Neutral Principles", *Virginia Law Review* 90.

Moore, C. 1998. *How the Fathers Made a Deal.* Toronto: McClelland & Stewart.

Nader, A. 1996. "Providing Essential Services: Canada's Constitution Under Section 36", *Dalhousie Law Journal* 19.

Noël, A. 2006. "Il suffisait de presque rien: Promises and Pitfalls of Open Federalism", in K. Banting *et al.* (eds.), *Open Federalism: Interpretations, Significance.* Kingston: Institute of Intergovernmental Relations, Queen's University.

Norman, W. 2006. *Negotiating Nationalism: Nation-building, Federalism, and Secession in the Multinational State.* Oxford: Oxford University Press.

Otis, G. 2000. "Informing Canadians – Public Accountability and Transparency", in A.-G. Gagnon and H. Segal (eds.), *The Canadian Social Union Without Quebec: 8 Critical Analyses.* Montreal: Institute for Research on Public Policy.

Peirce, C. 1997. "How To Make Our Ideas Clear", in L. Menand (ed.), *Pragmatism: A Reader.* New York: Vintage Books.

Petter, A. 1989. "Federalism and the Myth of the Federal Spending Power", *Canadian Bar Review* 68.

Phillips, S. 2003. "SUFA and Citizen Engagement: Fake or Genuine Masterpiece?" in S. Fortin, A. Noël, and F. St-Hilaire (eds.), *Forging the Canadian Social Union: SUFA and Beyond.* Montreal: Institute for Research on Public Policy.

Planiol, M. 1904. "L'inutilité d'une révision générale du Code civil", in *Le Code civil, 1804-1904: livre du centenaire*, vol. 2. Paris: Rousseau.

Post, R. and R. Siegel. 2007. "*Roe* Rage: Democratic Constitutionalism and Backlash", *Harvard Civil Rights-Civil Liberties Law Review* 42.

Postema, G.J. 2001. "Objectivity Fit for Law", in B. Leiter (ed.), *Objectivity in Law and Morals.* New York: Cambridge University Press.

Prakash, S.B. and J.C. Yoo. 2001. "The Puzzling Persistence of Process-Based Federalism Theories", *Texas Law Review* 79.

Putnam, H. 1995. *Pragmatism.* Cambridge, MA: Blackwell.

Quebec, Commission on Fiscal Imbalance. 2002. *Fiscal Imbalance in Canada: Historical Background: Supporting Document 1.* Quebec: The Commission.

Rawls, J. 1996. *Political Liberalism.* New York: Columbia University Press.

Raz, J. 2009. *Between Authority and Interpretation.* Oxford: Oxford University Press.

Roosevelt III, K. 2006. *The Myth of Judicial Activism.* New Haven: Yale University Press.

Sabel, C.F. 2001. "A Quiet Revolution of Democratic Governance: Towards Democratic Experimentalism", in OECD Secretariat, *Governance in the 21st Century.* Paris: Organisation for Economic Co-operation and Development.

Sabel, C.F. and W.H. Simon. 2003-04. "Destablization Rights: How Public Litigation Succeeds", *Harvard Law Review* 117.

Sabel, C.F. and J. Zeitlin. 2008. "Learning from Difference: The New Architecture of Experimentalist Governance in the EU", *European Law Journal* 14.

Sager, L.G. 2004. *Justice in Plainclothes: A Theory of American Constitutional Practice.* New Haven: Yale University Press.

Saywell, J.T. 2002. *The Lawmakers: Judicial Power and the Shaping of Canadian Federalism.* Toronto: University of Toronto Press.

Schauer, F. 1995. "Giving Reasons", *Stanford Law Review* 47.

Scott, J. and J. Holder. 2006. "Law and New Environmental Governance in the European Union", in G. de Búrca and J. Scott (eds.), *Law and New Governance in the EU and the US.* Portland: Hart.

Siegel, N.S. 2005. "A Theory in Search of a Court, and Itself: Judicial Minimalism at the Supreme Court Bar", *Michigan Law Review* 103.

Simeon, R. 2006. "Making Federalism Work", in K. Banting *et al.* (eds.), *Open Federalism: Interpretations, Significance.* Kingston: Institute of Intergovernmental Relations, Queen's University.

Simeon, R. and D. Cameron. 2002. "Intergovernmental Relations and Democracy: An Oxymoron If There Ever Was One?" in H. Bakvis and G. Skogstad (eds.), *Canadian Federalism: Performance, Effectiveness and Legitimacy.* Don Mills: Oxford University Press.

Simon, W.H. 2006. "Toyota Jurisprudence: Legal Theory and Rolling Rule Regimes", in G. de Búrca and J. Scott (eds.), *Law and New Governance in the EU and the US.* Portland: Hart.

Stone, A. 2008. "Judicial Review without Rights: Problems for the Democratic Legitimacy of Structural Judicial Review", *Oxford Journal of Legal Studies* 28.

Stone, G.R. 2008. "The Roberts Court, Stare Decisis and the Future of Constitutional Law", *Tulane Law Review* 82.

Strauss, D. 1988. "The Ubiquity of Prophylactic Rules", *The University of Chicago Law Review* 55.

Sunstein, C.R. 1999. *One Case at a Time: Judicial Minimalism on the Supreme Court.* Cambridge, MA: Harvard University Press.

Sunstein, C.R. and A. Vermeule. 2003. "Interpretation and Institutions", *Michigan Law Review* 101.

Swinton, K. 1990. *The Supreme Court and Canadian Federalism: The Laskin-Dickson Years.* Toronto: Carswell.

Thayer, J.B. 1893. "The Origin and Scope of the American Doctrine of Constitutional Law", *Harvard Law Review* 7.

Tushnet, M. 1995. "Policy Distortion and Democratic Deliberation: Comparative Illumination of the Countermajoritarian Difficulty", *Michigan Law Review* 94.

Vermeule, A. 2006. *Judging under Uncertainty: An Institutional Theory of Legal Interpretation.* Cambridge, MA: Harvard University Press.

Vipond, R.C. 1989. "1787 and 1867: The Federal Principle and Canadian Confederation Reconsidered", *Canadian Journal of Political Science* 22.

— 1991. *Liberty and Community: Canadian Federalism and the Failure of the Constitution.* Albany: State University of New York Press.

Waldron, J. 1999a. *Law and Disagreement.* Oxford: Oxford University Press.

— 1999b. *The Dignity of Legislation.* Cambridge, MA: Cambridge University Press.

Warren, N. 2008. "Reform of the Commonwealth Grants Commission: It's All in the Detail", *University of New South Wales Law Journal* 31(2).

Watts, R. 2005. "Autonomy or Dependence: Intergovernmental Financial Relations in Eleven Countries", Working Paper 2005(5). Online: Institute of Intergovernmental Relations, Queen's University at www.queensu.ca/iigr/working/watts.html.

Wechsler, H. 1959. "Toward Neutral Principles of Constitutional Law", *Harvard Law Review* 73.

Weiler, P. 1973. "The Supreme Court of Canada and Canadian Federalism", in J.S. Ziegel (ed.), *Law and Social Change.* Scarborough: Carswell.

Weinstock, D. 2001. "Towards a Normative Theory of Federalism", *International Social Science Journal* 53.

Westbrook, R.B. 2005. *Democratic Hope: Pragmatism and the Politics of Truth.* Ithaca: Cornell University Press.

Wheare, K.C. 1963. *Federal Government.* New York: Oxford University Press.

Williams, R.A. 2005. "Federal-State Financial Relations in Australia: The Role of the Commonwealth Grants Commission", *Australian Economic Review* 38(1).

IV

The Spending Power and Positive Law

10

Current Exercises of the Federal Spending Power: What Does the Constitution Say?

Andrée Lajoie

Le gouvernement fédéral a utilisé son pouvoir de dépenser pour renforcer la centralisation politique, soutient l'auteure de ce chapitre. Rien dans le texte de la Constitution ne légitime pourtant le pouvoir fédéral de dépenser et son utilisation comme instrument de centralisation, qui émanent en fait d'interprétations judiciaires de la répartition des pouvoirs et des pratiques subséquentes de l'État. Les spécialistes du droit et la jurisprudence sont divisés quant à la légitimité constitutionnelle de ce pouvoir, mais Ottawa n'en continue pas moins de dépenser dans les domaines de compétence provinciale. Ayant récemment amoindri les conditions assorties aux transferts financiers accordés aux provinces, il a entrepris en échange de verser des subventions directes aux entreprises et aux particuliers et de transférer des fonds spécifiquement destinés à certains programmes de compétence provinciale. Tout en restant inconstitutionnel, le pouvoir de dépenser serait ainsi devenu l'instrument de centralisation privilégié d'Ottawa.

INTRODUCTION

In federations, especially in former British colonies, centralization is the name of the game. The Canadian federal government is a constant winner at that game, which it plays with an array of tools, of which the "spending power" is but one. This tool is not a new one, having been used since 1912 when the federal government first implemented a program of conditional subsidies directed to agricultural education in the provinces (see Commission on Fiscal Imbalance 2002, 17). Despite having been used for decades, neither the existence of the federal spending power nor its use as a tool for centralization is justified by the text of the Constitution. Centralization is the product both of judicial interpretations of the division of powers and of the resulting government

Portions of this chapter draw substantially on one of the author's previously published works (Lajoie 2006). This material is used with the permission of the publisher.

practices. The federal government's use of the spending power as a tool for centralization erodes the constitutional framework of federalism and the provinces' exclusive jurisdiction over spending in certain areas.

I have written on this subject long enough, and those familiar with the field may recognize in this chapter elements of my first paper on the topic (Lajoie 1988a), a discussion that I updated and expanded in my report to the Séguin Commission in 2002.[1] I therefore touch only briefly on these well-known aspects of the subject and concentrate instead on its more recent evolution, both in case law and in government practice. I will also examine current exercises of the federal spending power, which show that it has become the federal government's preferred instrument of centralization.

WHAT DOES THE CONSTITUTION SAY?

The Initial Division of Powers

The *Constitution Act, 1867*, which establishes the Canadian federation, provides for the distribution of legislative powers between the federal and provincial levels of government. Section 91, "Powers of the Parliament", comprises twenty-nine areas of federal power including jurisdiction over the debt and public property,[2] general residual competence (ibid., s.91(29)), unemployment insurance (ibid., s.91(2A)), the raising of money by any mode or system of taxation (ibid., s.91(3)), quarantine and the establishment of marine hospitals, old age pensions[3] (which admittedly gives precedence to any applicable provincial legislation), and paramount jurisdiction over natural resource exports.[4]

As a counterpart to section 91, section 92 is entitled "Exclusive Powers of Provincial Legislatures". It lists sixteen areas of exclusive provincial jurisdiction, including "Direct Taxation within the Province in order to the raising of a Revenue for Provincial Purposes",[5] establishing and running hospitals and charities (ibid., s.92(7)), and residuary powers over matters of a merely local or private nature in the province (ibid., s.92(16)). To this list must

---

[1]Commission on Fiscal Imbalance (2002), from which large excerpts are used in this chapter with the authorization of the Quebec Department of Finance.

[2]*Constitution Act, 1867* (U.K.), 30 & 31 Vict., c. 3, s.91(1A), reprinted in R.S.C. 1985, App. II, No. 5.

[3]Ibid., s.94A. This section was added by the *Constitution Act, 1964* (U.K.), 12 & 13 Eliz. II, c. 73. Originally enacted by the *British North America Act, 1951* (U.K.), 14-15 Geo. VI, c. 32, s.94A, as rep. by the *Constitution Act, 1982*, being Schedule B to the *Canada Act 1982* (U.K.), 1982, c. 11.

[4]*Constitution Act, 1964*, ibid., s.92A. This section was inserted by the *Constitution Act, 1982*, ibid.

[5]*Constitution Act, 1867*, *supra* note 2, s.92(2).

be added education,[6] the provincial portion of the power over resources (ibid., s92A), and joint powers over immigration and agriculture (ibid., s.95).

By contrast, the powers of the executive are granted by a few provisions scattered throughout the text of the *Constitution Act, 1867*. These provisions incorporate the powers granted earlier to the executives of the colonies that formed the federation (ibid., ss.63-64), and include other powers over certain judicial appointments (ibid., s.96) and the expropriation of provincial lands for defence purposes (ibid., s.117). The spending power of the federal executive is not mentioned therein, nor is the spending power of the provinces. In considering the question of the division of powers of the executive in *Liquidators of the Maritime Bank of Canada v. Receiver-General of New Brunswick*, the Privy Council ruled that these powers were distributed along the same lines as the division of legislative powers in the *Constitution Act, 1867*.[7] This decision was recently affirmed by the Supreme Court of Canada in *Reference Re Secession of Quebec*.[8]

But it is not so much the original text of the Canadian Constitution that is responsible for the current centralization of legislative powers and their associated executive powers. Rather, this centralization has resulted from judicial interpretations of the division of powers and from government practices that have developed at the interpretive margins. The former centralizing factors include disallowances, now in disuse (ibid., 250); declarations to the general advantage of Canada based on section 92(10)(c) of the *Constitution Act, 1867*; and acquisitions of property either by purchase or expropriation. The latter include such interpretive theories as the ancillary power, the federal paramountcy, the residuary powers, the national dimensions theory, and the emergency powers.

Present Scope of the Spending Power within Canadian Federalism

The label that has been given to the federal centralization tool – the "spending power" – has led not only to confusion but has also given rise to one of the most spectacular attempts at ideological legitimization to be found in constitutional discourse.[9] Indeed, what could be more normal than for a government to spend? Can a government act in any way whatsoever without spending? More importantly, can we conceive of governments in a federal system with no spending power? Of course not. However, by presenting the spending power as the authority for fiscal intervention in areas of provincial legislative jurisdiction, the federal government invokes constitutional icons and seeks to give its actions an air of irrefutable validity.

---

[6]Covered in a separate provision in ibid., s.93.

[7][1892] 435 A.C. 437 (P.C.) at 441-42 [*Maritime Bank*].

[8][1998] 2 S.C.R. 217 at para. 56.

[9]The text of this section updates data found in Lajoie (1988b, 163-180); Lajoie (1988a).

To make matters worse, this gambit is partly justifiable. Indeed, it is clear that both the federal and provincial authorities can spend in the sphere of their respective legislative jurisdictions without violating the Constitution, as this is necessary to implement the legislative measures they legitimately adopt. For example, the federal authorities can and should pay for the army, for foreign affairs and for the post office, while the provincial authorities can and should pay for the public service, and for the courts, prisons, and hospitals. This is also the case when the Constitution makes express provision for spending by one level of government outside its own area of jurisdiction; for example, equalization payments, for which provision was introduced under section 36(2) of the *Constitution Act, 1982*: "Parliament and the government of Canada are committed to the principle of making equalization payments to ensure that provincial governments have sufficient revenues to provide reasonably comparable levels of public services at reasonably comparable levels of taxation."[10] However, the expression "spending power" does not refer to these constitutional practices of spending. Far from it: the Canadian constitutional jargon refers instead to the ideological affirmation of an arguably non-existent power, invoked by federal authorities to allow them to spend on a conditional basis in fields of provincial jurisdiction.

A Divided Legal Scholarship

Before arguing that the questions surrounding the constitutionality of the spending power are unresolved in Canadian jurisprudence, it should be noted that legal scholarship is also divided on the issue. Since the time of Pierre Trudeau, the spending power has drawn the attention of leading constitutional scholars, jurists, political scientists, and economists. Some of them (Pierre Blache [1993], Pierre Fortin [1988], Stefan Dupré [1988], and André Tremblay[11] in particular) have not expressed an opinion on the constitutional validity of the spending power but have been content to support it on normative grounds. Others have argued that the spending power of the federal state in fields of provincial jurisdiction is not part of our constitutional law. These scholars include Pierre Trudeau,[12] Jean Beetz (1965, 113ff), Jacques Dupont (1967) and, more recently, Andrew Petter (1988, 1989).

Among advocates of the constitutionality of the spending power, the "gift theory" predominates. According to this theory, federal authorities are allowed to distribute their tax revenues as gifts to the provinces or to legal or natural persons as they see fit. The recipients are under no obligation to accept

---

[10] *Constitution Act, 1982*, *supra* note 3, s.36(2).

[11] Tremblay (2001). It should be noted that the author's position at the time of the Meech Lake Accords implicitly approved the constitutionality of the spending power, the scope of which he sought to limit by clarifying it.

[12] Trudeau (1968). It should be noted that Trudeau, who reaffirmed here a position that he had first adopted in *Cité Libre* in February 1957, would implicitly dissociate himself from it two years later, when his government published a working document: Canada (1969).

these gifted revenues, which are justified either by virtue of the royal prerogative and common law, according to the oldest position held by Frank Scott (1955), or, more often, by virtue of the federal legislative power over public property, provided for in section 91(1A) of the *Constitution Act, 1867*.[13] If the recipients choose to accept these revenues, they subject themselves voluntarily to any normative conditions that the federal authorities may impose on the gift. Advocates of this theory claim that the federal government's ownership of public funds in the form of tax dollars gives it the right to spend these funds as it sees fit, including the imposition of normative conditions.

Other authors argue that sources of revenue other than tax dollars are also subject to conditional federal spending. Peter Hogg (1988), who incidentally argues that the spending power may be justified on the basis that it has been practised constantly by the federal government, invokes the grounds relied on in an isolated decision of the Alberta Court of Appeal, *Winterhaven Stables Ltd. v. Canada (A.G.)*.[14] The court held that the federal authorities can levy taxes to pay the expenses of the public service, and can presumably spend these taxes as they see fit by virtue of their constitutional jurisdiction to levy taxes[15] and to appropriate moneys for the public service (ibid., s.106). E.A. Dreidger (1981-82), in addition to that line of reasoning, argued that the federal power to create the Consolidated Revenue Fund also justifies the exercise of the spending power.[16] François Chevrette (1988) has taken the position that the spending power is part of Canadian constitutional law because it is inevitable, and because the expenses a government incurs as a government cannot be dissociated from those that it would incur as a simple legal entity. Lastly, Gerard La Forest and Michel Maher have adopted an intermediate position, arguing that the law is undecided on the question.[17]

---

[13]This view is advocated by Hogg (1988); Smiley and Burns (1969, 472); Hanssen (1966-67, 195); Schwartz (1987, 150-207).

[14][1988] 91 A.R. 114 (Alta. C.A.), leave to appeal to S.C.C. refused, 21262 (December 19, 1988) [*Winterhaven*].

[15]*Constitution Act, 1867*, *supra* note 2, s.91.3.

[16]*Constitution Act, 1867*, *supra* note 2, s.102. Also see Driedger (1981-82, 130):

> There is the principle that executive or prerogative power follows legislative power, but it does not follow that the authority of the federal or provincial executives to spend money is limited to subjects over which Parliament or the legislatures, as the case may be, have jurisdiction to make laws. Applying that principle to appropriations means only that the federal executive can direct authorized expenditures only from the Consolidated Revenue Fund of Canada [footnotes omitted].

[17]Gerard La Forest (1981) has leaned toward the constitutionality of the spending power, in which he favoured the constitutionality of the spending power while admitting that it had not been decided by the courts. Subsequently, following *Reference Re Canada Assistance Plan (B.C.)*, [1991] 2 S.C.R. 525 [*Canada Assistance Plan*], he expressed the view, in *obiter* in *Eldridge v. British Columbia (A.G.)*, [1997] 3 S.C.R. 624 at para. 25 [*Eldridge*], that the spending power had been constitutionalized: "(The constitutionality of this kind of conditional grant [from the federal government made to fund provincial health insurance programs], *I note parenthetically*, was approved by this court in *Reference Re Canada Assistance Plan (B.C.)*, [1991] 2 S.C.R. 525, at p. 567.)" (emphasis

A common qualification underlines the arguments in favour of the federal spending power in fields of provincial jurisdiction: that spending is justified when the revenues come from a specific source of federal public property. Hogg, Smiley and Burns, Hanssen, and Schwartz understood this source to be the Consolidated Revenue Fund (Hogg 1988; Smiley and Burns 1969; Hanssen 1966-67; Schwartz 1987, 151; Trudeau 1968, 98; Chevrette 1988). Trudeau (1968, 97) saw it to be monies other than income tax (i.e., public domain or federal property, spoils of war, profits of Crown corporations), and Hogg (1988) and Driedger (1981-82) understood it to be appropriations for the public service. Each author's favourite source would produce revenue that could be spent by the federal state under conditions of its own choosing – conditions imposed by virtue of the federal prerogative (Scott 1955), as the result of federal legislative power over public property (Hogg 1988; Smiley and Burns 1969; Hanssen 1966-67; Schwartz 1987), or because the state has a legal personality of general jurisdiction (Chevrette 1988). As such, according to some scholars, the federal government may dispose of the resources that constitute its "private property" (Trudeau 1968, 97) as if the funds were not part of the public domain.

The problem is that none of these theories – undoubtedly valid in a unitary state – can stand up within the context of a federation. Indeed, the Privy Council confirmed that the prerogative and the powers of the executive are divided along the same lines as legislative powers.[18] The Privy Council further indicated that the legal collection of taxes by the federal state in no way implied that it could dispose of them as it saw fit.[19] Nothing in the constitutional provisions relating to the Consolidated Revenue Fund or to appropriations for the public service authorizes conditional expenditures in fields of provincial jurisdiction. Further, the claim that the federal government has a legal personality and should be treated as a private enterprise, unlimited in its legal capacity by the Constitution, also disregards the federal character of the Canadian Constitution, which distributes these powers between the federal government and the provinces.

The precedents established by higher courts in both Canada and England do not lean in the same direction as the legal scholarship. Those courts instead reinforce the position that the spending power does not form part of Canadian constitutional law. Their precedents, none of which have resulted in any change to the constitutional status of the spending power, will be examined here from a historical perspective.

Inconclusive Judicial Discourse

As mentioned above, the question of the constitutionality of the spending power is still open for want of a binding Supreme Court decision, and the Court has not

added). Michel Maher (1996) would have liked to see the power constitutionalized in order to control it.

[18] *Maritime Bank*, *supra* note 7. Also see Lajoie (1972, 43ff).

[19] *Reference Re Employment and Social Insurance Act (Can.)*, [1937] 1 D.L.R. 684 (P.C.), (*sub nom. Canada (A.G.) v. Ontario (A.G.)*) [1937] A.C. 326 [*Unemployment Insurance Reference*].

indicated the direction it would take if confronted directly with the issue. In the 1930s, the Supreme Court of Canada commented favourably on the constitutionality of the spending power in the *Unemployment Insurance Reference*.[20] However, this interpretation was not confirmed by the Privy Council, which in the same case held a different view:

> That the Dominion may impose for the purpose of creating a fund for special purposes and may apply that fund for making contributions in the public interest to individuals, corporations or public authorities could not as a general proposition be denied ... But assuming that the Dominion has collected by means of taxation a fund, it by no means follows that any legislation which disposes of it is necessarily within Dominion competence.[21]

This statement expressly left the question open, and Professor La Forest (as he then was) acknowledged as late as 1981 that it remained unresolved, even though his personal normative position on the matter had evolved (*supra* note 17).

Since the *Unemployment Insurance Reference*, lower courts have rendered various decisions without settling the question. The Ontario Court of Appeal in *Central Mortgage and Housing Corp. v. Co-operative College Residences, Inc.*[22] and the Exchequer Court in *Porter v. R.*[23] both followed the earlier Supreme Court decision in *Employment and Social Insurance Act*. Although *Central Mortgage*, *Porter*, and a third case, *Angers v. M.N.R.*,[24] had been decided when La Forest updated his work on fiscal powers in 1981, he nevertheless concluded that the question was still open, as the first two cases had not been upheld by the Privy Council and the latter did not emanate from the Supreme Court (*supra* note 17). What is more, La Forest refuted the Exchequer Court's ruling in *Angers*, in which the authority for the federal spending power was based on the residual legislative competence of Parliament.

In three other decisions, the issue was raised indirectly and was again skirted by the courts. In *Re Lofstrom and Murphy*,[25] the Saskatchewan Court of Appeal decided that federal-provincial agreements setting up shared-cost programs for social benefits did not guarantee an individual right to those benefits, because only governments are parties to such agreements. Therefore, the status of the beneficiaries under the program was for the provinces to define. This position was confirmed by the Supreme Court in *Alden v. Gaglardi*,[26] but in that case Justice Ritchie stopped short of pronouncing on the constitutionality of

---

[20] [1936] S.C.R. 427.

[21] *Unemployment Insurance Reference*, *supra* note 19.

[22] (1977), 71 D.L.R. (3d) 183 (Ont. C.A.) [*Central Mortgage*].

[23] *Porter v. R.*, [1965] Ex. C.R. 200 [*Porter*].

[24] [1957] Ex. C.R. 83 [*Angers*].

[25] (1972), 22 D.L.R. (3d) 120 at 122 (Sask. C.A.).

[26] [1973] S.C.R. 199.

the agreement, as Justice Le Dain also did in *Finlay v. Canada (Minister of Finance).*[27] In *Reference Re Agricultural Products Marketing Act,*[28] Justice Pigeon held that even unconditional federal expenditures were unconstitutional in fields of provincial jurisdiction. Although that statement was part of the majority opinion of the Court, it has gone unnoticed in the spending power debate, undoubtedly because the case did not involve a shared-cost program.

Without giving them the status of precedents, two rulings from courts of first instance in Saskatchewan and Alberta must also be mentioned. Both were issued in the context of declaratory actions. The first, *Dunbar v. Saskatchewan (A.G.),*[29] dealt with the provincial spending power and sheds light on the matter of concern to us only by analogy. In that case, a grant of international aid by a provincial agency had been contested. Although the judge linked these grants to federal legislative jurisdiction over external affairs, he nevertheless concluded that the appropriation bills were constitutionally valid. The *ratio* of this decision, supported by two much earlier decisions at first instance,[30] seems to have been that the provincial legislature, in making those appropriations, did not purport to regulate activity within federal legislative competence. This same line of argument was also raised in *Lovelace v. Ontario,*[31] raising the possibility that the provincial spending power was valid only within provincial legislative competence, a universally accepted interpretation.

In contrast, the last decision I will discuss – *Winterhaven*[32] – did directly confront this question of the conditional use of the spending power. In a declaratory action, the Alberta Court of Appeal upheld the constitutionality of certain sections of the federal *Income Tax Act, 1971.*[33] These sections authorized the collection and transfer of money to the provinces in order to fund shared-cost programs in the fields of health, welfare, and post-secondary education, all matters falling within exclusive provincial jurisdiction. The provisions in question imposed conditions on the recipient provinces in the application of the

---

[27][1986] 2 S.C.R. 607.

[28][1978] 2 S.C.R. 1198 at 1292-93.

[29][1985], 11 D.L.R. (4th) 374 (Sask. Q.B.) [*Dunbar*].

[30]See ibid. at 378. The two cases were *Dow v. Black*, [1875] 6 L.R.P.C. 272 and *McMillan v. Winnipeg (City of)*, [1919] 45 D.L.R. 351 (Man. K.B.).

[31][2000] 1 S.C.R. 950 [*Lovelace*]. It must be noted that the grants were unconditional, and therefore do not qualify as an exercise of legislative power in a substantive field of jurisdiction, regardless of whether the grantor is the federal government or a provincial government. Consequently, the effect of such a decision, even though it emanated from a higher court, does not extend to conditional grants, which is what we are concerned with. I will not consider whether such grants fall within federal jurisdiction; certain international activities do indeed come within provincial authority, when they are directly linked to matters of exclusive provincial jurisdiction. See Morin (1984, 265).

[32]*Winterhaven, supra* note 14.

[33]Ibid. The provisions under contention were from the *Income Tax Act*, S.C. 1970-71-72, c. 63.

funds to these programs. The court considered the provisions valid because they dealt "in pith and substance" (ibid., 131) with raising money by taxation; it made no reference to the provincial purposes for which the money was earmarked. If the entire issue posed by the use of the federal spending power in fields of provincial jurisdiction is one of characterization, what has to be asked is whether the Alberta court correctly characterized the purpose of the challenged provisions of the *Income Tax Act* and whether it is permissible for Parliament to do indirectly what the Constitution prohibits directly. In any event, despite its thorough treatment of the question, this isolated decision by a provincial court of appeal cannot settle the question for all of Canada.

Since the decision in *Winterhaven* in 1988, four Supreme Court of Canada decisions have addressed the subject but only indirectly and in such a way that these rulings have not altered the substantive law.[34] In the first of these decisions, *YMHA Jewish Community Centre of Winnipeg v. Brown*,[35] in which the community centre participated in a federal job creation program, the Court decided that the power to establish the program is not founded in the federal government's exclusive jurisdiction over unemployment insurance. Justice L'Heureux-Dubé wrote on behalf of the Court:

> While Parliament may be free to offer grants subject to whatever restrictions it sees fit, the decision to make a grant of money in any particular area should not be construed as an intention to regulate all related aspects of that area. (ibid., 1533)

This statement was made in *obiter,* as Justice L'Heureux-Dubé confirmed in an explicit answer to my question at an unpublished session of the Association of Comparative Law at McGill University in 1990.

The second Supreme Court opinion was rendered by Justice Sopinka in *Canada Assistance Plan.*[36] The government of British Columbia had alleged that a federal law reducing health-care grants to the provinces was invalid because it was a breach of contract. The Court implicitly upheld the existing doctrine whereby Parliament has jurisdiction to cancel or modify contracts made by the Crown (see Lajoie 1984). In fact, this holding can be seen as being implicitly based on the validity of the federal-provincial agreement providing for the grants. However, the validity of that agreement had not been called into question by British Columbia. On the contrary, the province was demanding the performance of the contract because it saw no other way of obtaining the funds from the federal authorities. The existence of a federal power to spend conditionally in spheres of provincial jurisdiction was not raised before the Court or even discussed, so it cannot be concluded that the Court in this case confirmed the validity of that power.

---

[34]Such was the state of the law when two attempts were made to constitutionalize the spending power: included respectively in the Meech Lake Accord (1987) and the Charlottetown Accord (1992). Not having been ratified, these attempts did not alter the constitutionality of the spending power.

[35][1989] 1 S.C.R. 1532 [*YMHA*].

[36]*Canada Assistance Plan, supra* note 17.

The third case to indirectly address this question was *Eldridge v. British Columbia (A.G.)*.[37] The opinion of Justice La Forest that the spending power had been constitutionalized does not change matters, given that he made it in express *obiter*.[38] Moreover, this opinion was pronounced in a case that involved not the spending power but the application of the Canadian Charter to provincial laws. What is more, neither withdrawing federal grants to the provinces, nor placing a cap on these grants,[39] is equivalent to passing federal legislation in areas of provincial jurisdiction. It should go without saying that ending an unconstitutional practice by retracting unjustified federal grants is not itself unconstitutional. By stating this obvious point, the Court did not necessarily give an opinion on the constitutionality of the activity itself – an activity to which the federal executive put an end by withdrawing from shared-cost programs.

Finally, *Lovelace*[40] dealt with the spending power of the provinces and was decided entirely within the context of the qualification on equality rights enshrined in section 15(2) of the Canadian Charter of Rights and Freedoms.[41] The Court held that an Ontario casino project, contested by some First Nations, did not go to the essence of aboriginality (which would have brought it under federal jurisdiction) but rather that, like the *Dunbar* case (*supra* note 29), it involved the use of the provincial spending power in a field of provincial jurisdiction, which is indeed perfectly valid from a constitutional standpoint.

The above cases illustrate the Supreme Court's interpretation of the federal spending power as it stood when I wrote the second annex to the Séguin Commission report in 2004. Since then, two more decisions have referred to the issue: *Auton (Guardian ad litem of) v. British Columbia (A.G.)*[42] and *Chaoulli v. Quebec (A.G.)*.[43] In *Auton*, the Court stated in Annex B that the federal government "has authority under its spending power to attach conditions to financial grants to the provinces that are used to pay for social programs".[44] However, it must be kept in mind that this statement was made in an annex, and that the decision was explicitly based not on such considerations but on the absence of factual evidence of discrimination. Similarly, in *Chaoulli*, Justice Deschamps wrote:

---

[37]*Eldridge, supra* note 17.

[38]Ibid. and accompanying text.

[39]This issue is addressed in *Canada Assistance Plan, supra* note 17.

[40]*Lovelace, supra* note 31.

[41]*Supra* note 3, s.15. Section 15(2) states, "Subsection (1) does not preclude any law, program or activity that has as its object the amelioration of conditions of disadvantaged individuals or groups including those that are disadvantaged because of race, national or ethnic origin, colour, religion, sex, age or mental or physical disability".

[42][2004] 3 S.C.R 657 [*Auton*].

[43][2005] 1 S.C.R. 791 [*Chaoulli*].

[44]*Auton, supra* note 42, 682.

> Although the federal government has express jurisdiction over certain matters relating to health, such as quarantine, and the establishment and maintenance of marine hospitals ... it is in practice that it imposes its views on the provincial governments in the health care sphere by means of its spending power.[45]

Again, this pronouncement has nothing to do with the *ratio* for the decision, which was based on the Quebec Charter of Rights.

It is, however, important to watch for the forthcoming decision from the Supreme Court in *Syndicat national des employés de l'aluminium d'Arvida inc. v. Canada (A.G.).*[46] In the Quebec Court of Appeal, Chief Justice Michel Robert held that where some measures in the *Employment Insurance Act*[47] could not be validly adopted according to the jurisdiction of employment insurance itself, the federal spending power remains a sufficient jurisdiction.[48] He founded this element of his decision on Justice L'Heureux-Dubé's remarks in *YMHA* (*supra* note 35). As previously mentioned, Justice L'Heureux-Dubé later acknowledged publicly that these remarks had been made in *obiter*.

In short, Supreme Court pronouncements on the issue to date consist of four *obiter* statements, including one on the withdrawal of federal spending in a field of provincial jurisdiction, and two decisions on the spending power of a province in its own area of legislative jurisdiction. These statements have the effect of dissociating the Court from earlier judgments to the contrary by the Privy Council and, even more so, from the effect of amending the Constitution on this subject. The federal spending power, which imposes conditions that are equivalent to the exercise of normative power in fields of provincial jurisdiction, is still not a part of the Canadian Constitution – unless more weight is given to a decision of the Court of Appeal of Alberta than to all of the precedents of the Privy Council. In light of the direction and scope of these decisions, it still seems accurate to say that the law is not yet decided on the matter of the constitutionality of the federal spending power in areas falling under provincial legislative jurisdiction.

A final element, and not the least important, must be kept in mind. All of these decisions must be read in light of the principle of federalism that the Supreme Court reiterated several times in a recent judgment.[49] Admittedly, the concept of federalism is not completely unequivocal, and most Canadian constitutional scholars, to say the least, do not write prolifically on the theory of federalism[50] and especially on the differences between federalism and administrative decentralization. They agree, however, on a minimum threshold

---

[45]*Chaoulli*, *supra* note 43 at para. 16.

[46]2006 QCCA 1453; 157 A.C.W.S. (3d) 762, leave to appeal to S.C.C. granted, [2007] 1 S.C.R. xv [*Syndicat*].

[47]S.C. 1996, c. 23.

[48]*Syndicat*, *supra* note 46 at para. 140.

[49]*Reference Re Secession of Quebec*, *supra* note 8.

[50]Cf. Brun and Tremblay (1982) c. 4, who devote an important chapter to this question.

below which there may be no real federalism: that line is drawn when local authorities are subordinate to central authorities (see Hogg 2007, 110; Brun and Tremblay 1982, 294; Tremblay 1982, 88; Chevrette and Marx 1982, 219; Finkelstein 1986, 16-17; Beaudoin 1982, 11; Magnet 1983, 1). Except for Rémillard (1983, 48), who gears his discussion toward the federation/ confederation dichotomy and does not address the question of the minimal requirements of federalism, all Canadian constitutional scholars who have written on the subject are in agreement on that threshold (Whyte and Lederman 1977, 2-19; Brun and Tremblay 1982). Some authors even argue that the independence of local authorities from central authorities should be constitutionalized (see Tremblay 2001), or that local authorities must have sufficient fiscal powers to guarantee such independence (Whyte and Lederman 1977, 1-29).

But within this context, it is mainly the opinions of the Supreme Court that matter. The Court recently restated the principle of federalism in three landmark decisions[51] in the very words used by Lord Watson in *Maritime Bank*:

> The object of the Act was neither to weld the provinces into one, nor to subordinate provincial governments to a central authority, but to create a federal government in which they should all be represented, entrusted with the exclusive administration of affairs in which they had a common interest, each province retaining its independence and autonomy. (*supra* note 7 at 441-42)

It has further been suggested that

> the federal principle cannot be reconciled with a state of affairs where the modification of provincial legislative powers could be obtained by the unilateral action of the federal authorities. It would indeed offend the federal principle that "a radical change to ... [the] constitution [be] taken at the request of a bare majority of the members of the Canadian House of Commons and Senate". (Craik *et al.* 2006, 110 [footnotes omitted])

In sum, after this examination of the precedents of the Privy Council, the Supreme Court, and even the lower courts of competent jurisdiction, it may be stated that no judicial pronouncement having the force of precedent has affirmed the constitutionality of the federal spending power in fields of provincial jurisdiction.[52]

---

[51] *Reference Re Secession of Quebec*, *supra* note 8 at 250; *Reference Re Resolution to amend the Constitution*, [1981] 1 S.C.R. 753 at 819; *Reference Re Manitoba Language Rights*, [1985] 1 S.C.R. 721 at 751.

[52] Nor were things changed by Alain-G. Gagnon's recent examination of the "Canadian Social Union Without Québec," to plagiarize a title that has rightly become famous. See Tremblay 2001. The Social Union Framework Agreement is expressed as an administrative agreement and not a constitutional amendment, as there was no attempt to follow the formal procedures for amendment established by the *Constitution Act, 1982*. See *A Framework to Improve the Social Union for Canadians: An Agreement between the Government of Canada and the Governments of the Provinces and Territories*, Canada, 4 February 1999 [SUFA]. Even if the temporary nature of this agreement were to be changed by the passage of time, it would not constitute a "constitutional

CURRENT EXERCISES OF THE FEDERAL SPENDING POWER

It will now be apparent that conditional federal spending has taken different forms since the early twentieth century, including subsidy programs, tax rental agreements, conditional transfers and shared-cost payments to provinces, and direct grants to individuals. No matter what form it has taken, however, the federal government has always directly invaded provincial fields of jurisdiction: education, health, labour, income security, local economic development, and municipal institutions. This is a serious enough violation of the federal principle to warrant scrutiny of the forms that the conditional use of the federal spending power takes today. These forms fall into two categories: direct grants to provincial entities and individuals, and targeted grants to provinces. The first bypasses the authority of provincial governments by transferring federal funds directly to individuals and provincial entities through, for example, grants to municipalities, university professors, graduate students, and developers of natural resources. The second also bypasses provincial jurisdiction by seeing the federal government make fiscal transfers targeted to specific programs in the provinces.

Direct Grants to Provincial Entities and Individuals

Recently, instead of giving grants to provinces conditional on their being used in a certain field in accordance with certain restrictions, the federal government has been transferring money directly to individuals and to public and private corporations in the provinces. Thus, municipalities will get money for infrastructure, university professors will get research chairs, and graduate students will get scholarships in designated fields if they meet certain criteria. Natural resource companies affected by economic recession also get direct grants, which provincial governments are indeed asking for as if it were not an invasion of their jurisdiction. None of these exercises of the federal spending power are constitutionally valid, as they all entail indirect invasion of provincial jurisdiction. It is provincial law, enabled by the Constitution, that determines, what public money, and on what conditions, should go to municipalities, professors, scholars, and natural resources developers. According to sections 92(8), 92A(1), and 93, respectively, these fields are provincial. No regulation by federal authorities, direct or indirect, is authorized in these areas.

---

convention" (for Quebec at least) according to the definition of that term in *Reference Re Objection to a Resolution to Amend the Constitution*, [1982] 2 S.C.R. 793 at 802-803. Such a convention must receive the approval of the provinces whose legislative power is being affected, and the agreement does not meet that condition.

Targeted Grants to Provinces

The second way the federal government currently bypasses the authority of provincial governments is through targeted grants to the provinces. It should be noted that some transfers to provinces seem unconditional, as they do not outwardly imply conditions upon their use. This is the case for equalization payments, authorized by section 36 of the *Constitution Act, 1982*, and it would also be the case for other truly unconditional transfers. However, such transfers are not popular with the federal government, because it gets no electoral benefits from them. The federal government's preferred solution is therefore to transfer money attached to a certain field of provincial jurisdiction, especially health care and social welfare. However, the very targeting of these grants to a specific area of provincial jurisdiction interferes with the power of the provinces to allocate money to the areas of their choice, a power granted by section 92(2) of the *Constitution Act, 1867*.

CONCLUSION

The traditional federal tools of disallowance, declarations to the general advantage of Canada, and acquisitions of property by purchase or expropriation have become more difficult to use in the context of the socioeconomic well-being of the population. I think it is quite clear that the spending power has now become the preferred instrument of centralization for the federal government. Of course, such centralization may be the wish of the federal authorities and of some provinces in Canada – although not all, and especially not of Quebec. However, for this wish to become a reality, the Constitution itself must be modified. Until that happens, conditional federal spending in the realm of provincial jurisdiction is unconstitutional and disruptive to the federal principle and national harmony.

REFERENCES

Beaudoin, G.-A. 1982. *Le partage des pouvoirs*, 2d ed. Ottawa: Éditions de l'Université d'Ottawa.

Beetz, J. 1965. "Les attitudes changeantes du Québec à l'endroit de la constitution de 1867", in P.-A. Crépeau and C.B. Macpherson (eds.), *The Future of Canadian Federalism: L'avenir du federalisme canadien.* Toronto: University of Toronto Press.

Blache, P. 1993. "Le pouvoir de dépenser au cœur de la crise constitutionnelle canadienne", *Revue générale de droit* 24(1), 29-64.

Brun, H. and G. Tremblay. 1982. *Droit constitutionnel.* Cowansville: Yvon Blais.

Canada. 1969. *Federal-Provincial Grants and the Spending Power of Parliament: Working Paper on the Constitution.* Ottawa: Queen's Printer.

Charlottetown Accord (Special Joint Committee on a Renewed Canada). 1992. *Consensus Report on the Constitution.* Charlottetown.

Chevrette, F. 1988. "Contrôler le pouvoir fédéral de dépenser: un gain ou un piège?" in A. Costi (ed.), *L'adhésion du Québec à l'Accord du Lac Meech: points de vue juridiques et politiques.* Montréal, Thémis.

Chevrette, F. and H. Marx. 1982. *Droit constitutionnel.* Montréal: Presses de l'Université de Montréal.

Commission on Fiscal Imbalance. 2002. *The "Federal Spending Power": Supporting Document 2.* Québec: Bibliothèque nationale du Québec.

Craik, N. *et al.* 2006. *Public Law: Cases, Materials and Commentary.* Toronto: Emond Montgomery.

Driedger, E.A. 1981-82. "The Spending Power", *Queen's Law Journal* 7.

Dupont, J. 1967. "Le pouvoir de dépenser du gouvernement fédéral: 'A Dead Issue'?" *The University of British Columbia Law Review* (Centenneial Ed.) 69, 69-102.

Dupré, J.S. 1988. "Section 106A and the Federal-Provincial Fiscal Relations", in K.E. Swinton and C.S. Rogerson (eds.), *Competing Constitutional Visions: The Meech Lake Accord.* Toronto: Carswell.

Finkelstein, N. 1986. *Laskin's Canadian Constitutional Law*, 5th ed., vol. 1. Toronto: Carswell.

Fortin, P. 1988 "The Meech Lake Accord and the Federal Spending Power: A Good Maximin Solution", in K.E. Swinton and C.S. Rogerson (eds.), *Competing Constitutional Visions: The Meech Lake Accord.* Toronto: Carswell.

Hanssen, K. 1966-67. "The Constitutionality of Conditional Grant Legislation", *Manitoba Law Journal* 2.

Hogg, P.W. 1988. "Analysis of the New Spending Provision (Section 106A)", in K.E. Swinton and C.S. Rogerson (eds.), *Competing Constitutional Visions: The Meech Lake Accord.* Toronto: Carswell.

— 2007. *Constitutional Law of Canada*, student ed. Toronto: Thomson Canada.

La Forest, G.V. 1981. *The Allocation of Taxing Power under the Canadian Constitution*, 2d ed. Toronto: Canadian Tax Foundation.

Lajoie, A. 1972. *Expropriation et fédéralisme au Canada.* Montréal: Presses de l'Université de Montréal.

— 1984. *Contrats administratifs: jalons pour une théorie.* Montréal: Thémis.

— 1988a. "The Federal Spending Power and Meech Lake", in K.E. Swinton and C.S. Rogerson (eds.), *Competing Constitutional Visions: The Meech Lake Accord.* Toronto: Carswell.

— 1988b. "L'impact des Accords du Lac Meech sur le pouvoir de dépenser", in A. Costi (ed.), *L'adhésion du Québec à l'Accord du Lac Meech: points de vue juridiques et politiques.* Montréal, Thémis.

— 2006. "The Federal Spending Power and Fiscal Imbalance in Canada", in S. Choudhry, J.-F. Gaudreault-DesBiens, and L. Sossin (eds.), *Dilemmas of Solidarity: Rethinking Redistribution in the Canadian Federation.* Toronto: University of Toronto Press.

Magnet, J.E. 1983. *Constitutional Law of Canada.* Toronto: Carswell.

Maher, M. 1996. "Le défi du fédéralisme fiscal dans l'exercice du pouvoir de dépenser", *Canadian Bar Review* 75.

Meech Lake Accord (Library of Parliament, Research Branch, Law and Government Division). 1987. *The 1987 Constitutional Accord.* Ottawa: Minister of Supply and Services Canada.

Morin, J.-Y. 1984. "La personnalité internationale du Québec", *Revue québécoise de droit international* 1.

Petter, A. 1988. "Meech Ado About Nothing? Federalism, Democracy and the Spending Power", in K.E. Swinton and C.S. Rogerson (eds.), *Competing Constitutional Visions: The Meech Lake Accord.* Toronto: Carswell.

— 1989. "Federalism and the Myth of the Federal Spending Power", *Canadian Bar Review* 68, 448-479.

Rémillard, G. 1983. *Le fédéralisme canadien*, t. 1, "La loi constitutionnelle de 1867". Montréal: Québec/Amérique.

Scott, F.R. 1955. "The Constitutional Background of Taxation Agreements", *McGill Law Journal* 2(1), 1-10.

Schwartz, B. 1987. *Fathoming Meech Lake.* Winnipeg: Legal Research Institute of the University of Manitoba.

Smiley, D.V. and R.M. Burns. 1969. "Canadian Federalism and the Spending Power: Is Constitutional Restriction Necessary?" *Canadian Tax Journal* 17, 468-482.

Tremblay, A. 1982. *Précis de droit constitutionnel.* Montréal: Thémis.

— 2001. "Federal Spending Power", *The Canadian Social Union Without Québec: 8 Critical Analyses.* Montréal: Institute for Research on Public Policy.

Trudeau, P.E. 1968. "Federal Grants to Universities", in P.E. Trudeau (ed.), *Federalism and the French Canadians.* Toronto: Macmillan of Canada.

Whyte, J.D. and W.R. Lederman. 1977. *Canadian Constitutional Law*, 2d ed. Toronto: Butterworths.

11

The Spending Power, Cooperative Federalism, and Section 94

Marc-Antoine Adam

La thèse du pouvoir illimité de dépenser a longtemps servi à justifier les dépenses du gouvernement fédéral dans les domaines de compétence provinciale. Dépenser et réglementer seraient ainsi deux choses distinctes, selon cette thèse qui assujettit à la répartition des pouvoirs la seule action de réglementer. Il s'agit pourtant d'une thèse mal fondée en vertu de la Constitution et de la jurisprudence canadiennes, croit l'auteur, selon qui elle concorde tout aussi peu avec les principes de l'interprétation constitutionnelle. Sans compter qu'elle ne correspond pas à la réalité des dépenses fédérales dans les domaines de compétence provinciale, qui découlent rarement d'une action unilatérale mais généralement de discussions et de négociations. Or l'appui public aux programmes financés par le gouvernement fédéral nous aurait amenés à négliger l'absence d'un fondement de principe pour ces dépenses. Les provinces, le Québec notamment, ont de leur côté diversement résisté à une intervention fédérale censée empiéter sur leurs compétences, même lorsqu'elle allait dans le sens de leurs propres politiques.

En guise de solution de rechange, et pour éloigner la menace de contraintes fiscales, l'auteur propose une conception du pouvoir fédéral de dépenser reposant sur le consentement des provinces, qui pourraient de la sorte adhérer à un programme donné ou obtenir une compensation assurant l'égalité des chances à l'échelle du pays. Cette conception assouplie apaiserait les tensions entre les ordres de gouvernement et favoriserait à terme une meilleure intégration. À l'examen de plusieurs formules de fédéralisme coopératif, l'auteur estime que la section 94 de la Loi constitutionnelle de 1867 *offre les meilleurs fondements constitutionnels de cette variante du pouvoir de dépenser. En effet, observe-t-il, elle consiste essentiellement en un mécanisme législatif de délégation réciproque dont on peut faire une lecture suffisamment large pour inclure toutes les provinces et de très nombreux domaines, sans empêcher les provinces de se retirer d'un programme après y avoir adhéré. En agréant à la répartition des pouvoirs, un pouvoir fédéral de dépenser fondé sur la section 94 favoriserait la coopération intergouvernementale tout en respectant le caractère diversifié des provinces.*

The author is writing in his personal capacity.

INTRODUCTION

While the spending power issue first appeared in the mid-twentieth century, the events of the past 15 years, particularly the federal-provincial feud over the fiscal imbalance, have brought it back to centre stage. Tom Courchene suggests in his chapter that the most important triggering event was probably the 1995 federal budget, which led to severe cuts in the transfer payments to the provinces and effectively imposed on them a great deal of the burden of eliminating the federal deficit. More than ever before, that budget sent the provinces the signal that the spending power could have very real downsides. Hence, terms such as the "dispending power" or the "saving power" were coined.

When the federal deficit gave way to surpluses and the federal government set out to launch new initiatives in areas of provincial jurisdiction, instead of restoring its transfers to provincial governments to their previous levels, the provinces decided to act. Among other results, this led to the Social Union Framework Agreement (SUFA),[1] the main purpose of which was to circumscribe the use of the spending power. Although Quebec was a participant in the negotiations, it did not sign the final agreement as it feared the accord would be ineffective at curbing the use of the federal power and might be interpreted as legitimizing it (see, e.g. Tremblay 2000a, 175-177). Instead, the Quebec government appointed a commission of inquiry on the fiscal imbalance – the Séguin Commission. One of its chief conclusions was that the spending power, as defined by the federal government, had no foundation in the Canadian Constitution and had never been formally made law by a court of last resort (Quebec 2002).

By the time Paul Martin succeeded Jean Chrétien, SUFA had proven to be ineffective. Then the Conservatives took power in Ottawa with the promise to put formal limits on the spending power. However, despite repeated promises, including a pledge in the 2007 Speech from the Throne to legislate on this issue, no tangible progress has yet been achieved. Furthermore, the careful rewordings of the Conservative commitment to limit the spending power have led many – including Stéphane Dion,[2] former leader of the Liberal Party of Canada – to conclude that it was too narrow in scope, more so in fact than SUFA itself, to be useful given contemporary federal spending practices.

While these events were taking place on the political stage, two cases were brought before the courts by Quebec trade unions challenging, among other things, the constitutionality of the workforce-training measures in the federal *Employment Insurance Act* under the division of powers.[3] In response, the

[1]*Framework to Improve the Social Union for Canadians: An Agreement between the Government of Canada and the Governments of the Provinces and Territories*, 4 February 1999 [SUFA].

[2]House of Commons Debates, No. 002 (17 October 2007) at 15h55 (Hon. Stéphane Dion).

[3]*Syndicat national des employés de l'aluminium d'Arvida c. Canada (P.G.)*, 2006 QCCA 1453, 157 A.C.W.S. (3d) 762, leave to appeal to S.C.C. granted, [2007] 1 S.C.R. xv [*Syndicat national*]; *Confédération des syndicats nationaux c. Canada (P.G.)*, 2006

federal government argued that, even if the impugned provisions fell outside federal jurisdiction over employment insurance, they would nonetheless have to be declared valid on the basis of the federal spending power, which "is in no way limited by the division of powers".[4] The Quebec government intervened in both proceedings to oppose this argument and the cases are now under consideration by the Supreme Court of Canada.[5]

This eventful decade-and-a-half naturally generated a great deal of academic discussion around the issue of the fiscal imbalance and the governance of Canada's social union in general, and the spending power in particular. This volume and the associated conference attest to the high level of current interest. In 2006, at an earlier conference at Queen's University entitled Fiscal Federalism and the Future of Canada, I presented a paper suggesting that much of the difficulty encountered in governing Canada's social union is due to its shaky legal foundation: the unlimited spending power thesis.[6] After reviewing this thesis and highlighting its numerous weaknesses, I proposed an alternative solution drawing on a little known provision in the *Constitution Act, 1867*:[7] section 94.

In this chapter, I review and develop some of the legal arguments in support of my proposal, and I try to respond to the objections and criticisms it has generated. In the following section, I will scrutinize the unlimited federal spending power thesis by testing its validity against the written Constitution, what courts have said, constitutional theory, and current intergovernmental practice. In the second part, I will present my legal arguments supporting section 94 as a possible alternative to the spending power. In so doing, I will relate this provision to the broader context of cooperative federalism and particularly to legislative interdelegation, where I believe it belongs.[8]

QCCA 1454, [2006] R.J.Q. 2672, leave to appeal to S.C.C. granted, [2007] 1 S.C.R. viii [*Confédération des syndicats*]. The Court file numbers in the Quebec Superior Court were 150-05-001538-984 and 500-05-048333-999, respectively. These cases were decided together by the Quebec Court of Appeal.

[4]*Syndicat national des employés de l'aluminium d'Arvida c. Canada (P.G.)*, [2003] R.J.Q. 3188 (C.S.) (Defence, Attorney General of Canada at para. 40) [Defence] [translated by author].

[5]*Syndicat national*, *supra* note 3; *Confédération des syndicats nationaux*, *supra* note 3. [In the interval since the presentation of the paper, the Supreme Court has ruled on this matter, finding that the impugned active measures were indeed valid. See S.C.C. 511, 2008 SCC 68. (Eds.)]

[6]For a short version of this paper, see Adam (2007); for a long version, see Adam (2009).

[7](U.K.), 30 & 31 Vict., c. 3, reprinted in R.S.C. 1985, App. II, No. 5.

[8]While much of the material contained in this chapter was taken from my original paper, new sections have been added and the focus is more legal.

THE UNLIMITED FEDERAL SPENDING POWER THESIS

What Is the Issue and Why Does It Matter?

I believe that the two most relevant questions to ask with respect to the spending power are *why* and *how*. First, why does the federal government spend in areas of provincial jurisdiction? While there may sometimes be an element of pan-Canadian redistribution when the federal government uses its "spending power", that is not always the case, and when it is, the redistribution is often a mere side effect. However, a desire to bring some uniformity across the country is almost always a driver behind uses of the spending power; it is assumed that such uniformity would not exist if the federal government were not involved. We will address this goal of uniformity in the second part of this chapter.

The other central question is about the *means* used to bring about federal intervention in areas of provincial jurisdiction, in other words, the "how". Here, we enter the legal realm. In the name of flexibility and efficiency, the unlimited spending power thesis draws a distinction between, on the one hand, state spending, lending, and contracting and, on the other hand, state regulating. It then argues that the rules governing the federal division of powers do not apply to the former type of activity, even if the state's goals are the same as when it regulates.

For those who might be tempted to consider the debate surrounding the legality of the spending power a bygone issue, it should be noted that, quite independently of federalism, the use of contracts by governments for regulatory purposes is a growing trend in the Western world and has become a source of concern in the literature.[9] Efficiency, flexibility, and dispatch are often put forward as arguments in favour of these new regulatory methods, the same arguments, it may be noted, that are customarily made to support the unlimited spending power thesis. But it is legitimate to ask whether and to what extent the rules, and checks and balances – of a constitutional nature or otherwise – traditionally associated with governance can be waived when the state is not acting in a classical way. In other words, to what extent should we accept the creation of "public-law-free zones" as expedients?

For many, the "how" is a matter of technical detail, almost a source of annoyance. For lawyers, however, it should be an important issue. Federalism, like almost the entire body of public law, and constitutional law in particular, is about process, starting with the principle of the rule of law.

It should not come as a surprise that issues of process, such as those involved in the debate on the spending power, may seem trifling to most Canadians, nor should that fact be taken as an invitation to ignore such issues. On matters of process, the reactions of minorities are, in a sense, far more instructive than the attitude of majorities. Public law rules of process designed to restrain government action have usually been put in place precisely to shield

---

[9]See, e.g., Mockle (2002). Canada's spending power debate, far from being outdated, may be a precursor of wider debates to come.

vulnerable individuals or groups from the risk of arbitrary use of power by governments. Since power is held by the representatives of the majority in a democracy, the keenest concerns about its misuse are not likely to come from the majority. In a sense, minorities are like canaries in a mine: they are naturally more sensitive to potentially detrimental changes in their environment. Hence, even though the rule of law and constitutionalism are principles of the utmost importance for everybody because they afford stability and predictability, they are even more vital for minorities. While in a democracy such principles might mean curbing the will of the majority at times, this result scarcely needs to be explained or justified as far as the Canadian Charter of Rights and Freedoms[10] is concerned: it is broadly acknowledged and supported. However, the same logic is sometimes overlooked when it comes to the federal division of powers. As Hamish Telford has noted, because Quebec is the home of a "minority community" in this country, the federal division of powers gives Quebecers a form of constitutional protection in much the same way as the Charter does (Telford 2005). This is why, above and beyond the desirability of any specific federal spending program, the unlimited spending power thesis has always been a problem for Quebec.

The Constitution and the Spending Power

It is usually admitted that the federal spending power, as defined by the federal government in its defence to the constitutional challenge to workforce-training measures mentioned above,[11] is not spelled out in the text of the Constitution. A doctrinal construct that essentially appeared in the mid-twentieth century, it has been articulated in these terms by Peter Hogg:

> Parliament may spend or lend its funds to any government or institution or individual it chooses, for any purpose it chooses; and that it may attach to any grant or loan any condition it chooses, including conditions it could not directly legislate. There is a distinction, in my view, between compulsory regulation, which can obviously be accomplished only by legislation enacted within the limits of legislative power, and spending or lending or contracting, which either imposes no obligations on the recipient . . . or obligations which are voluntarily assumed by the recipient.... There is no compelling reason to confine spending or lending or contracting within the limits of legislative power, because in those functions the government is not purporting to exercise any peculiarly governmental authority over its subjects. (Hogg 2007, 6-18 to 6-19)

Although there is no unanimity among them, legal scholars supporting the unlimited spending power have attempted to infer it from various constitutional

[10]Part I of the *Constitution Act, 1982*, being Schedule B to the *Canada Act 1982* (U.K.), 1982, c. 11 [*Charter*].

[11]Defence, *supra* note 4.

provisions. The most frequently cited are sections 91(3), 91(1A), and 106 of the *Constitution Act, 1867* and section 36 of *Constitution Act, 1982*.[12]

None of these textual arguments are convincing. Sections 91(3) and 91(1A) essentially relate to the organization of the federal order of government, and are designed to enable it to perform its functions adequately. Such organic provisions must be distinguished from those that allocate jurisdiction between the two orders of government. Section 91(3), as it plainly states, deals exclusively with taxation. It grants to Parliament the power to raise autonomous revenues to meet the responsibilities assigned to it elsewhere in section 91: defence, for example. It provides no authorization for public policies other than taxing, let alone for spending conditionally in areas of provincial jurisdiction.[13] What is more, relying on the wording of section 92(2), which grants the provinces exclusive taxing power for provincial objects, the courts have in the past stated that section 91(3) had to be limited to taxation for federal objects. Even though this issue has largely remained theoretical because of the generality of our tax legislation, the constitutional text and the case law on it clearly militate against seeing section 91(3) as the constitutional foundation of an unlimited federal spending power.[14]

Section 91(1A), giving Parliament legislative authority over "The Public Debt and Property", must also be understood as an organic provision. It is designed to enable the federal order of government to manage its own property free of constraints that could otherwise arise from the provinces' general jurisdiction under section 92(13) over the field of property and civil rights. In other words, section 91(1A) provides a form of immunity.[15] Accordingly, the provinces do not need a parallel provision because of their general jurisdiction over property and civil rights.

As for section 106,[16] it is not even found in Part IV of the *Constitution Act, 1867*, which deals with the federal division of powers. It is therefore difficult to read it as granting the federal order any authority to interfere in areas of provincial jurisdiction. Section 106 is located in Part VIII, which contains various rather technical provisions on revenues, debts, assets, and taxation. It is

---

[12]Being Schedule B to the *Canada Act 1982* (U.K.), 1982, c. 11.

[13]See, e.g., *Reference Re the Insurance Act of Canada* (1931), [1932] A.C. 41 at 53 (P.C.).

[14]*Citizens Insurance Company of Canada v. Parsons* (1881), [1881-82] 7 A.C. 96 at 108-109 (P.C.); *Bank of Toronto v. Lambe*, [1887] 12 A.C. 575 at 585 (P.C.); *Caron v. R*, [1924] A.C. 999 at 1003-1004 (P.C.); *Forbes v. Manitoba (A.G.)*, [1937] A.C. 260 at 273-274 (P.C.); *Reference Re Agricultural Products Marketing Act*, [1978] 2 S.C.R. 1198 at 1233-1234.

[15]*Greater Toronto Airports Authority v. Mississauga (City of)* (2000), 50 O.R. (3d) 641 at paras. 62-63 (C.A.); *British Columbia (A.G.) v. Lafarge Canada*, 2007 SCC 23, [2007] 2 S.C.R. 86 at paras. 54-56; *Simon c. Oka (Municipalité d')*, [1999] R.J.Q. 108 at 117 (C.A.).

[16]"Subject to the several Payments by this Act charged on the Consolidated Revenue Fund of Canada, the same shall be appropriated by the Parliament of Canada for the Public Service": *Constitution Act, 1867*, *supra* note 7, s.106.

linked to the creation of the Consolidated Revenue Fund, and it awards a preferential rank to the specific charges mentioned under that title, many of which are now spent. The remainder of the section echoes the principle of the sovereignty of Parliament over the executive branch in respect of financial matters. A similar echo is found in section 53 of the same *Act*. The reference in section 106 to the "Public Service" must be understood to mean the federal public administration.[17]

Finally, some authors point to section 36 of the *Constitution Act, 1982*, and especially to section 36(1), as the potential legal foundation for the spending power. If one were to follow this view, it would have to be admitted that all of the federal spending programs in areas of provincial jurisdiction that existed before 1982 were unconstitutional. But reliance on section 36 must also be rejected. The provision has two distinct components. The first and more traditional component (Hogg 2007), found in section 36(2),[18] concerns intergovernmental fiscal transfers and inter-regional equity. The formula entrenched in 1982 essentially describes the federal equalization program as it existed then and still does today. Although the equalization program has existed since 1957, its roots are older. In the late 1930s, the Rowell-Sirois Commission had recommended the adoption of such a program in the aftermath of the Great Depression.[19] But one can look back even further to the transfer system put in

---

[17]This was common terminology in contemporary constitutional statutes of British origin. See, e.g., *The Union Act, 1840* (U.K.), 3 & 4 Vict., c. 35, ss. 50, 57, reprinted in R.S.C. 1985, App. II, No. 4; *An Act to remove Doubts respecting the Authority of the Legislature of Queensland, and to annex certain Territories to the Colony of South Australia, and for other Purposes* (U.K.), 24 & 25 Vict., c. 44, s. 6 [*Australian Colonies Act, 1861*]; *The South Africa Act, 1877* (U.K.), 40 & 41 Vict., c. 47, ss. 43, 48; *Commonwealth of Australia Constitution Act* (U.K.), 63 & 64 Vict., c.12, ss. 44, 52, 69, 84, 85; *Newfoundland Act* (U.K.), 12 & 13 Geo. VI, c. 22, Sch., s. 19, reprinted in R.S.C. 1985, App. II, No. 32.

[18]S.36(2): "Parliament and the government of Canada are committed to the principle of making equalization payments to ensure that provincial governments have sufficient revenues to provide reasonably comparable levels of public services at reasonably comparable levels of taxation."

[19]Royal Commission on Dominion-Provincial Relations (1940) [Rowell-Sirois Commission]. Despite the centralizing aspect of some of the Commission's recommendations, such as the transfer of unemployment insurance to Parliament by constitutional amendment, the Commission's recommendation with respect to unconditional "National Adjustment Grants" was clearly motivated by "the existence of pronounced differences in social philosophy between different regions in Canada" and "the presumption that existing constitutional arrangements [assigning social matters to the provinces] should not be disturbed except for compelling reasons": *ibid.* at 13. Hence, the proposed payments to provinces illustrated

> the Commission's conviction that provincial autonomy in the [social and education] fields must be respected and strengthened, and that the only true independence is financial security.... They are designed to make it possible for every province to provide for its people services of average Canadian standards and they will thus alleviate distress and shameful conditions which now weaken national unity and handicap many Canadians: ibid. at 125.

place at Confederation and provided for in sections 118[20] and 119 of the *Constitution Act, 1867*. A fundamental feature of all of these payments is that they were absolutely unconditional, in order to preserve complete provincial autonomy.

The second, more modern component of section 36 is found in subsection 1,[21] which, if it has any effect at all, does not grant powers to governments but rather spells out *commitments* toward citizens incumbent on each government acting in its own area of jurisdiction. Section 36(1) is more modern in the sense that it fits within the legal tradition of inscribing individual rights in constitutional documents. This is what the *Constitution Act, 1982*, with its Charter, is chiefly about. Further, the "rights" listed in section 36(1) are of a social and economic nature. These are a newer brand of rights to which jurisdictions around the world have been reluctant to give the same legal force as more classical individual rights and freedoms. This is why section 36(1) begins with a reserve clause stating that it does not alter federal and provincial legislative authority. This clause should be understood as protecting both the principle of parliamentary sovereignty and the division of powers. In other words, the "rights" in section 36(1) are not meant to have quite the same reach as Charter rights. Inasmuch as they commit the federal government and Parliament, it is only in respect of matters falling within federal jurisdiction. Indeed, it goes without saying that both orders of government have specific responsibilities that may impact on "the well-being of Canadians": both may play a role in "economic development", and both provide various "public services". In this last respect, section 36(1) works in the same way as the Charter; section 32(1) of the *Constitution Act, 1982* spells out that the Charter

---

In the Commission's view, it was clear that

> while the adjustment grant proposed is designed to enable a province to provide adequate services (at the average Canadian standard) without excessive taxation (on the average Canadian basis) the freedom of action of a province is in no way impaired. If a province chooses to provide inferior services and impose lower taxation it is free to do so, or it may provide better services than the average if its people are willing to be taxed accordingly, or it may, for example, starve its roads and improve its education, or starve its education and improve its roads – exactly as it may do today: ibid. at 84.

[20]This section was subsequently replaced by s. 1 of the *Constitution Act, 1907* (U.K.), 7 Edw. VII, c. 11, reprinted in R.S.C. 1985, App. II, No. 22, which in s. 1 provides for payments to every province "for its local purposes and the support of its Government and Legislature".

[21]Without altering the legislative authority of Parliament or of the provincial legislatures, or the rights of any of them with respect to the exercise of their legislative authority, Parliament and the legislatures, together with the government of Canada and the provincial governments, are committed to the following:

(a) promoting equal opportunities for the well-being of Canadians;

(b) furthering economic development to reduce disparity in opportunities; and

(c) providing essential public services of reasonable quality to all Canadians: *Constitution Act, 1982, supra* note 12, s. 36(1).

binds each order of government "in respect of all matters within the authority" of that order of government.[22]

In summary, neither section 36(1) nor section 36(2) can be interpreted as authorizing the federal government and Parliament to step into areas of provincial jurisdiction, or vice versa.

The Courts and the Spending Power

As we have just seen, the spending power is not found in the written text of the Constitution. But many will argue that it has been incorporated into Canadian constitutional law through the jurisprudence. A number of judgments rendered by the Supreme Court are usually cited in support of this view, starting with *YMHA Jewish Community Centre of Winnipeg Inc. v. Brown.*[23] As was demonstrated by the report of the Quebec Commission on Fiscal Imbalance[24] and by Andrée Lajoie in this volume, in each of these cases the comments made on the spending power were *obiter dicta*. As well, all of the comments were either statements by individual judges or notes appended to the Court's judgments. Further, they are all very brief, with no discussion of the sources or the precise boundaries of such a power. Given the extraordinary implications for Canadian federalism that would flow from the formal legal recognition of a federal spending power "in no way limited by the division of powers",[25] one should consider these comments with caution. After all, caution is the reason why *obiter dicta*, as opposed to the *ratio decidendi* of a case, are not considered to be binding.[26]

One last point should be made about the weight of these *obiter dicta*. While it is perhaps tempting to read them as a clear signal that the Supreme Court would not hesitate to recognize formally the validity of the unlimited spending power thesis, the fact remains that in all these years, it has never upheld the validity of a federal measure contested under the division of powers on the basis

---

[22]Charter, *supra* note 10, s.32(1). The fact that the reserve clause in s.36(1) speaks only of legislative authority, as in the case of s.32(1), should not be interpreted as a limitation of its scope to the legislative branch. That wording is simply attributable to the principle of parliamentary sovereignty.

[23][1989] 1 S.C.R. 1532. The other cases are *Reference Re Canada Assistance Plan (B.C.)*, [1991] 2 S.C.R. 525; *Finlay v. Canada (Minister of Finance)*, [1993] 1 S.C.R. 1080; *Eldridge v. British Columbia (A.G.)*, [1997] 3 S.C.R. 624 [*Eldridge*]; *Auton (Guardian ad litem of) v. British Columbia (A.G.)*, 2004 SCC 78, [2004] 3 S.C.R. 657; *Chaoulli v. Quebec (A.G.)*, 2005 SCC 35, [2005] 1 S.C.R. 791. Some lower court cases are also sometimes cited, but they obviously do not carry the same weight.

[24]The Commission examined all of the above-mentioned Supreme Court cases except the two last ones rendered after the issuance of its report (Quebec 2002).

[25]Defence, *supra* note 4.

[26]For authority for the proposition that not all *obiter dicta* are binding, see, e.g., *R. v. Henry*, 2005 SCC 76, [2005] 3 S.C.R. 609 at para. 57.

of the spending power. Indeed, there have been a few instances where the spending power was used by lower courts to validate federal legislation. This was notably the case in the Alberta Court of Appeal *Winterhaven Stables Ltd. v. Canada (A.G.)* judgment;[27] interestingly, the Supreme Court decided not to hear the appeal. It is also revealing that in several cases on the validity of spending measures under the division of powers that did reach the Supreme Court, the Court decided them on the basis of the "classical" heads of power. This was the case in the reference from Quebec with respect to parental benefits under the *Employment Insurance Act*.[28] It was also the case in *Lovelace*,[29] where the Court expressly characterized the impugned provincial measure as an exercise of the provincial spending power, but nonetheless found that since it was relating to a provincial matter and did not encroach upon federal jurisdiction, it conformed to the division of powers. In the coming months, it will be instructive to see how the Supreme Court decides the case, mentioned previously, involving the two Quebec unions.[30]

As several authors have recently pointed out (see Yudin 2002; see also Telford 2003), the only case that truly dealt with the federal spending power in an authoritative manner is the *Unemployment Insurance Reference*,[31] a 1937 decision of the Judicial Committee of the Privy Council that preceded the constitutional amendment transferring jurisdiction over unemployment insurance to Parliament. In that case, the federal government attempted to defend the validity of its legislation by construing it, on the one hand, as a taxation measure under section 91(3) of the *Constitution Act, 1867* and, on the other hand, as involving the disposition of federal property, and then by arguing that in disposing of such property, it was not constitutionally limited to areas of federal jurisdiction (so the argument ran). The Privy Council was not convinced by the federal characterization of the statute, but even supposing that characterization to be correct, the Court rejected the federal government's claim that its power to dispose of federal property was not limited by the distribution of powers.

In the first decades following the *Unemployment Insurance Reference*, the clearly dominant interpretation of the decision among scholars echoed that of

---

[27](1988), 53 D.L.R. (4th) 413 (Alta. C.A.), leave to appeal to S.C.C. refused, 21262 (19 December 1988).

[28]*Reference Re Employment Insurance Act (Canada), ss. 22 and 23*, 2005 SCC 56, [2005] 2 S.C.R. 669 [*Employment Insurance Reference*].

[29]*Lovelace v. Ontario*, 2000 SCC 37, [2000] 1 S.C.R. 950 at para. 111.

[30]*Syndicat national*, *supra* note 3; *Confédération des syndicats*, *supra* note 3. [See above, note 5. (Eds.)]

[31]*Reference Re Employment and Social Insurance Act (Can.)*, [1937] 1 D.L.R. 684 (P.C.), (*sub nom. Canada (A.G.) v. Ontario (A.G.)*) [1937] A.C. 326, aff'g *Reference Re The Employment and Social Insurance Act*, [1936] S.C.R. 427 [*Unemployment Insurance Reference*].

the Privy Council,[32] even though its implications displeased some. However, the unlimited spending power thesis eventually made a comeback.[33] The process by which the ruling of the Privy Council came to be disregarded by a majority of Canadian scholars is fascinating. Commentators first began treating the decision as unclear and looked to the Supreme Court's reasons, particularly those of its two dissenting judges, for guidance.[34] A number of commentators also considered the Privy Council's comments on the scope of the federal spending power to be *obiter*. Eventually, two distinctions were put forward to argue that, while the power of the federal government to spend "in areas of provincial jurisdictions" (note that the Privy Council never used these words) may have been somewhat limited by the Privy Council's decision, the bulk of federal spending remained unfettered. The first distinction sought to differentiate between federal expenditures made from a special fund and those made from the general consolidated revenue fund. A second, somewhat related distinction was proposed between pure federal expenses (which could nonetheless be conditional!) and expenses mixed with "compulsory" provisions, such as the requirement to pay premiums set out in the impugned *Unemployment Insurance Act*. As time went by, support for federal spending in areas of provincial jurisdiction became so strong in Canada, and its practice so common, that not only did these distinctions take hold but, by some ironic twist, the Privy Council's decision even came to be presented by some authors as the leading case recognizing the constitutionality of the federal unlimited spending power.[35]

With respect, these distinctions, and the resulting interpretations of the Privy Council's decision, fail to recognize a fundamental feature of the decision: Lord Atkin accepted the federal attorney's request to sever the compulsory provisions pertaining to premiums from the spending provisions pertaining to benefits, and to examine each operation separately. The federal government's contention was that the compulsory provisions were a valid federal tax under

[32]Keith (1937, 433-434); Commission royale des relations entre le Dominion et les provinces (1939, 20); MacDonald (1941, 77); Pigeon (1943, 439-440); Kennedy (1944, 157); Birch (1955, 162); Quebec (1956, 220-223); Ryan and Slutsky (1964-1966, 302-303; Beetz (1965, 132); Dupont (1967, 75-81).

[33]Many authors have noted that the Privy Council's ruling in the *Unemployment Insurance Reference* has been ineffective at restraining the spending power: Abel and Laskin (1975, 638); Petter (1989, 460); Tremblay (2000b, 304); Beaudoin (2000, 721).

[34]The reasons given in dissent by Duff C.J. in *Reference Re The Employment and Social Insurance Act*, [1936] S.C.R. 427, aff'd *Unemployment Insurance Reference*, *supra* note 31, are sometimes cited to support a broad interpretation of ss.91(1A) and 91(3), even though his suggestion that such powers entitled Parliament to raise and spend monies for any purpose it wanted and his conclusion that the impugned federal statute was therefore valid were clearly dismissed by both the Supreme Court majority and the Privy Council. For an example of reliance on Duff's reasoning, see Scott (1955, 3-4). Pierre Trudeau, before he became prime minister, noted this irony (Trudeau 1967, 87).

[35]On this evolution, see Scott (1955); Smiley (1962, 62); Hanssen (1966-67); La Forest (1981, 48); Cameron and Dupré (1983, 339); Chevrette and Marx (1982, 1040-1041); Rémillard (1983, 355-356); Schwartz (1987-88, 64-66); Choudhry (2002, 184-187); Brun, Tremblay and Brouillet (2007, 429); Beaudoin (2004).

section 91(3) of the *Constitution Act, 1867*, on the basis that there should be no distinction between general taxation and taxation to constitute a specific fund. The federal government then argued that the distribution of benefits was valid because of an unlimited federal spending power, which it presented in these terms: "Parliament is not confined in the appropriation of the funds to objects which are within the enumerated heads of section 91 of the *British North America Act*."[36]

In the end, Lord Atkin found it unnecessary to resolve the issues raised by the characterization of the premiums as tax because he flatly rejected the unlimited spending power thesis:

> But assuming that the Dominion has collected by means of taxation a fund, it by no means follows that any legislation which disposes of it is necessarily within Dominion competence. It may still be legislation affecting the classes of subjects enumerated in s.92, and, if so, would be ultra vires.... If on the true view of the legislation it is found that in reality in pith and substance the legislation invades civil rights within the Province, or in respect of other classes of subjects otherwise encroaches upon the provincial field, the legislation will be invalid. To hold otherwise would afford the Dominion an easy passage into the Provincial domain (ibid., 366-367).

Constitutional Theory and the Spending Power

The Privy Council decision in the *Unemployment Insurance Reference* is seldom mentioned in the contemporary literature supporting the unlimited spending power thesis and has never been discussed, let alone overturned, in the judicial decisions that are alleged to have "recognized" such a power. Clearly, what has allowed the unlimited spending power thesis to survive is the continuing and expanding practice of federal interventions in areas of provincial jurisdiction that came with the advent of the welfare state. In the legal literature, this led to some interesting intellectual gymnastics, first to skirt around the decision of the Privy Council, and second to skirt around the distribution of powers. This is how state spending, and the legislation authorizing it, have come to be differentiated from "compulsory regulation" and portrayed as a gift that could be made freely, irrespective of the assignment of responsibilities provided in the Constitution.[37] To achieve this result, three things occurred. First, words were read into sections 91 and 92 of the *Constitution Act, 1867*. Thus, these sections, effecting the distribution of powers, no longer applied to all legislation "in relation to" the matters listed, as is written; they applied only to the legislation actively "regulating" such matters. Second, it was argued that conditions attached to spending, no matter how detailed and restrictive on provincial autonomy they may be, do not amount to "regulation", even if such conditions admittedly

[36] *Unemployment Insurance Reference, supra* note 31 at 358.

[37] For an early articulation of the unlimited spending power thesis, see Scott (1955, 6). The most complete contemporary articulation is probably provided by Hogg (2007). Accordingly, it serves as the backdrop for the discussion set out in this chapter.

indirectly achieve the same outcome. Finally, we were told that the purpose of the spending is not to be taken into account even though purpose has always been a central element in determining the validity of legislation in disputes over the distribution of powers.

Indeed, one of the very first points that had to be addressed by the courts in deciding cases on the division of powers was how to analyze legislation in order to assess its conformity with the Constitution. Hence, the first step of the test developed by the courts consists of identifying the "pith and substance" of the legislation, and in doing so it was decided that the inquiry should go beyond examining the mere legal effects of the legislation to investigate its purpose. The logic here is to prevent not only direct infringements but also attempts to control indirectly matters within the jurisdiction of the other level of government. That is why, when analyzing the effects of legislation, both legal and practical effects may be considered.[38] As the Supreme Court recently has reminded us, the goal behind this teleological method of analysis is to provide predictability and maintain a balance between the two orders of government over time.[39] The idea that the purpose of any spending program is simply to spend and that the inquiry should end there is incompatible both with this method and the reasons for adopting it. No government spends merely for the sake of spending.

It should therefore come as no surprise that the unlimited spending power thesis is sometimes seen by non-lawyers as defying common sense. As Donald Smiley once put it:

> Although it is not within my competence to judge the constitutionality of the various uses of this power ... it appears to a layman to be the most superficial sort of quibbling to assert that when Parliament appropriates funds in aid of say, vocational training or housing, and enacts in some detail the circumstances under which such moneys are to be available that Parliament is not in fact 'legislating' in such fields. (Smiley 1962, 61)

The underlying rationale provided for the unlimited spending power thesis is that we should distinguish situations where the state acts as a "public power" – that is, in a "compulsory" manner – from cases where it acts as a "private actor", such as when spending, lending, and contracting. In the latter cases, it is argued, the state should be no more constrained by the Constitution than would be a private individual (Hogg 2007). It is interesting that no one has ever seriously attempted a similar public/private distinction with respect to the Charter by arguing that it ought not to apply to a government spending program. Clearly, there is a double standard at work here.[40]

---

[38]See Hogg (2007, 15-13 to 15-17). For a relatively recent judicial statement of the test, see *Kitkatla Band v. British Columbia (Minister of Small Business, Tourism and Culture)*, 2002 SCC 31, [2002] 2 S.C.R. 146 at 171ff.

[39]*Canadian Western Bank v. Alberta*, 2007 SCC 22, [2007] 2 S.C.R. 3 at paras. 24-25 [*Canadian Western Bank*].

[40]Limiting the applications of division of powers but not the Charter to instances where the government acts in a compulsory manner is all the more inconsistent when one considers that s.32 of the *Constitution Act, 1982*, which sets out when the Charter is to be

Taken to its logical conclusion, the unlimited spending power thesis implies that the provision of public services of any kind would largely be excluded from the purview of the distribution of powers, for it is essentially spending. The fact that "compulsory" taxation provides the means for such services seems irrelevant to the proponents of this thesis, as does the fact that the provision of public services is now the core mission of the modern state. Moreover, little explanation is provided to account for the presence of several items in sections 91 and 92 that allocate exclusive public services or spending responsibilities between the federal and the provincial legislatures.[41] Nor are we told why exactly we needed to amend the Constitution to allow the federal government to assume responsibility for providing unemployment insurance and old age pensions (ibid., ss.91(2A), 94A.).

In truth, the unlimited spending power thesis is a major case of constitutional revisionism with very profound implications. This is certainly plain when we set it against the understanding of Canadian federalism fleshed out by the Privy Council when it was called upon to arbitrate the first lawsuits between the provinces and federal government after Confederation:

> The object of the Act was neither to weld the provinces into one, nor to subordinate provincial governments to a central authority, but to create a federal government in which they should all be represented, entrusted with the exclusive administration of affairs in which they had common interest, each province retaining its independence and autonomy. That object was accomplished by distributing, between the Dominion and the provinces, all powers executive and legislative, and all public property and revenues which had previously belonged to the provinces; so that the Dominion Government should be vested with such of these powers, property, and revenues as were necessary for the due performance of its constitutional functions and that the remainder should be retained by the provinces for the purposes of provincial government.[42]

Despite what the unlimited spending power thesis seems to suggest, it was established long ago that the reach of the division of powers is not limited to the legislative branch, let alone to legislation of a compulsory nature, but extends to the executive branch. This is explicit in sections 12 and 65 of the *Constitution Act, 1867*.[43] Correctly understood, the distribution of powers contained in the

---

applied, simply refers to the distribution of legislative powers contained in the *Constitution Act, 1867*: see *infra* note 41.

[41]*Constitution Act, 1867*, *supra* note 7. For example: postal service at s.91(5); marine hospitals at s.91(11); ferries at s.91(13); hospitals, asylums, charities and eleemosynary institutions at s.92(7). Sections 91(8) and 92(4) are also interesting in that they specify what government has exclusive jurisdiction to pay which civil servants!

[42]*Liquidators of the Maritime Bank of Canada v. Receiver-General of New Brunswick*, [1892] A.C. 437 at 441-442 (P.C.).

[43]*Bonanza Creek Gold Mining Co., Ltd. v. R.*, [1916] 1 A.C. 566 (P.C.); see also *Kootenay & Elk Railway v. Canadian Pacific Railway*, [1974] S.C.R. 955 at 1013-1014.

Canadian Constitution is in essence a division of sovereignty.[44] Furthermore, it is exhaustive.[45] The fact that the language of sections 91 to 95 refers to the distribution of legislative and not executive powers is simply due to the principle of parliamentary sovereignty. There are numerous other constitutional provisions that echo the same principle, including section 32 of the *Constitution Act, 1982*. This last provision is particularly instructive as it is much more recent, and yet determines the scope of application of the Charter by merely referring to the legislative distribution of powers set out in the *Constitution Act, 1867*. Accordingly, the reach of the federal division of power and that of the Charter is intended to be the same.[46]

Another instructive provision is section 53 of the *Constitution Act, 1867*,[47] which provides that the raising and appropriation of public revenue must be authorized by parliamentary statute and originate from the House of Commons. This means that not only is spending subject to the division of powers, like all state action, but that it is also the preserve of the legislative branch and, accordingly, must be specifically authorized by an act of Parliament. In other words, a spending program should be seen as delegated legislation, akin to regulation.

The unlimited spending power thesis is at odds with many constitutional provisions and principles.[48] It is therefore not surprising that its legal foundations keep being called into question.[49] Among the most important principles at stake are constitutionalism and the rule of law and, in particular, the requirement to create and maintain "an actual order of positive laws which preserves and embodies the more general principle of normative order".[50] But perhaps the greatest conflict of all is with the principle of federalism itself. Over the

---

[44]Under Canadian federalism, both orders of government are said to be sovereign in their own areas of jurisdiction, in the same manner and to the same extent as independent states. And one of the central elements of sovereignty is independence, that is, protection from the interference of another government.

[45]The principle of the exhaustiveness of the distribution of powers was established very early on by the Privy Council in *Ontario (A.G.) v. Canada (A.G.)*, [1912] A.C. 571 at 584 [*Reference Appeal*]: "Whatever belongs to self-government in Canada belongs either to the Dominion or to the provinces, within the limits of the *British North America Act*."

[46]See *Operation Dismantle Inc. v. Canada*, [1985] 1 S.C.R. 441 at 463-464, where the Court held that the scope of the Charter, just like that of the division of powers, extended to Crown prerogatives.

[47]See also *Constitution Act, 1867*, *supra* note 7, s.106.

[48]For an excellent and thorough case of all the constitutional provisions and principles that militate against the unlimited spending power thesis, see Petter (1989). Many of the points made in this chapter are found in his work.

[49]See Petter (1989); Yudin (2002); Telford (2003); Gaudreault-DesBiens (2006); Kellock and LeRoy (2007).

[50]*Reference Re Manitoba Language Rights*, [1985] 1 S.C.R. 721 at 747-750. For a discussion of these principles in the context of the unlimited spending power thesis, see Gaudreault-DesBiens (2006).

past decade, starting with the *Quebec Secession Reference*,[51] the Supreme Court has reaffirmed on many occasions the importance of keeping federalism alive:

> The fundamental objectives of federalism were, and still are, to reconcile unity with diversity, promote democratic participation by reserving meaningful powers to the local or regional level and to foster co-operation among governments and legislatures for the common good. To attain these objectives, a certain degree of predictability with regard to the division of powers between Parliament and the provincial legislatures is essential. For this reason, the powers of each of these levels of government were enumerated in ss.91 and 92 of the *Constitution Act, 1867* or provided for elsewhere in that Act. As is true of any other part of our Constitution – this "living tree" as it is described in the famous image from *Edwards v. Attorney-General for Canada*, [1930] A.C. 124 (P.C.), at p. 136 – the interpretation of these powers and of how they interrelate must evolve and must be tailored to the changing political and cultural realities of Canadian society. It is also important to note that the fundamental principles of our constitutional order, which include federalism, continue to guide the definition and application of the powers as well as their interplay. Thus, the very functioning of Canada's federal system must continually be reassessed in light of the fundamental values it was designed to serve.[52]

Intergovernmental Practice and the Spending Power

In the end, the imperative to provide a legal explanation for federal interventions in provincial areas of jurisdiction constitutes the main selling point of the unlimited spending power thesis. Even Professor Hogg seems to admit this point (Hogg 2007, 6-17 to 6-18). But if one examines the situation carefully, one notices that this thesis does not capture accurately the practices on the ground either, where negotiation is much more often the rule than unilateralism. Ironically, this state of affairs has led some observers to conclude that there was a significant gap between the "*de facto* spending power" and what is generally assumed to be the "*de jure* spending power"![53]

Indeed, according to the unlimited spending power thesis, the distribution of powers is irrelevant when it comes to spending measures; the federal government and Parliament can act freely. This is certainly what happens with respect to spending in areas of federal jurisdiction. However, even though the federal government has always had the upper hand, its spending measures in areas of provincial jurisdiction have generally been the subject of federal-provincial discussions, if not negotiations and agreement. In fact, the bulk of federal-provincial relations today, with hundreds of meetings at various levels yearly, is related to such exchanges. Even federal programs taking the form of direct transfers to individuals and organizations are often discussed (for

[51] *Reference Re Secession of Quebec*, [1998] 2 S.C.R. 217 at para. 55.

[52] *Canadian Western Bank*, *supra* note 39 at paras. 22-23.

[53] Comments made at June 2008 Roundtable convened in Ottawa by the Institute for Research on Public Policy.

example, the Millennium Scholarship Fund, the National Child Benefit and, more recently, the creation by the federal government of the Mental Health Commission of Canada).

While there may be uncertainty about the respective constitutional rights of the federal government and the provinces over the issues being discussed and negotiated, few would dispute the necessity of such discussions and negotiations.[54] The federal government itself has on several occasions presented provincial consensus as a precondition for its interventions. SUFA was essentially an attempt – however disappointing – to codify some of the "rules" in this respect.[55] Incidentally, in January 1999, a week before the signing of SUFA and after nearly two years of intense collaborative work on this issue, all the provinces including Quebec had agreed on a comprehensive text laying out the rules that should govern Canada's social union. This text is known as the Victoria Proposal.[56] It was pushed aside by the federal government, which put $3 billion on the table for the provinces on the condition they sign another text of its own making, which became SUFA. The Victoria Proposal included the two following principles:

- Federal spending in an area of provincial jurisdiction that occurs in a province or territory must have the consent of the province or territory involved; and
- The federal government will provide full compensation to any provincial or territorial government that chooses not to participate in any new or modified Canada-wide program, providing it carries on a program or initiative that addresses the priority areas of the new or modified Canada-wide program.

In the aftermath of the failure of the Victoria Proposal and SUFA, the federal Conservative government's promise to legislate in order to limit the use of the spending power is yet another attempt to translate those rules.

Hence, the distribution of powers does seem to matter. Consider that, if the unlimited spending power thesis were the law, the federal government would have the right to withdraw all of its funding to the provinces for health and post-secondary education and open up its own hospitals and universities instead. Conversely, nothing would prevent the provinces from having their own armies, postal services, or currencies!

The notion of an absolute, unfettered federal power to intervene unilaterally by way of conditional spending in areas of provincial jurisdiction was probably

---

[54]See, e.g., Perry (1997, 27). In Quebec, legislation requires in many instances that the Quebec government or Minister approve agreements with other Canadian governments, including those governing federal spending in areas of provincial jurisdiction, for said agreements to be valid: *An Act respecting the Ministère du Conseil exécutif*, R.S.Q. c. M-30, s. 3.6.2ff.

[55]On this issue, see Leslie, Neumann, and Robinson (2004, 218); see also Cameron and Simeon (2002).

[56]*Securing Canada's Social Union into the 21st Century (The Victoria Proposal)*, reprinted in Gagnon and Segal (2000).

never widely supported as a sustainable proposition to guide the operation of Canadian federalism. This is why several rounds of constitutional negotiations have sought in one way or another to prescribe limits to federal spending.[57] In retrospect, given what has happened to efforts at constitutional reform, choosing this course instead of an outright constitutional challenge may have been a mistake. As we have seen, after the failure of the Charlottetown Accord,[58] the same endeavour was again attempted through the administrative route, just as unsuccessfully. The incentive to find an effective, permanent, and sustainable mechanism that would allow the federal government to play a constructive and collaborative role in areas of provincial jurisdictions has never been sufficiently strong or widely shared to bear fruit. The temptations of unilateralism stirred up by the unlimited spending power thesis have always prevailed.

Yet, what many Canadians want to see is collaboration between the two orders of government in the management of what they perceive to be pan-Canadian issues. However, the difficulty with satisfying this desire is twofold. First, often it is not equally shared by Quebecers. To be sure, there have been instances of opting out that have succeeded in smoothing over this difference of opinion, but these were ad hoc arrangements and only came after hard fought political battles.[59] The second difficulty is the apparent lack of a legal framework in the Constitution to sustain this vision of federalism.

COOPERATIVE FEDERALISM

For some in the academic world studying Canadian politics, cooperative federalism is what intergovernmental relations should ideally be about, but

---

[57]This was the case for the Victoria Charter in 1971 with its provisions granting federal jurisdiction over social policy subject to provincial paramountcy. Even though the "spending power" terminology was not used, the intent was to allow the federal government to intervene in the social field, subject to certain rules. The Meech Lake Accord in 1987 and the Charlottetown Accord in 1992 sought to accomplish the same thing, but this time, starting from the assumption that Parliament already had such a power through spending programs and attempting to circumscribe its exercise.

[58]Special Joint Committee on a Renewed Canada, *Consensus Report on the Constitution* (Charlottetown, 1992) [Charlottetown Accord].

[59]The major gains in this respect date back to the 1960s (Canada Pension Plan, health care, student aid, etc.). The level of political tension between Quebec's Lesage Liberal government and Ottawa's Pearson Liberal government before the first opting-out agreement could be secured in 1964 is not often mentioned but was considerable. See, e.g., Morin (1972, 19-31). More recent cases of "opting out" could include the Canada-Quebec agreement over manpower training in 1997, the Canada-Quebec agreement over parental leave of 2004 and, to some extent, the side agreement over health care of 2004. The first of these agreements was reached after decades of discussion and in the aftermath of the 1995 Quebec referendum, where the sovereigntist option nearly succeeded. The second was reached after the Quebec Court of Appeal declared the federal regime unconstitutional further to legal proceedings undertaken by the government of Quebec. See *Employment Insurance Reference*, *supra* note 28.

seldom are. For others, especially in the policy industry, it is an open invitation to disregard the Constitution and the division of powers. For many in the general public, it has become an empty political phrase. What has perhaps been forgotten is that cooperative federalism was once the subject of serious legal studies in Canada. The original inspiration came from the Privy Council in the 1930s when the courts were asked to decide on the validity of a number of economic and social pieces of federal legislation put forward in the aftermath of the Great Depression. The *Unemployment Insurance Reference* was but one of a string of cases where the judiciary confirmed that many such measures fall within provincial areas of jurisdiction.[60] In light of this result, the challenges at the root of the notion of cooperative federalism consisted of finding ways in which to reconcile a strict division of exclusive powers with changing needs and values within the Canadian population, and overcoming the growing difficulty of neatly deliniating contemporary issues (Tuck 1945). One way to meet this challenge, of course, was to try to amend the division of powers, as was done in 1940 regarding unemployment insurance. But this route, which then involved going to London, was considered too slow. Besides, such amendments required unanimity – hence an all or nothing symmetrical formula – which was not regarded as the most practical approach to foster greater integration due to the predictable resistance in some regions of the country, particularly Quebec, to the erosion of provincial autonomy.[61]

Inter-Delegation

To overcome the difficulties associated with piecemeal constitutional amendments, the Rowell-Sirois Commission recommended proceeding through a general power of delegation between Parliament and the provincial legislatures subject to mutual consent (Royal Commission on Dominion-Provincial Relations 1940, 72-73). The question then became whether it was possible to put in place such a power through ordinary statutes or whether the Constitution needed to be amended to provide for it.

Indeed, the notion of delegation of powers in the absence of clear constitutional text authorizing it appeared suspicious to many, either because it was perceived as an abdication of parliamentary sovereignty, a sacred principle in the British legal tradition (Chevrette and Marx 1982, 93-94, 102-103), or because it was perceived to be a breach of the principle of constitutional separation of powers, an equally sacred principle in the American legal tradition (Tuck 1945, 83ff).

---

[60]See also *Reference Re Natural Products Marketing Act*, [1936] S.C.R. 398, (*sub. nom. British Columbia (A.G.) v. Canada (A.G.)*) [1937] A.C. 377 at 389 (P.C.), where the Court specifically referred to the need for federal-provincial co-operation.

[61]For comment on the difficulty of amending the Constitution and the unanimity required, see Tuck (1945, 81).

In Canada, the big test came with the *Inter-Delegation Reference*[62] in 1951. In that case, the Supreme Court of Canada had to decide whether a Prince Edward Island statute allowing for the delegation of legislative authority to Parliament over employment matters normally falling within exclusive provincial jurisdiction, and vice versa, was constitutional. The answer was negative. Many commentators consider this decision unfortunate because it deprived the Canadian federation of a most convenient consensual tool. Still, it did not completely close the door to legal cooperative federalism. Indeed, the *Inter-Delegation Reference* dealt with one form of delegation, which is sometimes called legislative or horizontal interdelegation: in other words, a direct transfer of powers between two legislative assemblies. The decision left untouched many other devices capable of achieving analogous results.[63]

One such alternative is administrative interdelegation. This occurs when Parliament or a provincial legislature enacts a statute and entrusts its implementation to an agency or to the executive branch of another order of government. This may involve bestowing a power to grant licences and even some regulatory powers. The courts have validated administrative delegations, such as allowing a single administrative body to regulate both intra-provincial and inter-provincial commerce.[64]

Another alternative is through the technique of incorporation by reference where, instead of devising its own rules concerning an issue falling within its jurisdiction, a legislative assembly decides to make applicable to this issue the rules adopted by the legislature of another order of government to deal with similar issues. This too has been validated by the courts.[65] For a time, there was some doubt as to whether the reference could only incorporate rules in existence at the time it was made or whether it could include future amendments to these rules as well. Again, the concern was that the latter might be seen as a form of abdication of parliamentary sovereignty. Nevertheless, the courts decided that so long as the intention to include future amendments was clear, such a reference was valid too. A good example of this technique is provided by the *Indian Act*, which incorporates all general provincial laws for the purpose of regulating activities on Indian reserves that would otherwise fall under provincial jurisdiction.[66]

A third, somewhat related, alternative approach is conditional legislation. This takes place when the laws passed by a legislative assembly will apply, cease to apply, or apply differently subject to conditions determined by the other order of government.[67] Gerard V. La Forest thought that the provisions allowing

---

[62]*Nova Scotia (A.G.) v. Canada (A.G.)* (1950), [1951] S.C.R. 31 [*Inter-Delegation Reference*].

[63]Several scholars have written about these devices. See, e.g., Lederman (1967).

[64]*Prince Edward Island (Potato Marketing Board) v. H.B. Willis Inc.*, [1952] 2 S.C.R. 392.

[65]See *Coughlin v. Ontario Highway Transport Board*, [1968] S.C.R. 569.

[66]R.S.C. 1985, c. I-5, s. 88.

[67]See , e.g., *R. v. Furtney*, [1991] 3 S.C.R. 89 at 101-106.

provinces to opt out of social programs created by the federal government fell into this category (La Forest 1975, 138). The recent parental leave agreement between Quebec and Ottawa provides a good example of this.[68]

At this point it is worth noting that all of the techniques just described are, in effect, legal instruments of asymmetrical federalism, many of which are currently used in various situations without raising any controversy. Their validation has led many observers to conclude that much of what was prohibited by the Supreme Court in the *Inter-Delegation Reference* can now be achieved indirectly (Chevrette and Marx 1982, 263). However, as noted by several authors after a careful analysis of the case law, it is still forbidden for the legislative assembly of one order of government to enlarge the powers of a legislative assembly of the other order of government, enabling it to enact a statute that it would not have had the jurisdiction to adopt independently of the delegation (Hogg 2007, 14-32). In other words, these alternative techniques are of little assistance when truly exclusive areas of jurisdiction are involved.

One way around this problem, so as to allow the federal government to play a larger role in areas of provincial jurisdiction, particularly in the social domain, has been to advocate the existence of a spending power that would not be limited by the division of powers. As this concept was originally accompanied by generous federal subsidies (thanks to Ottawa's post-war fiscal resources), many of the provinces were initially quite happy to go along with it. Indeed, the literature on this topic tends to contrast two distinct periods. Generally, the system is perceived to have worked rather well until the mid-1970s, when money became scarce and it broke down.[69] Thus in 1967, Lederman confidently saw the unlimited spending power as yet another tool of cooperative federalism (Lederman 1967, 428-429). However, with hindsight, one may today question whether the notion of an unlimited federal spending power has indeed promoted cooperation between the federal government and the provinces. In his chapter, Tom Kent suggests that Ottawa should now simply bypass the provinces altogether and use its spending power to exert its influence over the provincial domain through direct transfers to individuals. This is perhaps the best evidence that cooperative federalism and the unlimited spending power thesis do not necessarily go hand in hand. In my opinion, if anything, this thesis has hindered the search for new and innovative ways to enhance genuine cooperative federalism, notably with respect to delegation (La Forest 1975, 131).

A number of arguments against legislative interdelegation were raised by the Supreme Court in the 1951 *Inter-Delegation Reference*. Essentially, it was felt that this was tantamount to amending the Constitution. The court stated,

---

[68]See the Entente de principe Canada-Québec sur le régime d'assurance parentale. Online: Conseil de gestion de l'assurance parentale at www.cgap.gouv.qc.ca/publications/index_en.asp?categorie=0401401 and the Entente finale Canada-Québec sur le régime québécois d'assurance parentale. Online: Régime québécois d'assurance parentale at www.rqap.gouv.qc.ca/publications/pdf/RQAP_entente_conges_parentaux.pdf, respectively signed in 2004 and 2005.

[69]See Lazar (2000); Meekison, Telford, and Lazar (2004); Papillon and Simeon (2004); Leslie, Neumann, and Robinson (2004); Noël (2005).

> The Constitution does not belong either to Parliament, or to the Legislatures; it belongs to the country and it is there that the citizens of the country will find the protection of the rights to which they are entitled. It is part of that protection that Parliament can legislate only on the subject matters referred to it by section 91 and that each Province can legislate exclusively on the subject matters referred to it by section 92.[70]

In making this point the Court emphasized that the Constitution distributed exclusive powers to each order of government. Although the proposed scheme of delegation allowed for the possibility of revocation, the Court distinguished it from a delegation of duties to a subordinate body. The Court suggested that in practice it could become very difficult among equally sovereign orders of government for one to reclaim a power once it had been exercised for a certain time by the other one. Justice Tashereau from Quebec raised the additional concern that too permissive an approach regarding informal modulations of the division of powers could eventually set Canada on a course towards a unitary regime.[71] Lederman agreed with the Supreme Court and added two further objections: legislative interdelegation might confuse citizens about the respective roles and responsibilities of their governments which, in turn, would reduce accountability (Lederman 1967).

There is merit to all of these arguments. However, all of these drawbacks are with us now because they apply to the spending power and fiscal federalism with even greater force. What is more, theoretically, following the unlimited spending power thesis, even the mutual consent of governments is not required, let alone that of legislative assemblies. In 1992, David Schneiderman made a similar observation in a paper where he explored the potential of delegation as a solution that could satisfy every region of the country (Schneiderman 1992). Indeed, following the suggestion of the Rowell-Sirois Commission, and given the 1951 Supreme Court decision, several proposals to amend the Constitution to provide for a general delegation mechanism have been advanced. Possibly the most comprehensive proposal came with the Fulton-Favreau formula in the early 1960s in the form of an expanded section 94: section 94A (see Hurley 1996, 187-188).

Legislative Inter-delegation and Section 94 of the Constitution Act, 1867

In the *Inter-Delegation Reference*,[72] one of the reasons given by the Supreme Court for dismissing the idea that the Constitution implicitly allowed legislative interdelegation was the existence of section 94 – an explicit but limited mechanism for legislative delegation. Briefly, section 94 allows Parliament to legislate in relation to property and civil rights, but only with the consent of the

---

[70] *Inter-Delegation Reference, supra* note 62, 34.

[71] Ibid. at 45.

[72] *Supra* note 62.

legislatures of the provinces where the federal legislation is to apply. The section reads:

> Notwithstanding anything in this Act, the Parliament of Canada may make Provision for the Uniformity of all or any of the Laws relative to Property and Civil Rights in Ontario, Nova Scotia, and New Brunswick, and of the Procedure of all or any of the Courts in those Three Provinces, and from and after the passing of any Act in that Behalf the Power of the Parliament of Canada to make Laws in relation to any Matter comprised in any such Act shall, notwithstanding anything in this Act, be unrestricted; but any Act of the Parliament of Canada making Provision for such Uniformity shall not have effect in any Province unless and until it is adopted and enacted as Law by the Legislature thereof.[73]

Section 94 is essentially the only provision[74] in the Constitution that contemplates in general terms the possibility of the federal government intervening in an area of exclusive provincial jurisdiction, namely, property and civil rights. As we know, property and civil rights constitutes the bulk of the provincial domain.

Section 94 expressly refers to only three provinces: Ontario, Nova Scotia, and New Brunswick – that is, to the three original common law provinces. It is clear that the intention of its framers was to exclude Quebec from its ambit on account of its distinct civil law tradition. In practice, under section 94, Parliament would adopt a piece of legislation after it was discussed and agreed upon with the relevant provincial authorities. This statute would subsequently be adopted by the provinces who so wished and from there on become valid and binding federal law in their territories (see Scott 1942, 536-537). In other words, section 94 is an opt-in formula that allows for asymmetrical federalism.[75] The federal government could decide, for economic and political considerations of its own, to make its intervention under section 94 conditional on a required number of provinces endorsing it. It could even require that all the provinces to which this section applies be on board. But there is no legal constraint in this respect.

In my original paper on section 94,[76] I argued that although it has never been formally used, section 94 could provide a more solid legal foundation for Canada's social union than the unlimited spending power thesis, and one that better reflects the actual dynamics at play in the practice of Canadian federalism: the desire for greater uniformity, the need for collaboration and federal-provincial agreement, and the possibility for Quebec to opt out. I believe that

---

[73]*Constitution Act, 1867, supra* note 7, s.94.

[74]Some could also view the federal declaratory power under s.92(10) and the federal remedial power under s.93 in this light; however, these are much more limited in scope and purpose than s.94, ibid.

[75]See, e.g., La Forest (2005); Pelletier (2005); Milne (2005); Courchene (2006); Brown (2005); Smith (2005).

[76]See *supra* note 6.

considerable benefits could ensue from such a change in legal paradigms in terms of transparency, accountability, effectiveness and quality of programs, reduced political tensions and, ultimately, Canadian unity. From a public law standpoint, perhaps the greatest benefit of all would be that this would allow us to reconcile the Canadian practice of federalism, in particular the governance of Canada's social union, with the principles of constitutionalism and the rule of law.

Anticipating possible objections to my proposal, I had also identified a number of legal issues that would have to be addressed concerning section 94 and attempted to provide arguments as to how they could be approached so that this constitutional provision could be put to use today. These issues are (a) whether section 94 applies to all common law provinces or just the three that are specifically mentioned; (b) whether its scope is wide enough to cover social programs; (c) whether it is reversible or not; and (d) whether non-participating provinces, including Quebec, would be entitled to receive compensation in the event of financial prejudice flowing from the use of section 94.

Since my original paper, I have had the benefit of a number of comments from various corners. On the whole, objections to my proposal came mostly in the form of scepticism that the courts would be willing to convey to section 94 a broad enough meaning to meet present needs if they were confronted with this matter (see, e.g., Petter, this volume).

For my part, I see section 94 as an enabling provision. It does not take away rights but rather offers new possibilities, so long as the consent of the relevant actors is secured. I therefore find it difficult, especially in the current context of constitutional paralysis, to see why the courts – and the Supreme Court in particular – would adopt a rigid approach in interpreting section 94. In the following paragraphs, I will review and develop the arguments that militate in favour of a broad interpretation of section 94 in respect of each of these issues.

The Geographic Scope of Section 94

The Rowell-Sirois Commission examined section 94 in the course of its investigation and dismissed it as a vehicle for adapting Canada's division of powers to modern demands. Essentially it did so for two reasons. First, it believed that section 94 could only apply to the three provinces listed in the section. Second, it believed that a transfer of powers pursuant to this provision would be irreversible, and that provinces would accordingly be very reluctant to use it (Royal Commission on Dominion-Provincial Relations 1940, 73).

F.R. Scott, who saw much potential in section 94 as a mechanism that would allow the federal government to play a leading role in building the welfare state, strongly disagreed with the Commission's conclusion on the first point.[77] He argued that section 94 would now apply to all the common law provinces. In fact, most scholars today are in agreement (see La Forest 1975, 132; Pelletier 1996 at 270, n. 799).

---

[77]Scott (1942). Scott submitted a brief to the Rowell-Sirois Commission.

Indeed, many provisions in the *Constitution Act, 1867* that are still in force have language that refers to only the original provinces. For example, section 5 reads: "Canada shall be divided into Four Provinces, named Ontario, Quebec, Nova Scotia and New Brunswick." Today, of course, we must interpret such provisions as also applying to the provinces that were added after Confederation. This result is ensured by express provisions contained in the constitutional statutes that incorporated the latter provinces into Canada such as section 2 of the *Manitoba Act*,[78] which reads as follows:

> The provisions of the *British North America Act, 1867*, shall, except those parts thereof which are in terms made, or, by reasonable intendment, may be held to be specially applicable to, or only to affect one or more, but not the whole of the Provinces now composing the Dominion, and except so far as the same may be varied by this Act, be applicable to the Province of Manitoba, in the same way, and to the like extent as they apply to the several Provinces of Canada, and as if the Province of Manitoba had been one of the Provinces originally united by the said Act.

There is compelling historical evidence to suggest that the framers intended section 94 to apply to the "whole" of the provinces except for Quebec. This is made clear by the fact that section 29(33) of the Québec Resolutions, the precursor of section 94, adopted in 1865, also listed Newfoundland and Prince Edward Island, which at the time were still negotiating to become original members of the new federation.[79] The purpose behind section 94 is obvious: the framers of Confederation foresaw that although they had agreed upon a federal-provincial distribution of powers, there would eventually be a desire for further integration among the common law provinces. The framers also foresaw that this would not be true for Quebec given its specificity.

Actually, with the help of the techniques that I have alluded to above – namely, incorporation by reference and administrative interdelegation – even Quebec could now indirectly opt into a section 94 scheme, with slightly different legal effects,[80] but with essentially the same practical result. Indeed, if by virtue of section 94, Parliament legislated in the domain of property and civil rights and its legislation was in force in some of the common law provinces, we would not be in a situation where the federal law "would have no significance and validity independent of the delegation" made by Quebec (Hogg 2007, 14-32); therefore, the Quebec National Assembly could resort to interdelegation effectively to opt in without violating the prohibition established in the *Inter-*

---

[78]S.C. 1870, c. 3.

[79]"The Québec Resolutions, October, 1864 (The 72 Resolutions)" (2005), online at Library and Archives Canada at www.collectionscanada.gc.ca/confederation/023001-245-e.html.

[80]The essential distinction would be that Quebec would formally be governed by Quebec legislation while the other provinces would formally be governed by federal legislation, with slightly different rules applying in the event of a conflict of law with other provincial statutes.

Delegation Reference. To conclude, I believe that today all the provinces could benefit equally from the opportunities offered by section 94.

The Material Scope of Section 94

Another potential issue with section 94 is its seemingly limited material scope: "property and civil rights". The same expression is used in section 92(13). Even so, we must remember that this is the most comprehensive head of provincial power. A lot can already be achieved under it. And, as Barbara Cameron once reminded me, social programs were originally conceived as public insurance – this is how they came to be classified as matters of provincial jurisdiction under this all embracing category, as was decided in the *Unemployment Insurance Reference*.[81]

If we return to the origins of this phrase in the 1774 *Quebec Act*,[82] we can understand why section 92(13) has become a kind of provincial residuary clause akin to "peace, order and good government" (Hogg 2007, 17-1 to 17-3, 21-2 to 21-3). The legal category of "property and civil rights" was originally conceived as an inclusive formula to allow for the restoration in Quebec of French law (which had been abolished pursuant to the British conquest) in all matters but criminal law, external trade, and a few others. This is evidenced by the way the *Quebec Act* is structured: it establishes in section VIII, in the broadest terms possible, the general principle of the restoration of French law in all matters related to "property and civil rights" and subsequently sets limits or carves out exceptions to this principle, such as the one concerning criminal law. Indeed, the expression "property and civil rights" would have included criminal law had it not been for its expressed subtraction in section XI (ibid., 2-7 to 2-8).

Interestingly, the expression "civil rights" was unofficially translated in 1774 as "droits de citoyen" (citizen rights), thus reflecting the wide meaning ascribed to it at the time. Accordingly, the conventional assimilation of the notion of "property and civil rights" to the field of "private law", as opposed to "public law", may be historically inaccurate. Aside from criminal law, there were other principles of English public law that were meant to continue to rule the inhabitants of Quebec, not necessarily because such principles fell outside the scope of the expression "property and civil rights" by definition. Rather, these English principles persisted because section VIII of the *Quebec Act* made clear that the rights of Quebecers "to hold and enjoy their Property and Possessions, together with all Customs and Usages relative thereto, and all their other Civil Rights ... [as] determined [by] the Laws of Canada [in other words, old French law]" had to be exercised in a manner consistent "with their Allegiance to his Majesty, and Subjection to the Crown and Parliament of Great Britain". In other words, it is only to the extent of an actual inconsistency with their duty of loyalty toward their new Sovereign, or otherwise in face of some

[81] *Supra* note 31.

[82] (U.K.) 14 Geo. III, c. 83, s. 3, reprinted in R.S.C. 1985, App. II, No. 2.

threat to English sovereignty, that Quebecers were to be governed by English law as opposed to their own pre-existing law.[83]

Of course, today, the scope of the provincial jurisdiction under section 92(13) is much more limited. That is because when the phrase "property and civil rights" was recycled in the *Constitution Act, 1867*, further subtractions were made to its scope by assigning a number of other subject matters in addition to criminal law and external trade – for instance bankruptcy and insolvency – to Parliament (Brun, Tremblay, and Brouillet 2007, 422). The majority of the federal heads of power can be seen in this light. In turn, such assignments to Parliament of matters related to property and civil rights led to further refinements in regard to section 92 so as to avoid any risk of confusion. That is why there are in section 92 many items other than section 92(13) that deal with property and civil rights: for example, provincial undertakings (section 92(10)), incorporation of companies with provincial objects (section 92(11)), and solemnization of marriage (section 92(12)). As can be seen, many of the subsections both in sections 92 and 91 were carved out of the legal category of property and civil rights in order to fine-tune the division of powers in this area. Section 92(7) (hospitals, asylums, charities, etc., other than marine hospitals) and section 93 (education) may well be other examples of this.

What does this mean when it comes to defining the material scope of section 94? Should it be limited to the residual matters of section 92(13), or should it extend to the other matters found in section 92 – or elsewhere in Part VI – that can also be included in the notion of property and civil rights? I believe that the second view is the better one. Excluding the "offspring" of section 92(13) would not make much sense, because it is often their close proximity with matters assigned to Parliament that has led to their express mention in section 92. Accordingly, they might be viewed as ideal candidates to be transferred to Parliament under section 94. Would it make sense, for instance, to prevent the unification of corporate law under section 94 – assuming there was a wish for it – simply because the incorporation of companies with provincial objects is specifically provided for in section 92(11)?

Reversibility of a Section 94 Transfer

Another difficult legal issue with section 94 is the potentially irreversible character of a regime adopted under its terms. Supposing the federal government did have recourse to it and some provinces did adopt the ensuing federal legislation, would it be possible for the parties subsequently to change their

[83]The relatively narrow scope of this restriction is evidenced by a judgment rendered by the Privy Council in 1835 with respect to a lawsuit arising out of Quebec. In short, it was held that, by virtue of the *Quebec Act*, "[t]he Prerogative of the Crown with regard to aliens [in this case the *droit d'aubaine*], must be determined by the laws of [Canada, i.e., old French law] … and not by the law of England, which is only to be looked at in order to determine who are, and who are not, aliens": *Donegani v. Donegani* (1835), 12 E.R. 571 at 571 (P.C.).

minds and return to the status quo *ante*? The possible irreversibility of a section 94 transfer was, together with its apparent limited geographical scope, the main reason why the Rowell-Sirois Commission in 1939 chose to disregard it as a potential solution for adapting Canada's division of powers to the needs of the twentieth century. The Commission viewed this as a non-starter from a provincial standpoint. In support of this second point, the Commission referred to an analogous provision in the 1900 Australian Constitution,[84] section 51(XXXVII), which up until that time had been a dead letter as well (Royal Commission on Dominion-Provincial Relations 1940, 73).

Controversy surrounding the issue of reversibility stems from the use of the word "unrestricted" to qualify the power invested in Parliament once a provincial legislature has adopted the federal statute. According to one interpretation, this means that recourse to section 94 is in essence a constitutional amendment and that there can be no transfer back (Scott 1942). Following another interpretation, section 94 is a delegation device and the word "unrestricted" was inserted simply to make sure that the delegated power was not limited to the terms of the original statute but also covered future amendments made by Parliament (La Forest 1975, 132). The possibility that the term "unrestricted" would mean both an irreversible grant of power to Parliament akin to a constitutional amendment, as well as the federal capacity thereafter to modify the law at will, should be ruled out; it would be tantamount to granting Parliament a tool to change the distribution of power at will in respect of property and civil rights. This proposition is hardly compatible with federalism and the economy of section 94, which requires provincial consent each time recourse is had to this section.

It is helpful to analyze previous versions of section 94 drafted at the Quebec and London conferences, which tend to suggest that the use of the word "unrestricted" was intended to cover future amendments. This word did not appear in article 29(33) of the Québec Resolution of 1865, which ended as follows: "but any Statute for this purpose shall have no force or authority in any Province until sanctioned by the Legislature thereof". In a subsequent text prepared for the London conference, the following phrase was added: "and when so sanctioned the power of amending, altering or repealing such laws shall thenceforth be vested in the Parliament only" (O'Connor 1939, 121). This, in the final version of the *Constitution Act, 1867*, would be replaced by the current notion of "unrestricted" power. Another reason based on historical text to dismiss the interpretation of section 94 as an "amending formula" is the fact that the *Constitution Act, 1867* contained elsewhere a provision expressly allowing provinces to effect "Amendment from Time to Time, notwithstanding anything in this Act, of the Constitution of the Province, except as regards the Office of the Lieutenant Governor" (section 92(1)). It begs the question why section 94 was devised as a separate provision, crafted very differently and carefully avoiding the term "amendment", if it were intended to serve as an amending formula.

[84] *Commonwealth of Australia Constitution Act* (U.K.), 63 & 64 Vict., c. 12.

Additional support for this interpretation can also be found in the new translation of the *Constitution Act, 1867*.[85] The text that was presented read:

> Nonobstant toute autre disposition de la présente loi, le Parlement du Canada peut prendre des mesures d'uniformisation totale ou partielle du droit relatif à la propriété et aux droits civils en Ontario, en Nouvelle-Écosse et au Nouveau-Brunswick, ainsi que de la procédure devant tout ou partie des tribunaux de ces trois provinces. En outre, nonobstant toute autre disposition de la présente loi, le Parlement, à compter de l'adoption d'une loi d'uniformisation, acquiert le pouvoir entier de légiférer en toute matière dont il est traité dans cette loi d'uniformisation, laquelle n'a toutefois effet dans une province que si sa législature lui donne elle-même force de loi.

Hence, this new French translation indicates very clearly that the legal authority ("force de loi") of a federal statute adopted pursuant to section 94 comes from the provincial legislature, which is, of course, an essential feature common to all delegations.

Finally, there are also compelling practical reasons to prefer this interpretation if section 94 is to play a useful role. While in 1867 Canada did not have a home-based amending formula to revisit the distribution of powers, it now has one – which even allows for asymmetry – under sections 38 to 40 of the *Constitution Act, 1982*. And we know that constitutional amendments are not easy. Unfortunately, Canada still lacks a simple mechanism to allow valid interdelegation of legislative powers, unless section 94 was partly meant to provide one.

Interestingly, the same debate over the issue of reversibility took place in Australia concerning their section 51(XXXVII). For a long time, doubts subsisted about its reversible character and it remained a dead letter. But eventually, the opinion that it is indeed reversible as well as the appeal of such a flexible cooperative came to prevail, and in recent years its use has grown considerably. For instance, it is through this mechanism that the Australians have succeeded in creating a national securities regulator. The Australian states have even developed a practice of inserting automatic revision clauses in their enabling statutes to ensure effective reversibility, the validity of which was confirmed by the Australian courts (see, e.g., Tate 2005; French forthcoming).

Compensation under Section 94

There is one last difficult legal issue that needs to be addressed: financial compensation for non-participating provinces under section 94. I believe that in

[85]Comité de rédaction constitutionnelle française, *Rapport définitif du comité de rédaction constitutionnelle française chargé d'établir, à l'intention du ministre de la Justice du Canada, un projet de version française officielle de certains textes constitutionnels: Loi de 1867 sur l'Amérique du Nord britannique — Texte no 1* (Minister of Justice), at www.justice.gc.ca/fra/pi/const/loireg-lawreg/p1t1-3.html. This translation was undertaken pursuant to s.55 of the *Constitution Act, 1982*, *supra* note 12, in order to give Canada an official French version of the *Constitution Act, 1867*.

the context of today's welfare state, to be faithful to the spirit of this provision, it must be possible for provinces to exercise a genuine choice between retaining their autonomy or opting for uniformity. And this can only be ensured if non-participating provinces are entitled to compensation. Otherwise, the same kind of coercion and tension at present associated with the unlimited spending power thesis would continue, which, in the end, would be detrimental to both autonomy and uniformity.

As section 94 was drafted in the nineteenth century with the classical liberal model in mind, it is silent on the issue of compensation, even with respect to Quebec. In those days, the provision of social services was ensured by religious and private organizations. Therefore, the substantial costs now associated with areas of provincial jurisdiction were not readily foreseeable. However, ever since the topic of interdelegation came to the fore in the twentieth century, discussions over potential reallocation of powers between the two orders of governments have included the issue of fiscal adjustments, particularly in view of potential asymmetrical outcomes. When large sums of money are involved, current instances of asymmetrical arrangements using the various techniques I described earlier nearly always involve some fiscal adjustments. These adjustments often take the form of a transfer of resources from the delegating province to the federal government as is the case, for example, when the Royal Canadian Mounted Police acts as a provincial police force.

When it comes to Canada's social union, a solid textual argument can be made that the commitment to promote equality of *opportunity* for the well-being of Canadians while respecting the division of powers constitutionalized in section 36 of the *Constitution Act, 1982* would require that non-participating provinces under a section 94 scheme be compensated. Compensation could take the form of transfers to the non-participating provincial governments or lower federal taxes for their residents, as with the existing Quebec abatement. Indeed, it would create inequality of opportunity among Canadians if Parliament were to put in place a social program in some provinces without some form of compensation for those that exercised their constitutional right to make different choices in ensuring the well-being of their residents. Similarly, given that Ottawa has, under section 36(2), a constitutional duty to equalize the fiscal capacity of provinces in order to compensate for external inequalities among them, it would be surprising if it were free to create through section 94 fiscal inequalities of its own volition.

There is uncertainty about the justiciability of section 36 stemming, notably, from the use of the term "committed" rather than the language of "rights".[86] But even if section 36 was not deemed to create enforceable rights, this would not mean that it should be devoid of any legal effects. Section 36 combines and articulates two very important contemporary Canadian values: equality of opportunity and respect for diversity. It may still serve to interpret other, older, provisions of the Constitution such as section 94. These same values may also be inferred in other provisions of the *Constitution Act, 1982*, such as sections 38

---

[86]See *Manitoba Keewatinowi Okimakanak Inc. v. Manitoba (Hydro-Electric Board)* (1992), 91 D.L.R. (4th) 554 at 557-558 (Man. C.A.). See also pages 254-257, above, for more on the distinction between Charter rights and s.36 commitments.

and 40. These provide that a constitutional amendment transferring provincial jurisdiction to Ottawa will have no effect in a province that has not consented to it, and if such power touches upon education or any other culturally sensitive matter, reasonable compensation will have to be awarded to that province.

A further argument could be made on the basis of section 15 of the *Charter*, the essence of which is also to protect the values of equality and respect for diversity, but unlike section 36, it is clearly enforceable. The fiscal prejudice incurred by the residents of a non-participating province as a result of Ottawa's refusal to compensate them or their provincial government could constitute a violation of the right to equality under section 15. The Supreme Court has established that violation of this right can result from omission[87] and has explained that victims can be individuals or groups:

> Discrimination may be described as a distinction, whether intentional or not but based on grounds relating to personal characteristics of the individual or group, which has the effect of imposing burdens, obligations, or disadvantages on such individual or group not imposed upon others, or which withholds or limits access to opportunities, benefits, and advantages available to other members of society. Distinctions based on personal characteristics attributed to an individual solely on the basis of association with a group will rarely escape the charge of discrimination, while those based on an individual's merits and capacities will rarely be so classed.[88]

The Supreme Court has suggested that the province of residence could in some instances be considered as a basis of discrimination prohibited under section 15. However, it has ruled that a federal law that applies differently from one province to the other in order to respect the various preferences expressed by these provinces could not be considered discriminatory because such differences are "a rational part of the political reality in the federal process".[89] Presumably, a federal measure that penalized the residents of a province whose legislature and government exercised their constitutional right to abstain from transferring to Ottawa power over a matter of exclusive provincial jurisdiction would be regarded differently. Far from being sensitive to provincial differences, such a policy would quite simply be a denial of the federal process.

Some Policy Concerns with Section 94

Among the responses to my proposal to revive section 94, there are two that relate more to its substance as a framework to govern Canada's social union than to its legal basis. The first one comes from a fear that the requirement for provincial consent, together with the obligation to compensate non-participating

---

[87] *Eldridge supra* note 23.

[88] *Andrews v. Law Society of British Columbia*, [1989] 1 S.C.R. 143 at 174-175.

[89] *Haig v. Canada (Chief Electoral Officer)*, [1993] 2 S.C.R. 995 at 1047. See also *R. v. S.(S.)*, [1990] 2 S.C.R. 254; *R. v. Turpin*, [1989] 1 S.C.R. 1296.

provinces, would deprive Ottawa of the necessary financial tools to induce provinces and would remove all incentive for further integration, even among the common law provinces. I think that this view is overly pessimistic.

First, an argument could be made that the current system, where the federal government claims it has a unilateral right to intervene and uses its financial leverage to pressure the provinces, is not truly conducive to provincial collaboration. Under such a paradigm, accepting Ottawa's involvement in a given area is tantamount to recognizing Ottawa has rights over the field. While a given Ottawa initiative may have some appeal, there is always the risk of creating a precedent that will be problematic when the next (not so appealing) federal initiative comes around. Accordingly, a good deal of intergovernmental energy on the part of provinces is spent curbing current initiatives to prevent future invasions of their jurisdiction. Recourse to section 94 would largely remove this concern.

Would pan-Canadian solutions be possible if provinces were free to opt in or out? I firmly believe the answer is yes. The voluntary movement towards greater integration is a deep trend being felt throughout the Western world quite independently of any fiscal inducement. There is powerful economic logic at play. Within Canada this movement is naturally strengthened by a sense of national community. In those matters where seamless solutions are desirable, provincial governments conduct themselves according to the wishes of their populations. For evidence of this we can look at the work underway at the Council of the Federation (2008) – where the federal government is not even at the table – in the area of labour mobility, for instance. There is no need for Ottawa to coerce provincial governments since they are moving in that direction by themselves. If classical universal social programs are perceived to be on the decline, it is not because of a lack of shared will to integrate; it might unfortunately simply be because of a lack of widespread popular support for the development of such programs today.

It might even be the case that less pressure to integrate and more openness to provincial differences would provide a more favourable environment for the creation of innovative social programs. In this regard, the uniformization that is associated with Ottawa's spending power may in fact hinder innovation. A good example is Quebec's $7 per day child-care program, which nearly never came into existence and continues to be threatened by Ottawa's refusal to adapt its existing uniform fiscal policies on this matter of provincial jurisdiction. Pan-Canadian solutions usually require a wide political consensus, which means that results are hard to achieve, watered down, and hard to reform once in place. The current general stasis affecting the health-care system may be a good example of that.

In the end, asymmetry rather than uniformity may be the best approach to foster innovation and the growth of new programs, be it in a single province or in partnership with other governments. Not requiring all provinces to join in, in order to move forward with a common venture, may make the difference between doing something significant and arguing but accomplishing nothing. If the member states of the European Union had not accepted the principle of asymmetry, there would still be separate currencies and border controls in all of them.

On the issue of asymmetrical federalism linked to section 94, the other policy concern that has been raised is what is sometimes called the "West Lothian question" in reference to the United Kingdom and Scotland where it has been a topic of intellectual discussions for decades. Essentially, the concern is that if given subject matters are devolved to subnational governments in some but not all regions, the legitimacy of the elected representatives in the central institutions who come from the more autonomous regions will become problematic, particularly when they are called on to vote for the remainder of the country on matters that have been devolved to their home regions. In search for a solution to this perceived problem, some interesting suggestions have occasionally been put forward in academic circles, such as reducing the total number of representatives coming from those regions with more autonomy or requesting that they abstain from voting on devolved matters, in order to avoid an unfair treatment of the other regions.

While the West Lothian question presents an interesting theoretical problem, in practice it would become a real issue only in the presence of extensive asymmetry. In the United Kingdom, where Scotland and Wales have their own parliaments with substantial autonomous legislative and fiscal powers while England has none, the issue barely has traction. In Canada, as Tom Courchene shows in his review in this volume, there have been and still are numerous instances of asymmetrical arrangements, particularly involving Quebec, and yet no one, to my knowledge, has ever requested that a Member of Parliament remain seated on a vote because of such arrangements (Courchene, this volume, 115).

Specifically in relation to section 94, additional factors can alleviate the West Lothian fear. First, if Quebec can opt into a section 94 scheme through the combined techniques of incorporation by reference and administrative interdelegation as I have suggested, using that section would not necessarily result in asymmetry, as demonstrated by the case of Australia. Second, contrary to the situation in the United Kingdom, the asymmetrical arrangements contemplated by section 94 are not available only to certain provinces. Any province can benefit from such arrangements, so that possible distortions in political representation would even out to a certain extent. Third, again contrary to the current situation in the United Kingdom, section 94 is not about a downward devolution of powers to one province, but about an upward transfer of powers to the central government on a voluntary basis. Accordingly, each province always has the option of refraining from transferring its powers, or, as we have seen, the option of reclaiming them, if it feels ill-served by the political representation in Parliament. Fourth, building on the third point, the representation issue might actually serve as a salutary check to prevent the indirect defederalization of some regions of the country resulting from an overuse of section 94. Indeed, I believe there is a point beyond which formal constitutional reform, as opposed to legislative interdelegation, would become the appropriate means to effect major changes.

Finally, it must be noted that sections 38(2) and (3) of the *Constitution Act, 1982* specifically allow for the possibility of asymmetrical constitutional transfers of powers from some provinces to Parliament without requiring any adjustment to the popular representation of the various provinces in Parliament.

Who Could Revive Section 94?

Whether governments would by themselves revive section 94 is difficult to predict at this juncture. Such a move into new territory would have to be driven by a sense of necessity. This might happen in areas such as securities regulation, as in Australia. After all, this is an instance of state activity traditionally associated with property and civil rights, and section 94 would appear to apply quite naturally in this context. In the social domain, much of the fortunes of section 94 would depend on what happens with the unlimited spending power thesis.

Much of what will happen with this thesis, and federalism more generally, will depend on the Supreme Court. Some argue that courts are no longer apt to police federalism due to the growing complexity of governance. If this were the case, we should start worrying about the future prospects of federalism. However, I find this argument unconvincing, particularly when we consider how much courts throughout the Western world have become involved in the policy process through the adjudication of individual rights under such instruments as the Charter. If anything, policing federalism as opposed to the Charter should be easier because, in doing so, courts are not asked to decide what should or should not be done; they are simply asked to decide who can do it.

CONCLUSION

In this chapter I have tried to demonstrate, as others have done before me, that the unlimited spending power thesis does not work. It has no basis in the Constitution and is at odds with many of our constitutional rules and principles. Nor has it been endorsed by the Privy Council or the Supreme Court of Canada. The unlimited spending power thesis is best described as an *ex post* construct designed to provide a legal explanation for Ottawa's involvement in areas of provincial jurisdiction, particularly in the social field in the aftermath of the Great Depression. As it is currently articulated, it is incompatible with constitutional federalism, a crucially important concept in Canada, if only from Quebec's perspective, because constitutional federalism protects minority rights. This may well explain why the unlimited spending power thesis has never been formally accepted by the Supreme Court. Furthermore, despite what is often assumed, acceptance of this radical thesis would not simply confirm the status quo; it would completely upset the workings of the Canadian federal system because it would promote unilateralism rather than cooperative federalism. The unlimited spending power thesis does not reflect the dynamics at play on the ground where intergovernmental negotiations and flexible arrangements, often involving Quebec, have always been prominent.

Even if the shortcomings of the unlimited spending power thesis are acknowledged by many, agreeing on what to do next is tricky. Although some would advocate a complete disentanglement between Ottawa and the provinces, going back to the original division of powers and strictly abiding by its terms is not a realistic solution. Others would advocate constitutional reform, but this too is hardly realistic in the current context. Then there are those who, in the name of realism, suggest that governments should simply ignore the Constitution and try to cut "administrative" (or "para-constitutional" or "non-legal") deals to regulate their actions. In my view, the problem with this approach is twofold. First, it does not work well: it tends to generate a lack of transparency and accountability and a great deal of political tension, and all attempts to agree on and abide by permanent voluntary rules have failed. Second, it boils down to relinquishing the principles of constitutionalism and the rule of law, and this is a slippery slope. Constitutional constraints are there for a reason.

Accordingly, before setting aside the Constitution, it is important to explore all of the possibilities it affords. After all, the dynamics at play, particularly in the relationship between Quebec and the rest of Canada, but also between central Canada and the other regions of the country, are not new; we could say they are as old as Canada itself. For this reason, I have tried to shed light on what is probably the least known of all the division of powers provisions in the *Constitution Act, 1867*: section 94. I think this section captures many of the subtleties of Canadian federalism.

Of course, section 94 also raises a number of legal issues, particularly if it were to be considered as the legal foundation for Canada's social union. Its wording dates back to another period and can be confusing to a modern reader. Unlike other provisions of the Constitution, it has not benefited from successive judicial restatements carrying its meaning through to the twenty-first century. As I have tried to show, however, these issues can be resolved in a way that would allow section 94 to play a meaningful role in addressing Canada's present needs. This exercise, which would take a living tree approach, might sometimes require us to move beyond the precise wording of that provision. Nevertheless, I contend that it would represent a much more straightforward reading of Canada's Constitution than the unlimited spending power thesis, and one that is much closer to the spirit of federalism.

REFERENCES

Abel, A.S. and J.I. Laskin. 1975. *Laskin's Canadian Constitutional Law: Cases, Text and Notes on Distribution of Legislative Power*, 4th ed. Toronto: Carswell.

Adam, M.-A. 2007. "Federalism and the Spending Power: Section 94 to the Rescue", (March) *Policy Options* 30. Online: Institute for Research on Public Policy at www.irpp.org/po/archive/mar07/adam.pdf.

— 2009. "Fiscal Federalism and the Future of Canada: Can Section 94 of the *Constitution Act, 1867* Be an Alternate to the Spending Power?" in J.R. Allan, T.J. Courchene, and C. Leuprecht (eds.), *Transitions: Fiscal and Political Federalism in an Era of Change.* Kingston: Institute of Intergovernmental Relations, Queen's University.

Beaudoin, G.-A. 2000. *Le fédéralisme au Canada.* Montreal: Wilson & Lafleur.

— 2004. "Un pouvoir limité", *La Presse* (September).

Beetz, J. 1965. "Les attitudes changeantes du Québec à l'endroit de la Constitution de 1867", in P.-A. Crépeau and C.B. Macpherson (eds.), *L'avenir du fédéralisme canadien.* Montreal: Presses de l'Université de Montréal.

Birch, A.H. 1955. *Federalism, Finance and Social Legislation in Canada, Australia and the United States.* Oxford: Clarendon Press.

Brown, D. 2005. "Who's Afraid of Asymmetric Federalism? – A Summary Discussion", *2005 Special Series on Asymmetric Federalism.* Online: Institute of Intergovernmental Relations at www.queensu.ca/iigr/working/archive/Asymmetric/papers/16.pdf.

Brun, H., G. Tremblay, and E. Brouillet. 2007. *Droit constitutionnel*, 5th ed. Cowansville: Yvon-Blais.

Cameron, D.M. and J.S. Dupré. 1983. "The Financial Framework of Income Distribution and Social Services", in S.M. Beck and I. Bernier (eds.), *Canada and the New Constitution: The Unfinished Agenda,* vol. 1. Montreal: Institute for Research on Public Policy.

Cameron, D. and R. Simeon. 2002. "Intergovernmental Relations in Canada: The Emergence of Collaborative Federalism", 32:2 *Publius: The Journal of Federalism* 49.

Chevrette, F. and H. Marx. 1982. *Droit constitutionnel: Notes et jurisprudence.* Montreal: Presses de l'Université de Montréal.

Choudhry, S. 2002. "Recasting Social Canada: A Reconsideration of Federal Jurisdiction over Social Policy", 52 *University of Toronto Law Journal* 163.

Commission royale des relations entre le Dominion et les provinces. 1939. *Expédients constitutionnels adoptés par le Dominion et les provinces,* by L.M. Gouin and B. Claxton. Ottawa: J.-O. Patenaude, O.S.I.

Council of the Federation. Communiqué. 2008. "Labour Market: Meeting the Requirements of the 21st Century" (18 July). Online: The Council of the Federation at www.councilofthefederation.ca/pdfs/COMMUNIQUE_EN_Labour_marketJuly 13clean.pdf.

Courchene, T.J. 2006. "Variations on the Federalism Theme", *Policy Options* (July).

Dupont, J. 1967. "Le pouvoir de dépenser du gouvernement fédéral: 'A Dead Issue?'" *University of British Columbia Law Review* 69.

French, R.S. forthcoming. "The Referral of State Powers – Cooperative Federalism Lives", *University of Western Australia Law Review.* Online: Federal Court of Australia at www.fedcourt.gov.au/ aboutct/judges_papers/speeches_frenchj6.rtf.

Gagnon, A.-G. and H. Segal, eds. 2000. *The Canadian Social Union without Quebec: 8 Critical Analyses.* Montreal: Institute for Research on Public Policy.

Gaudreault-DesBiens, J.-F. 2006. "The Irreducible Federal Necessity of Jurisdictional Autonomy, and the Irreducibility of Federalism to Jurisdictional Autonomy", in S. Choudhury, J.-F. Gaudreault-DesBiens, and L. Sossin (eds.), *Dilemmas of Solidarity: Rethinking Redistribution in the Canadian Federation.* Toronto: University of Toronto Press.

Hanssen, K. 1966-67. "The Constitutionality of Conditional Grant Legislation", 2 *Manitoba Law Journal* 191.

Hogg, P.W. 2007. *Constitutional Law of Canada*, looseleaf. Toronto: Thomson Carswell.

Hurley, J.R. 1996. *Amending Canada's Constitution: History, Processes, Problems and Prospects.* Ottawa: Canada Communication Group.

Keith, A.B. 1937. "The Privy Council Decisions: A Comment from Great Britain", 15 *Canadian Bar Review* 428.

Kellock, B.H. and S. LeRoy. 2007. "Questioning the Legality of the Federal 'Spending Power'", 89 Public Policy Sources. Online: The Fraser Institute at www.fraserinstitute. org/commerce.web/publication_details.aspx?pubID=4943.

Kennedy, W.P.M. 1944. "The Interpretation of the *British North America Act*", 8 *Cambridge Law Journal* 146.

La Forest, G.V. 1975. "Delegation of Legislative Power in Canada", 21 *McGill Law Journal* 131.

— 1981. *The Allocation of Taxing Power Under the Canadian Constitution*, 2d ed. Toronto: Canadian Tax Foundation.

— 2005. "The Historical and Legal Origins of Asymmetrical Federalism in Canada's Founding Debates: A Brief Interpretive Note", *2005 Special Series on Asymmetric Federalism.* Online: Institute of Intergovernmental Relations at www.queensu.ca/iigr/working/archive/Asymmetric/papers/8.pdf.

Lazar, H. 2000. "In Search of a New Mission Statement for Canadian Fiscal Federalism", in H. Lazar (ed.), *Canada: The State of the Federation 1999-2000: Toward a New Mission Statement for Canadian Federalism.* Montreal: McGill-Queen's University Press.

Lederman, W.R. 1967. "Some Forms and Limitations of Co-operative Federalism", 45 *Canadian Bar Review* 409.

Leslie, P., R.H. Neumann, and R. Robinson. 2004. "Managing Canadian Fiscal Federalism", in J.P. Meekison, H. Telford, and H. Lazar (eds.), *Canada: The State of the Federation 2002: Reconsidering the Institutions of Canadian Federalism.* Montreal: McGill-Queen's University Press.

MacDonald, V.C. 1941. "Taxation Powers in Canada", 19 *Canadian Bar Review* 75.

Meekison, J.P., H. Telford, and H. Lazar. 2004. "The Institutions of Executive Federalism: Myths and Realities" in J.P. Meekison, H. Telford, and H. Lazar (eds.), *Canada: The State of the Federation 2002: Reconsidering the Institutions of Canadian Federalism.* Montreal: McGill-Queen's University Press.

Milne, D. 2005. "Asymmetry in Canada, Past and Present", *2005 Special Series on Asymmetric Federalism.* Online: Institute of Intergovernmental Relations at www.queensu.ca/iigr/working/archive/Asymmetric/papers/1.pdf.

Mockle, D. 2002. "Gouverner sans le droit? Mutation des normes et nouveaux modes de régulation" 43 *Collège de Droit* 143.

Morin, C. 1972. *Le pouvoir québécois ... en négociation.* Quebec: Editions du Boréal Express.

Noël, A. 2005. "'A Report No One Has Discussed': Early Responses to Quebec's Commission on Fiscal Imbalance", in H. Lazar (ed.), *Canadian Fiscal Arrangements: What Works, What Might Work Better.* Montreal: McGill-Queen's University Press.

O'Connor, W.F. 1939. *Report Pursuant to Resolution of the Senate to the Honorable the Speaker by the Parliamentary Counsel relating the Enactment of the British North America Act, 1867, any lack of consonance between its terms and judicial construction of them and cognate matters.* Ottawa: Canada.

Papillon, M. and R. Simeon 2004. "The Weakest Link? First Ministers' Conferences in Canadian Intergovernmental Relations", in J.P. Meekison, H. Telford, and H. Lazar (eds.), *Canada: The State of the Federation 2002: Reconsidering the Institutions of Canadian Federalism.* Montreal: McGill-Queen's University Press.

Pelletier, B. 1996. *La modification constitutionnelle au Canada.* Scarborough: Carswell.

— 2005. "Asymmetrical Federalism: A Win-Win Formula!", *2005 Special Series on Asymmetric Federalism.* Online: Institute of Intergovernmental Relations at www.queensu.ca/iigr/working/archive/Asymmetric/papers/15a.pdf.

Perry, D.B. 1997. *Financing the Canadian Federation, 1867 to 1995: Setting the Stage for Change.* Toronto: Canadian Tax Foundation.

Petter, A. 1989. "Federalism and the Myth of the Federal Spending Power", 68 *Canadian Bar Review* 448.

Pigeon, L.-P. 1943. "Le problème des amendements à la Constitution", 3 *Revue de la Banque du Canada* 437.

Quebec, Commission on Fiscal Imbalance. 2002. *The "Federal Spending Power" – Supporting Document 2.* Quebec: Commission on Fiscal Imbalance.

Quebec, Commission royale d'enquête sur les problèmes constitutionnels. 1956. *Rapport de la Commission royale d'enquête sur les problèmes constitutionnels*, vol. 2. Quebec: Province of Quebec.

Rémillard, G. 1983. *Le fédéralisme canadien*, vol. 1. Montreal: Québec/Amérique.

Royal Commission on Dominion-Provincial Relations. 1940. *Report of the Royal Commission on Dominion-Provincial Relations*, vol. 2. Ottawa: J.-O. Patenaude, I.S.O. [Rowell-Sirois Commission].

Ryan, E.F. and B.V. Slutsky. 1964-66. "Canada Student Loans Act – Ultra Vires?" 2 *University of British Columbia Law Review* 299.

Schneiderman, D. 1992. "The Delegation Power Past and Present", 3 *Constitutional Forum constitutionnel* 82.

Schwartz, B. 1987-88. "Fathoming Meech Lake", 17 *Manitoba Law Journal* 1.

Scott, F.R. 1942. "Section 94 of the British North America Act", 20 *Canadian Bar Review* 525.

— 1955. "The Constitutional Background of Taxation Agreements", 2 *McGill Law Journal* 1.

Smiley, D.V. 1962. "The Rowell-Sirois Report, Provincial Autonomy, and Post-War Canadian Federalism", 28 *Canadian Journal of Economics and Political Science* 54.

Smith, J. 2005. "The Case for Asymmetry in Canadian Federalism", *2005 Special Series on Asymmetric Federalism.* Online: Institute of Intergovernmental Relations at www.queensu.ca/iigr/working/archive/Asymmetric/papers/6.pdf.

Tate, P. 2005. "New Directions in Co-operative Federalism: Referrals of Legislative Power and Their Consequences". Paper presented at the Constitutional Law Conference, Sydney, 18 February 2005. Online: Gilbert + Tobin Centre of Public Law at www.gtcentre.unsw.edu.au/publications/papers/docs/2005/5_PamelaTate.pdf.

Telford, H. 2003. "The Federal Spending Power in Canada: Nation-Building or Nation-Destroying?" 33:1 *Publius: The Journal of Federalism* 23.

— 2005. "Survivance Versus Ambivalence: The Federal Dilemma in Canada", *2005 Special Series on Asymmetric Federalism.* Online: Institute of Intergovernmental Relations at www.queensu.ca/iigr/working/archive/Asymmetric/papers/13.pdf.

Tremblay, A. 2000a. "Federal Spending Power", in A.-G. Gagnon and H. Segal (eds.), *The Canadian Social Union without Quebec: 8 Critical Analyses.* Montreal: Institute for Research on Public Policy.

— 2000b. *Droit constitutionnel: principes*, 2d ed. Montreal: Thémis.

Trudeau, P.E. 1967. *Le fédéralisme et la société canadienne française.* Montreal: HMH.

Tuck, R. 1945. "Delegation – A Way Over the Constitutional Hurdle", 23 *Canadian Bar Review* 79.

Yudin, D.W.S. 2002. "The Federal Spending Power in Canada, Australia and the United States", 13 *National Journal of Constitutional Law* 437.

12

Building Firewalls and Deconstructing Canada by Hobbling the Federal Spending Power: The Rise of the Harper Doctrine

Errol P. Mendes

C'est en toute connaissance de cause que l'actuel gouvernement conservateur du premier ministre Stephen Harper cherche à miner l'application du pouvoir fédéral de dépenser, observe l'auteur, qui qualifie de « doctrine Harper » cette démarche visant à favoriser une politique traditionnellement préconisée par les dirigeants du Québec, à savoir la restriction maximale sinon la suppression totale de la capacité d'Ottawa de dépenser dans les domaines de compétence provinciale.

Retraçant l'historique du pouvoir de dépenser tel qu'il est établi dans l'Entente-cadre sur l'union sociale (ECUS) de 1999, l'auteur ne met pas en cause sa légitimité constitutionnelle et rejette la possibilité de l'inscrire dans la Constitution en étendant la portée de la section 94 de la Loi constitutionnelle de 1867. *Il estime en effet que la section 36 de celle-ci, jumelée à l'ECUS, suffit à légitimer l'exercice responsable de ce pouvoir dans l'intérêt des Canadiens et le respect de l'autonomie provinciale. Il conclut par une mise en garde contre l'éventuel héritage du premier ministre Harper, qui pourrait gravement paralyser la capacité politique des prochains gouvernements d'utiliser leur pouvoir de dépenser pour renforcer le tissu social du pays.*

INTRODUCTION

During the 2006 federal election, in an effort to gain more seats in the province of Quebec, Conservative Party leader Stephen Harper campaigned on the promise to "limit the federal spending powers that the Liberals have so badly abused" (Harper 2007a). Once elected prime minister, he did not immediately follow up on this promise, and this opened the door for Quebec Premier Jean Charest to call for the creation of a Charter to strictly limit the federal spending power (Charest 2007). After the February 2007 federal budget and the subsequent provincial election in Quebec, the new Conservative government in

Ottawa seemed unconcerned about whether federal equalization payments made to Quebec were being properly used. In spite of this, federal Finance Minister Jim Flaherty gave Quebec an additional $2.3 billion in equalization funds for the 2007-08 fiscal year, including $700 million in an equalization adjustment.

In contrast to previous governments, the Harper government did not attach any conditions to these transfers. To the astonishment of many, including large parts of the electorate in Quebec, Premier Charest committed this amount to tax cuts. Such federal acquiescence in the abuse of equalization payments has the potential to turn the federal government into a postal service for the transfer of federal funds. One Quebec commentator suggested that this seemed to be a variation on bribing voters with their own money (see MacDonald 2008) – or, more accurately, an attempt to bribe them with other people's (in this case, other provinces') money.

BACKGROUND INFORMATION

Equalization Payments

Equalization payments are provided by the federal government to provincial governments without attached conditions; provinces are free to spend the money as they wish. In the words of section 36(2) of the *Constitution Act, 1982*, equalization payments are primarily intended to "ensure that provincial governments have sufficient revenues to provide reasonably comparable levels of public services at reasonably comparable levels of taxation".[1] The actual amount of such equalization payments is determined by complex formulas that measure the ability of every province to raise revenues – commonly known as the fiscal capacity of each province.[2]

As can be seen in the wording of section 36(2) above, there is a social-justice purpose behind equalization payments. These monetary transfers were established to counter fiscal disparities among the provinces that would otherwise create unacceptable levels of inequality across the Canadian federation. In theory, such payments give the less prosperous provinces the ability to provide their residents with public services that are reasonably comparable to those in the more prosperous provinces, while allowing for a reasonably comparable level of taxation to exist across the country. There is considerable doubt that equalization payments were ever intended to be used to justify tax cuts.

---

[1] *Constitution Act, 1982*, being Schedule B to the *Canada Act 1982*, (U.K.), 1982, c. 11 [*Constitution*].

[2] For further analysis of how equalization payments are calculated under the present Conservative government see references Department of Finance Canada.

Watertight Compartments and Firewalls

In his famous decision in *Labour Conventions* – a judgment handed down before the rise of the modern welfare state – Lord Atkin put forth the "watertight compartments" theory of Canadian federalism: "While the ship of state now sails on larger ventures ... she still retains the watertight compartments which are essential to her original structure."[3] The watertight compartments of Lord Atkin's extended metaphor refer to a restrictive interpretation of the federal/provincial division of powers found in the Canadian Constitution that militates against any form of intrusion by one level of government into the jurisdiction of another. Favoured not just by Lord Atkin but by the majority of British Lords in the Privy Council, this early interpretation of the Canadian Constitution did not anticipate the vast increase in both provincial and federal responsibilities that have arisen with the modern welfare state.

At the core of the Canadian welfare state is a fundamental commitment made by citizens and governments alike to reject the policies of economic and social Darwinism that would prevent revenues from the wealthy regions of Canada from being used to assist the less fortunate regions of our country. The modern welfare state requires that social inequalities do not reach a level where social stability is at risk. This is central to the rationales both for establishing the system of equalization payments and for the rise of the federal spending power. Indeed, as Hogg has stated, to stick to the watertight compartments interpretation is "to attribute a narrowness of vision to the framers which is thoroughly at odds with what we know of them. This is indeed the 'watertight compartments' view of federalism carried to an extreme" (Hogg 2007, 174).

Prime Minister Harper seems to be returning to just such an extreme interpretation of federalism when attacking the federal spending power. In a 2001 open letter to Ralph Klein, then premier of Alberta, Harper and five other Albertan "political and academic right-wingers" advocated the erection of a jurisdictional "firewall" around the province (Harper 2005). They urged Klein to "build firewalls around Alberta, to limit the extent to which an aggressive and hostile federal government can encroach upon legitimate jurisdiction" (ibid.). Harper's rhetoric is the modern day equivalent of Lord Atkin's naval metaphor; the Prime Minister uses "firewalls" to describe the watertight compartments he wishes to create. Unfortunately, regardless of which term is used, a restrictive interpretation of the division of powers effects the equalization payments by impliedly forbidding the richer regions of Canada from helping the poorer ones.

THE HARPER DOCTRINE

In this chapter, I will refer to the current Conservative government's largely unspoken policy on the federal spending power as the Harper Doctrine. Prime

---

[3]*Reference Re Weekly Rest in Industrial Undertakings Act, Minimum Wages Act and Limitation of Hours of Work Act*, [1937] 1 D.L.R. 673 at 684 (P.C.) (*sub nom. Canada (A.G.) v. Ontario (A.G.)*), [1937] A.C. 326 [*Labour Conventions*].

Minister Harper claims that he is determined to end what he terms the "domineering and paternalistic federalism" (Harper 2007b) of the previous government and promote what Quebec leaders have traditionally demanded: severe restrictions on federal spending in areas of provincial jurisdiction. While the Harper government has not publicly articulated how it intends to proceed with this agenda, it may be by slowly suffocating the spending power by making sure that there is very little money to spend.

Evidence of this agenda comes from one of Harper's ideological mentors: Tom Flanagan.[4] Flanagan has been quoted as saying that tightening the screws on the federal government would leave more money in the taxpayer's pocket and make it harder for the government to spend (Panetta 2008). While left unspoken by Harper himself, this agenda has been furthered by three Conservative budgets that have increased spending within express federal jurisdiction, such as defence, while slashing the federal capacity to raise revenue. The two percentage-point cut in the Goods and Services Tax (GST) between 2006 and 2007 reduced the federal purse by over $11 billion annually – close to $60 billion over five years. This is an amount that could have been used to establish many shared-cost programs. Income and corporate tax cuts, tax credits aimed at particular groups of voters (such as the kids' sports tax credit in the 2008 budget), and the tax-sheltered savings account have further emptied the federal coffers. Finally, adding to all these cuts, the use of any budget surplus for massive national debt reductions spells the death knell of any major federal spending in provincial jurisdiction. Even before the full impact of the recent financial credit and housing crisis in the United States was felt, both Flaherty and independent financial experts were predicting that the budget surplus would shrink from $13 billion in 2007 to $2.3 billion for the fiscal year that started 1 April 2008 – a drop of 77 percent from the previous year. While both Minister Flaherty and Bloomberg estimated that the surplus would drop further to $1.3 billion in 2009-10, the smallest since 1998; other analysts, however, predicted that surpluses might be higher.[5]

The economic downturn in the wake of the worldwide credit crisis means that the only feasible method of funding new federal spending in areas of provincial jurisdiction would be to raise taxes so significantly that it would result in huge political costs to any governing party. Flanagan is quoted as saying that through this dismantling of federal revenue capacity, the Harper government has "gradually re-engineered the system" (Panetta 2008). He continues:

> I'm quite impressed with it ... They're boxing in the ability of the federal government to come up with new program ideas ... The federal government is

---

[4]Flanagan was Harper's campaign chair for the 2004 federal election and also was his former chief of staff.

[5]Bloomberg is a U.S. financial analysis company. See www.bloomberg.com/apps/news?pid=20601082&sid=aBK2SuxOt.lA&refer=canada. However, the Conference Board of Canada is of the view that these figures may be too low. See Beltrame (2008).

now more constrained, the provinces have more revenue, and conservatives should be happy. (ibid.)

Flanagan seems particularly proud that the Harper government has been able to undermine the federal spending power quietly and without causing an outcry (ibid.). This has also put opposition parties in a straitjacket regarding any promises to resurrect federal spending in areas of joint or provincial jurisdiction, such as pharmacare and child care, or to improve conditions in First Nations communities, as envisioned in the Kelowna Accord.

The government's hostile rhetoric on the spending power has led many to fear that there might be a formal surrender of the federal government's ability to initiate new nationwide shared-cost programs, and that existing programs, such as universally administered and accessible health care, might be undermined. However, the worst fears to this effect were not borne out in the Throne Speech of October 2007. Instead, on the surface, the government promised to do no more than seek to legislate the Social Union Framework Agreement (SUFA) (Canada 1999) established by the Liberal government of Jean Chrétien eight years earlier. In the words of the Throne Speech, the Conservative government promised it would "place formal limits on the use of the federal spending power for new shared-cost programs in areas of exclusive provincial jurisdiction"[6] and "allow provinces and territories to opt out with reasonable compensation if they offer compatible programs" (ibid.). Apparently ignoring what had actually transpired with SUFA, the Harper government asserted in the Throne Speech that this intended legislation would be proof of its "federalism of openness" (ibid.).

As reported by the *Canadian Press*, reactions were mixed. The senior Quebec minister, Lawrence Cannon, argued that the intended legislative limits on the spending power would contrast sharply with the Liberals' "centralizing federalism" (Bryden 2007) aimed at keeping "Quebec in its place" (Cannon 2007). However, Gilles Duceppe, the leader of the federal separatist party, the Bloc Québécois, condemned the intended legislation as amounting to nothing other than SUFA, which had been "unanimously rejected in Quebec" (Duceppe 2007) although the other provinces had endorsed it. Cannon responded that the separatists should wait until they see the legislation curtailing the federal spending power, which he promised would "stop the isolation of Quebec" (Cannon 2007). To understand what the promised legislation could encompass and what could follow it, a brief digression into the details of SUFA is warranted.

THE SOCIAL UNION FRAMEWORK AGREEMENT

Since its inception, a distinguishing feature of Canada as a federal state has been the relationship between the autonomy of different levels of government and the

[6] *Debates of the Senate*, Vol. 144, No. 1 (16 October 2007) at 4 (Rt. Hon. Michaëlle Jean).

unifying role of the federal government in promoting a common citizenship. The federal government and Parliament have a role to play in protecting the quality of life and social opportunities of Canadians, wherever they reside in this vast country. This unifying role became critical in the aftermath of the Great Depression and the reconstruction period during and after the Second World War. Few would have contested in the "dirty thirties" that the federal government had to assist in alleviating the severe social and economic hardships experienced by so many Canadians, even if that meant spending federal funds in areas of provincial jurisdiction. Given that during these challenging times the revenues of the federal government greatly surpassed those of the provinces, it would have been inconsistent with any idea of federalism not to expend some of those federal revenues in areas of great need in the provinces. Indeed, this universally accepted need for a fair sharing of revenues across Canadian society led the Royal Commission on Dominion-Provincial Relations in 1940 (the Rowell-Sirois Commission) to recommend the establishment of a system of equalization payments by the federal government (Canada 1940).

The continued expansion of the Canadian welfare state in the post-war years and the introduction of a constitutional amendment saw the emergence of shared-cost programs, such as the family allowance program in 1944, the unemployment insurance program in 1956, and the hospital insurance program in 1957. Another constitutional amendment gave rise to the old age pension program in 1951 through section 94A of the *Constitution Act, 1867.*[7]

The favoured mechanism for realizing this vision of nation-building has been that of federal fiscal transfers, whether through equalization payments, direct grants, or the use of the federal spending power. However, concerns about intrusions into key areas of provincial jurisdiction led to interminable meetings between provincial and territorial leaders and between them and the federal government, especially in the late 1990s. The desire for a reconciliation of provincial and federal interests as regards the federal spending power was spurred by the failure of the Meech Lake Accord (Library of Parliament 1987) of 1987 and the Charlottetown Accord (Special Joint Committee on a Renewed Canada 1992) of 1992, which were aimed, in part, at accommodating the traditional demands of Quebec, including restraining the federal spending power. The Charlottetown Accord would have added a new section, 106A, to the Constitution to entrench the opting-out mechanism for any new shared-cost programs in areas of exclusive provincial jurisdiction. Reasonable compensation would have been provided under the amendment if the opting-out province had an equivalent program consistent with national objectives.[8]

The desire to reconcile the federal interest in promoting national standards of social development with respect for provincial spending priorities reached a high point in 1997-98, when the provinces and territories met several times to

---

[7]*Constitution Act, 1867*, (U.K.) 30 & 31 Vict., c. 3, reprinted in R.S.C. 1985, App. II No. 5.

[8]For multiple critiques of the Charlottetown Accord, see McRoberts and Monahan (1993).

discuss among themselves a social union with the federal government. The federal government then joined the negotiations, and on 4 February 1999, the Social Union Framework Agreement was signed. It represented a non-constitutional, non-legislated consensus between the federal government and the provinces – with the exception of Quebec. SUFA was a result of the federal government's increasing sensitivity to the resentment of provincial governments toward federal intrusion into the provinces' budgetary priorities. Even the allegedly centralizing government of Prime Minster Trudeau, in a 1969 Working Paper on the Constitution, admitted that new shared-cost programs should be based on a broad national consensus and that there should be a mechanism for opting out without any fiscal penalty (Canada 1969, 36).

The fundamental preconditions and principles set down by the federal government for SUFA are hard to characterize as demands of a domineering central authority. Essentially, they were intended to:

- promote equal opportunities for Canadians, regardless of their place of residence;
- improve cooperation between the two levels of government, to better serve Canadians; and
- enhance accountability to Canadians in terms of the results obtained (Asselin 2001, 2).

For their part, the provincial and territorial governments had agreed on a set of preconditions and principles that, according to the federal government, were seemingly compatible with those of Parliament:

- to establish, within a non-constitutional framework, rules governing the role of the federal government in relation to social programs;
- to avoid duplication and promote harmonization in social policy; and
- to promote greater intergovernmental cooperation in relation to social policy (ibid. [footnotes omitted]).

Under SUFA, the signatory governments agreed to work cooperatively to embody the above principles in any new national initiatives on health, education, or welfare, and to identify and collaborate on national social priorities and objectives. The federal government agreed not to introduce any new shared-cost social initiatives without the consent of a majority of provincial governments. Finally, the provinces and territories obtained the implied right to opt out of new, national shared-cost programs. However, it was made clear that a "provincial/territorial government which, because of its existing programming, does not require the total transfer to fulfill the agreed objectives would be able to reinvest any funds not required for those objectives in the same or a related priority area" (ibid., 11 [footnotes omitted]).

These critical provisions of SUFA represented the de facto entrenchment of the principle of asymmetrical federalism within the most important social programs, where the federal spending power has been used since the Second World War. Asymmetrical federalism has found favour with federalist Quebec governments, but it was perhaps inevitable that the province would not sign on to that agreement given its traditional antipathy to the federal spending power. This antipathy – which can be traced to the early years of the Duplessis provincial government in the 1940s, was reflected in the findings of the 1953 Tremblay Commission (ibid., 4), and crested during the Quiet Revolution of the 1960s – arose out of a desire to safeguard Quebec's distinctive social developments through strengthened fiscal autonomy (Ministère du Conseil exécutif du Québec 1998).

The Quebec government may also have found objectionable that SUFA excluded from the opting-out provision certain new initiatives in social programs outside the areas of health, education, and welfare. Additionally, its refusal to sign on could have been a form of protest against the federal government's use of direct transfers to individuals or agencies to create new national programs such as the Millennium Scholarships.[9] Whatever the government's reasons, antagonism toward SUFA persists among the Quebec intellectual and political elite, who continue to imagine the existence of an "unlimited spending power" of the federal government with all sorts of dire consequences for provincial autonomy and especially for the Francophone majority in Quebec (Adam 2007, 31). This antagonism is not lessened by the fact that politically and administratively the "unlimited spending power" does not exist.

The post-SUFA argument against the spending power also maintains that because the agreement is not entrenched within a constitutional framework, it somehow violates constitutionalism and the rule of law (ibid.). This is, of course, easily refutable when one considers that federal-provincial agreements such as SUFA are a fundamental part of Canadian constitutionalism and the rule of law and that they have not been the product of "arbitrariness of the power holders of the day" (ibid.). In short, the core principles of SUFA hardly qualify as examples of a domineering federalism or an "outrageous spending power". Opponents of the Harper Doctrine would contest such characterizations of the federal spending power, claiming instead that it has been a vital instrument in creating a unique society in North America – one that emphasizes community, caring, and sharing before survival of the fittest or, at least, survival of the fittest province (see Lazar 2000, 22). Moreover, supporters of the spending power have also noted that decentralization may reduce both efficiency and equity (see Boadway 2000, 53). We would conclude, therefore, that, rather than being "outrageous", the core principles of SUFA are quite compatible with the amorphous concept of "Open Federalism" promoted by the Conservative government.[10]

---

[9]This hypothesis is based on my conversation with a senior Quebec government official on 8 January 2008 at the Faculty of Law, University of Ottawa. While my conversation may have been confidential, the accuracy of my hypothesis should become public knowledge in the future.

[10]Prime Minister Harper gives the following definition of his concept of "Open Federalism":

- taking advantage of the experience and expertise that the provinces and territories can contribute to the national dialogue

THE CONSTITUTIONALITY OF THE FEDERAL SPENDING POWER

While the hostility toward the "unlimited spending power" has led to debate regarding its constitutionality,[11] Professor Peter Hogg is strongly of the view that "the federal Parliament may spend or lend its funds to any government or institution or individual it chooses, for any purpose it chooses; and that it may attach to any grant or loan any conditions it chooses, including conditions it could not directly legislate" (Hogg 2007, 174). According to Hogg, the spending power must therefore be inferred from the constitutional power to levy taxes (section 91(3)), the power to legislate in relation to public property (section 91 (1A)), and the power to appropriate federal funds (section 106) (ibid., 173). If Parliament has these revenue-raising powers, it must also have the power to dispose of its own property. Hogg makes a distinction between compulsory regulation, which can be enacted only within jurisdictions permitted by sections 91 and 92, and the spending, lending, and contracting abilities, which impose neither binding nor voluntary obligations on the recipient.[12] In support of this view, Hogg refers to the Supreme Court of Canada's decision in *Reference Re Canada Assistance Plan (B.C.)*,[13] which he considers to be a

> clear affirmation of both of the Parliament's power to authorize grants to the provinces for use in fields of provincial jurisdiction and the power to impose conditions on the recipient provinces. Provided Parliament's intervention does not go beyond the granting or withholding of money, there is no unconstitutional trespass on provincial jurisdiction. (Hogg 2007, 175-176)

The arguments in favour of the constitutionality of the federal spending power made by Hogg and other leading jurists have been vigorously critiqued by Quebec academics and Quebec provincial bodies as equating public monies and property with private property and private contracting (Commission on the Fiscal Imbalance 2002). A leading critic, Professor Andrée Lajoie, canvasses the arguments of the major writers supporting the constitutionality of the spending

---

- respecting areas of provincial jurisdiction
- keeping the federal government's spending power within bounds
- full cooperation by the Government of Canada with all other levels of government, while clarifying the roles and responsibilities of each.

Stephen Harper, quoted in Office of the Prime Minister (2006).

[11]For scholars who contest the constitutionality of the spending power see Quebec (1956, 217-233). See also Beetz (1965); Dupont (1967); Trudeau (1968); Petter (1989).

[12]Ibid. at 170-171. It is assumed that Hogg is referring to any method of federal expenditure of financial resources through shared-cost programs (spending), giving loans or guarantees (lending), or entering into contracts to provide services without requiring financial compensation (contracting).

[13][1991] 2 S.C.R. 525 [*Canada Assistance Plan (B.C.)*].

power and attempts to demolish them by claiming that nothing in the text of the Constitution justifies the exercise of the spending power in fields of provincial jurisdiction (see Chapter 6, pp. 11-12).

Lajoie further argues that decisions such as *Canada Assistance Plan (B.C.)* deal only with situations where provinces are seeking to obtain funds from the federal authorities and are therefore trying to secure performance of the federal-provincial agreement. Lajoie concludes that the Supreme Court's decision merely amounted to a statement that to stop doing something unconstitutional is not in itself unconstitutional (Hogg 2007, 175). In other words, Lajoie is arguing that a Supreme Court decision that the federal government is perfectly entitled to cease its unconstitutional actions does not suddenly retroactively make those actions constitutional – an interesting constitutional twist on the old common-law rule *ex injuria non oritur ius* (a right cannot arise from a wrong).

The real thrust of critiques of the spending power is revealed by references to Privy Council decisions, such as the 1937 *Labour Conventions* case.[14] As discussed earlier, the *Labour Conventions* decision, based on the prevailing "watertight compartments" jurisprudence of the Privy Council, denied the federal government a treaty-implementing power. After appeals to the Privy Council were abolished, the Supreme Court of Canada rejected the "watertight compartments" interpretation, and did so in cases dealing with (among other things) the incorporation of international treaty obligations into domestic Canadian law.[15]

It is puzzling why Quebec writers such as Lajoie do not also object that the spending power of the Quebec government is unconstitutional when exercised outside the legislative jurisdiction of the province. Such spending would include promoting Quebec interests through quasi-diplomatic delegations in Brussels, London, Mexico City, New York, Paris, and Tokyo. To the knowledge of this author, there has been no assertion by the federal government that such spending by the Quebec government outside its legislative jurisdiction is unconstitutional.

Opponents of the federal spending power omit from their analysis of the *Canada Assistance Plan (B.C.)* decision that the province of Manitoba, as an intervener, attempted to challenge the power of the federal government to make grants to the provinces in a field of provincial jurisdiction (Hogg 2007, 175). Justice Sopinka, speaking for a unanimous court, responded as follows:

> The written argument of the Attorney General of Manitoba was that the legislation "amounts to" regulation of a matter outside of federal authority. I disagree. The Agreement under the *Plan* set up an open-ended cost-sharing scheme, which left it to British Columbia to decide which programmes it would establish and fund. *The simple withholding of federal money which had previously been granted to fund a matter within provincial jurisdiction does not amount to the regulation of that matter*.[16]

---

[14]*Supra* note 3.

[15]See *MacDonald v. Vapour Canada Ltd.* (1976), [1977] 2 S.C.R. 134; *R. v. Crown Zellerbach*, [1988] 1 S.C.R. 401.

[16]*Canada Assistance Plan (B.C.), supra* note 14 at 567 [emphasis added].

This view of the constitutionality of the federal spending power has received support from the Alberta Court of Appeal in *Winterhaven Stables Ltd. v. Canada (A.G.).*[17] With leave to appeal from this court subsequently refused by the Supreme Court, the conclusion that the constitutionality of the federal spending power is not substantially in doubt has been further reinforced. However, the antagonism voiced by Lajoie and other Quebec jurists toward the federal spending power has led to fanciful suggestions of how to entrench the "unlimited spending power" for those provinces who want to be subject to it while allowing Quebec and any other province to fully opt out using an expanded reach of the unused section 94 power of the Constitution.

Section 94 of the Constitution Act, 1867

Section 94 of the Constitution is an archaic and, some would argue, an obsolete provision as it is more suitable to a unitary state that allows the federal government to take over provincial powers with the consent of the relevant province. The provision allows the federal Parliament to legislatively intrude into the property and civil rights jurisdiction of those provinces that would agree to this serious incursion. The subsequent legislation would be binding federal law in the province (Adam 2007, 33).

Those who find authority for the spending power in section 94 are unconcerned that this provision shows its obsolescence by referring only to Ontario, Nova Scotia, and New Brunswick. One proponent in particular, Marc-Antoine Adam, has suggested that "[t]he weight of historical evidence and expert opinion is that section 94 would now apply to all common law provinces" (ibid.). However, it is hard to see how section 94 could be used without a constitutional amendment that would expressly allow it to apply to other provinces. Hogg gives a much more convincing account, noting that there is no express power of legislative interdelegation in the Canadian Constitution, as there is in the Australian Constitution. Moreover, the decision in *Nova Scotia Inter-Delegation*[18] has made it clear that such interdelegation should not be allowed in the absence of clear authority in the Constitution. Given that it refers only to the three founding common law provinces and deliberately excludes Quebec, section 94 does not provide that sort of unambiguous authority. As the late W.R. Lederman put it, "perhaps this is the reason why it has never been used" (1967, 421, n. 20). In addition, section 94 does not provide any compensation for provinces that do not want the intrusion of federal law and money into their territory. Nevertheless, those who support the use of this esoteric and obsolete provision would find some kind of penumbra entitlement to compensation based on section 36(1), which commits the Parliament and legislatures and their respective governments

[17][1988] 91 A.R. 114 (Alta. C.A.), aff'g [1986] 29 D.L.R. (4th) 394 (Alta. Q.B.), leave to appeal to S.C.C. refused, 21262 (19 December 1988).

[18]*Nova Scotia (A.G.) v. Canada (A.G.)* (1950), [1951] S.C.R. 31 [*Nova Scotia Inter-Delegation*].

- to promote equal opportunities for the well-being of Canadians;
- to further economic development to reduce disparity in opportunities; and
- to provide essential public services of reasonable quality to all Canadians.[19]

Reinforcing this implied penumbra entitlement is section 36(2), which states: "Parliament and the government of Canada are committed to the principle of making equalization payments to ensure that provincial governments have sufficient revenues to provide reasonably comparable levels of public service at reasonably comparable levels of taxation" (ibid., s.36(2)). This provision imposes a constitutional obligation to equalize the fiscal capacity of provinces and compensate for existing disparities.[20] The federal government, through a resurrected section 94, could then create the same fiscal inequities by not compensating non-participating provinces (Adam 2007, 34).

This argument is contradictory given the antagonism by some jurists, especially from Quebec, who decry the adequacy of SUFA to limit the federal spending power as it is only an administrative agreement, not a constitutionally entrenched framework. However, the possibility of a penumbra entitlement based on section 36(2) of the Constitution is much weaker than a federal-provincial agreement such as SUFA. In contrast to the tortured interpretation of section 94, combined with teasing out some penumbra entitlement from section 36, it is suggested that the ordinary meaning of section 36 gives constitutional support to a federal spending power that is exercised responsibly in the interests of a common Canadian citizenship, while SUFA works with section 36 to avoid as much as possible the undermining of provincial autonomy and spending priorities.

UNMASKING THE HARPER DOCTRINE

The Harper Doctrine is driven in part by an ideological position that the federal spending power is a by-product of excessive taxation by successive federal governments. According to this Conservative view, the best way to begin attacking both the federal spending power and excessive taxation is to first reduce the federal government's revenue-raising ability. Harper succeeded in doing this through his 2 percent reduction of the GST, taking tens of billions of dollars out of the Canadian treasury. The next step is to increase spending in areas that are clearly within federal jurisdiction and that reinforce the Conservative agenda. Defence and military procurement has become a top priority in this regard, especially with the extension of the military mission in Afghanistan until 2011. As of the end of 2007, Canada had spent approximately $7.2 billion in Afghanistan in six years of warfare. It has been reported that, since the start of the Afghan mission, "national military spending has increased

[19] *Constitution*, *supra* note 1, s.36(1).

[20] Some scholars would disagree, given the horatory language in s.36(2).

by 27 per cent and is at its highest level in 55 years" (Goar 2007). According to one think tank (the Rideau Institute), Canada's military spending in 2007-08 alone will reach $18.24 billion after major expenditures on military heavy-lift transport planes and other equipment; in adjusted dollars, it will surpass Canada's spending on the military during the peak of the Cold War (1952-53) by 2.3 percentage points (Staples and Robinson 2007, 1). The increased spending in such areas will hinder future governments from creating new national shared-cost programs in areas of provincial jurisdiction such as the national child-care program, which was in the planning stages before Prime Minister Paul Martin's government fell in the 2006 election.

Providing compensation to an opting-out province through tax points also seriously damages the federal government's ability to be an instrument of national social development and an equalizer of disparities. Once these tax points have been given, they cannot be taken back as it would be politically impossible to justify vacating taxing space to the provinces only to reoccupy it. Evidence of this may be found in the Canada Health and Social Transfer (CHST). The CHST replaced Established Program Financing, which covered health care and post-secondary education; and the Canada Assistance Plan, which dealt with social assistance and welfare services. Introduced in 1996 as part of the Liberal government's drastic deficit cutting, the CHST combined these two programs into single block funding (Asselin 2001, 13-15), which the federal government claimed would give the provinces more autonomy in implementing social programs. Established Program Financing and the Canada Assistance Plan were conditional block-funding programs financed equally by cash transfers and tax-point transfers. Under the CHST, the provinces can more easily set their own health, education, and social spending priorities. The federal government has essentially given up its right to set conditions for the funding of health and social programs, with the exception of the *Canada Health Act* standards (ibid., 12). Undeniably, the deficit cutting that underlay the CHST establishment has generated conflict with the provinces over the evolution of the spending power in Canada. However, with the ratio of cash transfers to tax points increasing under the CHST, the federal government will eventually lose the leverage to be "domineering" or "centralizing". Cash transfers are the only potential carrot and stick available to the federal government to encourage nationwide social development and to promote equity among the provinces.

The above discussion leaves one to wonder what more the Conservative government could do to curtail legislatively the federal spending power. Some have speculated that the Prime Minister's objective is to construct a firewall around the federal spending power. However, what the Conservative government could do to further restrain the federal spending power by legislative rather than constitutional means is a perplexing question. The following is an educated guess as to how the Harper government might attempt to accomplish this task:

- First, the Conservative government under Stephen Harper might raise the number of provinces required to consent to any new shared-cost program to a two-thirds majority. This might well be the death knell of any new shared-cost programs such as child care or pharmacare.

- Second, the federal government might use legislation to severely limit its ability to initiate any new direct transfer programs, such as the Millennium Scholarships, which are funded solely by the federal government. This might be accomplished, for example, by individual agreements with each province that restrict the ability of the federal government to initiate new direct transfer programs and promise full compensation without any conditions should direct transfers be initiated with other provinces.
- Finally, the Conservative government might concede to demands by Quebec (or any other province) to legislate the option of a de facto "no strings attached" transfer to a province choosing to opt out of new shared-cost programs that have been sanctioned by a majority or super majority of provinces. This could take the form of the offer of tax points, without the sanction of a withdrawal of actual cash if there is no adherence to the national objectives agreed to under the new shared-cost program. Hogg has suggested that a "no strings attached" opt-out could also take the form of a federal grant to provinces of similar value to the federal share of the shared-cost program; however, the grant would not be tied to a required provincial program, but rather could be used by the province for its own spending priorities (Hogg 2007, 174).

CONCLUSION

The danger behind the possible legislative additions to the 1999 Social Union Framework Agreement implicit in the Harper government's stated desire to legislate restraints on the federal spending power is that, if realized, such changes could hobble the spending power by making it impractical and unrealistic in both economic and political terms to create any new national shared-cost programs, such as child care or pharmacare. These restrictions on new shared-cost programs would in effect put a firewall around the spending power, which might well have been the objective of both Prime Minister Harper and his Quebec government allies.

If this is the ultimate goal of the Harper Doctrine, it may be undone by the fact that it can be achieved only by federal legislation. While such legislation might be enacted by the current government, it could be repealed by any subsequent government that did not agree that destroying the ability of the federal government to promote vital national objectives in social development was conducive to meeting the real challenges of a competitive global economy. For this reason, Harper's rhetoric about the "outrageous spending power" might be mere symbolic sound and fury, signifying not very much other than an attempt to lure Quebec voters. The major danger with this political manoeuvring, however, is that the very attempt to build firewalls through the use of tax points could not only permanently hobble the spending power but undermine one of the very foundations of federalism itself.

REFERENCES

Adam, M.-A. 2007. "Federalism and the Spending Power: Section 94 to the Rescue", *Policy Options* (March).

Asselin, R.B. 2001. *The Canadian Social Union: Questions about the Division of Powers and Fiscal Federalism.* Ottawa: Library of Parliament. At dsp-psd.pwgsc.gc.ca/Collection-R/LoPBdP/BP/prb0031-e.htm.

Beetz, J. 1965. "Les attitudes changeantes du Québec à l'endroit de la Constitution de 1867", in P.-A. Crépeau and C.B. Macpherson (eds.), *The Future of Canadian Federalism.* Toronto: University of Toronto Press.

Beltrame, J. 2008. "Inflation Helping Ottawa Grow Budget Surplus", *CNews* (27 August), at cnews.canoe.ca/CNEWS/Canada/2008/08/27/6587271-cp.html.

Boadway, R. 2000. "Recent Developments in the Economics of Federalism", in H. Lazar (ed.), *Canada: The State of the Federation 1999/2000: Toward a New Mission for Canadian Fiscal Federalism.* Kingston: McGill-Queen's University Press.

Bryden, J. 2007. "Spending Limits in Provincial Jurisdiction Affect New Programs Only", *Canadian Press* (16 October), at www.thestar.com/News/Canada/article/267520.

Canada. 1940. *Report of the Royal Commission on the Dominion-Provincial Relations*, Books 1, 2 & 3. Ottawa: King's Printer.

— 1969. *Federal-Provincial Grants and the Spending Power of Parliament,* Working Paper on the Constitution. Ottawa: Queen's Printer.

— 1999. *Framework to Improve the Social Union for Canadians: An Agreement between the Government of Canada and the Governments of the Provinces and Territories*, 4 February 1999 [SUFA].

Canada, Department of Finance. N.p. "Federal Transfers to Provinces and Territories: Equalization Program", at www.fin.gc.ca/FEDPROV/eqpe.html.

Cannon, L. The Honourable. 2007. Quoted in "Spending Limits in Provincial Jurisdiction Affect New Programs Only", *Canadian Press* (16 October), at www.thestar.com/News/Canada/article/267520.

Charest, J. 2007. Quoted in "Don't Lose the Flexibility", Editorial, *Globe and Mail* (15 August), at proquest.umi.com/pqdweb?did=1320129631&Fmt=3&clientId=14119&RQT= 309&VName=PQD.

Commission on the Fiscal Imbalance. 2002. *The "Federal Spending Power".* Quebec: Legal Deposit, Bibliothèque nationale du Quebec. At www.desequilibrefiscal.gouv.qc.ca/en/pdf/pouvoir_en.pdf.

Duceppe, G. 2007. Quoted in "Spending Limits in Provincial Jurisdiction Affect New Programs Only", *Canadian Press* (16 October), at www.thestar.com/News/Canada/article/267520.

Dupont, J. 1967. "Le pouvoir de dépenser du gouvernement fédéral: 'A Dead Issue'?" *University of British Columbia Law Review.*

Goar, C. 2007. "Canada: Big Military Spender", *Toronto Star* (29 October) AA06.

Harper, S. 2005. Quoted in John Geddes "Meet the Real Stephen Harper", *Maclean's Magazine* (5 May), at www.macleans.ca/article.jsp?content= 20050509_105134_105134&source=srch.

— 2006. Quoted in Office of the Prime Minister, "Prime Minister Promotes Federalism", *Government Press Release* (21 April), at pm.gc.ca/eng/media.asp?id=1123.

— 2007a. Quoted in "Don't Lose the Flexibility", Editorial, *Globe and Mail* (15 August), at proquest.umi.com/pqdweb?did=1320129631&Fmt=3&clientId=14119&RQT=309&VName=PQD.

— 2007b. Quoted in "Weaken Ottawa, Hobble the Nation", Editorial, *Toronto Star* (14 August), at proquest.umi.com/pqdweb?did=1319608041&Fmt=3&clientId=4119&RQT=309&VName=PQD.

Hogg, P.H. 2007. *Constitutional Law of Canada*, student ed. Toronto: Thomson Canada.

Lazar, H. 2000. "In Search of a New Mission Statement for Canadian Fiscal Federalism", in H. Lazar (ed.), *Canada: The State of the Federation 1999/2000: Toward a New Mission Statement for Canadian Fiscal Federalism.* Kingston: McGill-Queen's University Press.

Lederman, W.R. 1967. "Some Forms and Limitations of Co-operative Federalism", *Canadian Bar Review* 45.

Library of Parliament, Research Branch, Law and Government Division. 1987. *The 1987 Constitutional Accord.* Ottawa: Minister of Supply and Services Canada.

MacDonald, L.I. 2008. "Charest and Harper Still Need Each Other", *Montreal Gazette* (16 January), at www.canada.com/montrealgazette/news/editorial/story.html?id=8e99b38c-1dbc-49fd-9edb-7ed9b70d418d.

McRoberts, K. and P. Monahan, eds. 1993. *The Charlottetown Accord, the Referendum and the Future of Canada.* Toronto: University of Toronto Press.

Ministère du Conseil exécutif du Québec. 1998. *Quebec's Historical Position on the Federal Spending Power 1944-1998.* Quebec: Secretariat aux Affaires. At www.saic.gouv.qc.ca/publications/documents_inst_const/positionEng.pdf.

Office of the Prime Minister. 2006. "Prime Minister Promotes Federalism", *Government Press Release* (21 April), at pm.gc.ca/eng/media.asp?id=1123.

Panetta, A. 2008. "Harper Gradually 'Tightening the Screws' on Government, Ex-advisor Says", *Canadian Press NewsWire* (2 March), at proquest.umi.com/pqdweb?did=1438261971&Fmt=3&clientId=14119&RQT=309&VName= PQD.

Petter, A. 1989. "Federalism and the Myth of the Federal Spending Power", *Canadian Bar Review* 68.

Quebec.1956. *Report of the Royal Commission of Inquiry on Constitutional Problems*, vol. 2. Quebec City: Province of Quebec.

Special Joint Committee on a Renewed Canada. 1992. *Consensus Report on the Constitution.* Charlottetown [Charlottetown Accord].

Staples, S. and B. Robinson. 2007. "More than the Cold War: Canada's Military Spending 2007-08", *Foreign Policy Series* 2(3).

Trudeau, P.E. 1968. "Federalism Grants to Universities", in *Federalism and the French Canadians.* Toronto: Macmillan of Canada.

V

The Spending Power in Perspective

13

The Federal Spending Power Is Now Chiefly for People, Not Provinces

Tom Kent

Le pouvoir fédéral de dépenser est indispensable à la prestation équitable et efficiente des services collectifs au-delà des frontières provinciales, soutient l'auteur. Mais comme il est politiquement irréaliste d'envisager une péréquation d'une rigueur absolue, il nous faut adopter d'autres approches de ce pouvoir. Dans les années 1960, le partage des coûts avait permis la création d'un État-providence moderne que l'action de la classe politique fédérale a depuis irrémédiablement anéanti. À défaut de quoi Ottawa devrait aujourd'hui privilégier les programmes axés sur des transferts directs d'argent aux entreprises et aux particuliers. Cette application du pouvoir de dépenser serait mieux adaptée aux réalités politiques actuelles et ferait progresser les objectifs sociaux du pays, tout en renforçant la productivité et la résilience de son économie. En assurant plus d'autonomie à la population, elle incarnerait aussi une volonté démocratique soutenue et favoriserait la collaboration intergouvernementale indispensable au fédéralisme canadien.

Some people reject the evidence that man-made emissions are increasingly changing the climate. Some lawyers and academics deny the existence of the federal spending power. Nevertheless, in both cases, the practical issue is not whether to act. It is how to act.

The spending power is the ability to use tax money for objectives outside the scope for which the federal government can itself deliver public services. Like all power, it can be misused. Its proper use is essential to the Canadian federation. Otherwise, many necessary public services could not be equably and efficiently provided.

One major use of the spending power is not open to any debate. Since 1982, it has been required by the Constitution that Ottawa must spend federal money to help some provinces finance activities in their jurisdiction. Specifically, "Parliament and the government of Canada are committed to the principle of making equalization payments to ensure that provincial governments have sufficient revenues to provide reasonably comparable levels of public services at reasonably comparable levels of taxation".[1]

Strict "equalization" would at present require Ottawa to transfer to all other provinces enough money to enable them to provide the Alberta level of services at the Alberta level of taxation. So massive a transfer is out of the question. Albertans, and many others, would rise in revolt against paying the federal taxes required. Well short of that point, federal politicians would be driven to desperation by the taxation needed to finance both their own responsibilities and massive transfers for provincial politicians to spend.

Consequently, while for fifty years equalization has been part of the glue of Canada's federal union, it is necessary but far from sufficient. As much as is politically possible should be done to finance, by a principled equalization program, provincial services that are not unreasonably diverse. But that leaves much to be done by other federal-provincial collaboration, for which other uses of the spending power are required.

Those other uses are the topic of this chapter. Its thesis can be summarized in four statements. First, in the 1960s it was essential that we find ways to deploy the federal power for social purposes, to build a modern welfare state throughout Canada. Had we not done so, it is questionable whether our political union would have survived the twentieth century. The main method then used was cost-sharing. That is, Ottawa reimbursed provincial treasuries for part (broadly, 50 percent) of the costs they incurred in delivering certain defined services.

This worked well, for a time; indeed, it worked so well that advocates of good causes that are provincial responsibilities still almost automatically demand cost-sharing as the way to get things done. They are, however, calling in vain. My second statement is thus that cost-sharing is now an instrument broken beyond repair, broken not by wish of the provinces but by federal politicians.

Nevertheless, and this is my third statement, extensive deployment of the spending power is needed now more than ever, both for social purposes and for the productivity and resilience of the economy. However, the uses of the spending power that fit contemporary circumstances require transfers not to provincial treasuries but to individuals and organizations, and their nature is to empower civil society in a market economy.

That is the fourth statement that I hope to justify.

Federalism distinguishes separate activities for the two orders of government. Today those activities in total are far more intensive than they were in 1867, but even then the *British North America Act*[2] recognized that the division of powers could not be absolute. For agriculture and for immigration, jurisdiction was made concurrent, though with firm federal precedence: provincial legislation "shall have effect in and for the Province as long and as far only as it is not repugnant to any Act of the Parliament of Canada" (ibid., s.95).

---

[1] *Constitution Act, 1982*, s.36(2), being Schedule B to the *Canada Act 1982* (U.K.), 1982, c. 11.

[2] *Constitution Act, 1867* (U.K.), 30 & 31 Victoria, c. 3, reprinted in R.S.C. 1985, App. II, No. 5 [*British North America Act*].

Again, provincial power to legislate on "Local Works and Undertakings" was made subject to specific restrictions and, more generally, it excluded "Such works as, though wholly situate within the Province, are before or after their Execution declared by the Parliament of Canada to be for the general Advantage of Canada or for the Advantage of Two or more of the Provinces" (ibid., s.92(10)).

Nevertheless, despite such qualifications, the Constitution is considerably more precise about the division of powers than about dividing the resources needed to exercise them. There is effectively no separation of tax fields. The tariffs that provinces cannot impose are now unimportant as sources of money. Otherwise, Ottawa and the provinces have the same access to revenue, except that all provinces have prior claim to raise it from natural resources within their borders.

What is different between the two orders of government is the use they can make of money. A province is limited to spending on its own activities. It may impose "Direct Taxation within the Province in order to the raising of a Revenue for Provincial Purposes" (ibid., s.92(2)). The federal Parliament, by contrast, can legislate for "The raising of Money by any Mode or System of Taxation" (ibid., s.91(3)). There is no restriction of purpose. Ottawa is not limited to spending on its own activities. It can subsidize provincial governments. It can provide money to individuals and to organizations of all kinds, on such terms as Parliament legislates.

Public spending is not solely the writing of cheques. It includes measures that forego taxes in order to encourage or assist people in defined ways. In the form of refundable credits, such tax expenditures can powerfully redistribute income to people in need. Most of those now operative, however, have a different motive. Many are directed to business activities. Others serve purposes as diverse as subsidizing savings for retirement, encouraging charitable giving and small donations to political parties, and helping to pay for health care not covered by provincial programs and for the day care of children of working parents. The characteristic common to many of these measures is that the benefit is greater the higher one's income.

The tax expenditures of more recent times are thereby in contrast with the earlier uses of the federal spending power in the dominant programs of the 1940s-60s period. The first of those was the Family Allowance: a universal payment of great significance to low-income mothers and especially to those too poor to pay taxes. Old Age Security, originally introduced thanks to a 1951 constitutional amendment,[3] has equally rested on the spending power since it was freed from the pretence of being a contributory pension by having specific taxes dedicated to it.

The emphasis in deployment of the spending power soon shifted, however, from direct federal programs to cost-sharing. There are still politicians and propagandists who like to represent this as power-hungry Ottawa using its money to barge into the jurisdiction of reluctant provinces. That is not at all the

[3] *Old Age Security Act,* R.S.C. 1985, c. O-9.

way it was. The impulse came, naturally, from the provinces. They were the seducers, Ottawa initially a slow respondent.

Saskatchewan started the affair by introducing its own hospital insurance. People liked it. Other provinces came under strong pressure to save their citizens from the high costs of going to the hospital. Their politicians were held back by a little ideological and much financial concern. They looked to Ottawa for help. The St-Laurent government, by then tired and complacent, resisted, until the Conservative government of Ontario became particularly insistent. Even so, the federal legislation provided for cost-sharing to begin only when a majority of provinces had adopted the program. It was not until the arrival of the Diefenbaker Conservative government that this barrier was lifted and any province got federal money as soon it started hospital insurance.

With that, the key to the federal treasury was indeed turned. It had to be. In the late 1950s, after two decades of remarkable economic growth had replaced the Great Depression, Canadians were eagerly ready for the welfare state. The provinces were too diverse in fiscal capacity to proceed at anything close to comparable speed. The Canada-wide welfare state could come only with federal cost-sharing. That federal intervention was inherent in the politics of the federal-provincial relationship that was emerging.

But it was not, in 1958, quite there. In Quebec's *ancien regime*, social affairs were still the business of the church more than the state. Diefenbaker's move could have produced a deep division in the federal union. Fortunately, there came the Quiet Revolution. With the Lesage government of 1960, Quebec soon replaced Saskatchewan as the most activist of provincial administrations. It was in the forefront of wanting medicare and the rest. It sought more room for provincial taxes to pay for them. But Lesage was an economic realist as well as a social reformer. He wanted to do things Quebec's way but knew it must be much the same as the rest of Canada's way. In particular, Quebec taxes could not be far out of line with the rest. He was therefore all for use of the federal spending power to share costs.

There was, however, a condition. Earlier cost-sharing had been appropriately labelled as the conduct of "joint" programs. Hospital insurance, categorical social assistance, and the short-lived technical and vocational training program had all been provincial services operated according to provisions stipulated in the federal legislation that authorized sharing of their costs. Such compromise of provincial jurisdiction had been acceptable in the continuing aftermath of wartime centralization. Fifteen years on, it was unacceptable in Quebec and resented everywhere.

Nevertheless, it was thanks to federal taxes providing half of the costs that medicare was instituted nationwide; post-secondary education was vastly extended; social services were sophisticated; and social assistance according to need, without discrimination according to cause, was made universal. The triumph of cooperative federalism in the 1960s was to achieve all this without compromising the constitutional division of powers. Federal legislation did not prescribe provincial programs. It stated only broad principles that would enable Ottawa to contribute half of the cost. Provinces separately legislated everything else. National finance simply made it all possible.

There was still some debate, and grumbling. It is not in the nature of provincial politicians to give much credit to the feds. The Social Credit government of Alberta disliked medicare in principle. Conservative governments saw political Machiavellianism in federal Liberal policy. But there was no word of objection to the spending power as such, from either the provinces or from the federal Conservatives who voted for all the 1960s social legislation.

A similar consensus secured nationwide contributory pensions. Lesage wanted to exercise the primacy of provincial jurisdiction. He badly needed pension capital to modernize Quebec's infrastructure and industry. But again he recognized that a big difference from the rest of Canada would spell trouble. In practice, we were able to agree on identical plans.

In sum, Canada's social programs were not created by federal dominance over provincial jurisdiction. They were created by federal and provincial governments in a consensus driven by democratic will, by a tide of public opinion. Some governments rode the surf with pleasure and skill. Some were more like drifters with the tide. But all ended on the same shore and found it, for a time, smooth and warm.

Not, however, for long. Within a decade, the political foundations of cost-sharing had cracked. The cause was not in the provinces. They did not turn against the federal spending power. Ottawa did. It let the provinces down. It reneged on the promises with which the programs began.

The reason was simple and is enduring. The politicians of the 1960s had known the stagnation of the Great Depression and had experienced the role of federal leadership in war and in the post-war economy. Though the new social programs were run by the provinces, Ottawa was confident of receiving its due credit for them. It misjudged the changing times. A new generation, less aware of the contrast with depression and war, soon took the welfare state for granted. Precisely because it went well, the committed fiscal transfers that underpinned it became routines of no public interest. Credit for them disappeared. A new set of federal politicians quickly came to resent raising taxes for provincial politicians to spend and get the credit.

The initial break, the 1977 legislation on the financing of established programs,[4] was accompanied by flim-flam about the provinces getting more program flexibility in exchange for imposing the taxes that Ottawa graciously ceded to them. In fact, public opinion ensured that the reduced transfer was increasingly used to meet the rising costs of medicare, at the expense of using less for post-secondary education. The flexibility was that the provinces shuffled the federal purposes for the transfer.

Through the 1980s, as the federal government increasingly failed to manage the economy, mounting interest costs became mounting excuses to renege further on the cost-sharing with which the programs had been started. Finally, the 1995 budget ended all vestige of federal commitment to a defined share in costs. The spending power is still used to transfer federal revenue to provincial

---

[4]*Federal-Provincial Fiscal Arrangements and Established Programs Financing Act, 1977*, S.C. 1977, c. 10.

treasuries. But these "health and social" transfers are block amounts fixed by political pressures and the state of federal finances. They are subsidies that owe their survival to a different past.

The 1995 slashing of transfers profoundly changed the federal-provincial relationship. Morally and politically, Ottawa was put on the defensive. The provinces thereby gained a much stronger hand in negotiations. They promptly used it. They formulated their agreed ideas about federal money, ideas embodied in the Social Union Framework Agreement (SUFA),[5] which Ottawa had to sign in 1999. It established rules for future intergovernmental transfers. These transfers are to be conditional on nothing tighter than "agreed Canada-wide objectives" and "respect [for] the accountability framework", which each province can meet in its own way and thereby be entitled to its share of Ottawa's money (ibid.).

That was a brilliant way to write an obituary without declaring death. If provincial programs need to be no more than vaguely similar, supporting them with federal money would yield neither influence nor political benefit for Ottawa. Only the most short-sighted of governments would use its taxes that way. It is true that the Martin government proposed to do so, in its late, despairing days. It offered block grants extending for some years as the way to kick-start wider provision of early childhood care. It negotiated with the provinces individually in a hasty, disjointed improvization that would have created too many anomalies to survive. The Harper government immediately cancelled the program, without political pain.

There will no doubt continue to be federal transfers to particular provinces for particular projects, notably the infrastructures that appeal to politicians of all stripes for the photo-ops they provide. But thoughts of continuing transfers for new programs are ghosts from the past. In light of SUFA, block funding is ruled out equally with cost-sharing. It is not in any event a sound base for an effective, steady program. It cannot be believably offered for the long term. It is even more exposed to being cut, if attitudes change or Ottawa is in financial trouble, than cost-sharing proved to be. Provincial governments will foolishly take the risk only if tempted by very lavish terms in the short run, while the federal government invites future trouble for only short-term political benefit. Any such program would be a measure of desperation, not use of the spending power for the efficient, stable collaboration good federalism requires.

For that, we now need to look to the other use of the spending power. The SUFA obituary was strictly for new program transfers to the provinces. It was not for the spending power. On the contrary, SUFA fully recognizes its direct use, for individuals and organizations, as a federal right: "Another use of the federal spending power is making transfers to individuals and to organizations in order to promote equality of opportunity, mobility, and other Canada-wide objectives" (ibid.). Such programs are not hedged by the conditions attached to transfers to the provinces. The only restraint is that before implementing "new Canada-wide initiatives funded through direct transfers to individuals or

---

[5] *Framework to Improve the Social Union for Canadians: An Agreement between the Government of Canada and the Governments of the Provinces and Territories,* 4 February 1999 [SUFA].

organizations", the federal government will "give at least three months' notice and offer to consult" (ibid.).

Constitutionally and practically, the federal government thus has full scope to establish a national framework of social policy, a framework on which provincial governments can build as they choose. The instrument is the spending power used directly to help Canadians individually. That use is not limited either by the Constitution or by provincial opposition. The limits are set by considerations of practicality and sustainability, by finance, and by the collaborative spirit within federalism.

In that spirit, this chapter briefly reviews a broad range of possible programs from which to choose priorities.

The first, in my view, is a basic measure of family income support. At present, low incomes are taxed too much. I have suggested that the basic allowance should be increased and that a substantial part of it – say, initially, $10,000 for one person, and a combined $15, 000 for a couple – should become a refundable credit. The Canada Child Tax Benefit should be at a corresponding level of $5,000 for the first two dependants, somewhat lower for larger families. The result would be to establish, in effect, a modest guaranteed income of, for example, $15,000 for a childless couple and for a single parent with one child, and $25,000 for a couple with two children (adjusted, of course, for increases in the cost of living). That would be below the poverty level, particularly in large cities, but it would be a solid national base to which provinces and municipalities could add, for example, housing allowances, health benefits not covered by medicare, and other social services and assistance.

A second major program would be a return, in a sense, to a brief period in the past. Ottawa should take clear, countrywide responsibility for upgrading the skills of unemployed and underemployed Canadians. It should support them by allowances while they take training courses; it should ensure that courses are available by standing ready to purchase them from appropriate sources, which in addition to provincial colleges and schools might include various kinds of private agencies.

Such a program would be a major part of the investment in human capital now recognized to be crucial to a productive economy. Another component is post-secondary education. The present confusion of provincial financing, erratic loans, and bureaucratically variable repayments is in urgent need of reform. It could best be replaced by interest-bearing advances of up to the full costs of taking diploma, bachelor, and graduate courses. (Doctoral studies fit better with research financing.) Repayment would be income-contingent, through a graduated surtax on subsequent income above, say, the national average of individual full-time earnings.

It must be noted, however, that some graduates are internationally mobile and will be increasingly so. While this is entirely desirable, the incidental effect is to enlarge opportunities for tax avoidance. Countering it requires a legal base we have not established but the United States has. American citizens have the same liability to pay American taxes wherever in the world they live. Canada can follow that good example. The major reason for doing so is to combat tax evasion generally, but it is of some special importance that working abroad should not enable people to avoid repayment of public investment in their post-secondary education. Such financing should therefore be available only to citizens, not other residents.

The other two priority uses of the spending power would apply to all children resident in Canada. Early childhood education is at last widely recognized as an essential investment in our most important, and increasingly scarce, resource. In most of Canada, however, early childhood education is gravely deficient. Much of the organized child care available is little more than babysitting and even so is too expensive for many parents. There are other considerable obstacles. Long bus journeys are not how preschool children should spend their time. The ideal child-care centres, with extensive services and an adequate number of professional staff, are therefore impracticable outside cities and sizeable towns. Everywhere there are parents who want to keep their offspring at home or just down the street.

In time, a lower entry age for compulsory schooling might become acceptable, but the time is not now. Meanwhile, and probably for the foreseeable future at ages below four, the appropriate public policy is to finance the consumer demand. This demand is strong. The role of government is to make it effective. The need is countrywide and urgent. It will not be well met by provincially operated programs, however financed. The way that would be more democratic, fairer, and faster is for the federal government to reimburse parents, on a sliding scale related to income, for fees paid for the kind of early educational care they choose for their children. Municipalities with underused school space now on their hands, as well as community groups and non-profit agencies, would be eager to respond. While competition as well as public spirit would do much to ensure adequate standards, fee scales would be agreed upon by the provinces and paid only for services licenced and supervised by them.

Public opinion would ensure that the needed, close collaboration was willing collaboration. Both orders of government would have everything to gain by it, not only initially but permanently. Ottawa would get continuing political credit for its cheques going to people, and the provinces could be sure that the feds would never get away with reneging on kids as they did on obscure transfers to provincial treasuries. While this chapter is not the place to attempt to discuss all the careful detail required for such a program, the main point is surely clear. The federal spending power is the appropriate instrument available for this major national purpose, provided it is deployed not to finance provinces but to empower people.

That applies equally to my fifth suggestion, which is for health policy. Canada's medicare is, despite its weaknesses, a fine public service to cherish. But in one respect it has stayed too close to its origins. It began because the costs of being treated for illnesses were often impossible for many people and financially disastrous even for the well-to-do. But, to quote Tommy Douglas, the goal of public policy is healthy people, "not just patching them up when they're sick".

Medicare, however, was geared to do the patching, and medical science makes it increasingly able to do the job. More and more sicknesses can be more effectively treated – at higher and higher costs. The financial strain encourages sticking with the established job. Measures to prevent sickness, to foster good health, are crowded out. Preventing is not only better than curing but also, in the long run, cheaper. In the short run, however, preventive measures are an additional expense. They are not, of course, ignored. There have been some improvements. But, inevitably, preventive measures take second place to the immediate needs within a system that cannot afford all it could do to patch up the sick.

The dilemma is plain. The longer we are deficient in preventing sickness, and the more the costs of treating it increase, the harder it becomes to find the money for prevention. The money will not come, anywhere near sufficiently and quickly enough, from within the present process. It will not come from the federal government increasing its health transfer to the provinces, as it did in 2000, 2003, and 2004. That may shorten some wait times for some treatments. It will not lessen sicknesses.

The need is for a break from the old way, for a different kind of initiative to put new vitality into the noble work of building a healthy community. Measures to promote good health are more effective the earlier in life they begin. The best initiative would be to mount a comprehensive range of services for child health. But if that were attempted by putting more money into the existing health transfer, much of it would inevitably be lost amid all the pressing demands that medicare puts on provincial treasuries. The effective initiative would make children truly the priority. Additional federal action should now be directed specifically and firmly toward them. Later, the whole federal health transfer, which in its present form runs to 2014, will require reformulation by careful consideration and thorough consultation. It should aim for the fullest practicable reimbursement of the costs of preventive services, especially in youth.

The transfers for which the federal spending power is needed now are not only to individuals but also to some organizations. One priority is research and development. Much of our industry is deficient in this area. While post-secondary education is best served by financing the students, universities also have a major role in research. For that, federal funding is now significant but not sufficient.

The more controversial organizational funding is for industrial reconstruction and development. The controversy over the often wasted grants and easy loans that government has traditionally provided comes to the fore in a recession. In our financial system, it is not only some business investors and private consumers who get funding all too easily. So, often, do established corporations, especially for mergers and acquisitions. Capital for innovation and for the growth of small businesses is much scarcer, even in the recent times of so much financial splurging.

The requirement is for risk capital, and that is what government aid should be. The appropriate contribution through the spending power is not to make grants or easy loans but to provide additional equity for industrial enterprise. Public money should share both in the risk and in the return from venturing. It should not, however, buy power to interfere in private management. Government capital in industry should be in the form of special shares, carrying a normal right to dividends but not to voting in company business. Responsibility would then be properly shared through a public-private partnership in enterprise.

The initiatives I have briefly outlined here are in my view important policies, but their merits or demerits are incidental to this discussion. They are examples to illustrate what I consider to be the central truth for Canadian federalism today. For a generation, half a century ago, the federal spending power was used to share, nationwide, the provinces' costs of instituting new programs that transformed our society. In that form, it was the right instrument for the times. In that form, it has had its use. It does not fit the present times. But it is only the form that is outmoded. The spending power is as essential as ever. It is essential to our economic as well as our social betterment. This time, however, it has to be used primarily for transfers to people.

The change is appropriate to the spirit of the century, to the widening opportunities of the information society, to the increasing independence of individual choice that advancing technology makes possible. Broadening freedom for all requires, however, a reliable framework of public policy. Transfers between government treasuries proved to be unreliable. Transfers that go directly to people are transfers not easily chopped and changed in the manoeuvres of politics. The spending power so used for all Canadians can be a sustained expression of democratic will, and thereby a firm assertion of the stable collaboration between governments that is essential to our federalism.

14

Constitutional Change in the Twenty-First Century: A New Debate over the Spending Power

Sujit Choudhry

Pour étayer son analyse du débat sur l'avenir du pouvoir fédéral de dépenser, l'auteur examine tout d'abord les visées initiales de la Constitution canadienne du XIXe siècle et l'évolution qu'elle a connue au siècle suivant face à la redéfinition du rôle de l'État moderne et à la place du Canada dans le monde. Il soutient ainsi que le débat actuel procède des frictions qui opposent la dimension politique de la Constitution du XIXe siècle et la dimension financière de celle du XXe. À propos du siècle actuel, il prédit que le débat procédera essentiellement des changements démographiques. Des changements qui mettront à l'avant plan l'enjeu de la représentation politique et soulèveront des questions clés sur le rôle des dépenses fédérales au regard des politiques économiques et sociales du pays.

INTRODUCTION

The contemporary debate over the federal spending power fills me with a sense of both déjà vu and nostalgia – déjà vu because it has gone on for so long, and nostalgia because of my own involvement in it.

As a country, we have been debating the questions of whether there are justiciable limits on the federal spending power, and whether we should amend the Constitution to include such limits, ever since the Privy Council announced the existence of that power in the *Unemployment Insurance Reference*.[1] Indeed,

This chapter is based on my rapporteur's remarks at Open Federalism and the Spending Power conference, held at Queen's University in January 2008, as well as comments delivered at the Institute for Research in Public Policy/Canadian Medical Association Roundtable, "Defining the Federal Government's Role in Social Policy: The

controversies over the federal spending power have been at the heart of the politics of social policy, which in turn have been at the very centre of federal-provincial relations since the rise of the Canadian social union after the Second World War. Throughout, debates about the federal role in social policy have not merely been debates over the design of social programs, or even about the appropriate division of labour between the federal and provincial governments. Rather, the politics of social policy have been a terrain for competing nationalisms. In the post-war period, the construction of the welfare state has been central to a pan-Canadian nationalism, centred on the federal government. Though the origin of modern Quebec nationalism is a complex story, to a considerable extent it was a defensive response to this federally led nation-building project. Federal social-policy activism meant an increase in the importance of federal institutions, especially the federal bureaucracy, which worked in English and in which francophone Quebecers were a small minority.

For over a decade, I have contributed to these debates myself. There are three strands to my work. First, I have devoted considerable attention to the legal framework governing shared-cost programs, in particular the design and enforcement of federal statutes authorizing transfers to the provinces and territories conditioned on compliance with national standards for medicare (Choudhry 1996, 2000; Canada, Royal Commission on the Future of Health Care in Canada 2002). In short, I have argued that national standards have rarely been enforced by the federal government. In addition, I have suggested that they be fundamentally rethought. These standards should be converted into self-imposed provincial benchmarks, with provincial performance assessed and publicly reported on by an independent third-party agency (such as the Health Council of Canada), and with enforcement left to the provincial political process.

Second, I have turned my mind to the constitutional architecture within which these arrangements have developed (Choudhry 2002, 2003). Two constitutional assumptions underlie the development of the social union: the federal government lacks direct jurisdiction over the design and delivery of social programs, and intergovernmental agreements are judicially unenforceable. I have tried to suggest that these should now be reconsidered. In particular, I have argued that the strongest criticism of the federal spending power – the incoherence of granting the federal government fiscal jurisdiction in areas where it lacks regulatory jurisdiction – does not necessarily lead to the conclusion that it should not be able to make conditional transfers to underwrite provincial social programs. Rather, in light of the modern Supreme Court of Canada's expansive conception of federal jurisdiction, an argument could be crafted under

---

Spending Power and Other Instruments", held in Ottawa in June 2008. I thank the organizers of both events – Marc-Antoine Adam, John Allan, Tom Courchene, Mel Cappe, Hoi Kong, William Tholl, and Leslie Seidle – for their invitations to speak. All remaining errors are mine.

[1]*Reference Re Employment and Social Insurance Act (Can.)*, [1937] 1 D.L.R. 684 (P.C.), (*sub nom. Canada (A.G.) v. Ontario (A.G.)*) [1937] A.C. 326 [*Unemployment Insurance Reference*].

the "peace, order and good government" (POGG) power for federal jurisdiction over social policy.

This chapter extends arguments that I have developed in the third and most recent strand of my work (Choudhry, Gaudreault-DesBiens, and Sossin 2006a; Choudhry, Gaudreault-DesBiens, and Sossin 2006b; Choudhry 2006; Choudhry, Gaudreault-DesBiens, and Sossin 2006c). Rather than diving into the familiar legal and political debates once again, I have suggested that how we think about the federal role in social policy, and about redistribution more generally, has started to shift in response to the profound demographic change that is beginning to put strain on a number of dimensions of our constitutional structure. I posit, for example, that the rise of the "cities agenda" – especially as advanced by the mayors of Canada's major urban centres – will strain the federal-provincial transfer system, as cities emerge as nascent sites of political identity and fuel demands to reduce financial transfers – which are considerable – from urban to rural areas through the federal tax and transfer system. In this chapter, I take this line of analysis one step further, and ask what other changes we can expect to see in the politics of the federal spending power in the twenty-first century.

THE NINETEENTH VERSUS THE TWENTIETH CENTURY

To get at that question, I want to reflect on where the contemporary controversy over the federal spending power comes from. These debates arise from the manner in which Canada has managed constitutional change over the last century. The constitutional provisions governing the federal division of powers are found in the *Constitution Act, 1867*.[2] The key sections are sections 91 and 92, which contain lists of "exclusive" areas of jurisdiction. Some areas of jurisdiction – consider criminal law and procedure – remain central areas of public policy. Many of the grants of jurisdiction in these uninspiring lists now appear rather narrow (for example, weights and measures, beacons and buoys, saloons and taverns). But more importantly, they reflect a nineteenth-century conception of what the state does, and what the Canadian state in particular was expected to do.

One of the principal goals of Confederation was to create and empower a federal government that could undertake the expansion of European settlement of the western half of the northern half of the continent, and integrate that part of North America, economically and politically, with the rest of Canada. International relations were left to the Empire. This is reflected in section 132, on the implementation of Imperial treaties – the only reference to international treaties in the constitutional text (ibid., s. 132). To be sure, there have been important amendments to the provisions governing federalism since 1867. In the social policy field, for example, there have been amendments conferring

---

[2]*Constitution Act, 1867* (U.K.), 30 & 31, Vict., c. 3, ss. 91-92, reprinted in R.S.C. 1985, App. II, No. 5.

jurisdiction on the federal government over unemployment insurance (1940),[3] old age pensions (1951),[4] and supplementary benefits including survivors' and disability benefits irrespective of age (1964).[5] But sections 91 and 92 have survived largely intact.

It is beyond dispute that if the division of powers were drafted today, it would look rather different. By way of comparison, consider the 1996 South African Constitution, one of the leading examples of a contemporary federal constitution. It refers explicitly, and at length, to the welfare state.[6] It allocates jurisdiction over health care, social assistance, and housing (ibid.). In addition, it assigns responsibility for the environment, consumer protection, labour relations, competition policy, economic development, and telecommunication and broadcasting, among other areas (ibid.). It also speaks to international relations, including the power to make and implement treaties (ibid., ss. 231-233).

This comparison between a constitution negotiated in the mid-nineteenth century and one negotiated at the end of the twentieth century highlights the enormous gap between what we need our Constitution to do and what its written text says. One of the central themes of Canadian constitutional development has been our attempts to deal with the encounter of our nineteenth-century Constitution with a dramatically changed sense both of what a modern state should be and of Canada's place in the world. In a nutshell, the Constitution has had to adapt to the demands of a regulatory, redistributive state, as well as to the fact of Canadian independence. None of this was foreseen in 1867.

Constitutional change in the federal division of powers occurred only rarely through constitutional amendment, and even then, never through large-scale, comprehensive constitutional change. For the most part, it occurred through two other mechanisms – ad hoc, incremental constitutional interpretation in the litigation process, and executive and legislative action.

Constitutional litigation on the division of powers has been driven in part by the gap between the nineteenth-century text and the public functions needed in a modern, independent Canada. In many cases, the courts have engaged in a process of *constitutional translation*, re-reading provisions drafted against the backdrop of nineteenth-century legal categories in a twentieth-century policy context. Far from being flatly counter-majoritarian, this process has often occurred at the invitation of one level of government, and has therefore been about the allocation of power between different political majorities. The interpretive metaphor of the "living tree" offers the doctrinal basis for this court-

---

[3]*Constitution Act, 1940* (U.K.), 3-4 George VI, c. 36.

[4]*British North America Act, 1951* (U.K.), 4-15 George VI, c. 32, as rep. by *Constitution Act, 1982*, Sch., being Schedule B to the *Canada Act, 1982* (U.K.), 1982, c. 11.

[5]*Constitution Act, 1964* (U.K.), 12-13 Eliz. II, c. 73.

[6]*Constitution of the Republic of South Africa 1996*, No. 108 of 1996, Sch. 4.

driven approach to constitutional development.[7] An excellent example is provided by the fairly recent decision in *Reference Re Employment Insurance Act (Can.), ss. 22 and 23*,[8] where the Court invoked the living-tree doctrine to reject a constitutional challenge to the maternity and parental-leave benefits provided under the *Employment Insurance Act*, notwithstanding their weak connection to the original rationale for the employment insurance system.

This mechanism of ad hoc incremental change remains an important, if underappreciated, form of judicial interpretation, which is likely to be deployed in the service of the ongoing project of constitutional adaptation. In challenges now pending against the *Assisted Human Reproduction Act*[9] and the *Personal Information Protection and Electronic Documents Act*,[10] as well as in the looming constitutional battle over the implementation of the Kyoto Protocol[11] and its successor agreement, the Court will have to translate the 1867 constitutional text to allocate jurisdiction over reproductive technologies, privacy, and international environmental protection.

In other cases, the Court has fashioned new constitutional powers to meet pressing social and political needs by literally filling constitutional gaps. Perhaps the most vivid examples are found in judicial attempts to adapt the Constitution to the reality of Canadian independence. The early cases on the implementation of international treaties (the *Aeronautics Reference*[12] and the *Radio Reference*[13]) suggested that the Court would respond to the *Balfour Declaration*[14] and the *Statute of Westminster*[15] by vesting treaty implementation in the federal jurisdiction. Although the Court stepped back from this conclusion

---

[7]*Reference Re British North America Act, 1867 s. 24* (1929), [1930] 1 D.L.R. 98 (P.C.), (*sub nom. Edwards v. Canada (A.G.)*) [1930] A.C. 124.

[8]2005 SCC 56, [2005] 2 S.C.R. 669.

[9]S.C. 2004, c. 2. Portions of this Act were found to be unconstitutional by the Quebec Court of Appeal in *L'Affaire du Renvoi fait par le gouvernement du Québec en vertu de la Loi sur les renvois à la Cour d'appel, L.R.Q. ch. R-23, relativement à la constitutionnalité des articles 8 à 19, 40 à 53, 60, 61 et 68 de la Loi sur la procréation assistée, L.C. 2004, ch. 2*, 2008 QCCA 1167.

[10]S.C. 2000, c. 5 [*PIPEDA*]. The Quebec government issued an order-in-council posing a reference question to the Quebec Court of Appeal on the constitutionality of *PIPEDA* under the division of powers on December 17, 2003. This proceeding does not appear to have moved forward. See *Concerning a reference to the Court of Appeal to the Personal Information Protection and Electronic Documents Act (S.C. 2000, c. 5)*, O.I.C. 1368-2003, G.O.Q. 2003.

[11]*Kyoto Protocol to the United Nations Framework Convention on Climate Change*, 10 December 1997, U.N. Doc FCCC/CP/1997/7/Add.1, (1998) 37 I.L.M. 22.

[12]*Re Regulation and Control of Aeronautics in Canada*, [1932] 1 D.L.R. 58 (P.C.).

[13]*Re Regulation and Control of Radio Communication*, [1932] 2 D.L.R. 81 (P.C.).

[14]Letter from Arthur James Balfour to Lord Walter Rothschild (2 November 1917), online: Yale Law School, *Avalon Project* at avalon.law.yale.edu/20th_century/balfour.asp.

[15]*Statute of Westminster, 1931* (U.K.), 22 & 23 Geo. V, c. 4.

in *Labour Conventions*,[16] the intuition that Canada's international legal personality had domestic constitutional implications was carried forward, through the "gap" branch of peace, order and good government, in cases on jurisdiction over the continental shelf.[17]

But it would be a mistake to conclude that the courts, and the litigation process, have been the principal agents of constitutional change outside the formal procedures of constitutional amendment. Another mechanism of adaptation has rested with political actors, acting through the executive and legislative branches of government. As Richard Simeon and Ian Robinson (1990) have argued, governments, confronted with the mismatch between twentieth-century policy responsibilities and nineteenth-century constitutional text, have engaged in a complex mix of competition and collaboration. Political competition has often culminated in epochal constitutional battles before the Supreme Court – for example, over natural resources[18] and broadcasting.[19] Yet political cooperation has been equally important. The principal constitutional devices that have facilitated federal-provincial policy cooperation are executive federalism and intergovernmental agreements. Neither is referred to in the constitutional text, yet both have evolved to enable governments to work the gears of a nineteenth-century Constitution in a modern context of overlapping jurisdiction and policy interdependence. Nor is either one legally required or legally enforceable, so that policy unilateralism is subject to few hard constitutional restraints. However, both devices are well-established political practices that are clearly of *constitutional* significance, in that they constrain the exercise of public power and fuel public expectations of appropriate political behaviour.

The point I want to make is that the constitutional politics of social policy are part of this much larger story of constitutional change. From the standpoint of the twentieth century, the failure to provide for the welfare state was one of the most conspicuous gaps in our nineteenth-century Constitution. To be sure, section 92(7) grants the provinces jurisdiction over hospitals, asylums, charities, and "eleemonsynary institutions." But these are arguably references to private forms of social provision, and they fall far short of giving clear jurisdiction over the welfare state which, as the Rowell-Sirois Commission accurately observed, was no doubt beyond the contemplation of the framers of the 1867 Constitution. Notwithstanding the lack of clear constitutional guidance on jurisdiction over

---

[16]*Reference Re Weekly Rest in Industrial Undertakings Act, Minimum Wages Act and Limitation of Hours of Work Act*, [1937] 1 D.L.R. 673 (P.C.), (*sub nom. Canada (A.G.) v. Ontario (A.G.)*), [1937] A.C. 326 [*Labour Conventions*].

[17]*Reference Re Offshore Mineral Rights*, [1967] S.C.R. 792; *Reference Re Newfoundland Continental Shelf*, [1984] 1 S.C.R. 86.

[18]See. e.g., *Canadian Industrial Gas & Oil Ltd. v. Saskatchewan*, [1978] 2 S.C.R. 545; *Central Canada Potash Co. v. Government of Saskatchewan* (1978), [1979] 1 S.C.R. 42; *Reference Re Proposed Federal Tax on Exported Natural Gas*, [1982] 1 S.C.R. 1004.

[19]See, e.g., *Capital Cities Communications v. CRTC*, [1978] 2 S.C.R. 141; *Public Service Board v. Dionne*, [1978] 2 S.C.R. 191; *Quebec (A.G.) v. Kellogg's Co.*, [1978] 2 S.C.R. 211.

social policy, Canadians have managed, by a variety of means, to change the Constitution to create a uniquely Canadian version of the welfare state, and one that was adapted to the reality of federalism.

The courts have played an unusual role in this constitutional story. On the one hand, their place in it has been central. It was the courts that created the constitutional space for the social union, through the Privy Council's pivotal judgment in the *Reference Re The Employment and Social Insurance Act*.[20] While finding that the federal scheme of mandatory, contributory unemployment insurance was unconstitutional, the Privy Council affirmed the constitutionality of conditional federal grants to individuals, institutions, and other levels of government – a power that is nowhere referred to in the constitutional text. This judgment raised a number of important questions about the contours of the spending power, such as when a federal condition shades into a colourable intrusion into provincial jurisdiction, questions one would have expected to give rise to subsequent litigation. But although these contours have been the subject of intense political dispute, the spending power has never been brought back to the courts by governments, largely because governments have found that the risks of constitutional litigation would outweigh the potential benefits.

Political institutions have taken the lead in crafting the constitutional instruments that constitute and regulate the social union. Intergovernmental agreements, such as those entered into under the former Canada Assistance Plan, were one way to codify the results of federal-provincial negotiations. The Social Union Framework Agreement, although of questionable practical importance, is also in this tradition. But of far greater importance are the various statutes creating shared-cost programs. In their current form, these statutes have a complicated genealogy, deriving from those creating medicare[21] and shared-cost programs in the social assistance area,[22] and providing for financial transfers.[23] The genealogy is tied not only to health insurance and social assistance but also to the unconditional transfers that are part of equalization.

So, layered on top of our nineteenth-century political Constitution is a twentieth-century fiscal Constitution consisting of constitutional doctrine, intergovernmental agreements, and federal statutes creating shared-cost programs and equalization. But the fit is far from perfect. At its root, the problem is one of competing constitutional logics. The logic of the nineteenth-century Constitution is to align jurisdiction over policy areas with policy instruments. A powerful illustration is provided by the *Labour Conventions* case, which established the important point that jurisdiction over treaty implementation tracks sections 91 and 92 – that is, the mere fact that a treaty

---

[20] *Labour Conventions*, *supra* note 16.

[21] *Hospital and Diagnostic Insurance Act*, R.S.C. 1970, c. H-8; *Medical Care Act*, R.S.C. 1970, c. M-8; *Canada Health Act*, R.S.C. 1985, c. C-6.

[22] *Canada Assistance Plan Act*, R.S.C. 1985, c. C-1.

[23] *Federal-Provincial Fiscal Arrangements Act*, R.S.C. 1985, c. F-8.

was on the table did not serve to modify the division of powers.[24] Extended to the federal spending power, this reasoning would render unconstitutional *any* condition attached to federal monies in areas of provincial jurisdiction. However, that has not occurred because our twentieth-century fiscal Constitution clearly divorces the federal government's regulatory jurisdiction from its fiscal jurisdiction. Similarly, the twentieth-century Constitution distinguishes between treaty negotiation, which by constitutional practice vests with the federal crown, and treaty implementation, which tracks the division of powers. It is the friction between the nineteenth- and twentieth-century Constitutions and, more fundamentally, the clash between their underlying logics that more than anything else has generated more than five decades of conflict over the federal spending power.

THE TWENTY-FIRST CENTURY

Viewed in broader historical perspective, the constitutional politics of the spending power are the product of a larger process of constitutional adaptation. This raises the following question. Suppose our Constitution comes under pressure to change again. What will the constitutional politics of the spending power look like in the twenty-first century? To answer this specific question, I will identify an emerging set of pressures on our broader constitutional arrangements, and then come back to the issue of the spending power. In short, I will suggest that our Constitution is increasingly out of sync with some key demographic facts.

First, although Canada's population grew considerably over the twentieth century, that growth is increasingly and disproportionately concentrated in certain provinces. For example, between 1981 and 2006, the country's population grew from 24.3 million to 31.6 million. Of this growth, 82 percent occurred in Ontario, Alberta, and British Columbia, whose share of total population continues to rise. Every other province has seen its relative share decline over the same period. In absolute terms, Saskatchewan experienced no growth, and Newfoundland and Labrador's population actually declined.[25] Moreover, a variety of scenarios project that population growth will continue to be concentrated in Ontario, Alberta, and British Columbia, both in absolute and relative terms.

Second, Canada has become an urban nation. In 1901, 37 percent of Canadians lived in urban regions. By 2006, that figure had risen to 80 percent. Within urban Canada, the population is increasingly concentrated in our largest urban centres, known as Census Metropolitan Areas (CMAs), which are now home to 68 percent of Canadians. Even more dramatically, 10 million people

---

[24] *Supra* note 16 at 682: "[N]o further legislative competence is obtained by the Dominion from its accession to international status, and the consequent increase in the scope of its executive functions."

[25] These calculations are based on figures in the 1981 and 2006 censuses. The projections are from Statistics Canada (2005).

now live in metropolitan Toronto, Montreal, and Vancouver, although those cities account for only 0.1 percent of Canada's total territory. The rise of urban Canada has been fuelled by two kinds of migration: international and internal. Over time, immigrants have increasingly tended to settle in Toronto, Montreal, and Vancouver. Nearly three-quarters of the immigrants who arrived in Canada between 1991 and 2001 settled in those three cities, 43 percent in Toronto alone. The migration pattern of persons born *in* Canada has been equally dramatic, with people moving in large numbers to CMAs around Toronto, Montreal, and Vancouver, and away from rural Canada.[26]

Third, Canada's population is aging. In 1946, its median age was twenty-eight. By 2006, it had risen to thirty-nine. Even assuming immigration at present or higher levels, the median age is projected to continue to rise to between forty-five and fifty by 2056. As a consequence, Canada's dependency ratio – the number of persons not of working age for every hundred of working age – will increase rapidly. In 2005, this was forty-four. In 2031, it is projected to be as high as sixty-one. Moreover, the aging of Canada's population intersects with the other two demographic trends mentioned above. The youngest parts of Canada will overlap considerably with those where population is increasingly concentrated: urban Canada, Ontario, and Alberta. Rural Canada and the Maritime provinces are, and will remain, the oldest demographically. The fact that persons between the ages of fifteen and twenty-nine are the most likely to migrate from rural to urban areas has played a key role in the aging of rural Canada.

A new issue for constitutional politics in the twenty-first century is how our institutions will respond to these profound demographic changes. At the most fundamental level, the question is this: will votes, political power, and public expenditure follow people as they make choices about where to work and live and, in the process, fundamentally alter the geographic distribution of Canada's population? This basic question is already forcing itself onto the constitutional agenda, and will continue to play out in three interrelated arenas: political representation, economic policy, and social policy.

The first arena is *political representation*. The allocation of House of Commons seats across provinces will be one flashpoint. As I have argued elsewhere, the rules governing the allocation of seats in the House of Commons, both across provinces and within provinces, have produced enormous disparities in riding sizes (Pal and Choudhry 2007). Ridings in Ontario, Alberta, and British Columbia have significantly more people than ridings in other provinces. Moreover, within all provinces, urban ridings are more populous than rural ridings. As a consequence, although all adult Canadians enjoy formal equality with respect to the right to vote, the weight of their votes varies widely. These variations are deliberate, and are arguably designed to protect the minority of voters who live in smaller provinces and rural areas. However, these disparities are producing a House of Commons that is increasingly at odds with the principle of one person, one vote. By my count, in the current House of Commons of 308 seats, Alberta, British Columbia, and Ontario are under-

[26]Data from Statistics Canada (2007).

represented by eighteen seats. As population growth continues to be concentrated in these provinces, this gap will grow considerably. Dealing with this increasing disparity is likely to be controversial, as was illustrated by Bill C-22, which proposed to address it, but only for Alberta and British Columbia.[27] Not surprisingly, it was attacked by Ontario's provincial government and has sparked a furious political controversy.

Another area of controversy is Senate reform, as reflected in Ontario and Quebec's opposition to Bill C-20.[28] Bill C-20 proposed to create a system of Senate "consultations" that would in practice function no differently than elections. Of the many objections to the Bill, one is that it would clothe the upper chamber with democratic legitimacy without addressing the other dimensions of Senate reform. One of these dimensions, regional representation, was of central importance during both the Quebec and Canada rounds of constitutional negotiations in the 1980s and 1990s. It is well known that our Senate is demographically anachronistic, with the Maritime provinces enjoying greater relative representation than the larger provinces of Alberta and British Columbia because they once had a greater share of the national population. But another issue underlies Ontario's strenuous objections to C-20: when our upper chamber was designed, no one contemplated that a single province would have 40 percent of the country's population, a proportion that is projected to increase well into this century. In every federation, the upper chamber is structured on the basis of a principle of representation that departs to some extent from representation by population. We must turn our minds to crafting an upper chamber that will reflect Canada's great population asymmetry, especially if we democratize the process of selecting Senators.

Now consider cities. They are creatures of provincial legislation, and traditionally have been viewed as minor players in public policy. But for major metropolitan centres, that perception in changing. As Richard Florida (2002) has famously argued, global city-regions have a central role in economic prosperity in the information age. Should we begin to think of major urban areas as a third order of government? If so, should their juridical status, and regulatory and revenue-raising powers, change to reflect their importance? Should they be formally regarded as actors in intergovernmental relations, able to engage in direct discussions with the federal government on matters of urban policy?

Political representation is linked to a second arena in which demographics will affect the constitutional agenda: the arena of *economic policy*. Consider

---

[27]Bill C-22, *An Act to amend the Constitution Act, 1867 (Democratic representation)*, 2nd Sess., 39th Parl., 2007 (as given first reading in the House of Commons 14 November 2007). See also its predecessor Bill C-56, *An Act to amend the Constitution Act, 1867 (Democratic representation)*, 1st Sess., 39th Parl., 2007 (as given first reading in the House of Commons 11 May 2007).

[28]Bill C-20, *An Act to provide for consultations with electors on their preferences for appointments to the Senate*, 2nd Sess., 39th Parl., 2007 (as given first reading in the House of Commons 13 November 2007). See also its predecessor Bill C-43, *An Act to provide for consultations with electors on their preferences for appointments to the Senate*, 1st Sess., 39th Parl., 2006 (as given first reading in the House of Commons 13 December 2006).

major urban areas again. In the literature on the cities agenda, one of the most common assumptions is that the only appropriate response to the importance of cities is their jurisdictional and fiscal empowerment, with the ultimate goal of turning them into city-states. However, this would be a serious mistake. Even the most expansive vision of urban autonomy in Canada would leave many important policy areas in federal jurisdiction. Macroeconomic policy, innovation policy, and immigration policy are core areas of federal jurisdiction. For the cities agenda to succeed, the federal government, in its areas of responsibility, must make the economic health of Canada's major urban centres a national priority (see Courchene 2007). However, our Constitution imposes two obstacles to getting a federally led, urban agenda off the ground – for example, on the matter of rapid transit, which is necessarily focused in metropolitan areas. First, cities lie within provincial jurisdiction, an argument raised by Quebec in opposing federal policy activism on urban issues. Second, the possibility of getting traction on urban issues at the federal level is linked to another issue of political representation – the already-mentioned growing gap between the size of rural and urban ridings. The distorting effect of rural overrepresentation on federal public policy is perhaps best illustrated by the morphing of the Martin government's cities agenda into a cities and communities agenda, in response to pressure from rural MPs.

Finally, political representation is also linked to a third arena: *social policy*. In the social-policy arena, the size and shape of federal expenditures pursuant to the spending power is partly a function of underlying patterns of political representation. The overrepresentation of smaller provinces and rural areas in the House of Commons creates a set of political incentives that diminish the prospects of having social policies specifically directed at urban ills. Infusing the Senate with democratic legitimacy could compound this effect; Senators appointed on the basis of "consultations" could very well depart from the long-established convention of deferring to the legislative priorities and decisions of the House of Commons. Indeed, given that Senate consultations would be provincewide, Senators might even conclude that they had more legitimacy than MPs elected at riding level. This would enhance the political power of provinces that are in absolute and relative population decline, at the expense of those parts of Canada where people are choosing to live.

In the social-policy arena, political conflict fuelled by this demographic gap could play out in the following way. The federal-provincial transfer system is sustained by narratives of solidarity with the "other Canada" – the idea that our fellow citizens in all parts of the country deserve a basic level of services, no matter where they are born or where they live. But increasingly, the other Canada is also to be found in the growing enclaves of urban poverty that are taking on an increasingly racialized character. If narratives of social citizenship undergird the federal-provincial transfer system, then changing those narratives to emphasize bonds of solidarity that are much more local could have dramatic implications for Canada's fiscal constitution. There may be a demand that the kind of energy and resources we have long invested in regional development projects in Northern and Atlantic Canada now be directed at our deprived inner cities and immigrant populations. The growing chasm between our institutions of representation and the emerging patterns of political identity would be manifest in a new type of debate over the spending power – a debate that would give voice to the larger, underlying pressures that are building for constitutional change. If we examine debates over the spending power in isolation, we will not fully understand what is at stake.

Let me conclude with this point. Debates over the conditions to be attached to the exercise of the federal spending power – prior provincial consent, opt-outs with compensation, and so on – are debates of the twentieth century. We are now in a new century, and new issues are already upon us. How we talk about the spending power will necessarily change as part of a larger reconfiguration of political and economic power.

REFERENCES

Canada, Royal Commission on the Future of Health Care in Canada. 2002. *Strengthening the Foundations: Modernizing the Canada Health Act,* by C.M. Flood and S. Choudhry. Discussion Paper No. 13. Ottawa: Health Canada.

Choudhry, S. 1996. "The Enforcement of the *Canada Health Act*", *McGill Law Journal* 41(2).

— 2000. "Bill 11, The *Canada Health Act* and the Social Union: The Need for Institutions", *Osgoode Hall Law Journal* 38(1).

— 2002. "Recasting Social Canada: A Reconsideration of Federal Jurisdiction over Social Policy", *University of Toronto Law Journal 52.*

— 2003. "Beyond the Flight from Constitutional Legalism: Rethinking the Politics of Social Policy post-Charlottetown", *Constitutional Forum Constitutionnel* 12(3), 77-83.

— 2006. "Redistribution in the Canadian Federation: The Impact of the Cities Agenda and the New Canada", in S. Choudhry, J.-F. Gaudreault-DesBiens, and L. Sossin (eds.), *Dilemmas of Solidarity: Rethinking Redistribution in the Canadian Federation.* Toronto: University of Toronto Press.

Choudhry, S., J.-F. Gaudreault-DesBiens, and L. Sossin, eds. 2006a. *Dilemmas of Solidarity: Rethinking Redistribution in the Canadian Federation.* Toronto: University of Toronto Press.

— 2006b. "Introduction: Exploring the Dilemmas of Solidarity", in S. Choudhry, J.-F. Gaudreault-DesBiens, and L. Sossin (eds.), *Dilemmas of Solidarity: Rethinking Redistribution in the Canadian Federation.* Toronto: University of Toronto Press.

— 2006c. "Afterword: Solidarity Between Modesty and Boldness", in S. Choudhry, J.-F. Gaudreault-DesBiens, and L. Sossin (eds.), *Dilemmas of Solidarity: Rethinking Redistribution in the Canadian Federation.* Toronto: University of Toronto Press.

Courchene, T.J. 2007. "Global Futures for Canada's Cities". *Policy Matters* 8(2), Montreal: IRPP.

Florida, R. 2002. *The Rise of the Creative Class: And How It's Transforming Work, Leisure, Community and Everyday Life.* New York: Basic Books.

Pal, M. and S. Choudhry. 2007. "Is Every Ballot Equal? Visible Minority Vote Dilution in Canada", *Choices* 13(1). Montreal: IRPP.

Simeon, R. and I. Robinson. 1990. *State, Society and the Development of Canadian Federalism.* Toronto: University of Toronto Press.

Statistics Canada. 2005. *Population Projections for Canada, Provinces and Territories: 2005-2031,* by A. Bélanger, L. Martel, and É. Caron-Malenfant. Ottawa: Minister of Industry.

— 2007. *Demographic Changes in Canada from 1971 to 2001 Across an Urban-to-Rural Gradient,* by É. Caron-Malenfant *et al.* Ottawa: Ministry of Industry.

CONTRIBUTORS

Marc-Antoine Adam, Member, Quebec Bar. Director of the Direction de la réflexion stratégique at the Secrétariat aux affaires intergouvernementales canadiennes in the Government of Quebec. The ideas contained in this paper were developed while the author was a Visiting Fellow at the Institute of Intergovernmental Relations at Queen's University. The author wrote in his personal capacity.

John R. Allan was, at the time of the Conference, Associate Director, Institute of Intergovernmental Relations, Queen's University, Kingston, Ontario. He is also Vice-President Emeritus and Professor of Economics Emeritus of the University of Regina.

Marc Chevrier, Professeur, Département de science politique, Université du Québec à Montréal.

Sujit Choudhry, Faculty of Law, Department of Political Science and School of Public Policy and Governance, University of Toronto.

Thomas J. Courchene, Jarislowsky-Deutsch Professor of Economics and Financial Policy and Senior Scholar, Institute for Research on Public Policy, Montreal. At the time of the Conference, he was Director, Institute of Intergovernmental Relations at Queen's University.

Tom Kent, Companion of the Order of Canada; Lifetime Fellow, Institute for Research on Public Policy; Fellow, School of Policy Studies, Queen's University.

Hoi Kong, Assistant Professor of Law, Faculty of Law, McGill University, Montreal, Quebec.

Andrée Lajoie, Professor Emeritus, Faculty of Law, Université de Montréal.

Harvey Lazar is a senior research associate, Centre for Global Studies, and adjunct professor, School of Public Administration, University of Victoria. He is also a fellow of the Institute of Intergovernmental Relations and adjunct professor, School of Policy Studies, Queen's University.

Roderick A. Macdonald, F.R. Scott Professor of Public and Constitutional Law, McGill University.

Errol P. Mendes, Faculty of Law, University of Ottawa, Editor-in-Chief, National Journal of Constitutional Law.

Alain Noël, M.Sc. (Montréal), Ph.D. (Denver), Professeur titulaire, Département de science politique, Université de Montréal.

Andrew Petter, Professor, Faculty of Law, University of Victoria.

John D. Whyte, Law Foundation of Saskatchewan, Professor of Law, College of Law, University of Saskatchewan.

Queen's School of Policy Studies (SPS) was established in 1987 in order to create an organizational focus to build upon Queen's long and venerable tradition as a leading contributor to Canadian public affairs and public policy. Toward this end, Queen's School of Public Administration (est. 1969) came under the SPS umbrella in 1993 so that SPS now offers a Masters in Public Administration (MPA) and a part-time Professional MPA. The School of Industrial Relations with its Masters in Industrial Relations (MIR) and its new part-time Professional MIR, along with the Institute of Industrial Relations, merged with SPS in 2003. Other policy-related institutes/centres/programs within SPS include: the Institute of Intergovernmental Relations (IIGR), the Queen's Centre for International Relations (QCIR), the Centre for the Studies on Democracy and Diversity (CSDD), Queen's University Institute for Energy and Environmental Policy (QIEEP) and the Canadian Opinion Research Archive (CORA) as well as Defence Management Studies and the Third Sector Initiative. For more information on the publications and activities of the SPS visit www.queensu.ca/sps.

Recent Publications

A full catalogue and ordering information may be found on their web site (http://mqup.mcgill.ca/).

Institute of Intergovernmental Relations

The Evolving Canadian Crown, Jennifer Smith and D. Michael Jackson (eds.), 2012. ISBN 978-1-55339-202-6

The Federal Idea: Essays in Honour of Ronald L. Watts, Thomas J. Courchene, John R. Allan, Christian Leuprecht, and Nadia Verrelli (eds.), 2011. Paper ISBN 978-1-55339-198-2 Cloth ISBN 978-1-55339-199-9

Canada: The State of the Federation 2009, vol. 22, *Carbon Pricing and Environmental Federalism*, Thomas J. Courchene and John R. Allan (eds.), 2010 Paper ISBN 978-1-55339-196-8 Cloth ISBN 978-1-55339-197-5

The Democratic Dilemma: Reforming the Canadian Senate, Jennifer Smith (ed.), 2009 Paper ISBN 978-1-55339-190-6

Canada: The State of the Federation 2006/07: Transitions – Fiscal and Political Federalism in an Era of Change, vol. 20, John R. Allan, Thomas J. Courchene, and Christian Leuprecht (eds.), 2009 Paper ISBN 978-1-55339-189-0 Cloth ISBN 978-1-55339-191-3

The following publications are available from the Institute of Intergovernmental Relations, Queen's University, Kingston, Ontario K7L 3N6
Tel: (613) 533-2080 / Fax: (613) 533-6868; E-mail: iigr@queensu.ca

The Role of the Policy Advisor: An Insider's Look, Nadia Verrelli (ed.), 2008
ISBN 978-1-55339-193-7

Open Federalism, Interpretations Significance, collection of essays by Keith G. Banting, Roger Gibbins, Peter M. Leslie, Alain Noël, Richard Simeon, and Robert Young, 2006
ISBN 978-1-55339-187-6

Publications prior to 2005 may be downloaded from the IIGR website:
http://www.queensu.ca/iigr/pub/archive.html
The Institute's working paper series can be downloaded from our website www.iigr.ca

School of Policy Studies

Where to from Here: Keeping Medicare Sustainable, Stephen Duckett, 2012.
ISBN 978-1-55339-318-4

International Migration in Uncertain Times, John Nieuwenhuysen, Howard Duncan, and Stine Neerup (eds.), 2012. ISBN 978-1-55339-308-5

Centre for the Studies on Democracy and Diversity

Jimmy and Rosalynn Carter: A Canadian Tribute, Arthur Milnes (ed.), 2011
Paper ISBN 978-1-55339-300-9 Cloth ISBN 978-1-55339-301-6

Unrevised and Unrepented II: Debating Speeches and Others By the Right Honourable Arthur Meighen, Arthur Milnes (ed.), 2011 Paper ISBN 978-1-55339-296-5
Cloth ISBN 978-1-55339-297-2

Queen's Centre for International Relations

Security Operations in the 21st Century: Canadian Perspectives on the Comprehensive Approach, Michael Rostek and Peter Gizewski (eds.), 2011 Paper ISBN 978-1-55339-351-1

Europe Without Soldiers? Recruitment and Retention across the Armed Forces of Europe, Tibor Szvircsev Tresch and Christian Leuprecht (eds.), 2010
Paper ISBN 978-1-55339-246-0 Cloth ISBN 978-1-55339-247-7

John Deutsch Institute for the Study of Economic Policy

The 2009 Federal Budget: Challenge, Response and Retrospect, Charles M. Beach, Bev Dahlby and Paul A.R. Hobson (eds.), 2010 Paper ISBN 978-1-55339-165-4
Cloth ISBN 978-1-55339-166-1

Discount Rates for the Evaluation of Public Private Partnerships,
David F. Burgess and Glenn P. Jenkins (eds.), 2010
Paper ISBN 978-1-55339-163-0 Cloth ISBN 978-1-55339-164-7

For more information about new and backlist titles from Queen's Policy Studies, visit http://www.queensu.ca/sps/books or visit the McGill-Queen's University Press web site at: **http://mqup.mcgill.ca/**